A REBEL TO HIS
LAST BREATH

Joseph
McCabe
and
Rationalism

A REBEL TO HIS
LAST BREATH

BILL COOKE

Foreword by John R. Burr, Ph.D.

 **Prometheus Books**

59 John Glenn Drive
Amherst, New York 14228-2197

Published 2001 by Prometheus Books

Inquiries should be addressed to
Prometheus Books
59 John Glenn Drive
Amherst, New York 14228–2197
VOICE: 716–691–0133, ext. 207
FAX: 716–564–2711
WWW.PROMETHEUSBOOKS.COM

05 04 03 02 01   5 4 3 2 1

Library of Congress Cataloging-in-Publication Data

Cooke, Bill, 1956–
    A rebel to his last breath : Joseph McCabe and rationalism / Bill Cooke.
        p. cm.
    Includes bibliographical references and index.
    ISBN 1–57392–878–X (alk. paper)
    1. McCabe, Joseph, 1867–1955. 2. Rationalists—Great Britain—Biography.
I. Title.

BL2790.M35 C66 2001
211'.4'092—dc21
[B]   2001020489

Printed in Canada on acid-free paper

For *Arthur* and *Florence*

Contents

Acknowledgments   9

Foreword
  John R. Burr, Ph.D.   11

Introduction. Joseph Who?   15

1. The Rise and Fall of Father Antony   23

2. The Rise and Fall of Joseph McCabe   35

3. The Trained Athlete of Disbelief   67

4. Past and Present: McCabe As Historian and Social Commentator   89

5. "A Future More Splendid Than Any Poet Can Imagine":
McCabe and Science   117

6. Edwardian Feminist: Gender, Politics, and Sex   151

7. The Apprehended Shadow: McCabe and Religion   179

8. Was McCabe an Anti-Catholic Bigot?   211

9. A Twentieth-Century Diderot   239

8   CONTENTS

Appendix 1. A Bibliography of Works by Joseph McCabe   269

Appendix 2. Articles by McCabe in the *Literary Guide*   289

Appendix 3. Lectures and Debates Given by Joseph McCabe   297

Bibliography   319

Index   327

Acknowledgments

There is a dauntingly large number of people to whom I owe thanks for helping me complete this work. Three people read an early draft of this work, and their encouragement and criticism was critical in my decision to extend the early draft to a book-length study. They are Professor John G. Burr of the Department of Philosophy at the University of Wisconsin, Oshkosh (and author of the entry on McCabe in the *Encyclopedia of Unbelief*); Professor H. James Birx, of the Department of Anthropology and Sociology at Canisius College, Buffalo, New York; and Nigel Sinnott, a historian of freethought based in Australia. Professor Burr encouraged me to enlarge the earlier draft into a book-length study, and I am grateful to him for that advice.

I am also grateful to the very fine historian and scholar Nicolas Walter, who retired after a long career with the Rationalist Press Association in London. Tragically, Nicolas died within weeks of his retirement, on March 7, 2000, and will not see this book as a finished item. Other people have lent important assistance in providing me with scarce material or information on McCabe. They are Timothy Binga, director of the Center for Inquiry Library at Amherst, New York; Jennifer Jeynes, librarian of the very fine collection owned by the South Place Ethical Society in London; Joe Zamecki of the American Atheists organization; Nigel Collins, a seller of freethought material based in England; and Ray Dahlitz, another freethought historian based in Australia. Other people who have lent valuable assistance in this area include David Tribe and Fred Whitehead, freethought historians based in Australia and Kansas, respectively, and Sanal Edamaruku, general secretary of the Indian Rationalist Association. I am also grateful to Warwick Don, retired senior lecturer in zoology at the University of Otago in New Zealand, who provided important assistance with chapter 5. Deborah Crowe provided some needed encouragement and criticism at a crucial stage in the book's development, for which I am thankful.

10   ACKNOWLEDGMENTS

I am especially grateful to Jenifer Blenard, Joseph McCabe's granddaughter. Jenifer and her husband, Stuart, were extraordinarily welcoming and helpful to this stranger who turned up out of the blue talking about her grandfather. Mr. and Mrs. Blenard provided insights into McCabe as a family man that can only come from within the family.

I am also particularly grateful to Mike Lloyd-Jones, who has a very fine collection of McCabe titles, and who provided me with important information about several aspects of McCabe's life and career. Mr. Lloyd-Jones undertook a serious study of McCabe's life some time ago, and has been unusually open and generous with his research findings. I want also to acknowledge the assistance of Ron Carden, who was instrumental in arriving at the list of works McCabe ghostwrote for Bishop William Montgomery Brown.

I am indebted to the New Zealand Association of Rationalists and Humanists, which has one of the finest freethought libraries in the world, for its generous policy of allowing me unrestricted access to its extensive collection of McCabe material, and for a host of other generous considerations given to me while this book was being written. If ever one wants evidence of eupraxophy in action, it can be found in this fine organization. Excellent as the McCabe collection is here, I have still relied on some sleuths to track down rare McCabe titles for me: Ian Hambly and Peter Murphy in New Zealand have been particularly successful in this regard. Irving Yablon, from the United States, was generous enough to send me some titles I could not otherwise have had access to. A New Zealand friend, David Ross, took enormous trouble to proofread and criticize the entire manuscript. Rae West of England and Belinda Kusabs of New Zealand have also rendered useful assistance.

I would also like to thank Manukau Institute of Technology, which provided me with generous funding in 1999 to undertake research in London. This funding has been indispensable to the integrity of this book. Chapters 4, 8, and 9 all began as papers presented at conferences and all benefited from subsequent criticism and comment. Chapters 4 and 9 began as papers that were given at a conference called "Science and Society," cohosted by the Russian Academy of Sciences, St. Petersburg Branch, and the St. Petersburg University philosophy department. This conference was held between June 21 and 25, 1999. The precursor to chapter 8 was given as a paper at a conference of the New Zealand Association for the Study of Religions, Otago University, in Dunedin, New Zealand, which was held between July 6 and 9, 1998. The bibliography of McCabe's works was originally published in the *New Zealand Rationalist and Humanist*, spring 1997 issue. I am pleased to be able to publish an updated version of that bibliography here.

Lastly, I would like to thank my partner, Bobbie Wallace, for practical assistance such as reading chapters, but also for less tangible assistance and support while I grappled with this project. Naturally, none of these individuals or institutions is responsible for the opinions expressed in this book, the responsibility for which is mine alone.

Foreword

John R. Burr, Ph.D.

At the close of my article on Joseph McCabe in *The Encyclopedia of Unbe-lief*, edited by Gordon Stein and published by Prometheus in 1985, I lamented, "McCabe has not received the attention his life, ideas, and writings deserve, and no full studies of him have been published." This present volume proves that I no longer have any reason for complaint.

Dr. Cooke's *A Rebel to His Last Breath* is a clearly and engagingly written and scrupulously researched study of the character of the man, his writings, his ideas, his almost lifelong campaign to educate the general public, and his continuing sig-nificance today. Although the author describes this work as "principally an intel-lectual biography" because no comprehensive biography of McCabe is known to exist and most of his papers were destroyed by his housekeeper shortly after his death, *A Rebel to His Last Breath* does convey a vivid sense of his personality not only in his early monastic years but throughout his career, by never failing to describe, where the evidence permits, McCabe's relations to those immediately around him and their reactions to him. Reading Dr. Cooke's study leaves no doubt that if ever the old saying that the writing is the man were true of anyone, it is of McCabe's style. It is clear, flowing, almost conversational; one might be listening to the man talk over a glass or two of beer. A few intimate, personal details about himself and others might be mentioned now and then to illustrate some point, but he leaves no doubt that it is the point, not the personal, that is the most impor-tant. McCabe clearly emerges as one of those unusual people to whom what appears to be the truth after the most careful and thorough investigation genuinely matters. Indeed, as Dr. Cooke brings out, it matters more than financial success, celebrity, the sensitivities of colleagues, and even long-standing friendships. Any biography of McCabe, no matter how complete, inevitably would have to be intellectual, for he was an immensely painstaking scholar whose learning covered an unusually large number of subjects from history, religion, and philosophy to the physical and social sciences; and, what is rare for most scholars, he devoted an immense amount of time and energy to bringing the fruits of his scholarship to the general public. However, in the end what most impresses about McCabe and his writings and what Dr. Cooke highlights is the relentless intellectual honesty of the man, his mien of speaking straight from the shoulder, of telling you exactly what he thinks about what he considers important whether you agree with him or not. In our politic age such individuals startle, puzzle, and irritate many. People don't know what to do with such men and often end up ignoring them. Such a fate of "internal exile" has befallen McCabe much to our loss. Yet he deserves to be revisited, not only because of his bracing and refreshing character, but because he devoted his life to a cause more imperative than ever.

That cause is the promotion of public enlightenment, a contemporary version of the eighteenth-century Enlightenment. As Dr. Cooke's book makes so clear, McCabe saw that the tremendous, ever-accelerating development of science was forcing on humanity a pervasive and fundamental reconstruction of all human culture. For McCabe, true enlightenment meant not only keeping abreast of the latest scientific discoveries and technological developments but, above all, fearlessly and honestly facing the revisions they demand in basic beliefs and institutions, particularly in economics, politics, morality, and religion.

What sharply differentiates McCabe from so many today, especially those loosely called "postmodernists," is his optimistic view of science and its methods of solving problems. That optimism was rooted firmly in his vision of the *humane* or humanistic potentialities of science, of its future promise and already partial achievement of better lives for all. McCabe called the nineteenth century a "century of stupendous progress" because the successful utilization of science to improve the standard of living of more people than ever before in human history was beginning to be demonstrated. It proved his optimistic vision was realistic and not delusive. McCabe's cause was not enlightenment merely but public enlightenment. McCabe was convinced that if the general public could be brought to share that vision of the humanistic potentialities of science its realization would become irresistible. Therefore, for McCabe the crucial battlefront ran between those who promoted pubic enlightenment and those who opposed it as a mortal threat to their special privileges or, in McCabe's own words, "bishops, preachers, exploiters of the poor, millionaires, parasites, dictators and liars and crooks generally."

Although *A Rebel to His Last Breath* certainty is no hagiography, blind to its subject's flaws and foibles, but rather a measured assessment of the man and his writings, the author emulates his subject's candor by making no bones of the fact that he shares McCabe's optimistic vision and cause. As the growth of science or simply knowledge, as McCabe preferred to call it, touches us ever more deeply and intimately down to the genetic structure of our being, so resistance to it grows apace. That opposition ranges from the crudest forms of religious fundamentalism to sophisticated postmodernist rejections of the ideals of the eighteenth-century Enlightenment as a temporary historical aberration and their snide depiction of science or knowledge and its cultural implications as so many stories, no truer than any others, that we tell ourselves. The author argues cogently that what McCabe courageously stood for in his time is more relevant and needed today than ever, that McCabe's struggle for genuine public enlightenment is our struggle. *A Rebel to His Last Breath* is a worthy contribution to that struggle.

Introduction
Joseph Who?

The twentieth century was a bad century for reason—among other things. In 1900, Reason, suitably armed with a capital letter, could be sent out into the world with confidence to eradicate superstition and ignorance. But a century on, many people contrive to portray reason as nothing more than a discredited weapon of deceit with which to manipulate a hegemonic discourse with a view to marginalizing dissent. In 1900 it was a good thing to be "coldly rational," which meant to be dispassionate, and thus able to analyze something sensibly, free from the nebulous phantoms of irrationality or prejudice. But, at the beginning of the twenty-first century, to be "coldly rational" is to make an attempt, one that will necessarily fail, to couch one's prejudices in the language of late capitalism. And this is a Bad Thing.

The fate of reason in the twentieth century can be illustrated by following the changing fortunes of the three most important philosophers of the century: Bertrand Russell, Ludwig Wittgenstein, and Martin Heidegger. The rationalism of Russell (1872–1970) has given way to the cryptic mysticism of Wittgenstein (1889–1951), which has in turn been overshadowed late in the century by the return to prominence of Heidegger's (1889–1976) byzantine and antirational obfuscation.

Alongside this sidelining of reason and Heidegger's return to prominence has come the replacement of clear writing with tortuous and jargon-packed prose. Such writing is thought to be more profound than the simple and

15

digestible language of the rationalists. No clearer contrast can be found as that between the writing of Russell and Heidegger. And Heidegger, along with Friedrich Nietzsche, is often hailed as the intellectual foundation for contemporary postmodernism. When I speak of postmodernism, I will use the description given it by the American political philosopher Gregory Bruce Smith. He describes it as "fundamentally a sign of disintegration, of transition, of waning faith in the modern ideas of Reason and Progress, and the Enlightenment project in general."[1] Postmodernists claim that all experience is based on nothing more than one's own interpretation. This is so, they say, because all the foundations of knowledge have been eroded. Science, in particular, has no privileged access to knowledge, because all languages are local and perspectival.[2] Strangely, they also insist that universal claims are impossible.

These are the main tenets of postmodernism according to the English postmodernist Michael Luntley. I use him because his language is less abstruse and extravagant than his better-known French brethren, and because his rendering of postmodernism is more conducive to analysis.[3] Whatever the other variations within this eclectic trend, the most consistent feature of the postmodernist hall of mirrors is the notion, for them reassuring, of a discredited rationalism. And many theorists who are not regulation postmodernists would agree that, whatever else may be the case, rationalism has been discredited. Alongside this antirationalism has come a loathing of science, followed by execrations of scientism and historicism and the marginalizing of dissent. We have also seen some ferocious attacks on those who profess an admiration for both reason and science. An English critic and journalist a few years ago described Bertrand Russell as "one of the most fabulously stupid men of our age" and accorded him the status of chief villain.[4]

One postmodernist scholar, the sociologist Zygmunt Bauman, has seen fit to write off all modernity as "a long march to prison." In preference to modernity he advocates a postmodernity that "splits the truth, the standards of the ideal into already deconstructed and about to be deconstructed." Bauman credits Heidegger as the pioneer of this "second Copernican revolution" away from the totalitarian bonds of modernity.[5] That Bertrand Russell spent his life combating totalitarianism and Martin Heidegger devoted his life to providing totalitarianism with a semimystical halo seems to count for little. Other, more moderate postmodernist scholars like Michael Luntley have recognized that a postmodernist critique is one thing, but antirationalism (Luntley's phrase) is quite another, and serves no one. But, while wishing to preserve rationality, Luntley is just as adamant that the most distinctive features of the Enlightenment are now in ruins.[6]

This book is an attempt to look at some of the apparently discredited notions of rationalist humanism and ask whether they are in fact as bankrupt as is commonly supposed. By rationalist humanism I mean the trend in modernity to value the processes of reason, of science, of informed skepticism, and of humanism. Until the final chapter, when I discuss all this in detail, I shall use both "rationalist" and "humanist" interchangeably. "Rationalist" will get the most use, simply because it was the word McCabe used most of the time. When I speak of rationalism I do not mean the great tradition of rationalist philosophy of René Descartes, Baruch du Spinoza, and G. W. Leibniz. I have in mind people like Bertrand Russell, particularly as we know him from his popular writings. But rather than study someone like Russell who, fortunately, has many able contemporary defenders, this account intends to introduce readers to another thinker from this tradition who is now virtually unknown.

The reason for choosing Joseph McCabe goes back to the time I was writing my doctorate, which examined the history and beliefs of the New Zealand Association of Rationalists and Humanists. Time and time again I came across McCabe's name. And time and time and again I sought some confirmation, refutation, or even acknowledgement of his ideas from other sources—almost always unsuccessfully. There have been very few references to McCabe since his death in 1955. And yet he had an enormous influence and a very wide readership around the world.

One of the few recent references to McCabe I *have* come across made the important point that he was a man who had many imitators.[7] This is a point we will return to over and again through the course of this book. Whether in history, popular science, feel-good popular psychology, or a host of other genres, McCabe was a pioneer. I am not, of course, claiming that all those who followed McCabe consciously imitated him. But I am saying that their work owes at least an oblique nod in McCabe's direction.

So how is it that a person who has written over two hundred books and monographs comes to be so completely ignored? McCabe was one of the most remarkable polymaths of the twentieth century, and yet is unknown, even by specialists working within relevant fields. How is it that a man who once featured regularly in the English *Who's Who* and was acknowledged as an expert on the Roman Catholic Church, and a popularizer of science with a worldwide reputation, is now rarely mentioned, even in passing?

There are several possible answers to this question. The answer we will hear most often is that, now that we are all postmodern, it is hardly necessary to examine a long-dead advocate of reason and science. We've done all that, and both are now discredited and unwanted. I disagree, for (at least) two reasons. I disagree because I dispute the postmodernist assumption of intellectual hegemony. I also reject the sneers of Jacques Derrida, who declares that this sort of study cannot be made in good faith. The second half of the 1990s saw a significant counterattack against postmodernism by rationalists and scientists around the world. The turning point, it has been suggested, was Alan Sokal's brilliant scuttling of the prominent postmodernist academic journal *Social Text*. The New York–based physicist wrote a scandalously overwritten and nonsensical parody of postmodernist thinking, replete with glaring errors of fact—and *Social Text* printed it! Postmodernist pretensions to academic credibility have looked fragile ever since. Since the rout of *Social Text*, several important books have emerged and the general feeling of a fight back is in the air. I am a historian, and this study of McCabe is intended as my contribution to that fight back. It also seeks to embolden the rationalists of the twenty-first century with the knowledge of a doughty and courageous predecessor.

As part of its contribution to the struggle against the tide of irrationalism, this book will question many of the standard objections made about the rationalism of the early first half of the twentieth century. It has been accused of incurable scientism, historicism, sexism, racism, technocentrism, and desacralization. By making a study of this lesser-known figure, we may get a clearer picture of the credibility of these charges. Many studies have been made of better-known rationalists of the twentieth century, like Bertrand Russell, but perhaps a study of a lesser figure will be more revealing. Truly great minds like Russell's are capable of substantially resetting the intellectual outlook. McCabe was not a truly great mind in the sense of being original in a significant way. But not being the equal of Bertrand Russell is hardly a rebuke—only two other men of the twentieth century were his equal, and even then their equality to Russell was confined strictly to the intellectual field.

So why study Joseph McCabe? He has, after all, sunk without trace from nearly every field of academic study. Maybe he deserves to? Obviously I think not. Joseph McCabe was, I will argue, one of the finest all-around intellects and communicators of the twentieth century. He was one of the century's most remarkable *philosophes*: a formidable scholar, a fine writer, a trenchant smiter of humbug, and a relentlessly honest man. McCabe deserves to be placed beside, if not ahead of, the best popularizers of history and science one would care to name. He was also a pioneer and prophet without honor in his own time.

Surely, though, if McCabe had been all these things, he would be remembered now? But he isn't, and this book also is an attempt to provide some explanation for this. Let us begin by looking at some of the problems associated with a study of Joseph McCabe. To begin with, McCabe died in 1955, and a comprehensive biography of him is probably not possible now. No biography of any sort has been written about him, and so there is nothing to build on. Gorden Stein (1941–1996), the American historian of freethought, wanted to write one a while ago, but abandoned the project for lack of information.[8] Some years after McCabe's death, the majority of his papers were destroyed by his housekeeper, who had inherited his property. So, of necessity, this account of McCabe is principally an intellectual biography. But even here there are massive problems. McCabe traveled and lectured widely, from Scotland to the South Island of New Zealand, from Bulgaria to British Columbia. So a fully comprehensive biographical account of this man's impact on his contemporaries would require the biographer to follow in his footsteps around large parts of the world. Lacking, as I do, the riches of Croesus, this enjoyable task remains to be done.

Neither is there any center devoted to collecting McCabe's works. The first half of his publishing career was centered in London; the second half, mainly in

Kansas, meaning that McCabe's vast output is scattered around the world. As with biographical work, there is virtually no current analytical work about him to build on, and no library with an authoritative collection of his works. Many of the monographs written in the second half of his career were wretchedly printed on poor paper and are disintegrating. So, in order to get some idea of this extraordinary man, the first two chapters will present what purely biographical information is still available to us. Having given an impression of the person, I will, in the next chapter, outline the extent of his influence around the world. The remaining six chapters will explore significant aspects of McCabe's intellectual outlook and will seek to defend the rationalist humanism that inspired it.

But we need to return to the question: Is it possible that his work is simply too flawed or outdated now to bother with? No, and not the least reason being that if McCabe's work was so badly flawed, I suspect it would have attracted the attention of religious apologists or postmodernist jeremiahs, keen for an easy victory. It is true that much of McCabe's work was time-sensitive, but this is often the fate of the popularizer. And writing time-sensitive material is not a flaw, especially for a popularizer. This will be one of the themes of chapter 5. But, again, this doesn't really explain why his material should have been so neglected.

Part of the explanation of McCabe's almost total obscurity might be that he has been lumped in with the large cohort of anti-Catholic writers. Much of this sort of writing, usually from Protestants, is so intellectually flatulent and mean-spirited that many people are unwilling to be associated with it, even for the purposes of study. I enter this area with some trepidation myself, as I am not keen to suffer the years of vilification that McCabe did. Religious studies scholarship has wanted to concentrate on the positive aspects of the phenomenon of religion, so sectarianism has not been a popular field of study. Any prejudices, except those against unbelievers, are now so frowned upon that even studying the area can expose the scholar to calumny. Chapter 8 is devoted to showing that McCabe was an opponent of the Roman Catholic Church—an intelligent, astute, and pertinent critic. The significant difference between McCabe and virtually all other anti-Catholic writers is that McCabe's position was completely transparent at all times. It would be unjust to include him with the majority of anti-Catholic writers, whose prime motivation is simple hatred. What is more, all honest critics recognized this.

One of the disciplines that might have been expected to have studied McCabe is religious studies. This discipline has developed tremendously since the Second World War, but it has tended to ignore the phenomenon of freethought, which has suffered from this neglect. Freethought, here used as a catchall title to include all varieties of unbelief, has tended to fall down the cracks between intellectual history, religious studies, philosophy, and the history of science. Theologians have continued to show some interest in atheism, but their research has hardly been conducive to a balanced picture, motivated as they are by their prior goal of proving that their brand of theism is true.

So, there have been few academics with the inclination to devote time to what is not a central area in their discipline. A related problem is that McCabe wrote so broadly that few scholars would feel competent to judge with equal authority his views on embryology, the state of education in the papal states, astronomy, the religious anthropology of the Fuegians, existentialism, the philosophy of mind, and the literary merit of George Bernard Shaw—among other things. This has certainly been an issue for me, and several fields deserving closer study have been neglected by me, largely because I am simply not able to comment on them with any authority.

McCabe has also been neglected because he was not an established academic himself. Thinkers outside the universities are often treated as examples of trends in thought, rather than as people whose thought deserves consideration on its own terms. Academics of McCabe's time were usually content to dismiss him as an amateur, a generalist, and a popularizer. More recently, as I have suggested, they have seen little profit in studying someone whose *weltanschauung* is so clearly obsolete. And given the pressures of specialization, many academics would be severely challenged to comment sensibly on such a wide range of subjects as McCabe traversed.

Another reason McCabe has been forgotten was predicted very soon after his death. "One thing only will militate against his speedy recognition; he was a militant Freethinker, Atheist and Materialist."[9] Another crime could be added: McCabe was also an outspoken feminist and advocate of sexual liberty. Any one of these grave sins might have been forgivable in the first half of the twentieth century, or perhaps two of them, so long as a discreet silence was kept. But to endorse publicly all four of these heresies—that was unforgivable. It is difficult to appreciate quite how reviled atheism and materialism have been—and in many parts of the world still are—and that a public profession of atheism or materialism often came at considerable social cost. Few people knew this more than McCabe. A public profession of atheism in McCabe's day was often seen as a public confession of moral and intellectual bankruptcy. More recently, philosophers like Wallace Matson, J. J. C. Smart, Antony Flew, J. L. Mackie, J. C. A. Gaskin, and Michael Martin have banished this ancient prejudice and have put atheism well and truly on the intellectual map. The same has happened to materialism even more recently thanks to thinkers like Daniel Dennett, Paul and Patricia Churchland, Richard Dawkins, and Richard Vitzhum. As a result, both atheism and materialism are recognized as intellectually respectable positions far more than was the case in McCabe's day. And, of course, Western societies have undergone a comprehensive revolution in our attitudes toward sexuality and what are now called gender issues. So, again, there is little need to bother with McCabe.

This seems unjust. Joseph McCabe deserves to be remembered. He deserves to be remembered as an atheist/materialist voice in the wilderness, if a biblical allusion is not inappropriate. McCabe was a lone, often despised, pioneer for systems of thought that are now breaking tremendous new ground. He deserves to be remembered as an extraordinary scholar—as one of the twentieth century's most complete polymaths. He also deserves respect for his commitment to the Enlightenment ideals of education, informed skepticism, and the power of reason. His writings were always directed to the general reader. And as such, he deserves to be remembered as a man who has indeed had many imitators.

NOTES

1. Gregory Bruce Smith, *Nietzsche, Heidegger, and the Transition to Postmodernity* (Chicago & London: University of Chicago Press, 1996), p 8. Smith is critical of contemporary postmodernism, but uses Nietzsche and Heidegger to fashion what he claims is a truly postmodern outlook.

2. Michael Luntley, *Reason, Truth and Self* (London & New York: Routledge, 1995), pp. 15–16.

3. I am, of course, under no obligation to provide definitions of postmodernism, which freely admits its own incoherence and preference for moods, mayhem and metaphor, but do so anyway.

4. Bryan Appleyard, *Understanding the Present* (London: QPD, 1992), pp. 237–39.

5. Zygmunt Bauman, *Intimations of Postmodernity* (London & New York: Routledge, 1993), see introduction.

6. Luntley, *Reason, Truth and Self*, p. 84.

7. This observation was made by Michael Coren in his biography of G. K. Chesterton. See *Gilbert: The Man Who Was G. K. Chesterton* (London: Jonathan Cape, 1989), p. 151.

8. I am grateful to Mike Lloyd-Jones for this insight, as I am for a great many others.

9. G. H. Taylor, "Joseph McCabe—A Tribute," *Freethinker* (April 2, 1955): 34.

1

The Rise and Fall
of Father Antony

John Ralston Saul, in his irreverent *Doubter's Companion*, wrote of Voltaire that there is no convincing evidence that writers do their job by being nice. "Nice writers are usually working for someone or senile or in the wrong business. Those who have done the most good, as Voltaire pointed out, have 'mostly been persecuted.' "[1] For reasons that will become obvious as this book develops, I can think of few better introductions to Joseph McCabe.

Joseph Martin McCabe was born on November 11, 1867, the second of eight children, four of each. Both his parents were Catholics, although of different stamps. His father, William Thomas McCabe, was born in Ireland and had inherited the faith, which he wore with a genial tolerance. Like so many of his compatriots, he had fled famine and poverty in Ireland, and ended up in the Lancashire slums. Joseph's mother, Harriet Kirk, was English and converted to Catholicism on marrying William McCabe. Her adopted faith remained bright for the rest of her life. Piety seemed to be a family inheritance. It was Harriet's maternal great-grandfather, the story went, who was sent to arrest Thomas Paine. On finding Paine's bed empty he was reputed to have thrust his sword deep into it. The sword became a treasured family heirloom.[2]

Determined to raise good Catholic children, Harriet named her second-born Joseph in the hope that he would follow his namesake's lead and enter the church. McCabe recalled late in his life that his middle name, Martin, was to commemorate being born on St. Martin's day. However, as if to complicate what should be a simple matter of fact, McCabe's birth certificate actually states he was born on November 12. We can only speculate about what is happening here.

It seems unlikely that McCabe, an accomplished historian, spent his entire life giving the wrong date for his own birthday. It is more likely that, as Joseph was from a poor family, undue precision over the correct date on the birth certificate was not thought to be necessary, and so he was declared born on the following day. We will never know for sure.[3]

We do know that Joseph was born in Macclesfield, Cheshire, where his father worked as a silk weaver. Before Joseph was three, the family moved into a two-up, two-down terrace house in Gorton, a drab outer suburb of Manchester, then one of the industrial powerhouses of the world. William McCabe slowly improved his position, rising to become a foreman. Harriet worked in one of the downstairs rooms in their house as a milliner. "Facing our new house, across the narrow street, were the church and monastery of St. Francis. The church, a handsome Gothic structure designed by the distinguished Catholic architect, Pugin, rose, narrowly, high above the squalid clusters of houses and etched itself in my mind."[4] This church is now in a very advanced state of disrepair.

The McCabe children attended the local Catholic schools, with Joseph standing out as a model pupil and zealous believer. "I recall vividly how at times I knelt in rapt adoration before the altar, dressed in a pretty lace surplice (as an 'altar boy') and the expression of a cherub, and wondered why God did not send down a fiery chariot for *me* as he did for Elijah of old."[5] While God may have missed the pious altar boy with the cherubic expression, certain adults near to him did not. While writing a work on the inferiority complex in 1940, at the age of 73, McCabe made a startling admission about child abuse. "I remember vividly attempts of men, on two or three different occasions, to induce me to do something of the kind when I was eleven or twelve years old." He had been discussing what we now call repressed memory syndrome, about which, incidentally, he was skeptical. He noted quietly that instances of abuse "are hardly matters which a child of eleven or twelve is likely to forget."[6] This is the only time McCabe ever specifically mentions this abuse. Neither does he give any indication of the offender. He would still have been at his Catholic school at this stage, and we have had all too much evidence of the sorry record of these institutions in the last couple of decades of the twentieth century not to be understandably suspicious. On one occasion, in 1914, McCabe was discussing pederasty (a "repugnant vice") among the Greeks, and went on to exonerate the Greeks from sole responsibility for this practice. McCabe assured his readers that, contrary to the boasting of a contemporary apologist, "unnatural vices" are still "prevalent in Europe today, even in England. . . ."[7] There is little to be gained by indulging in speculative psychoanalysis about the consequences of this abuse on McCabe's later behavior, but it is important to bear this incident in mind.

McCabe was not simply exposed to moral dangers at his school. Being a school for poor children, the hygiene standards were abysmal. All the lavatories for the school of several hundred "emptied into a common large open pit (open to the playground), which was emptied by the 'night-soil men' only once in a few months."[8] The stink from the pit and even from the streets of his grubby section of Manchester was something McCabe recalled with horror half a century later. Either way, with education costing anything up to sixpence a week, McCabe's education was never going to be protracted. At thirteen he left school and joined the workforce. McCabe describes the culture he entered into:

> Fighting and copulation were the outstanding pleasures of life, the only pleasures for which they paid nothing. At 12, usually, the boy or girl entered the shop or factory, and there was commonly, at the end of the first day, a ceremony of initiation, for boy or girl, churchgoer or not, that I need not describe. From that day their ears were drenched with obscene talk. On Saturday they saw their elders flock to the squalid public houses, and by evening the streets were enlivened with group-fights.[9]

McCabe started his career at Rutlands warehouse as an errand boy, and rose quickly to take the position of clerk. But in June 1884, at the age of sixteen, he left his job and began to study for the priesthood. Joseph's parents, while proud of the thought of a son of theirs rising to become a priest, put no undue pressure on him, and assured him of a warm welcome should he decide the life was not for him. Nonetheless, the boy did feel himself to be under some pressure. "I had been conscious throughout of merely yielding to circumstances, to the advice and exhortation of my elders; there was no definite craving for the life on my part, certainly no 'voice speaking within me' to which I felt a duty to submit."[10]

The new entrant was placed in a class with seven others for a year's training prior to becoming a novice. The training was almost exclusively the rote learning of Latin grammar. His year of study was a success, thanks largely to his own efforts, for the standard of teaching was low. By the end of the year McCabe had a sound grasp of the elements of Latin, having read all of Cicero and most of Virgil. McCabe had a natural flair for languages. Later on in life, he was to become fluent not only in Latin, but also Greek, German, French, Spanish, and Italian.

At the end of 1885, McCabe entered his novitiate year where, "dead to the world," he was renamed Brother Antony. Were this to be the pious life of a saint, we could at this point wax lyrical about divine prescience in choosing Antony of Padua (1195–1231/2) as the young man's new name. But it is not, so we will be content with an ironic smile. St. Antony, despite being small and with a gentle, almost soft demeanor, was in fact a scourge of ill-living clergy and was known as the "hammer of heretics." He was known as an excellent biblical scholar and preacher, one who could be understood by the learned and simple alike.[11] Seven centuries later, Joseph McCabe would share these characteristics, although he came to hammer humbug rather than heresy.

But in the meantime, the young novice repaired to the monastery at Killarney, County Kerry, in Ireland. The novitiate year was to be a test of faith and preparation for taking the solemn vows of chastity, poverty, and obedience. His first impression of the substantial limestone building was of "profound melancholy and discontent."

> The interior of the monastery with its chill, gloomy cloisters, its solemn and silent inmates, conveyed at once a deep impression of solitude and isolation. When we sat down to supper at the bare wooden tables on the evening of our arrival—my first community meal—widely separated from each other, eating in profound silence, and with a most depressing gravity, I felt that my monastic career would be a short one. A young friend had entered their novitiate the previous year and had ignominiously taken flight two days after his arrival: I found myself warmly sympathizing with him.[12]

Brother Antony pulled himself together and settled into the life of the monastery. He was not able to abandon his intellectual pursuits, however. At one point he was reprimanded for reading a Greek grammar, not a common offense among seventeen-year-old boys, then or now. He would have had plenty of opportunity for repentance and chastisement, as his monastery practiced flagellation. Three times a week the friars would retire to their cells in order to flog themselves with knotted cords. "Knowing that our instructor used to listen at our doors during the performance, we frequently gave him an exaggerated impression of our fervor by religiously flogging the desk or any other resonant device."[13] Brother Antony also developed dyspepsia from the rich food and large quantities of alcohol that was the staple fare of the monks. But neither the flagellation nor the alcohol could expel the first twinges of doubt.

> One month I would sit, ill, in the garden moodily contemplating the melancholy blue Kerry hills beyond the lakes. Next month I would rally and face the holy treadmill. And gradually there emerged from the grey waters of my thoughts the fundamental doubt that was to haunt me for the next ten years and in the end lead me to sanity and freedom.[14]

He spoke of his doubts at one stage in a confession and was treated to what he came to know as the "blush argument"—ridicule. "How dare I, an ignorant boy, doubt what such legions of great men believed!"[15] Suitably chastened, Brother Antony would plunge back into monastic life. "I was," he wrote,

> during the periods when doubt departed from me, profoundly religious and most devoted to the models of the medieval saints. In my early twenties I would frequently spend an hour in wordless prayer or a state closely akin to that which is known as ecstasy, or differing from it only in the degree of intensity.[16]

Doubtless emboldened by these spates of piety, the novice overcame his doubts, and took his vows in the middle of 1886. The church young Father Antony entered into was going through what even contemporaries could see was a dark phase of its long career. Ever since 1870 the pope had been in a self-imposed exile in the Vatican, as a protest against the loss of the papal states. The newly created state of Italy had already seized the northern two-thirds of the papal territories in 1860. Once an electoral roll was established, a vote was held, and the overwhelming majority favored incorporation into Italy. Pius IX had begun his career a liberal but, frightened by the 1848 troubles, quickly became a reactionary. From 1850 to 1870 Pius IX ruled in Rome only due to the support of French and (for a while) Austrian troops to prevent rebellion. When the last French troops withdrew in 1870, the Italians marched in and incorporated the city of Rome and its immediate hinterland, known as the Patrimony. Again, an electoral roll had to be established, and the subsequent vote was embarrassingly comprehensive in favor of incorporation to Italy. In the Patrimony, 133,681 voted for inclusion into Italy, with a desultory 1,507 wanting to stay with the pope. In Rome itself 40,785 voted for Italy while only 46 voted for the Papacy.[17]

Not surprisingly, Pius IX developed a lasting dislike for democracy and for all the trappings of modernity. Pius's successor, Leo XIII (1878–1903), though outwardly more conciliatory, was in fact just as reactionary as he was. Leo had been instrumental in the construction of the *Syllabus of Errors* during Pius's pontificate. The *Syllabus* was a comprehensive condemnation of the eighty "principal errors of our times," culminating in a rejection of "progress, liberalism, and modern civilization."[18] Leo also decreed, in *Aeterni Patris* of 1879, the works of St. Thomas Aquinas to become foundational in higher Catholic education. As a Catholic historian has commented, "'Leo saw Thomism not as a starting point of theological inquiry, but as the end of it. . . . Within a generation of the publication of *Aeterni Patris*, 'Thomism' had itself become an ossified orthodoxy in the Roman schools."[19] Leo followed *Aeterni Patris* with *Providentissimus Deus* in 1890, which affirmed the complete inerrancy of the Bible.

Father Antony was to become very familiar with the Catholic education system during Leo's pontificate. Soon after making his simple vows (the final, "solemn" vows happened after three years at Forest Gate), he was transferred to the central training college of the Franciscans, known as Forest Gate, actually the Church of St. Anthony, in Upton, London, where he studied for five years. After fifteen months studying Latin classics and rhetoric, another fifteen months studying scholastic philosophy, the bulk of the program (another two and a half years) was taken up with the study of theology. Under that broad title was included ecclesiastical history, canon law, and moral and dogmatic theology. Their lecturer in dogmatic theology was Father David, who went on to serve on the Church's Biblical Commission under Pius X, where he would insist on the Mosaic authorship of the Pentateuch.[20] This, indeed, was part of the problem. McCabe noted in *Twelve Years in a Monastery* that the main problem with his philosophical training was its "narrow exclusivism."

At Cambridge, the program of philosophical authors is so delightfully impartial that few students find themselves in possession of definite philosophical views after reading it; in every seminary and monastic college the impression made upon the student is that the scholastic system is so clearly and uniquely true that all opponents are either feeble-minded or dishonest—usually the latter alternative is urged.[21]

This exclusivism was to rankle for many years after his departure from the church. And with good reason, because Leo's successor, Pius X, was considerably more reactionary and suspicious of intellectual activity even than his predecessors. Not surprisingly, given this climate, the serious problem with Forest Gate was the quality of its teaching. The student body during his five years earned a reputation for being difficult. Father Antony quickly became the spokesperson for the students, and, altogether, they were responsible for the removal of no fewer than six of the teaching staff. One of their victims, "a Belgian friar of noted eccentricity" would dictate the questions *and the answers*, and would the next day wish them to be repeated verbatim. McCabe noted that "a family of parrots could have passed his examinations as brilliantly as we did."[22] Another became "alarmingly broad and familiar," to the extent that "absolute dementia is the kindest hypothesis to urge in its defense."[23] The mind boggles. Nevertheless, Father Antony did so well in this study, he was appointed professor of philosophy and ecclesiastical history there in 1890, aged only twenty-three.

In the three years Father Antony lectured at Forest Gate, he acquired a reputation for his staunch advocacy of the need to improve the educational quality of the clergy. The monastery at Killarney had, he later found out, been a place of exile for monks who had disgraced themselves elsewhere, and the general standard of lecturers at Forest Gate left a lot to be desired. He writes movingly of fellow priests driven mad by sexual frustration, ruined by drink, or sunk into a banal triviality as the only means of surviving the unnatural regime they found themselves in.

Father Antony's campaign to improve the standard of education for the clergy was bound to ruffle feathers, implying, as it did, that the current standard set by those in charge was inadequate. At no point in his own training, for instance, had he been given any training in science. This was frowned upon because of the danger such an education was thought to have of predisposing the student to the evils of materialism. He even incurred suspicion for recommending a friend with a toothache to visit a dentist. It smacked of rationalism not suggesting to the afflicted one to pray for deliverance. Father Antony's last sermon as a Catholic brother was an appeal for a better quality education for the clergy.

Now holding the chair of philosophy at Forest Gate, Father Antony devoted his spare time to extinguishing the skepticism that was assailing his waking hours. "My skepticism," he wrote, "was partly the effect of temperament, partly a natural desire to verify the opinions which I found myself acting upon.

. . . I knew that philosophy alone could furnish the answer to my doubts, if such an answer were obtainable."[24] Father Antony put himself under the guidance of Father David, his old dogmatic theology lecturer, "and for seven years he was informed, almost weekly, of the growth of my thoughts."[25] Eventually, he came to see the limits of Father David's apologetical resources, which only served to increase his isolation.

It was at Forest Gate where the young man heard his first confession; "a London maid of twenty-four or so—I never saw her face—and a small-minded, raw youth of twenty-four usurping the function of God and forgiving sin!" Father Antony's mind was drastically enlarged by the many lurid, often formulaic and embellished accounts of sexual adventures he heard at confession. Indeed, they were his first real encounters with sexuality.[26] Father Antony developed a lasting dislike for the confessional.

Father Antony spent 1893–94 studying philosophy and oriental languages at the Catholic university at Louvain in Belgium. It was thought by his superiors that he was a suitable candidate to take on the next professorship of Hebrew at Grey Friars. "Weary with struggles against doubt and with premature ministerial activity, I eagerly accepted and made my way to the monastery of our order at Louvain."[27] Louvain had for a long time been one of the most important centers for training promising young priests, although its position was under threat in the 1890s, with Washington University in the United States and Innsbruck in Austria fast becoming significant rival centers. During the year McCabe spent at Louvain, he was among fifty clerical students out of a student body of sixteen hundred. Fully a third of the student body neglected their duty to attend Mass, and McCabe described the piety of the rest as of a "painfully evanescent character."

Less evanescent was the predilection for alcohol, which McCabe found shocking. He recalled arriving one day for dinner among fellow friars in Ghent:

> . . . and after dinner (with the usual pint of strong ale) four of us sat down to five or six bottles of good claret: I drew the line at six glasses and at once attracted as much suspicion as a "water-bibber" of ancient Greece or Rome. At three o'clock a second pint of strong ale had to be faced, and at seven a third; when wine reappeared after that I violently protested—and never recovered their good opinion.[28]

As a scholar, Father Antony prospered. Quite in any way the most outstanding scholar at Louvain that young priest came across was Mgr. Désiré Joseph Mercier, "a gentleman of refined and sympathetic character and one of the ablest living exponents of Catholic philosophy."[29] Mercier (1851–1926) took a shine to Father Antony as well, and invited him to stay at his own house. Franciscan regulations forbade that, but the two got to know each other well during Father Antony's year in Louvain. Mercier had a genuine love of philosophy, so much so, writes the *Catholic Encyclopedia*, that he saw it as a purely rational discipline, to be kept quite distinct from theology, let alone apologetics.[30] In other words, Mercier was a Modernist who was familiar with current philosophical trends. McCabe remembered Mercier speaking disparagingly of traditional doctrines such as eternal punishment.[31] However, Mercier had been installed at Louvain to implement Pope Leo's *Aeterni Patris* decree, which had the effect of reducing the "philosophy" component of his study to little more than rote learning of St. Thomas Aquinas and more recent Thomist apologetics. McCabe later recalled that none of the philosophical authorities of the time: John Stuart Mill, Herbert Spencer, T. H. Green, Nietzsche, Rudolf Lotze, F. H. Bradley, Andrew Seth, or Josiah Royce (McCabe's list) were studied in his philosophy training.[32] And yet one of McCabe's most truculent critics in later years, Father Vincent McNabb, hailed *Aeterni Patris* as a significant advance for philosophy brought on by a farsighted and courageous Leo XIII.[33] Father Antony's year at Louvain was the turning point in his life. Mercier had managed to reconcile the demands of *Aeterni Patris* and *Providentissimus Deus* with contemporary thought, and lesser intellects were reveling in what they took to be a victory for true philosophy. But it was becoming increasingly difficult for Father Antony to do either of these things. Despite all this, he was an outstanding student, and was offered a Ph.D. for his work, but was required to refuse, as accepting such honorifics was forbidden in the Franciscan order.

It is worth noting that, almost fifty years later, the state of Catholic higher education was just as lamentable. The young Anthony Kenny, who later left the church and became a prominent philosopher, remembered that his tertiary education gave "little encouragement to read the works of the great Catholic divines, [and] we were positively forbidden to read theological works by any writer who was not a Catholic."[34]

In the middle of 1894, Father Antony was recalled to Forest Gate, and to the ministry. A fresh batch of students required his instruction. But by this time the "clouds of doubt became dark and permanent."[35] He tried to bury his doubts in work, and returned to his campaign to improve the educational standards of the priests. This problem was emerging in his ministry.

> I have been asked by wives and sisters in the confessional to visit men who were understood to be wavering in faith; I referred them to their parish priests, and was answered that they had so low an estimate of their parish priests that they refused to discuss with them. And where they do meet a Catholic who shows an interest in an acquaintance with modern literature, they are suspiciously forward in urging the restrictions imposed by the Index.[36]

Recognizing an impending crisis, Father Antony decided on a change in his life. Late in 1895, he secured an appointment as principal of the newly established Catholic College of St. Bernardine in Buckingham. Father David, his old mentor from Forest Gate, persuaded him to take the position, in recognition of his campaign to improve the educational standards of the priesthood. Tired and ill, Father Antony took this position to find time in a rural setting to wrestle with his conscience and bring to a head the doubts that were becoming a permanent feature of his life.

These proved to be the final months of Father Antony's life. Over the Christmas break of 1895 he descended into his final crisis of faith. "During the Christmas vacation I settled resolutely to my task, and uninterruptedly, all day and half the night, I went solemnly back over the ground of my studies. Point by point the structure of argument yielded under pressure. Before many days a heavy and benumbing consciousness weighed upon me that I was drifting out into the mist and unknown sea."[37]

"I took a sheet of paper and—was it the Manchester influence?—divided it into debit and credit columns on the arguments for God and immortality. On Christmas Eve I wrote 'Bankrupt' at the foot."[38] "And it was on Christmas morning 1895, after I had celebrated three masses, while the bells of the parish church were ringing out the Christ-message of peace, that, with great pain, I found myself far out from the familiar land—homelessly, aimlessly drifting. But the bells were right after all; from that hour I have been wholly free from the nightmare of doubt that had lain on me for ten years."[39]

It was by now common knowledge that Father Antony was teetering. Father David was sent to Buckingham to ascertain the situation. He arrived in the afternoon and the two men sat and talked amiably of their days at Forest Gate. The next morning Father David's demeanor had changed. "Without further ceremony he handed me the form of deposition from my position, and an order to retire to the friary at Chilworth, in Surrey. Out of curiosity I asked him why I was deposed, and he replied that he did not know."[40] It was Ash Wednesday. Father Antony refused the orders and walked away from St. Bernardine's College and the Catholic Church.

For several months McCabe worked as a clerk in the town for a paltry sum. This was an ugly time for him, as the church harassed him with petty criminal charges, none of which came to anything. Not long after he seceded, he met on the streets of London a Catholic teacher he had known in the church. "He turned pale, either with anger or fear, and asked me, very seriously, if I was not afraid that the earth would open up and let me down to where I belonged."[41] For many years to come McCabe was the target of constant streams of slander and vitriol. Rumors were spread that he had left in order to indulge his apparently numerous vices, variously given as drink, theft, or philandering. Reactions from his immediate family varied. His sister, a schoolmistress at a Catholic school, on one occasion actually went around Manchester tearing down posters advertising a McCabe lecture. Years later, by this time holding more liberal theist beliefs, she and Joseph were reconciled. Harriet, his aged mother, also had a very difficult adjustment to make, as her beloved son was now that most feared of beings—an apostate. But while she never renounced her own Catholicism, neither did she renounce her son. Having heard of his decision, Harriet wrote to her son as only a mother could: "I do not understand, Joe, but I know you."[42] And as for William McCabe, he couldn't suppress his pride in seeing the family name printed in such big letters.

In many ways the most hurtful thing about this sad episode is the church's inability to concede that anyone could secede from it in good faith.[43] Another former colleague, of whom McCabe had thought highly enough to feel the need to explain his secession, said that he would not listen a word of it, and left McCabe to "the worm of conscience."[44] McCabe had truly wanted to believe. He had, in many ways, a believer's temperament. But his head refused to succumb. "With all my privileges and opportunities for study it cost me the better part of ten years of constant reading and thought to come to a final and reliable decision."[45] McCabe could easily have followed the thousands of other priests who found they had lost their faith. He could have suppressed his doubts and settled into the easy life or he could slowly have tried to embalm his doubts with alcohol. Some people, such as the outspoken journalist W. T. Stead, tried to persuade the young man to remain in the church, so as to modernize from within.[46] But he didn't do these things; he left the church. Despite the appalling dislocation to the only life he knew, McCabe had to follow the dictates of his reason. Postmodernists and others for whom a struggle for personal integrity is little more than an amusing aside in a novel may well find such a conclusion anachronistic. What they fail to understand is that McCabe genuinely believed that a life spent in pursuit of truth is a life well spent. This is the main point that all belief systems—whether religious or secular—have in common. And it is the main point of difference between belief systems and the various brands of irrationalism that go by the collective label of postmodernism.

McCabe was now about to embark on a whole new direction in his life. He was still only twenty-eight, and had emerged intact from a profound crisis of faith that would have broken many people. He had developed a formidable ability for intellectual work as well as the discipline to sustain effort through thick and thin. Penniless and homeless, McCabe had to start again. With the help of 20/20 hindsight, we can also see that McCabe went into the world remarkably naive. He recalled later that he had to buy for himself a guide to etiquette, so unfamiliar was he with the outside world.[47] Having undergone such a demanding crisis of faith and commitment, it took him a while to appreciate that others are more prepared to backslide and take the easier route. He never quite came to terms with that when he found it in senior and respected freethinkers. It was to lead him into strife with those who should normally have been counted as his natural allies.

NOTES

1. John Ralston Saul, *The Doubter's Companion* (London: Penguin, 1995), p. 306.

2. Joseph McCabe, *Can We Save Civilization?* (London: The Search, 1932), p. 196.

3. I am grateful to Nicolas Walter for drawing my attention to the alternative date. It was his opinion that November 12 was the correct date of McCabe's birth.

4. Joseph McCabe, *Eighty Years a Rebel* (Girard, Kan.: Haldeman-Julius, 1947), p. 7.

5. *Literary Guide* (December 1924): 203–204.

6. Joseph McCabe, *The Inferiority Complex Eliminated* (Girard, Kan.: Haldeman-Julius, 1940), p. 84.

7. Joseph McCabe, *The Sources of the Morality of the Gospels* (London: Watts, 1914), p. 117.

8. Joseph McCabe, *1825–1925: A Century of Stupendous Progress* (London: Watts, 1925), p. 47.

9. McCabe, *Eighty Years a Rebel*, p. 9.

10. Joseph McCabe, *Twelve Years in a Monastery* (London: Smith Elder, 1897), p. 18.

11. See Donald Attwater, *The Penguin Dictionary of Saints* (London: Penguin, 1985), p. 48.

12. McCabe, *Twelve Years in a Monastery* (1897), p. 36.

13. Ibid., p. 48.

14. McCabe, *Eighty Years a Rebel*, p. 13.

15. Ibid.

16. Joseph McCabe, *Key to Love and Sex* (Girard, Kan.: Haldeman-Julius, 1929), vol. 4, p. 35.

17. Joseph McCabe, *Crises in the History of the Papacy* (London: Watts, 1916), pp. 408–409.

18. Joseph McCabe, *Rome's Syllabus of Condemned Opinions* (Girard, Kan.: Haldeman-Julius, 1950), p. 9.

19. Eamon Duffy, *Saints and Sinners: A History of the Popes* (New Haven, Conn.: Yale University Press in association with S4C, 1997), p. 241.

20. See the footnote in the revised third edition of *Twelve Years in a Monastery* (London: Watts, 1931), p. 70.

21. McCabe, *Twelve Years in a Monastery* (1897), pp. 71–71.

22. Ibid., p. 73.

23. Ibid., p. 65.

24. Ibid., pp. 108–109.

25. Ibid., p. 110.

26. Joseph McCabe, *The Popes and Their Church: A Candid Account* (London: Watts, 1918), pp. 175, 179.

27. McCabe, *Twelve Years in a Monastery* (1897), p. 141.

28. Ibid., pp. 151–52.

29. Ibid., p. 144.

30. See "Mercier, Désiré Joseph" in *New Catholic Encyclopedia* (New York: McGraw-Hill, 1967), vol. 9, pp. 671–72.

31. Joseph McCabe, *The Totalitarian Church of Rome*, Black International, no. 11 (Girard, Kan.: Haldeman-Julius, 1942), p. 19.

32. McCabe, *The Popes and Their Church*, p. 223.

33. Vincent McNabb, *The Catholic Church and Philosophy* (New York: Macmillan, 1927), pp. 119–20.

34. Anthony Kenny, *A Path from Rome* (Oxford: Oxford University Press, 1986), p. 75.

35. McCabe, *Eighty Years a Rebel*, p. 17.

36. McCabe, *Twelve Years in a Monastery* (1897), pp. 170–71.

37. Joseph McCabe, *Twelve Years in a Monastery* (1897), The Thinker's Library, no. 3 (London: Watts, 1930), p. 202.

38. McCabe, *Eighty Years a Rebel*, p. 19.

39. McCabe, *Twelve Years in a Monastery* (1930), pp. 202–203.

40. McCabe, *Twelve Years in a Monastery* (1897), p. 241.

41. Joseph McCabe, *How the Faith Is Protected*, Black International, no. 17 (Girard, Kan.: Haldeman-Julius, 1942), p. 15.

42. Isaac Goldberg, *Joseph McCabe: Fighter for Freethought: Fifty Years on the Rationalist Front* (Girard, Kan.: Haldeman-Julius, 1936), p. 6.

43. McCabe returned to this theme quite often. See *The Popes and Their Church*, pp. 160–61, for a discussion on some of the more draconian papal remedies proposed as late as 1901 to deal with apostates and heretics. See also McCabe, *Twelve Years in a Monastery* (1931), p. 217.

44. McCabe, *How the Faith Is Protected*, p. 15.

45. McCabe, *Twelve Years in a Monastery* (1897), p. 226.

46. F. J. Gould, "The 'Guide,' 1885 to 1899," *Literary Guide* (January 1936): 4. Stead was later to lose his life on the *Titanic*.

47. Joseph McCabe, *The Tyranny of Shams* (London: Eveleigh Nash/Dodd Mead, 1916), p. 256.

2

The Rise and Fall of Joseph McCabe

FROM ROME TO RATIONALISM

Joseph McCabe was twenty-eight, penniless, and dependent on the support of a small circle of friends when he left the Catholic Church on Ash Wednesday 1896. It was obvious he couldn't stay in Buckingham, and before the end of the year he left for London. He spent the next couple of years drifting through a series of positions there and elsewhere, including a six-month sojourn in Nice as the private secretary to the Hon. Mrs. Ives, a wealthy widow, so old, McCabe recalled, she had "been presented to three sultans and three popes and had seen Napoleon."[1] He also began writing. Very soon after arriving in London, he arranged to meet with F. J. Gould (1855–1938), a member of a small group called the Rationalist Press Committee. Gould later recalled meeting this "unassuming, spectacled young man, with a very firm mouth" and suggested he write a pamphlet about his experiences. McCabe agreed, and *From Rome to Rationalism* was published later in the year.[2] The following year he expanded on the theme in another short work called *Why I Left the Church*. Later in 1897 he combined the autobiographical account with the summary of his thoughts on the state of the church in *Twelve Years in a Monastery*.

The London of the late 1890s was full of young men anxious to impress with their literary talents but McCabe was soon standing out from the crowd. He was introduced to Sir Leslie Stephen (1832–1904), a fellow of the British Academy, honorary associate of the Rationalist Press Association, respected writer, critic, and agnostic. McCabe had already written his experiences up as fiction, but it

35

was Stephen who persuaded him to write it as nonfiction. Stephen provided the young man with much-needed encouragement and introduced him to important people. It was Stephen who recommended the manuscript of *Twelve Years in a Monastery* to the publishing firm Smith Elder, and later on Stephen urged his friend Herbert Duckworth publish McCabe's *Peter Abélard* and *St. Augustine and His Age*. Years later, a lifelong friend of McCabe acknowledged that Stephen's help had been critical for "winning McCabe to Rationalism."[3] In gratitude, McCabe dedicated his biography of St. Augustine to Stephen. In his letter of thanks, Stephen wrote that "I can assure you that, though your gratitude pleases me, it makes me ashamed. I feel how very little I have done for you, though the will has not been wanting. I have thoroughly liked and respected all that I have known of you and your work, and wish you all success. . . ."[4]

The respect clearly went both ways and McCabe was to remain intensely loyal to Stephen's memory for the rest of his life. *Twelve Years in a Monastery* was to do much to establish McCabe's reputation as a writer, scholar, and controversialist. It remains one of the titles most referred to from what was to become one of the most extraordinary literary outputs by one person in the history of writing. And McCabe was to make his living from writing and lecturing for the rest of his days.

As well as the accounts of his experiences in the Catholic Church, both in fiction and nonfiction form, McCabe also wrote *Modern Rationalism* in 1897. He was obviously encouraged by the critical success of his first works. The reviewer of *From Rome to Rationalism* in the *Literary Guide*, the journal of the Rationalist Press Committee, had called on McCabe to set out in a future volume his positive views, and *Modern Rationalism* was his attempt to answer that call.[5] This was a general survey of modern knowledge as it referred to theology, biblical criticism, philosophy, science, and ethics. In each case he found the church's teachings at variance with the conclusions of contemporary scholarship. He was later to describe this book as "dreadfully stodgy" and *Twelve Years in a Monastery* as devoid of humor and adolescent in style. While these descriptions are too harsh, it is true that both books were written in an atmosphere that was, in McCabe's own words, "radiant with adolescent fire."[6] *Twelve Years* is certainly the better-written book of the two. These two books, plus his translation of Ernst Haeckel's *The Riddle of the Universe*, contain the basic material that McCabe was to spend the next half century reworking and refining. And it was this newfound zeal for rationalism and his strong loyalties to his mentors in these crucial early years after his secession that were to shape much of the rest of his life.

In his autobiography McCabe recalled the high expectations he had of freethought organizations. He was convinced that "anti-clerical movements would be entirely honest and courageous. I found at once that my expectation had the enthusiasm of youth and inexperience."[7] But underneath his fierce certainty, McCabe was almost hoping the world would prove as wicked as his sermons had once represented. McCabe was never entirely comfortable with intellectual or moral gray areas. Things were usually black or white with him. He never came to terms with the fact that people arrive at whatever brand of freethought they embrace by a bewildering mixture of routes. He had taken the passionate route of the betrayed believer, one that had cost twelve years of his life and a large amount of suffering and isolation. McCabe always found it difficult to accept that others, whose path to freethought was different, were equally sincere. None of this was obvious at the time, however, as McCabe began a long, and for many years rewarding, career as a spokesman for the Rationalist movement.

An important opportunity came up for McCabe in 1898 when the Leicester Secular Society decided to appoint a full-time organizer and lecturer. The Leicester organization was one of the largest and most important bodies in the country to retain the "Secular" title. Secularism had been founded by George Jacob Holyoake (1817–1906) in the middle of the nineteenth century. Holyoake intended Secularism to put unbelief on a sound philosophical basis in its disputes with Christianity, and absorb remnants of the Owenite and Chartist movements into a broader, cooperative rationalist reform movement. The Secularist movement was in decline at the end of the nineteenth century, having given ground to, among other things, the more militant atheism of the National Secular Society, the organization founded by Charles Bradlaugh. The appointment of McCabe as full-time lecturer was intended to arrest this decline. In many ways McCabe was an inspired choice, but he lasted in the job for less than a year, returning to London in 1899.

The main reason for McCabe failing at Leicester, I think, was that it was at Leicester. He was ideologically sympathetic to the secularist programme, but was impatient to develop the contacts and opportunities that were opening to him in London. And, having left the church, McCabe was not comfortable with a role that had any pastoral aspect to it. This said, he did not leave Leicester on bad terms. McCabe retained close relations with the Leicester Secular Society for the rest of his life. Along with the Glasgow Rationalists, Leicester was one of the most-frequented venues for his lecture tours. And while at Leicester, McCabe met Beatrice Lee (1881–1960), an eighteen-year-old daughter of a hosiery worker. A year later they were married.

Back in London, McCabe returned to the circle of his mentor, Sir Leslie Stephen, who was just beginning his second term as president of the West London Ethical Society. It was thanks to the support of Stephen that McCabe was introduced to the principal lecturer of the ethical movement at the time, the dynamic and headstrong American activist Stanton Coit (1857–1944). McCabe became part of a team of lecturers working for a School of Ethics that Coit had established. As is often the case among spokespeople for openness and collegiality, Coit was a dictatorial titan, and he and the young McCabe did not get on at all. Nevertheless, McCabe taught at Coit's School of Ethics from 1901 until 1904, doing courses on church discipline in the Roman Catholic Church in 1901, logic and applied logic in 1902–1903 and ecclesiastical history in

1903–1904. With a young family to support and an uncertain future outside the freethought movement, McCabe's options were limited—even within the movement. He had written for the *Freethinker*, the paper of the National Secular Society, in 1899, but was even less able to get on with its editor, G. W. Foote (1850–1915) than he was with Coit. The *Freethinker*, England's most militantly secular magazine, was founded by Foote in 1881, and was very much his creation. McCabe was a young man in a hurry, but he was moving among some formidable self-made men who were not going to be hurried by a new arrival.

It was among two other freethought organizations that McCabe found a home. The Rationalist Press Committee quickly recognized McCabe's ability. Early in 1898, the *Literary Guide* announced that McCabe was to become a regular contributor. He was also actively involved the following year when the committee reconstituted itself as the Rationalist Press Association (RPA), serving on its directorate until 1902. He had the honor of writing the first book the RPA published, *Religion in the Twentieth Century*. Here McCabe gave vent to his tremendous optimism for the future. He saw religious thought moving inexorably toward rationalism "unless science is a mockery and the truth of history a delusion."[8] A century later a coterie of postmodernist academics would be saying just these things—and getting paid for it.

The other organization in which McCabe found a convivial home was the South Place Ethical Society. This extraordinary body was originally founded in 1793 as a Dissenting Protestant chapel but moved fairly soon to Unitarianism. By the time McCabe came along, South Place was a humanist organization. Coit had been involved with South Place until 1891 but left to work for the wider Ethical movement. The first formal involvement McCabe had with South Place was to take part in a discussion on the subject of "The Place of Authority in Things Ethical," in September 1900, with J. M. Robertson, W. H. Hudson, and Mr. Swinny, a Positivist.

McCabe was quickly building a reputation for himself. Another man he met through Sir Leslie Stephen was Stephen's onetime research assistant, Ramsay MacDonald. Clearly a man on the way up, his home at Lincoln Inn Fields took on the role of "a kind of socialist salon" under the guidance of MacDonald's sociable wife Margaret Gladstone.[9] This friendship came to nothing, McCabe giving the reason that MacDonald became wary of his heretical aquaintance.

The next twenty years were a blur of frantic activity as McCabe built a family, a reputation, and a respectable income. Joseph and Beatrice had four children, two boys and two girls. Frank was born in February 1902, Athene in September 1905, Dorothy sometime in 1907, and Ernest in January 1909. The young family lived for a while in Cricklewood, before moving to Bridge Lane in Golder's Green. Each summer they went off to Southwold in Suffolk for their family vacation. There must, however, have been long periods when the children would have had to play outside because "Daddy's working." Between 1899 and 1914 McCabe wrote in the neighborhood of fifty-seven books and translated a further sixteen works from German, French, and Spanish. This averages out at, approximately, a book written or translated every ten weeks. This was on top of a staggering schedule of public lectures in all parts of the country as well as a continuous stream of articles for many different magazines. Most of his more scholarly books (in the conventional sense) were from this early period in his publishing career. The books McCabe wrote, and the ones he translated, were among the more popular books published by the RPA at the time, and contributed significantly to its financial success. The outstanding example of this was his translation of Ernst Haeckel's *The Riddle of the Universe*. We will examine the extraordinary success of this book in the next chapter.

With each passing year McCabe became more senior in the Rationalist Press Association. Up until 1906 J. M. Robertson (1856–1933) was unquestionably the most senior RPA author and thinker, but Robertson was elected in the Liberal landslide of that year as Member of Parliament (MP) for Tyneside and remained in national politics until 1918. McCabe's rise after 1906 was rapid. In 1908 he was nominated an honorary associate of the RPA, although, as we will see later, this honor had the flavor of a consolation prize. McCabe also rose in seniority among the journalists and reviewers writing for the *Literary Guide*, the RPA's journal. In 1913 he was put in charge of a new series of short works to be published by the RPA called The Inquirer's Library, which was designed to bring rationalist perspectives on religion to the general reader. McCabe himself authored the first in the series, called *The Existence of God*, and a lifelong friend, the London lawyer E. S. P. Haynes, contributed the second in the series, *The Belief in Personal Immortality*. Other authors in the series included Edward Clodd, Charles Gorham, and Edward Pilcher ("Chilperic Edwards"), all well-known controversialists in their time. By 1914, McCabe could with justice be labeled the "leading spirit of the Rationalist Press Association."[10]

This rise in McCabe's fortunes was done on the back of a staggering workload. As well as the many books, he wrote an uncounted number of articles, including a lengthy contribution each year for the annuals put out by the RPA. It would now be virtually impossible to gather an even remotely accurate estimate of how many magazine articles he wrote. Appendix 2 is an attempt, primarily from English sources, to give an idea of the scale of McCabe's output. And as was the custom, book reviews went unsigned in those days, so it is reasonable to suppose that he wrote his fair share of those. And not all of McCabe's work was for the rationalist press. From 1916 to 1919 he wrote for the wartime Information Department, where his fluency in several languages and extensive contacts must have been invaluable. McCabe held a senior position in the section dealing with the neutral countries. As an example of his work there, he devoted a lot of time scotching rumors that the war had been engineered by England in order to ruin a resurgent German economy.

When McCabe was not writing, he was in heavy demand on the lecture circuit. McCabe came of age in the second half of the great era of the itinerant lecturer, when working men and women thirsted after knowledge their lowly status denied them. At the time of his autobiography, McCabe estimated he had given more than four thousand lectures. As with the magazine articles, it is no longer possible to compile anything like a comprehensive list of McCabe's lecture engagements. Appendix 3 has a reasonable spread of his English lectures and some from his tours of New Zealand, but it is necessarily incomplete. This extraordinary career began, as we saw, in various arms of the London Ethical movement at the turn of the century.

In 1907 South Place decided to name four appointed lecturers in place of its previous system of having one minister. McCabe was among the four lecturers invited to take the post up. He continued to lecture for the South Place Ethical Society until the last years of his life. But McCabe was also a very active lecturer for the Rationalist Press Association. The RPA Annual Report for 1908 boasted that Joseph McCabe, "whose energies are apparently inexhaustible, has been addressing crowded audiences most week-nights during the season as well as twice on Sundays."[11] Twelve years later the report noted simply that a "complete list of his engagements for the RPA alone would occupy more than a page of this report."[12] Furthermore, attendance at McCabe's lectures was extremely impressive. Just as an example, in October 1907, McCabe was lecturing on evolution and religion to five hundred people on each of two evenings to the Plymouth Rationalist Society. Usually the reaction was favorable, even from those who disagreed with him. McCabe recalled an elder of the Kirk in northern Scotland, who told him at the end of the evening, "It was a gran' lecture. Of course it was a pack o' lees, but it was a gran' lecture."[13]

Like most successful lecturers, he developed a knack for staggering his programs, and often repeated lecture programs in short seasons. For instance, between October 20 and November 19 in 1908, he gave a program of four lectures, one a week, complete with 180 lantern slides on the evolution of mind, to two separate audiences. For over thirty years the lantern slide was the most impressive high-tech accompaniment a lecturer could possess. He gave the lecture to the South Place Ethical Society on one day of the week, then two days later, give it again to a public audience at the Fulham Town Hall. He then wrote the lectures up and Adam & Charles Black published them in 1910 as *The Evolution of Mind*. The book was reprinted twice, in 1911 and again in 1921. McCabe's prodigious energy on the lecturing circuit beggars belief. Some of his contemporaries gave vent to their envy at his success. Chapman Cohen (1868–1954), himself an energetic lecturer, spoke dismissively of "Little Jo and his magic lanterns." Years later a historian of the South Place Ethical Society acknowledged McCabe as the best lecturer on evolution in Britain.[14]

Not only was McCabe an indefatigable lecturer, he was also a formidable debater. Over his long career, McCabe took part in about a dozen major debates with theologians, archbishops, creationists, and spiritualists. In the days before television, debates and lectures were an important source of public instruction and entertainment. Looking back on the printed versions of these debates in an age of television sound bytes, one can only admire the attention span of the audiences. Inevitably, these debates took place during an already crowded schedule. For example, a fortnight before this frantic program of lectures in 1908, McCabe took part in a public debate that went over two evenings at Essex Hall. The topic was "The First Chapter of Genesis and Modern Science" and his opponent was Rev. John Tuckwell. The texts of McCabe's debates were usually published jointly by the RPA and a publisher nominated by his opponent. In this case it was generally thought that Tuckwell had done such a bad job there was little point in doing so.

In November of the following year a gentleman by the name of G. W. de Tunzelmann challenged McCabe to a debate on the rather grand topic of "Theism and the Problem of the Universe." De Tunzelmann had a complicated mathematical argument, derived from Sir James Jeans, that the universe had a beginning, and therefore had to be created. Sadly, the audience was not given the opportunity to discern the soundness of his argument, as de Tunzelmann asked that it be "taken as read."[15] When McCabe was abroad the following year de Tunzelmann unilaterally published a heavily revised report of the debate. McCabe was described as "the luminary of some Little Bethel" and each of his addresses were peppered with ad hominem footnote comments added later by de Tunzelmann.[16]

Despite these unfortunate episodes, and McCabe's increasingly daunting reputation, most debates he was involved in were held in an atmosphere of mutual respect and good manners. Debating issues is almost a sacrament to rationalists. In the course of a debate in 1923 on the argument to design, McCabe made his views clear.

> It must make plain to those on both sides, who are disposed to dismiss with disdain all dissent from their position, that impatience or arrogance of that kind is superficial. Mr. Shebbeare and I have engaged in this discussion in entire friendliness, mutual respect, and freedom from those personal or sectarian influences which very commonly make such discussion unprofitable. We take one single issue, on which we may concentrate our attention; and the evidence consists, not of statements of fact which it requires a laborious scholarship to verify, or upon which divergent authorities may be quoted, but of simple observations of Nature which must lie within the memory of every reader. Yet our differences in interpreting this evidence are profound, and the patient endeavor to reach the roots of those differences can hardly fail to communicate a little of our mutual respect to others.[17]

To respect the process of civilized debate between knowledgeable disputants is essential to rationalism. Doubtless it can be disparaged as "bloodless," but then so can many essential features of the open society. And despite McCabe's fearsome reputation as a difficult man, he was almost always a gracious and honorable opponent, even when his opponent was not.

The last significant debate McCabe was involved with was held at Welfare Hall in Pyle, Glamorgan, in 1939, a month short of his seventy-second birthday. His opponent on this occasion was an old adversary, Father Vincent McNabb, and the discussion was "that Roman Catholicism is a false religion." McNabb was a friend of Hilaire Belloc (1870–1953) and G. K. Chesterton (1874–1936), and shared their hostility to modernity and pluralism. These two had crossed swords in 1916, when McNabb had written a hostile and condescending review of McCabe's *The Influence of the Church on Marriage and Divorce*. Responding to McNabb's call that he should withdraw the book from circulation, McCabe replied, "I will not. But after this exhibition of foul tactics and revolting misrepresentation I will— write something stronger."[18] McCabe would more than honor that pledge.

As well as all this, McCabe found time to lend active support to campaigns for secular education, birth control, and women's suffrage. McCabe showed great generosity with his time and skills for causes he believed in, and was unconcerned with the effect they had on his reputation, something that mattered quite a lot to someone whose sole source of income was writing and lecturing.

McCabe's advocacy for secular education led to his admiration for New Zealand, which was then the envy of the world for its education which, since 1877, had been declared free, secular, and compulsory. New Zealand was, for McCabe, the prime example of a country with a sensible, progressive, and practical attitude toward social improvement that he recommended to his readers throughout his career. He wrote two books on this topic as well, *The Truth About Secular Education* (1906) and *A Hundred Years of Educational Controversy* (1907). In both books the education systems of Australia and New Zealand were contrasted favorably with that of the United Kingdom.

APOSTOLIC TOURS

In all likelihood, it was his curiosity about these countries that led him to accept invitations from rationalists in those countries to tour them in 1910, 1913, 1920, and finally in 1923. McCabe had been to parts of Europe before 1910, but this was his first major tour away from Britain. Between 1910 and 1930, McCabe toured Europe, North America, and Australasia extensively. For some tours, he was away for months at a time. As he was usually being paid by his host organizations, he had to save money as best he could. He always traveled alone, and in the economy classes. He usually spent his sea passages writing but was occasionally recognized and ended up giving impromptu lectures to delighted fellow passengers.

McCabe's first trips abroad were to Europe. His two earliest trips were also among the two most significant. The International Freethought Congresses in Rome in 1904 and Paris in 1905 were very well attended and were formidable experiences for McCabe. The Rome congress was held in the face of bitter protests from the Catholic Church, from Pope Pius X down. To McCabe's pleasure the "Italian Government's only reply was to grant the heretics all the privileges that were ever given to the great Catholic pilgrimages: to put at their disposal its finest institution, the Collegio Romano, and to send its Minister of Public Instruction to open the Congress."[19] The memory of the significant troop presence surrounding the congress remained with many delegates for years to come. He was to meet many significant European thinkers at these congresses, chief among them was Ernst Haeckel, several of whose works McCabe had translated. In 1907 McCabe made a special visit to Jena and met Haeckel personally. Fond references to this visit are scattered throughout McCabe's writings.

Equally significant was his flying visit in 1909 to France and Spain to gather information about the recent murder of the Spanish educationist Francisco Ferrer. Within a month he had produced an angry indictment of Ferrer's murder, which quickly sold out and was to be very influential. The First World War interrupted McCabe's travels in Europe, but following his stint in the wartime Information Department he did a two-month lecture tour of British troops stationed in the Rhineland in 1919. He visited Greece in 1922, then in the final stages of its defeat by Turkey. He wrote up his experiences and impressions of this last trip as a special correspondent for one of tabloid papers. On his way out there, McCabe spent a week in Vienna. "One day, standing in a crowd of workers on the steps of the Opera House I saw the sabers of the mounted police flash in the sun as they threatened to charge, and I ran with the crowd."[20]

In 1925 he traveled through Spain and attended the Freethought Congress that was again being held in Paris. Times had changed, however, and this congress was a shadow of the huge freethought gatherings that had so impressed the young McCabe before the war. As well as being written up for the popular press, each of these tours provided McCabe with an extensive supply of anecdotes that livened up his writing. McCabe could describe with equal felicity and empathy a joyfully drunken train journey by Bulgarian peasants on a festival day, or a conversation with a world-renowned scholar on an erudite point of scholastic philosophy.

McCabe's experiences in Australia and New Zealand are in many ways representative of this apostolic (his term) part of his career. It is uncertain who invited him to make his first tour to New Zealand. The idea first came up in the rationalist press in July 1908 but it took another two years before McCabe finally set sail. His tour of Australia had been a huge success, although not without incident. McCabe had been given a police escort into a debate with Cardinal Moran in Sydney, having been received a threat to his life—the second in his career so far.[21] Generally, reaction to McCabe was wildly positive. In Melbourne, for instance, he was engaged to give five lectures, on evolution and on the death of Francisco Ferrer (see chapter 8). "Kind friends in England," McCabe later wrote, "who knew Australia, had prepared me for anything, from empty seats to overripe tomatoes; but no one had predicted the success we have had."[22] Eight hundred people attended his first lecture, and at the end of the fifth lecture he was prevailed upon to stay in the city for another five. The final lecture was held in

the Melbourne Town Hall and was attended by four thousand people. McCabe
was entertained at a reception at the Federal Parliament House by the newly
elected Labour premier. Taking a swipe at the fashionable literary pessimism of
his day, McCabe observed that "D'Annunzio's artistic dread of the 'gray flood of
democratic mud' would waver if he came out here."[23]

Flushed by the extravagant success of his Australian tour, McCabe arrived
in New Zealand late in June 1910. McCabe's reception in Wellington can be
seen as a typical example. Even before McCabe arrived in the city, he was
embroiled in controversy. The city council, in a display of pettiness McCabe was
to experience many times in his lecturing career, had decided not to permit
McCabe the use of the town hall. They were persuaded to rescind the ban only
after a deputation of respected civic leaders had approached them. The deputation included Professor Hugh McKenzie, a genial, expansive Highlander "with a
natural gift for heresy," and John Gemmel, a Unitarian minister.[24]

The day he arrived in the city he was the guest at a welcome function
attended by upwards of seventy people, including civic leaders and dignitaries.
The local paper reported the purpose of McCabe's tour as "broadening people's
minds and breaking down the barriers to liberal thought by opening up to them
vistas of a few thousand miles of space. By such broadening people were better
fitted for social, municipal, and any other problem."[25] Two nights later, McCabe
spoke to a crowded town hall on "Secular Education: The Question of the
Hour." Sir Robert Stout, New Zealand's chief justice, chaired the meeting.
McCabe defended the principle of secular education, and gave a series of historical examples of the benighted state of education during the Middle Ages. He
cited crime figures in New Zealand and Victoria to show that secular education
posed no dangers to the moral fabric of the nation. At the end of the meeting
the packed hall voted unanimously to form a National League for the Defense
of Secular Education.[26] This organization went on to keep the issue of secular
education alive in New Zealand for twenty years.

On the following day, McCabe spoke on "Christianity and Social Progress"
to an equally large audience at His Majesty's Theatre, although this lecture
received no press coverage at all. On July 4, McCabe lectured in the concert
chamber of the town hall on "The Evolution of Man." The paper reports people
having to be turned away, and his address being punctuated with applause.[27]
The next day, his last in the capital, McCabe gave two lectures. At 3:30 P.M.
McCabe spoke to a packed Unitarian church on "The Evolution of Woman"
and in the evening he was back at the town hall to address a large audience on
"The Evolution of Morals and Civilization." The only occasion when McCabe
faced dissent from the audience was in this final lecture when he expressed his
admiration for the high moral character of the Chinese.[28]

In addition to his three trips to Australasia, McCabe traveled North
America extensively, in 1914, 1917, again in 1925–26, 1928 (this trip including
Canada), and finally in 1929–30. While in New York in 1917, McCabe was

introduced to Theodore Roosevelt, the former president, at a dinner given in McCabe's honor at the Harvard Club. Roosevelt thoroughly appreciated McCabe's sense of humor and assertiveness. At the same time President Wilson was asking America to join the war against Germany, McCabe was a guest speaker at the Harvard Club. After a liberal succession of cocktails, McCabe was hoisted onto a three-foot-square table and gave an impassioned speech for an hour. "Many seemed to be hanging from the ceiling by their eyelashes, the room was so packed and enthusiastic." He then retired to drink beer and smoke pipes with a selection of the American military leadership.[29]

An extraordinary thing about McCabe was the breadth of his experience of different shades of humanity. While hobnobbing with the elites at the Harvard Club, he was also attending meetings of the New York Socialists. Quite the rudest person he met in this group of, as he puts it, "bloodthirsty pacifists" was Leon Trotsky, who insisted that under no circumstances whatever was it lawful to shed another's blood. McCabe noted that within a matter of months he would be minister of war in Russia "and athirst for slaughter."[30]

McCabe's other contacts, of course, were with American freethinkers, and it was among these people that he created the most lasting impression. One such American was George MacDonald, who later wrote a history of the *Truth Seeker*, one of America's longest-lasting freethought magazines. "I had difficulty," Mac-Donald wrote,

> adjusting Mr McCabe's personality to his huge and heavy literary product. . . .
> [H]e was a 135-pound Irishman below the medium height. Mr. McCabe belongs
> to the order of Little Giants, being less than middle sized but mighty.[31]

Without doubt, the most important introduction McCabe ever made in America was when he met Emanuel Haldeman-Julius (1889–1951). While lecturing in Kansas City toward the end of 1925, McCabe was invited to visit the wealthy, leftist publisher, who lived nearby. This was one of McCabe's busiest tours, which took in Mexico and Cuba, and in which McCabe gave forty major lectures and took part in six debates. Haldeman-Julius, a lifelong atheist, specialized in very cheaply produced tracts of a scientific, political, or social nature for the general reader. These were already well known in the United States as the People's Pocket Series. In 1924 Haldeman-Julius was looking for a new direction with this series, which had hitherto been mainly concerned with reprinting classics of literature. His first move was to rename this series the Little Blue Books, but the arrival of McCabe provided him with the excellent opportunity for an injection of fresh, approachable, and controversial material for his new series. An agreement for fifty Little Blue Books was made and McCabe wrote them all in just over twelve months. The first one he wrote in between lecturing engagements in Los Angeles early in 1926; the second, on the ship back to England from Cuba.

This friendship was to be enormously important for McCabe, particularly after his break with the RPA, because Haldeman-Julius became McCabe's most important publisher and source of income. In a report on his American trip, McCabe described Haldeman-Julius as "an outspoken, almost Voltairean Rationalist writer of great power. . . ."[32] And Haldeman-Julius's respect for McCabe was boundless. The American considered McCabe "the generation's greatest thinker and scholar," adding that his association with McCabe "had been enough to build a career for anyone."[33] He also noted that he had been warned about McCabe being a difficult personality. "Well, I can say, after almost 25 years, that we never exchanged an unfriendly, discourteous word. I've always found him sprightly, peppy, enthusiastic, cheerful, considerate, gracious, generous, and appreciative. In short, always a gentleman."[34] Like most people, McCabe enjoyed being appreciated, and it brought out the best in him in return. The two men's working relationship continued without a break until Haldeman-Julius's untimely death in 1951.

Two years and a mountain of trouble later, McCabe returned to North America for another lecture tour. We can follow the course of McCabe's North American tour of 1928–29 from mentions made of it while writing his eight-volume *Key to Love and Sex*. It shows what an extraordinarily busy life he had. Volume 1 was written in the prairies of Canada, during his lecture tour of that country; volume 2 was written in "a respectable hotel on Vancouver Island"; volume 3 in San Francisco; volume 4 between Arizona and Kansas, where the last chapter was written at the home of Haldeman-Julius; volumes 5 and 6 on the six-week voyage back to England; and volumes 7 and 8 at home in London. He was never to leave England again.

"THE STORY OF MY CALAMITIES"

It is not surprising that these extended trips abroad led to strains on his marriage. He was away from home for protracted periods at a time, and had been abroad at least every other year for fifteen years when his marriage to Beatrice ended in 1925. Even when in England his commitment to the lecture circuit meant he was away from home very regularly. McCabe admits that the marriage had been a dead letter for a while, and that "we parted by mutual consent."[35] This does not mean that the parting was amicable, however. On learning that the Hampstead Ethical Institute was still providing a platform for Beatrice, McCabe severed his links with the organization for good.[36] Beatrice remained in their marriage property and Joseph was soon to purchase another property nearby, where he remained for the rest of his life. He shared the house with a housekeeper, Ellen Newton, who remained staunchly loyal to McCabe to the end.

But the collapse of his marriage was only part of the story of his calamities. McCabe used this phrase in his autobiography to describe this dismal period of his life. He borrowed it from Peter Abélard, an early influence and subject of his first biography, whose life had been as tumultuous as his own. The 1920s fully justified this phrase for McCabe. Not only did relations with his wife break down irrevocably, but relations with his colleagues in both the South Place Ethical Society and the RPA became increasingly strained. He had been through a series of personality clashes with senior Rationalist figures from relatively early on, which culminated in a bitter estrangement from both organizations in 1928. As if these disasters were not enough, the financial collapse of 1929 and the Depression that followed caused ongoing financial difficulties for the remainder of McCabe's life.

Undoubtedly, McCabe was his own worst enemy. It was his bad luck to be controversialist with a thin skin. McCabe never managed to distinguish criticism of his views, however respectfully put, from personal abuse. This can be seen as early as 1899, when he was still a very junior figure in the Rationalist and Ethical movements. Following an article entitled "Impersonal Deities" in the August issue of the *Literary Guide*, a reader wrote in to differ with McCabe on a couple of points of abstruse theology. McCabe's reply was to describe this poor man as "evidently very limited in imaginative effort."[37] When someone else wrote to the *Guide* on the same controversy, McCabe lamented this man's "offensive attempts to caricature my opinions. . . ."[38] This tendency toward defensive postures in controversies was never far away and came to dominate his thinking over the years.

It is likely that McCabe's personality had a part to play in his rift with the South Place Ethical Society (SPES). In 1907 SPES decided to appoint a team of regular lecturers rather than look for a single replacement for the recently retired titan Moncure Conway (1832–1907). One of the four was Joseph McCabe, who was to lecture regularly at the society for over twenty years. There is little record available to the historian to suggest why this break came about. He was praised for his contributions to SPES in its Annual Report for 1921–22.[39] He was duly reappointed as lecturer at their annual general meeting of May 28, 1922. But it is apparent that all is not well. When, at the end of 1922, a SPES eminence, Herbert Burrows, died, the appreciation of his life from McCabe was terse and sardonic, in sharp distinction to all the other more appreciative, if formulaic, responses.[40] And then, on March 4, 1923, McCabe gave what was to be his last lecture for the SPES for more than a decade. The innocuous subject matter, "Renan As a Moralist," gives little away. The Annual Report for 1923–24 announced that the society had decided to reduce the number of lecturers from five (as it had risen to) to three.[41] McCabe was not one of them. The society had recently purchased a site between Red Lion Square and Theobald's Road in London and would soon begin building its own premises there. Understandably, this would have required that economies be made, and equally understandably, those economies would be made at the most troublesome points.

The story of McCabe's estrangement from the RPA is much more complicated, and to understand it properly, we need to go back to 1908. In that year he wrote an article for the *Literary Guide* about a recent prosecution of a soapbox atheist for blasphemy. McCabe supported the prosecution, declaring he had "not the faintest interest in securing for myself, or any other man, the liberty to attack Christianity in coarse, vulgar, or scurrilous terms."[42] McCabe went on to discuss recent blasphemy cases, claiming that the last genuine prosecution for atheism was that of his mentor George Jacob Holyoake. McCabe had only just finished writing a two-volume biography of Holyoake, having been commissioned for the job by the RPA. All more recent prosecutions, McCabe's article concluded, had involved an element of scurrility and thus were to some extent justifiable.

McCabe's article, and more particularly, his biography of Holyoake, caused grave offense among some of his colleagues and reopened an old division in the freethought movement between those who supported the rival claims of Holyoake or Charles Bradlaugh to be thought of as its most significant leader and shaper. Some people, notably G. W. Foote, founder of the *Freethinker* and an ardent follower of Bradlaugh, had been prosecuted for blasphemy since Holyoake. McCabe had imputed a degree of scurrility to the Foote case, and had therefore insulted the supporters of Bradlaugh within the movement. This was on top of other accusations against Foote in his Holyoake biography, including unnecessary coarseness in his propaganda and dishonesty in a controversy with a prominent churchman.[43]

The disputes over McCabe's views on blasphemy were merely a prelude and a cover for the larger struggle going on behind the scenes. Let McCabe tell the rest of the story:

> My book was printed and bound, and copies were sent to special members. Sir E Brabrook, who got one, at once wrote Bradlaugh's daughter and J M Robertson that certain letters of Ingersoll to Holyoake which I included were damaging to Bradlaugh, Foote, and other leading members of the Freethought movement in Britain, and they presented the Rationalist publishers with an ultimatum: unless these letters and some remarks in my work were struck out, though it meant breaking up hundreds of copies of the bound two-volume work and reprinting many pages, Brabrook, Robertson, Mrs Bradlaugh-Bonner, and other Bradlaughites would quit the Association.[44]

Tragically, the minutes of the RPA until 1934 are missing, so we will never get to the bottom of this episode, or of one or two others. But on the information available to us it seems that McCabe was right, and that the changes to the Holyoake biography were made. The *Literary Guide* of January 1, 1908 gives notice that the *Life and Letters of George Jacob Holyoake* is almost complete and parts of it is already going through the press. A loose flyer and order form for the book which accompanied that issue announced the publication date to be April 25.[45] But the May 1 issue advises readers that publication "has been deferred until the end of May."[46] No reason is given for the deferral. Only with the June issue does the review of the work appear. The review is duly appreciative, but concentrates more on Holyoake's life than McCabe's treatment of it.[47] It is definite, then, that publication of the Holyoake biography was deferred. What is not definite is the reason why this deferral took place. There are any number of reasons why publishing a book can be delayed, but there is no reason why McCabe's explanation is not the correct one in this instance.

While all this was going on behind the scenes, the shadowboxing continued in the *Literary Guide* over the blasphemy row McCabe had ignited. After an unconvincing protestation of admiration for McCabe's abilities, Hypatia Bradlaugh Bonner (1858–1935), Bradlaugh's daughter, came to her real point. McCabe's article about blasphemy represented "the position of the younger generation, and those who have come into the Rationalist Movement since the worst of the fight was over and the way was smoothed for their feet."[48] Such condescension could only have made McCabe's blood boil, given how difficult his path to rationalism had in fact been. Not surprisingly, the response from Foote's *Freethinker* was still less measured. McCabe's views were described as a "farrago of folly and falsehood" and "malignantly libelous."[49] Foote continued the attack:

> His taste is *the* standard for the Freethought party. We must, as it were, set our clocks and watches by him. To differ from him is an obvious error; to set him right on a matter of fact is a gross impertinence; to criticize him is a wilful sin; to argue with him is flat blasphemy. It is really grotesque.[50]

Foote's attack was unkind, but not entirely untrue. He had, it will be recalled, employed McCabe in 1899, but the two men had not gotten along. The split with Foote and the *Freethinker* lasted forty-six years. It survived Foote's death, with his successor as editor of the *Freethinker*, Chapman Cohen, continuing the enmity.

McCabe could have survived the estrangement of G. W. Foote and the supporters of the *Freethinker*, but his criticisms of Bradlaugh had offended important insiders within the RPA. The general view among Bradlaugh supporters was that Holyoake had been lukewarm in the advocacy of freethought and treacherous in his relations with Bradlaugh. McCabe's view was that relations between the two men were usually pleasant, if not warm, and generally improved "as Bradlaugh's character matured. . . ."[51] It is worth noting that McCabe was certainly not going out of his way to blacken Bradlaugh's memory, and noted his courage, leadership skills (which he acknowledged to be finer than Holyoake's), doggedness, and matchless powers of oratory.[52]

The irony of all this is that McCabe's biography of Holyoake, a man accused of trying to please everybody, ended up pleasing nobody. McCabe was adept at getting himself into this situation. It was his first public disagreement with his Rationalist colleagues, and it shook his naive notion that all freethinkers would be staunch battlers for the truth, united entirely by the justness of that struggle. It was a turning point in McCabe's life.

McCabe's estrangement from the Rationalist Press Association began from that date. From then on he had, as he put it, "a leaning for rebellion in the ranks of the rebels. . . ."[53] It is important to note, however, that relations did not deteriorate seriously for another fifteen years or more. In fact, 1908 was probably the high point of McCabe's influence within the RPA. That year he was made an honorary associate of the organization and gave the principal speech at its annual dinner. He praised the leadership of the director, Edward Clodd (1840–1930). But McCabe knew, and his adversaries in the movement knew, that these were little more than consolatory baubles.

In the years that followed, McCabe became increasingly impatient with the softly-softly approach to freethought advocacy preferred by some of his older colleagues like Edward Clodd, F. J. Gould, and, most importantly, Charles Albert Watts (1858–1946), director of the RPA since 1899 and chief executive officer of Watts & Co., the publishing house of the RPA. One example of the softly-softly approach that would have irked McCabe was Watts's consistent discouragement of married clergymen to leave their position upon finding that they have lost their faith. Watts remained convinced that secession would almost always entail destitution for the man's family and an inability to earn a living.[54] For McCabe, this was tantamount to counseling hypocrisy, which for him was contrary to the spirit of rationalism. He described the task of rationalism as to "attack superstition, correct clerical misstatements, and diffuse knowledge."[55] Watts and his supporters, however, disliked this approach. One of Clodd's many friends was Sir Frederick Pollock who put it this way:

My Dear Clodd

Rationalist I am, but Agnostic I am not—being a freethinking Idealist, which is another thing; and the RPA is too much like a dogmatic agnostic propaganda for my sympathy with it to be perfect; too much of its shooting is of the old muzzle-loading type.[56]

Letters such as these encouraged Clodd's natural dislike for McCabe's aggressive stance. And Clodd himself had been satirized by H. G. Wells as a militant agnostic in the manner of an alert customs officer of a materialistic age who examines "every proposition to see that the Creator wasn't being smuggled back under some specious new generalization."[57] So if Clodd could be characterized as a militant, how much more so McCabe?

But the ironies do not end there. While McCabe's differences with the moderates such as Clodd and Watts could be put down to differences in temperament, the problems with people like J. M. Robertson arose from too similar a temperament. They were too alike to be able to get along. Like McCabe,

Robertson came from a humble family and had risen to prominence as a prolific scholar, thanks to daunting self-discipline, prodigious learning, and a firm belief in himself. David Tribe, Bradlaugh's biographer, described Robertson as a "dour, uncompromising, prickly egghead from Edinburgh."[58] After McCabe's death, an unnamed commentator in the South Place Ethical Society's *Monthly Record* remarked that Robertson and McCabe shared similar lecturing styles. They were "essentially combative. At all times they enjoyed controversy and many of their admirers have said that any subject that lent itself to intellectual fisticuffs was plainly to their liking."[59] McCabe was always respectful of Robertson, but the two disagreed on important issues, including the historicity of Jesus and the relative importance of Charles Bradlaugh or George Jacob Holyoake to the development of freethought. After Robertson's electoral defeat in 1918, he returned to active work in the freethought movement. Trouble was not far behind. Robertson was one of the lecturers who remained in the pared-down team at SPES, and he would be an important figure in the assault on McCabe at the RPA. It is ironic that McCabe was disliked by staunch Bradlaughites like Robertson, while also getting the same reputation as Bradlaugh for being a difficult personality and militant atheist.

McCabe made efforts to get out of the trap he felt himself to be in. Early in 1924 he left the *Literary Guide* to establish his own paper. The goal of the *Tribune* was expressed in classically McCabean terms: It was designed to "put before its readers such little known or disregarded facts as may enable them to form a clear and firm judgement which every live citizen now demands."[60] This venture lasted less than three months, and by May 1924 a frustrated McCabe was back with the *Guide*. He then tried to effect some changes within the RPA. In March the following year, McCabe opened a discussion at their headquarters on the topic "Is a Militant Rationalist Policy Desirable?" The general opinion of the meeting was that it was, although it is significant that no senior RPA names were there. McCabe's meeting was criticized in the *Guide* by some moderates. Horace Bridges and Stanton Coit were critical of McCabe for seeing Unitarianism as different or even hostile to Rationalism.

One of McCabe's ideas to present a more militant face to the public was to produce a series of short works of popular science for the general reader. McCabe was just embarking on his series of Little Blue Books for Haldeman-Julius and suggested a similar series for English readers, to be called the Pocket Series. The scheme didn't go ahead at once, but when it did, it was very successful. It was eventually called the Forum Series, and included works by Julian Huxley, H. G. Wells, Cyril Joad, and Sir Arthur Keith, among others. While it was McCabe's idea, it was Charles Watts who actually put the series together.

As the Forum Series episode shows, the policy differences between McCabe and his RPA colleagues were not significant. It was the personality differences that determined the split. But it wasn't simply a question of McCabe the militant versus the rest. He was too militant for the moderates and too McCabean for the other militants. Outwardly, things continued as normal. In September of 1925 McCabe represented the RPA in a debate at Queen's Hall in London with the American fundamentalist George McCready Price on "Is Evolution True?" Within days of that debate, McCabe left for America and what was to prove a fateful sojourn in Chicago. Within a few short months the bond between McCabe and the RPA had been fatally torn, never to heal completely. What went wrong?

McCabe intimated, without ever actually stating so openly, that early in 1926 he was presented with some sort of ultimatum from the RPA. Significantly, among the many claims and denials when the quarrel went public in 1928, this was never denied by the RPA. In an article in the March 1926 issue of the *Guide*, written while on tour in North America, McCabe gave some indication of the current situation, and of his reaction to it:

> It seems my epistles bore superior people, are even deemed rather egotistic. It appears that my habit of hitting back is painful to Rationalists. It is to be understood, I gather, that I must take in silence all the sneers and criticisms and cheating I encounter. What a cantankerous little devil I must be, to want to smite back and to expose crookedness! But I fear I am incurably I, and must work so or not at all. Very well, I accept your decision.

Charles Watts, the *Guide's* editor, added a rather embarrassed rejoinder: "Judging by his contribution to our present issue, Mr McCabe has been having a rough and exciting time in the United States and Canada. Pioneer lecturing, it would seem, is not an ideal occupation."[61] He also cut out some sections of McCabe's vitriolic article. McCabe never wrote for the *Literary Guide* again and relations deteriorated very rapidly after that.

This had been the last straw, but other issues and grievances had dogged McCabe's relationship with the RPA going back, as we have seen, to 1908. Again, we need to retrace our steps a little in order to comprehend what went on between 1926 and 1928. One source of grievance is easily found. As he came to enjoy more and more success as an author, McCabe also grew impatient of what he saw as impertinent or inaccurate corrections to the proofs of the many books he continued to publish through the RPA. Charles Watts took a paternalistic interest in all the titles his firm published and, in its early years, submitted every book to close editing. As the firm grew, he maintained an editorial interest in many works, McCabe's among them, very likely having the Holyoake biography affair in mind. After Watts's death, his obituarist recalled that established authors "who were sometimes inclined to be sensitive and to regard their productions as verbally inspired, might at first resent his emendations, but in the end they were usually grateful to their competent and punctilious critic."[62] McCabe was not among them. While he did not view his works as inspired in any way, he keenly resented Watts' corrections to his argument and to his writing style.

Another dispute arose, McCabe later claimed, over Watts's decision to print a second edition of *The Evolution of Mind*, which came out in 1921. McCabe had written a preface for the new edition in 1916, but the book was not released until five years later. This was due, an anonymous note under McCabe's preface said, to the "disturbed conditions" of the time. McCabe claimed that the second edition, while advertising itself as a revised edition, had not, in fact, been revised at all. He also wanted the second edition to come out as a Cheap Reprint, to make it more affordable. The RPA was well known for its Cheap Reprint series, which brought the works of prominent scientists, historians, and freethinkers within the price range of working people. The RPA maintained that the second edition had in fact been revised and that printing costs required it to be sold in a format and at a price beyond the range of Cheap Reprint series. It is difficult to apportion blame fairly here. On the one hand, McCabe's point about the revised edition seems valid. I have been unable to find any evidence of the second edition having been revised in any way. But on the other hand, the RPA had bought the rights to the book from Adam & Charles Black, the publisher of the first edition, and were entitled to dispose of it in any way they saw fit. The RPA also denied that McCabe ever raised the issue of reprinting the work as a Cheap Reprint to them. The RPA went further than that, claiming that McCabe had not seen fit to raise this grievance with them until 1928, by which time it was far too late.[63]

McCabe later claimed that the *Evolution of Mind* imbroglio coincided with another dispute, this time involving statements made by McCabe in his *Tyranny of Shams*. He always thought highly of this book, and felt it in many ways to be the clearest one-volume summary of his worldview. It was, he later wrote "the full and candid social creed I had constructed for myself in seventeen years."[64] He also thought his views on sexual relations as expressed in *The Tyranny of Shams* were seen by his RPA colleagues as a liability.[65] So much so, McCabe claimed in his autobiography, that the book wasn't reviewed in the *Literary Guide*.[66] This is incorrect. The book was reviewed, quite positively, in the August 1916 issue. C. Turner, the reviewer, thought that we "may not be convinced that the mantle of Carlyle has fallen upon Mr McCabe (or indeed upon any one in particular); yet we cannot help being impressed by the vigor, insight and sincerity which are revealed by Mr McCabe's stimulating book."[67] Turner did not mention McCabe's views on sexuality, but we can infer little from that. While McCabe was wrong about the review, it is not unlikely that his Rationalist colleagues were uncomfortable with his advanced views on sexuality. We will examine this, and McCabe's opinions, more closely in chapter 6.

The only specific point of conflict between McCabe and the RPA that we can be certain actually took place outside McCabe's imagination lay in the disputes over financial accountability regarding his various trips around the world. By the time the conflict was public, McCabe claimed there had been problems over the fee he was to have received for his debate with Sir Arthur Conan Doyle in 1920 and regarding aspects of his second tour of Australia. But both sides agree that the problem really escalated over disagreements over liability for a debt incurred by McCabe during his lecture tour in Chicago. The Chicago lectures had been under the auspices of Percy Ward, who had ordered several hundred dollars worth of books from the RPA, only to default on the payments. As the order had been placed in the context of McCabe's lectures, the RPA decided that McCabe was liable.[68] Ward had proved unreliable with earlier orders of RPA material, but McCabe made a verbal undertaking to see that payments for the order coincident with his Chicago tour would be met. He then confirmed that obligation in correspondence with Charles Watts regarding this processing of this order.

It would seem that none of this was a problem until relations really broke down in 1926. As late as December 1925 McCabe was acknowledging his responsibility for the debt. But after March of the following year and the debacle of the (as it transpired) final article in the *Literary Guide*, McCabe insisted that the sum outstanding was not his liability. In the correspondence that ensued, the RPA sent rather confusing messages to McCabe. On the one hand it made a generous offer to end the quarrel with McCabe paying half the amount in dispute (or £66.5s.2d.) and writing the rest off. But on the other hand it made veiled threats of seeking legal recourse if no satisfactory conclusion could be reached.[69] The RPA later denied it intended any legal threats, but the damage was done. McCabe's reaction was volcanic. He adamantly refused to acknowledge any liability to the debt and refused equally adamantly to enter into any further negotiations.

There things festered for two years. The next step in this dreary episode was taken by a group of McCabe's supporters, but with his active connivance. One of these supporters, Mr. G. K. Holliday, called an Extraordinary General Meeting of the RPA, which was held on March 12, 1928. This meeting was an ill-judged attempt by McCabe's supporters to bring McCabe back into the fold, accompanied by some sort of apology or resignation from members of the RPA directorate. The meeting was a disaster for McCabe, for the RPA, and for rationalism generally. The speeches of Holliday and McCabe were intemperate and lacked any notion of a willingness to compromise or recognize fault. Holliday suggested, only half in jest, that the directors were in the pay of the Catholic Church, while McCabe lambasted them in a manner only he could do. McCabe read to the meeting one of the last letters he sent to the directors, part of which read:

> I have seen the Rationalist Press Association shrink under your direction from a fine educational force to a petty mutual admiration and mutual profit society at which the Churches smile. Now you who have accomplished this, some of you old personal opponents of mine, most of you parvenus in Rationalism, turn upon a man who has literally grown grey in the service of the Movement. . . .[70]

Not much room for compromise there! The speeches of J. P. Gilmour, chairman of the RPA Board of Directors, and J. M. Robertson were more diplomatic, but less transparent than McCabe's. Eventually, the meeting moved

> that, having heard the statements of the requisitionists and of Mr Joseph McCabe concerning his severance from the Rationalist Press Association, this meeting, recognizing in the fullest measure, Mr McCabe's great services to the Rationalist cause, expresses unabated confidence in the Board of Directors, and earnestly desires Mr McCabe to resume membership of the Association.[71]

Most people would have accepted this resolution as permitting each party to save face and start again. Joseph McCabe regarded it as a defeat. He was in no doubt as to the underlying reasons for the hostility of the RPA's directors:

> The causes of this feeling are not obscure; jealousy, detestation because I will not close my eyes to what is wrong in the movement, and the bitter hostility of the followers of Mr Bradlaugh (now numerous in the executive), ever since, twenty years ago, I vindicated the memory of that great pioneer of Rationalism, George Jacob Holyoake, from their unjust remarks.[72]

He was to repeat this claim in his autobiography.[73] McCabe was, I think, correct about this. Both J. P. Gilmour and J. M Robertson were ardent admirers of Bradlaugh. Other people on the board included Hypatia Bradlaugh Bonner, Bradlaugh's daughter, with whom McCabe had crossed swords in 1908. And it was Robertson who led the attack on McCabe at the March Extraordinary Meeting. However, McCabe is clearly wrong to cast this as the main reason for the breakdown in relations between him and the RPA. By the midtwenties, everyone in the organization, regardless of their position on Bradlaugh, was fed up with McCabe's combativeness and inability to work amicably with others. Even F. J. Gould, a resolutely amiable personality and one of the few veterans of the movement who defended McCabe at the Extraordinary General Meeting, acknowledged shortly afterward that McCabe had "for some considerable time ceased to co-operate in the work of the Association."[74] E. Royston Pike, who later became a prominent scholar, and between 1928 and 1932 was secretary of the RPA, attended this dreadful meeting. Royston Pike remembered the meeting as acrimonious. McCabe, he said, was "far too dogmatic, as much so as J. M. Robertson (which is saying something!)"[75] The RPA just wasn't big enough for *two* aging titans.

McCabe never really forgave the association. He was undoubtedly a difficult man to work with. The reason for this goes back to his personality. McCabe was never able to appreciate that there are many credible varieties of unbelief. McCabe was not the sort of person to rise through the ranks without rocking the boat. One veteran of the RPA remembered that when McCabe "disagreed on matters of policy there was not much hope of conciliation."[76] He became intolerant of forms of freethought that seemed to him to be shallow or held with insufficient passion. It is worthwhile to illustrate this point, because it is an important clue to understanding McCabe.

In 1903, while still a rising star within the RPA and with everything to work for, McCabe had this to say. Replying to some churchman who was bemoaning the "decay of reverence," McCabe told his readers:

> I know some men, writers and lecturers, who help to redeem the vulgarity and hypocrisy of life by their lingering presence with us; men who, like Huxley, made solemn vows "to smite all humbugs" and never compromise with lies; men who have carried their vow unbroken through a long and laborious career, and whose last days are lit up by a consciousness that they never told England what it wanted to be told, instead of what it ought to be told, because it paid better.[77]

Such zeal cannot survive a long life unbattered. Forty-four years later McCabe admitted that "from the year I entered the monastery and throughout the half-century of my public life I saw so much compromise with truth, from petty insincerities and posing to lying and deception, that in reaction I became suspicious, blunt and intransigent."[78] It is one thing to smite humbugs—a thoroughly worthwhile occupation—it is another thing to mistake people with whom one does not agree as humbugs. This was one aspect of his religious heritage he did not succeed in shedding. Tolerance of difference is the most important feature of the freethinker—and the most difficult to manage. McCabe admitted this himself in 1932, when he acknowledged that he had taken his bluntness too far on occasions, having made "more fuss than the occasion required."[79] That is an understatement.

RECLUSE

McCabe was approaching sixty by now, but the pressure to write in order to maintain an income did not lessen. Indeed, he was entering one of his most productive writing phases. Between 1927 and 1932 he wrote at least a dozen multivolume works for Haldeman-Julius, including the forty-volume *Key to Culture* (1927–29), a compendium of social, sexual, and psychological issues called *Key to Love and Sex* (eight volumes, 1929), *The Rise and Fall of the Gods* (six volumes, 1931) and *The History of Human Morals* (twelve volumes, 1931). Each of these volumes came in the shape of one of Haldeman-Julius's Big Blue Books. These were monograph-length publications of around sixty-four pages, with about six hundred words per page. Haldeman-Julius had begun this series in 1925, a year after his Little Blue Books. This series of multivolume works for Haldeman-Julius represents one of the least recognized feats of first-class scholarship of the twentieth century.

McCabe continued to publish in Britain as well, but these titles seem marginal and produced on order. Titles from these years include *Science Yesterday, Today, Tomorrow* (1927), *Can We Save Civilization?* (1932), and *Edward Clodd: A Memoir* (1932). It is worthwhile to note that McCabe's break with the RPA could not have been as drastic as he made out in his autobiography. The year after the break, the RPA reissued his *Twelve Years in a Monastery* and his translation of *The Riddle of the Universe* as titles in their new Thinker's Library series. While this did not require McCabe's consent, it could only serve to reopen wounds; unless there weren't many wounds to reopen. But it is even more significant that it was McCabe who wrote the memoir of Edward Clodd, one of the RPA's most senior figures, and one of the old guard of conservatives who supposedly never felt comfortable with his younger colleague. McCabe had full access to Clodd's diaries, and his memoir was well received as a generous account of a noble, if not a great, figure.[80] It is worth dwelling on this for a moment. While McCabe conducted his battles fiercely against the living, he did not (unlike Robertson) continue his vendettas beyond the grave. McCabe always argued honestly and transparently, and to an opponent capable of answering back. Neither did he abuse his position as a researcher. The entries on Foote, Cohen, Clodd, Robertson, and other opponents in his *Biographical Dictionary of Modern Rationalists* and *Rationalist Encyclopedia* are generous and free from rancor. This needs to be taken into account when assessing McCabe's personality.

The memoir of Clodd, while interesting, was of small moment to McCabe's overall output. Without question, McCabe's main economic lifeline was coming in these years from the United States. He had also agreed in 1928 to ghostwrite a series of books called *The Bankruptcy of Christian Supernaturalism* for Bishop William Montgomery Brown (1855–1937), an eccentric former American bishop who had been deposed for denouncing the idea of a personal god and the divinity of Jesus. McCabe produced a book a year for Brown until the bishop's death in 1937. He also wrote Bishop Brown's well-received discourse at the Chicago Parliament of Religion in 1933. When not ghostwriting for Bishop Brown, McCabe rewrote his 1912 *Story of Evolution*, which was published in 1931 as *The New Science and the New Evolution*. That book must have sunk without a trace, as it was completely overshadowed by H. G. Wells's blockbuster, *The Science of Life*.

This was a bad time for anybody to be publishing books. Haldeman-Julius was fighting a losing battle against the Depression and orders for more work from McCabe dried up. Nineteen thirty-three proved to be McCabe's leanest year for publications since 1904, with only a rewritten edition of *The Existence of God* and two Big Blue Books being released. As with the Clodd memoir, the RPA reprinting any McCabe title at this time suggests that the estrangement had not been as final as McCabe later made out. He also lost money on retirement investments he had made, and with maintenance commitments to his ex-wife over his normal running expenses, McCabe's late sixties were pretty hard.

But out of the blue came help, and from a surprising source. In the middle

of 1934 the RPA made tentative approaches to McCabe with a view to establishing a limited rapprochement. The person responsible for this was Surgeon
Rear Admiral Charles Beadnell (1872–1947), then a director of the RPA. Why
was this approach made at all? There are a number of reasons. The most simple
is that those most strongly opposed to McCabe, and in turn most despised by
McCabe, were now dead or retired. Edward Clodd had died in 1930 and J. M.
Robertson and Charles Gorham, in 1933. Of equal importance, Charles Watts
had retired from active duty in Watts & Co. in 1930. Hypatia Bradlaugh Bonner
was ailing, and was to die in 1935. The RPA must have realized that, with the
passing of these people, the core stable of Rationalist authors was thinning significantly. More than that, the RPA had suffered a much more broad-based challenge by a group of social and political radicals, notably J. A. Hobson (1858–
1940) and C. E. M. Joad (1891–1953). This attack, known later on as "the
Great Conway Hall Plot," had sought to broaden the RPA into a more generally
leftist social reform movement. The coup failed, but it may well have left the
RPA thinking that maybe McCabe wasn't so bad after all. McCabe was one of
the last of the original generation of RPA authors still active, and by far the best
known. The RPA needed McCabe.

Inevitably, the first sign of the rapprochement was that McCabe titles were
again published by the RPA. Things moved quite quickly, with what proved to
be one of McCabe's more successful books of the decade, *The Riddle of the Universe Today*, appearing later in 1934, the year Beadnell initiated the approach.
The following year they produced a relatively lavish edition of another new title,
The Splendor of Moorish Spain. McCabe also wrote for its popular and successful
Thinker's Library series, producing a summary of his arguments from *A History
of Human Morals* and *The Rise and Fall of the Gods*. The book was called *The
Social Record of Christianity*. Two years later still, McCabe's other big sellers of the
decade, *The Papacy in Politics Today* and *A History of the Popes*, were published
by the RPA. The publication of these books in England can only have helped
McCabe's precarious financial situation, as Haldeman-Julius was being forced to
withdraw from further publishing initiatives because of ever-declining sales as a
result of the depressed American economy. McCabe needed the RPA.

This symbiosis did not mean that all was forgiven, however. It was not long
before relations were again patchy. McCabe complained bitterly in his autobiography that *The Splendor of Moorish Spain* had received a "shabby and scanty notice
by a totally ignorant reviewer (an engineer, I learned) in the organ of the Association."[81] This is quite unfair. The review I found in the *Literary Guide* by Sir
Alexander Cardew praised the book intelligently, commenting only that, contrary to McCabe, some historians *had* drawn attention to the Moorish civilization
prior to his book.[82] Apart from that, Cardew was supportive, noting that it "is
right that this debt to the Arab genius should not be forgotten, and Mr McCabe
has done well in drawing attention to it."[83] The RPA took some trouble to produce an attractive book, including a colored frontispiece and eight plates.

This was a guarded rapprochement, with the RPA and its *enfant terrible* maintaining a suspicious distance between each other. On the one hand we see McCabe prepared to publicly defend the RPA once more, as he did in a short critique of the Church of England's report on doctrine in 1938.[84] But on the other hand, we don't see a return of McCabe to the *Literary Guide*. Once one of the *Guide's* most prolific contributors, McCabe contributed not a single article after the rapprochement, and neither was he ever interviewed for the various features the *Guide* ran. For instance, in 1939 and 1940, the *Guide* sent one of its main contributors at the time, minor novelist and journalist John Rowland, to interview rationalist notables such as H. G. Wells, C. E. M. Joad, George Bernard Shaw, and others. McCabe was not interviewed. In another feature, a large number of people were asked what books had influenced them to become rationalists. Again, McCabe was not among them, although many considerably less renowned people were. Blame for this cannot necessarily be laid at the hands of the *Guide*, however. It is quite possible that McCabe was invited to contribute but refused.

Certainly, the RPA cannot be accused of deliberately trying to keep McCabe at arm's length. There was, for instance, a belated recognition that McCabe's seventieth birthday should be marked. It had become a freethought tradition that the seventieth birthday of old campaigners should be honored with a financial testimonial. McCabe turned seventy in November 1937, but it was not until January 1938 that public recognition of this milestone was given. Moves by some of McCabe's friends to honor him were begun with a notice in the *Literary Guide* of the appeal having started with a donation of £10.10. The fund closed in June with a total collected of £241.17s.7d., the largest donation coming from the RPA itself. McCabe was grateful at the time, as his financial situation was very grim indeed. Ten years later, though, McCabe still saw fit to grizzle about the appeal being both late and relatively modest.[85]

Certainly, the testimonial was no reason for McCabe to refrain from criticism. At one of the Conway Discussion Circles, run jointly by the South Place Ethical Society and the RPA, McCabe fired broadsides at three younger and more fashionable rationalist commentators. Gerald Bullett came in for criticism over his apparent jeering at materialism, Lord Horder was rebuked for arguing that rationalism should do more than stick to negations of religion, and G. D. H. Cole was attacked for advocating a more political role for rationalism.[86] This is one of the reasons McCabe is not remembered today. Most of his contemporaries had been criticized by him at some point.

Not surprisingly, McCabe was beginning to find himself very unpopular, not only with the older veterans of the RPA, but also with the younger leaders rising to prominence. But even this does not explain why, in 1939 and 1940, McCabe produced two books for the RPA under a pseudonym. He wrote *The Liberation of Germany* and *Bureaucracy Run Mad* under the pseudonym Martin Abbotson. Martin being his middle name and Abbotson, meaning—as McCabe means—

"son of the abbot." McCabe claims this was suggested to him by the RPA because his "name was anathema." But if this was the case, why was he invited, in the same year, to edit an encyclopedia for the RPA under his own name? And why, between 1939 and 1948, did McCabe have a further eight works published in his own name by the RPA? It is not unlikely that this arrangement suited McCabe, as he could perhaps reach a wider readership under a different name. This would have been all to the good for him, as his financial situation was still desperate. And with no track record of comment in the areas the pseudonymous works covered, sales may well have been better than had they simply been two more works by Joseph McCabe.

McCabe's last major project with the RPA was the *Rationalist Encyclopedia*, which was designed to bring up to date his successful *Biographical Dictionary of Modern Rationalists*, which had come out in 1920. The *Biographical Dictionary* is, after the multivolume Haldeman-Julius series referred to earlier, McCabe's most outstanding scholarly achievement. The *Rationalist Encyclopedia* was not as successful as its predecessor but it is nevertheless a useful reference work. McCabe worked on it through the war and it was eventually published in 1948. His relationship with the RPA deteriorated steadily during this period, with acrimonious exchanges over the relevance, accuracy, and politeness of corrections made to proofs.

The dispute over the encyclopedia was a symptom of wider disagreements over the nature and future of Rationalism. In 1940 McCabe had complained to the *Literary Guide* that he was the only Honorary Associate of the RPA "who professes Atheism and Materialism, to say nothing of more deadly heresies."[87] As we will see in later sections, McCabe became less tolerant as he got older toward other styles of freethought, which he came increasingly to regard as soft options. The clearest outward sign of the breakdown in relations is that when the RPA decided on a fifth impression of Haeckel's classic, *The Riddle of the Universe*, in 1946, McCabe was not asked to provide the foreword—despite McCabe's reputation being so closely linked with the book. Sir Arthur Keith provided the foreword instead. However, even then the break was not final, because as late as 1951 the RPA published a rewritten version of *The Papacy in Politics Today*. And the following year McCabe took part in a RPA conference on "The Menace of Roman Catholicism." This was the last project between McCabe and the RPA. McCabe offered a monograph-length study called *Crime and Religion* to the RPA for publication, but they turned it down.[88] It was eventually published in 1954 by the American freethought magazine *Progressive World*, which also printed some of McCabe's last articles. Many of the younger intellectuals attracted to the RPA in the years after the Second World War were embarrassed by McCabe's anti-Catholicism. They saw it as a throwback to an earlier, more sectarian phase of the movement's history.

But even when McCabe did move with the times, he was not moving in the right direction with his new colleagues. As we will see in chapter 6, McCabe was never an uncritical disciple of the Soviet Union, although he came closest to that position during these last years of his life. Like many people, McCabe had been deeply impressed by the extent of the Soviet contribution to the defeat of Hitler during the war. He also shared the general anxiety about the postwar political situation, and the widespread fear of another war, this time with the Soviet Union. Where McCabe parted company with most of his contemporaries was his firm belief that it was not the Soviets who were planning the war.[89] McCabe complained bitterly in his autobiography of two of the younger academics coming into the RPA after the war snubbing him "most offensively" after his telling a Rationalist audience that there was a general agitation for war in the United States.[90] McCabe's fears, we now know, were not without foundation. His error was to couch his fears as facts. Rupert Crawshay-Williams observed a similar decline in the elderly Bertrand Russell, saying that "the elastic which drew him back from the extreme positions began to perish."[91] This was also true for McCabe and we will see this process with regard to his political views and his late views on Catholicism.

Once he had finished with the RPA, McCabe devoted all his writing energies to Haldeman-Julius. Once the United States began to pull itself out of the Depression, Haldeman-Julius was able to resume a heavy program of purchasing McCabe material. After virtually nothing in 1934 and 1935, McCabe wrote eleven Big Blue Books the following year. Between 1948 and 1951, when Haldeman-Julius died, McCabe wrote at least twenty monographs (the Big Blue Books) for his American publisher. The Little Blue Books took longer to recover. After his huge production of Little Blue Books in 1926 and 1927, things dwindled until 1931 and McCabe wrote no more until 1942. But then he returned with a vengeance, writing no fewer that forty-six in 1943 alone. Not surprisingly, these are among the most vituperative of all McCabe's publications. They remained intelligent and thoroughly readable to the end.

And despite the generally grim picture he presented, McCabe retained his optimism. In one of his last Haldeman-Julius books, *The Origin and Meaning of Ideas*, McCabe mentioned, again, "my friend Wells," who, he reminded us, "died a pessimist. I am still an optimist, singing 'Beulah Land' at the age of 83."[92] During his brief phase as a theist during the First World War, Wells had chided McCabe about his optimism. McCabe had plenty of reason to lose hope. Unlike Wells, his last years were very difficult financially. News of his plight even reached his old followers in New Zealand. The November 1950 issue of the *NZ Rationalist* featured an article outlining McCabe's career and asked the question: "How many are there who acknowledge with deep thanksgiving the influence of Joseph McCabe in causing them to become Rationalists? They must number thousands or even millions throughout the world."[93] The magazine launched a Joseph McCabe Fund to offset "the shocking inroads of taxation and literary expenses into the money he has been able to earn with his pen." The loyal Kiwis came up with the respectable total of £44.15s.6d. for their hero.

McCabe kept busy to the end. He wrote his last Little Blue Books, four of them, in 1947. The very last, No. 1844, was possibly autobiographical, and was called *The Erring Husband*. His main output came out as Big Blue Books, averaging about a half dozen a year, with the continual production of magazine articles. But all this came to a sudden end with the death of Haldeman-Julius in his swimming pool on July 31 1951. Haldeman-Julius had been found guilty earlier in the year of income-tax evasion. Earlier still, he had incurred the wrath of J. Edgar Hoover after criticizing the FBI. Hoover's men left no stone unturned to dig up what dirt it could find on Haldeman-Julius's business affairs.[94]

McCabe could have been forgiven for deciding that, on the death of Haldeman-Julius and at the age of eighty-four, his writing career was over. But he observed laconically in a letter to his son at the end of 1953 that "the market for serious work is appalling and to run contrary to the public's ideas, as I am so fond of doing, is suicidal. However, I keep on experimenting and no doubt will strike a vein sooner or later."[95] He wasn't joking, because at the time of his death two manuscripts were found among his possessions: a historical romance using the pseudonym of Robert Romaine and a detective story under the name of Dick Drummond.

After Haldeman-Julius's death, most of McCabe's output went to various American freethought publications. In 1954, he even contributed several articles to the National Secular Society's paper the *Freethinker*. He and Chapman Cohen, the longtime editor of the paper, had disliked each other intensely since the argument in 1908 between McCabe and Cohen's predecessor and mentor, G. W. Foote. For over forty years Cohen had virtually ignored McCabe. Once Cohen was dead, McCabe felt free to join the National Secular Society and contribute to the *Freethinker*. He continued to give lectures as well. A few days before his eighty-fifth birthday, McCabe addressed the West London National Secular Society about "Religion, Crime, and Secularism." He later developed this material into what was his last publication, the sixty-four-page monograph, *Crime and Religion*. This was to be the first of half a dozen works criticizing the Roman Catholic Church. Here he reiterated comments he had made a half century before about secular education and produced figures to demonstrate that religious indoctrination in schools had little or no influence in reducing crime. McCabe's last lecture was given to the South Place Ethical Society on February 28, 1954, and was entitled "The Character of Popular Revolutions."

Later the same year McCabe ended his final article with these words. After relating the shocking waste of wealth that twentieth century wars had involved, and the current danger of nuclear war, he wrote,

> Do not talk to me of the action of a God in such a universe. Do not talk to me about immortal souls and heavens. Do not talk to me about that jumble of ancient stories which is called Christianity. We shall gain enormously when we rule out the whole of this preposterous nonsense from the administration of our planet.[96]

McCabe died on January 10, 1955, and his funeral was conducted by his old friend F. A. Hornibrook, the New Zealand–born physical culture advocate and columnist. He had been unconscious for more than a week before dying of prostate cancer. He bequeathed the remainder of the lease of his house and all its contents to his housekeeper, Ellen Newton, "for her own use in recognition of more than 20 years of devoted service." McCabe left the not inconsiderable estate of £4765.17s.4d.[97]

As a young man of thirty-four McCabe had written of St. Augustine at the time of his death: "The strong will had sustained the slight frame through sixty years of untiring exertion, and left it with an integrity which few preserve."[98] How uncannily true that is of McCabe himself.

NOTES

1. Joseph McCabe, *Eighty Years a Rebel* (Girard, Kan.: Haldeman-Julius, 1947), p. 23.

2. F. J. Gould, *The Life-Story of a Humanist* (London: Watts, 1923), p. 74.

3. *Literary Guide* (April 1941): 47.

4. F. W. Maitland, *Life and Letters of Leslie Stephen* (London: Duckworth, 1906), p. 468.

5. *Literary Guide* (February 1, 1897): 119.

6. McCabe, *Eighty Years a Rebel*, p. 22.

7. Ibid., p. 26.

8. *Literary Guide* (January 1, 1900): 5.

9. A. J. Davies, *To Build a New Jerusalem* (London: Abacus, 1996), pp. 111–12.

10. C. L. Drawbridge, *Common Objections to Christianity* (London: Robert Scott, 1914), p. 20.

11. *Tenth Annual Report: 1908*, Rationalist Press Association Ltd., p. 8.

12. *Twenty-Second Annual Report: 1920*, Rationalist Press Association Ltd., p. 9.

13. McCabe, *Eighty Years a Rebel*, p. 44.

14. S. K. Ratcliffe, *The Story of South Place* (London: Watts, 1955), p. 66.

15. Joseph McCabe, *The Existence of God*, Inquirer's Library, no. 1 (London: Watts, 1913), p. 123.

16. See *Report of a Debate on Theism and the Problem of the Universe Between Mr. G. W. de Tunzelmann and Mr. Joseph McCabe* (Manchester: Sherratt & Hughes, 1910), p. 4.

17. Joseph McCabe and Rev. C. J. Shebbeare, *The Design Argument Reconsidered* (London: Watts, 1923), p. 84.

18. *Literary Guide* (August 1916): 114.

19. See McCabe's chapter attached to the revised edition of Wilhelm Bölsche, *Haeckel: His Life and Work* (London: Watts, 1909), p. 124.

20. Joseph McCabe, *The Papacy in Politics Today* (London: Watts, 1951), p. 63.

21. Joseph McCabe, *Vice in German Monasteries* (Girard, Kan.: Haldeman-Julius, 1937), p. 3.

22. *Literary Guide* (August 1, 1910): 113.

23. Ibid., p. 114.

24. J. C. Beaglehole, *Victoria University College* (Wellington: New Zealand University Press, 1949), p. 34.

25. *Wellington (N.Z.) Evening Post*, July 2, 1910, p. 3.

26. Ibid., July 4, 1910, p. 3.

27. Ibid., July 5, 1910, p. 9.

28. Ibid., July 6, 1910, p. 3.

29. McCabe, *Eighty Years a Rebel*, p. 65.

30. Ibid.

31. George MacDonald, *Fifty Years of Freethought: The Story of the Truth Seeker* (New York: Truth Seeker, 1931), vol. 2, pp. 476–77.

32. *Literary Guide* (December 1925): 206.

33. Emanuel Haldeman-Julius, "My Second 25 Years," *Critic and Guide* (1949): 17. I am grateful to Tim Binga of the Center for Inquiry Library in Amherst, New York, for providing me with this publication.

34. Ibid., p. 20.

35. McCabe, *Eighty Years a Rebel*, p. 78.

36. I am grateful to Nicolas Walter for helping me verify this.

37. *Literary Guide* (September 1, 1899): 142.

38. Ibid. (November 1, 1899): 173.

39. *Report of the Committee of the South Place Ethical Society, 1921–22* (London: South Place Chapel & Institute), p. 5.

40. *South Place Ethical Society*, January 1923, p. 7.

41. *Report of the Committee of the South Place Ethical Society, 1923–24* (London: South Place Chapel & Institute), p. 4.

42. *Literary Guide* (March 1, 1908): 1–3. Fundamentalists ignore statements such as this when they repeatedly accuse unbelievers of scurrility and vulgarity.

43. Joseph McCabe, *The Life and Letters of George Jacob Holyoake* (London: Watts, 1908), vol. 2, pp. 148, 258–60.

44. McCabe, *Eighty Years a Rebel*, p. 28.

45. *Literary Guide* (January 1, 1908): 8; and see accompanying flyer and order form.

46. Ibid. (May 1, 1908): 72.

47. Ibid. (June 1, 1908): 85–86.

48. Ibid. (April 1, 1908): 49–51.

49. Ibid., pp. 57–58.

50. *Freethinker* (March 29, 1908): 195.

51. McCabe, *The Life and Letters of George Jacob Holyoake*, vol. 2, p. 252.

52. Ibid., pp. 276–77.

53. McCabe, *Eighty Years a Rebel*, p. 29.

54. *Literary Guide* (July 1946): 103–104.

55. Joseph McCabe, *The Church and the People* (London: Watts, 1917), p. 93.

56. Joseph McCabe, *Edward Clodd: A Memoir* (London: John Lane, 1932), pp. 129–29.

57. H. G. Wells, *Boon, the Mind of the Race, The Wild Asses of the Devil, and the Last Trump* (London: T. Fisher Unwin, 1915), pp. 44–45.

58. David Tribe, *President Charles Bradlaugh MP* (London: Elek, 1971), p. 243.

59. *Monthly Record* (March 1955): 6.

60. Ibid. (February 1924): 36.

61. Ibid. (March 1926): 49, 54.

62. Ibid. (July 1946): 104.

63. See *Report of Extraordinary General Meeting held on March 12, 1928* (London: RPA, 1928), p. 41. I am extremely grateful to Nicolas Walter for providing me with a copy of this document.

64. McCabe, *Eighty Years a Rebel*, p. 34.

65. Joseph McCabe, *Key to Love and Sex* (Girard, Kan.: Haldeman-Julius, 1929), vol. 3, p. 53.

66. McCabe, *Eighty Years a Rebel*, p. 34. In all probability, "C. Turner" was in fact Charles T. Gorham (1856–1933), longtime RPA secretary and popularizer.

67. *Literary Guide* (August 1916): 118.

68. Gordon Stein, *Freethought: A Descriptive Bibliography* (Westport, Conn.: Greenwood Publishing Co., 1981), pp. 101–102.

69. *Report of Extraordinary General Meeting*, pp. 27–28.

70. Ibid., pp. 18–19.

71. *Literary Guide* (April 1928): 70.

72. Joseph McCabe, *A Letter from Mr. Joseph McCabe to the Members of the RPA* (self-published, 1928), p. 3.

73. McCabe, *Eighty Years a Rebel*, p. 82.

74. F. J. Gould, *The Pioneers of Johnson's Court* (London: Watts, 1929), p. 144.

75. Letter from Royston Pike to Mike Lloyd-Jones. I am grateful to Mr. Lloyd-Jones for this insight.

76. *Rationalist Review* 1, no. 12 (March 1955): iv.

77. *Literary Guide* (January 1, 1903): 2.

78. McCabe, *Eighty Years a Rebel*, p. 77.

79. Joseph McCabe, *Getting the Most Out of Life* (Girard, Kan.: Haldeman-Julius, 1932), p. 55.

80. *Times Literary Supplement*, January 21, 1932, p. 39; *Freethinker* (February 7, 1932): 89.

81. McCabe, *Eighty Years a Rebel*, p. 86.

82. This is true, and McCabe knew it. John William Draper had written about this in chapter 2 of *A History of the Intellectual Development of Europe* (London: George Bell & Sons, 1891). McCabe mentions Draper's books in both *A Biographical Dictionary of Modern Rationalists* (London: Watts, 1920) and *A Rationalist Encyclopedia* (London: Watts, 1948).

83. *Literary Guide* (August 1935): 153.

84. Joseph McCabe, *The Passing of Heaven and Hell* (London: Watts, 1938), pp. 2–4.

85. McCabe, *Eighty Years a Rebel*, p. 87.

86. *Literary Guide* (December 1938): 220.

87. Ibid. (November 1940): 172.

88. I am grateful to Mike Lloyd-Jones for this piece of information.

89. Only now, after the end of the Cold War, do we find out how correct McCabe was. See Martin Walker, *The Cold War* (London: Vintage, 1994), especially chap. 1.

90. McCabe, *Eighty Years a Rebel*, p. 87.

91. Rupert Crawshay-Williams, *Russell Remembered* (London: Oxford University Press, 1970), p. 140.

92. Joseph McCabe, *The Origin and Meaning of Ideas* (Girard, Kan.: Haldeman-Julius, 1951), p. 66.

93. *New Zealand Rationalist* (November 1950): 3.

94. See the entry "Haldeman-Julius, Emanuel" in Gordon Stein, ed., *The Encyclopedia of Unbelief* (Amherst, N.Y.: Prometheus Books, 1985), pp. 307–309.

95. Letter to Ernest McCabe, dated December 30, 1953, in possession of his granddaughter, Jenifer Blenard.

96. *New Zealand Rationalist* (April 1955): 3–4.

97. I owe the details of his will, which was drawn up on November 18, 1948, to Mike Lloyd-Jones.

98. Joseph McCabe, *St. Augustine and His Age* (London: Duckworth, 1902), p. 428.

3

The Trained Athlete of Disbelief

Having outlined McCabe's long and crowded life, we need now to step back and try to understand this extraordinary man. We have followed what he did, but what sort of person was he? Mention has already been made of how little we know of McCabe's parents or family. Despite the huge body of writing McCabe left behind, including a rather sullen and misanthropic autobiography, it is almost impossible to piece together important aspects of McCabe's life. Every now and then, McCabe permitted himself a short anecdote about his family, but these are all we have to go on for the foreseeable future.

His parents were loving, but strict. His father may well have had a fiery temper. At one stage he transferred his family to a new church after a blazing row with the priests at the one they had previously attended. This proved troublesome for young Joseph, then in the very first stages of entering the priesthood, as his father's outburst cast doubt for a while on the son's suitability. These flashes of temper seem to have been one of William McCabe's legacies to his son. There is no reason to suppose, in either man, that temper flared into violence. In both men it was more a testimony to their uncompromising sense of rightness, which manifested itself "inappropriately," as we would say now.

McCabe was deeply loyal to his friends, and loved nothing more than a good argument about matters of importance, preferably over a drink and a pipe or cigar. But while these were deeply enjoyable times for McCabe, he was always aware of how important these questions were, and of our duty to treat them as intelligently as we can. He never got used to people treating important questions of philosophy, religion, science, or history lightly. This has always been a central

67

element in rationalism, and its main inheritance from its puritan ancestors. He had hoped that the world of freethought would be a tight band of brothers, working with the same level of seriousness toward truth, as the monastic ideal aspired to be. Petty jealousies and ignoble little ambitions, whether among underemployed priests or prominent unbelievers, were equally intolerable to McCabe, and quickly exasperated him.

As is often the case with biographies—this one included—we can learn as much about the writer of the biography as we do of the subject. Such is the case with McCabe's early biography of Peter Abélard. McCabe's description of the medieval heretic sounds very much like McCabe himself.

> It is the general opinion of students of his life that his main object in [studying theology] was to make more secure his progress towards the higher ecclesiastical dignities. That he had such ambition, and was not content with the mere chair and chancellorship of the cloistral school, is quite clear. In his clouded and embittered old age he is said, on the high authority of Peter of Cluny, to have discovered even that final virtue of humility. There are those who prefer him in the days of his frank, buoyant pride and ambition.[1]

Without doubt, McCabe counted himself among that latter group. McCabe saw little that was commendable in falseness, even false modesty. Like Abélard, McCabe was a very capable man indeed, but also like Abélard, he had certain defects of character that ensured he would antagonize people unnecessarily. Unlike Abélard, McCabe never recanted, and never deviated from his chosen path.

H. J. Blackham, the new man in English humanism, recognized this flinty grit at the heart of McCabe's character. He remembered the old man as "lonely and embittered, and fighting. But this was not incompatible with his being friendly and genial by flashes."[2] Shortly after McCabe's death, S. K. Ratcliffe, an acquaintance of long standing from the South Place Ethical Society and the RPA wrote that "McCabe was wholly himself—independent, downright, and in intellectual conflict, uncompromising."[3]

McCabe did reveal several interesting facets of his personality in a monograph for Haldeman-Julius called *Getting the Most Out of Life*, originally written in 1932. Anticipating the flood of later pop-psychology theorists, McCabe wrote a down-to-earth humanist account of how to live what would later be called an authentic life. McCabe told his readers that the purpose of life is

> what we humans choose to make it; and, since we are no longer antagonistic units of savage life, but vitally connected parts of a social and industrial organism, it is what we choose to make it by common agreement. And the one thing on which we can agree, and have every right to agree, is that we want as many pleasant hours and as few unpleasant hours as possible in our short span of life, and work is a means to attain that end.[4]

All well and good, but McCabe was also quite practical about how this may be attained. He dismissed the sanctimonious moralizing about the blight of materialism. "We all want more money. I certainly do. I should like to live in a detached rose-girt little house instead of this dump muddled amongst putty-minded neighbours, with a few beautiful things round me and the means to travel when and how I liked." He offered no quick solutions to the amassing of money, noting that for ninety-nine out of a hundred of us, this would only be done by "cool, cheerful, conscientious industry."[5]

McCabe did not neglect his leisure time, though. Like Immanuel Kant before him, McCabe's leisure was nothing if not regular. "The talkies once a week (preferably humorous) or twice if anything good is offered, first class football matches in the winter (during eight months of the year in England), plenty of novels (preferably detective, humorous, and western, but at times for their literary quality), and my daily walk fill up my leisure; which is ample, as I only work six or seven hours a day, though with strict concentration."[6] When not out, McCabe would listen to the radio or read between eight o'clock and midnight.

Sex, too, was a perfectly legitimate leisure activity, and could be enjoyed simply because it is fun. He criticized Havelock Ellis and Bertrand Russell for seeing sex as "having an inherent taint which needs the consecration of love. . . . The sex-act is no more impure than kissing, and its legitimacy in each case must be judged by its consequences. If there are consequences for others, it falls under the same law of justice as all other acts."[7] In the language of a later generation, McCabe was insisting on rights, with due recognition of responsibilities. This, of course, if American calumniators of "secular humanism" are to be taken seriously, is precisely what such people do not do.

McCABE THE WRITER

But of course, it is as a writer that we know Joseph McCabe. Nobody knows how much McCabe wrote, and estimates vary. He claimed to be one of the most prolific writers of all time, citing more than two hundred titles over his career. In arriving at this figure, McCabe counted the five multivolume series he wrote for Haldeman-Julius as one title each. Gordon Stein, editor of the *Encyclopedia of Unbelief*, arrived at a larger figure by counting each title separately. The five multivolume works mentioned above, for instance, came as seventy-eight standalone Big Blue Books. Stein estimated McCabe wrote about two hundred books, a similar number of monograph-length publications, and about one hundred pamphlets.[8] Even allowing for Stein's method of counting, this figure is too high, although by how much it is very difficult to say. By my count, this is the figure as it stands so far:

Book-length titles	81
Pamphlets	12
Book-length titles for Haldeman-Julius	7
Big Blue Books for Haldeman-Julius	104
Little Blue Books for Haldeman-Julius	126
Translations	30
Ghostwritten book-length titles	7
Coauthored titles	14

By any standards this is a remarkable achievement. That adds up to 95 books, 104 monographs, and 138 pamphlets, plus the translations and coauthored titles. This figure is, as we have seen, arbitrary, as it is just as valid to count the titles as Stein did to arrive at his figure. I have counted the Haldeman-Julius monographs in the forty-volume, 2520-page *Key to Culture*, for example, as one title, and have not counted the five sections of the *Key* that were later sold off as stand-alone titles. Estimates of the number of his translations range from thirty to fifty, so it is quite possible that my list is still incomplete. I have only listed titles that I have actually seen or have direct evidence of. While some of his translations were nothing more than a means to earn an income, some were a labor of love for him because he thought they merited translation. McCabe was always more sensitive to trends in continental thought than rationalist thinkers were—or are—given credit for.

McCabe's writing career can be divided into two quite clearly defined phases, both spanning about thirty years and with 1926 as the pivotal year. Until 1926 most of McCabe's titles were published for Watts, the publishing house of the Rationalist Press Association. After that year his major publisher became Emanuel Haldeman-Julius. Before 1926, most of McCabe's publications were book-length whereas all his Haldeman-Julius titles were a monograph-length format.

Many of the book-length studies McCabe wrote for the RPA before and during the First World War were later reworked, either as shorter books for the RPA, or as monographs for Haldeman-Julius. For instance, the two-volume *Life and Letters of George Jacob Holyoake*, written in 1908, was reworked fourteen years later to appear as a 120-page book in the RPA's Life Stories of Great Men series. *Peter Abélard* (1901, 346 pages) reappeared three decades later as a Little Blue Book called *The Love Affair of a Priest and a Nun*. The Little Blue Books were not always blue, but they were always little. They measured about 5 by 3.5 inches and usually carried around fifteen thousand closely printed words. They were designed for the worker, without generous training or leisure, to read while on the bus to work, or at lunchtime.

On other occasions McCabe wrote shorter works in response to demand. In 1920, for instance, he recognized his audiences needed a short overview on evolution. Despite having already written two substantial works and three overviews on the subject, McCabe wrote *The ABC of Evolution* to fill that need. On other occasions McCabe rewrote material under the same heading. For example, *The Papacy in Politics Today*, originally published in 1937, was completely rewritten in 1942 and again in 1951, to keep up with events. Also, *The Existence of God*, written originally in 1913, was rewritten twenty years later, with attention given to the theistic speculations of Sir James Jeans and Sir Arthur Eddington. And, nineteen years after *The Story of Evolution*, McCabe wrote *The New Science and the Story of Evolution*, again, to bring the results of recent evolutionary studies to the notice of his readers. He also reused successful ideas; the most obvious example is *The Riddle of the Universe Today*, written in 1934, which was designed, like its famous predecessor, to provide the general reader with an overview of the world of science and its implications for modern thought.

The general pattern of McCabe's publishing history is clear. The first half of McCabe's writing career was itself made up of two uneasily coexisting components. On the one hand, he wrote biographies, histories, and general accounts of evolution. These were designed for the general, educated reading market, and were published by reputable firms such as Duckworth, Hutchinson, Putnams, Collins, Methuen, and so on. On the other hand, McCabe wrote shorter, more controversial studies of sensitive areas such as women's rights, the falsity of Christian apologetics, the folly of spiritualism, the conflict between religion and science, and—most damaging of all—sexual ethics. These books were mostly published by the Rationalist Press Association, and was probably only a matter of time before his activities as controversialist were going to impinge on his career as a society writer. Time and again his friends warned him that he was endangering his career. They were right, and the turning point came, as we will see, in 1916. After the First World War, as offers from the publishing houses dried up or were withdrawn, McCabe turned to translating. McCabe's future lay principally with rationalist controversialist writing; but then, of course, came the break with the RPA, and this dried up as well.

The main lost opportunity came early in the 1920s. Following on from the phenomenal success of H. G. Wells's *Outline of History*, a succession of other outlines were published to cash in on this innovative new publishing idea. One publishing house—McCabe never names it—reneged on a lucrative contract for McCabe to write an *Outline of Science*. McCabe later claimed that Wells himself had originally been invited to write the book but had said that McCabe was the only person who could write such a book. But one he began the book, the publishers were approached by J. Arthur Thomson, a prominent biologist with vitalist leanings, and "so many difficulties and unpleasantnesses were now put in my way that I had to accept a small compensation and retire."[9] Thomson was to oversee the production of a lavish two-volume *Outline of Science*, published by Cassell in England and Putnams in the United States in 1922. McCabe always regarded this episode as his greatest lost opportunity. This claim cannot be proved, but I see no reason to doubt it.

As opportunities slowly dried up in England, the link with Haldeman-Julius became correspondingly more important. Indeed, it is difficult to overestimate the importance of Haldeman-Julius to McCabe's writing career; had it not been for Haldeman-Julius, McCabe would not have had a writing career to speak of after 1926. Thanks to Haldeman-Julius, McCabe was able to write for another twenty-five years, and reach a very large audience. Generally speaking, the second half of McCabe's writing career, from 1926 onward, was taken up with controversial, scientific, historical writing.

But while McCabe's writing career has two noticeable phases, the subjects he wrote about remained pretty constant. As with the counting of titles, listing them by subject could be done in several different ways, but this is perhaps a fair indication of his areas of interest:

General outlines of McCabe's worldview	6
Catholicism	49
History	30
Topical issues	21
Religion	20
Biographies	18
Science	15
Controversies with religious apologists	10
Evolution	9
Reference	7
Sex/lifestyle issues	6
Miscellaneous	4

He retained an interest in these subject areas for most of his life, the only clear exception being biographies, the great majority of which were written in the first half of his career. Similarly, he did very few translations after 1926.

For over fifty years, McCabe would spend seven hours of the day writing. He would work from ten in the morning for three hours and then again from four until eight in the evening. This he would do four days a week. The other three would be spent researching at the British Museum.[10] McCabe came to know the British Museum as well as any other scholar and better than most. In the earlier phase of his career, when he was traveling extensively, travel by sea afforded a further opportunity to write. Many of his books were written at sea.

Early in his career he had taken courses on writing, but later confessed their limited use for him. He acknowledged that he was no artist. "Often do I fancy that the pen in my hand is a brush, but I know my limitations."[11] For McCabe, writing was always a means to an end, which was the propagation of ideas. He had a horror of verbiage and padding, and kept his writing simple, direct, and plain. Half a century after McCabe several thinkers have noted how fatal for one's career clear writing can be. John Passmore has noted that "it is the fate of those who write clearly, rather than opaquely and apocalyptically, to find themselves ignored, while the critics gyrate, in ever more fanciful paths, about the dozen or so esoteric writers who, by their obscurity, offer them endless opportunities for exegesis."[12] Richard Dawkins has gone one step further by speculating that this obscurity is deliberate, even necessary, for otherwise people will discover that they in fact have nothing to say.[13] McCabe has certainly suffered the fate of the clear writers.

McCabe's writing was so clear, in fact, that Edward Clodd complained that reading him was like having a pistol fired close to his ear.[14] The impression of a lot of McCabe's later writing is that the pistol is being aimed directly *at* one's ear. His early writing was direct, but polite and conventional. A review of one of his earliest books spoke of his writing as troubled by "no hesitating voice" and "no diffident touch."[15] As his confidence grew and as his impatience with what he saw as quibbling over details by academics and fellow rationalists also grew, he became more—to use his own word—truculent. He refused, he wrote shortly before his seventieth birthday, to be mellowed by age.[16] This is reflected in his writing, which became freer and less labored as he aged.

Neither McCabe as an individual nor his writing can be understood without appreciating that he was writing for the nonspecialist reader. He lived at the same time that some of the greatest popular writers of all time were active, the most prominent being H. G. Wells (1866–1946). McCabe admired Wells and referred to him throughout his works. At one point, McCabe likened Wells to Shelley: "Wells is very far from being a poet. But the fundamental ideas are the same; or at least no other powerful writer agrees so much with Shelley's basic ideas, and utters them so boldly."[17] Wells, in turn could, and occasionally did, appreciate McCabe's strengths. On one occasion Wells described McCabe as "the trained athlete of disbelief."[18] Looking over the list of McCabe's writings, it is difficult to avoid the impression of his living under the shadow of his great contemporary. Born a year apart, they both fought their way out of the uncomfortable border region between the working and middle classes they were born into. Like Wells, McCabe considered himself a prophet, but unlike Wells, he lacked the ability to really project himself into the future. Wells was always one, or even two, steps ahead of McCabe in getting his ideas across to the public and in thinking of original ways to do so. McCabe, as we have seen, joined the line of authors to publish an "outline" after the tremendous success of Wells's *Outline of History*. Between 1927 and 1929 McCabe wrote what was called the *Key to Culture*, which was an ambitious forty-volume encyclopedia that sought to cover all major areas of human endeavor. In the best Enlightenment tradition, this encyclopedia was designed to provide the general reader with all modern knowledge in a readily accessible style. McCabe's publisher later divided the encyclopedia into subject sections and sold them off as *The Complete Outline of History*, *The Foundations of Science*, *The Elements of Economics*, *The Outline of Literature*, and so on. Ten years after Wells wrote *The Salvaging of Civilization*, McCabe followed with *Can We Save Civilization?*

It is possible that this is also true regarding George Bernard Shaw. A year after Shaw's *Everybody's Political What's What*, McCabe came out with his *Outline of the World's Great 'Isms*. However, it is equally likely that this was coincidental and that both titles were being produced independently. McCabe never admired Shaw, whose cheerful unconcern for the facts of science was a constant source of irritation. Early in 1914 McCabe was invited to write a critique of Shaw. The *Times Literary Supplement* gave the book a lengthy and positive review; its only query being whether Shaw as philosopher was worth such a sustained examination.[19] For McCabe humbug was always worth smiting, regardless of the degree of seriousness in which it was offered.

INFLUENCES ON McCABE

While H. G. Wells was admired by McCabe, he couldn't be said to be his hero. Who, then, were McCabe's heroes? Who were the people whose memory inspired McCabe to carry on? As is the case with many remarkable individuals, McCabe considered himself deeply in the debt of other people. Three stand out. Two of them were identified by McCabe in 1917. There are, he wrote, "no men with whom I feel a closer kinship than the noble Robert Owen and his high-minded disciple George Jacob Holyoake."[20] One of the first articles McCabe wrote in the *South Place Magazine* was "Robert Owen As Thinker."[21] Twenty years later, McCabe expressed his admiration by supplying short biographies on both men for Watts's Life-Stories of Famous Men series, Owen in 1920 and Holyoake in 1922. He had already overseen a generous two-volume work on Holyoake in 1908. This two-volume work, *Life and Letters of George Jacob Holyoake*, was one of the largest works he ever produced.

It is not surprising that Robert Owen (1771–1858) should have been a source of inspiration for McCabe. Like McCabe, Owen had lived his life against the intellectual current of the time. While still a young man, Owen came upon a profound realization that our character is made for us, and not by us. He lived the rest of his life applying that principle in a variety of schemes and projects, most of which ended in failure. The most famous, and most successful, was Owen's experiment at the New Lanark cotton works in Scotland, which he took over in 1801. In fifteen years Owen transformed the small community. From a community of overworked, underpaid, poorly housed and fed victims of vicious alcohol abuse, gambling, prostitution, and appalling hygiene, Owen built what has become a model for communal living ever since. Owen reduced the hours of work without reducing the pay and released children from labor and put them in school instead. He improved housing, education, and health facilities for the workers. He slowly overcame their suspicion, and that of his business partners, because he found that the whole exercise even yielded better returns than the previous system of brutalizing exploitation.

With what can now be seen to be naive optimism, Owen went to London to persuade the politicians that his methods should be adopted across Britain. When Sir Robert Peel began proceedings to bring in a bill to abolish child labor in 1815, alarmed mill owners rallied to defeat the measure. The surest way to ensure Owen came to be seen as a liability was to highlight his heretical views on religion.

> Men who were fighting, with gross selfishness, for profits which were built up on the virtual slavery and debauch of little children asked gravely what were Owen's religious beliefs, and what were the religious principles on which he based the education of his children [at New Lanark]. It was a sordid and hypocritical business.[22]

McCabe repeatedly stressed the practical nature of Owen's work. "I protest once more against the fashion of calling it [Owen's central principle] an 'abstract principle.' It was a concrete and most comprehensive moral ideal, and it essentially implied a series of most drastic material and industrial changes."[23] Elsewhere he concluded that "some day the chief fount and source of the great English crusade against injustice will be recognized in the industrial experiment at New Lanark. . . ."[24] Owen was not a philosopher, a point in his favor for McCabe, but a man of practical intelligence, firm personal conviction, and social altruism. It was these features of Owen that McCabe admired the most.

As we will see so often in this book, McCabe was not given to uncritical adulation, and was more than aware of Owen's weaknesses. "Apart from his successes at New Lanark," he wrote in 1908, "he touched little that did not collapse. His enduring importance was as the disseminator of principles that would provoke more practical men to act. The spirit he brought into social service at the beginning of the nineteenth century was invaluable."[25] McCabe saw the Secularist, Rationalist, and Ethicist movements as the "proper heirs and successors" to Owen.[26]

McCabe's other source of inspiration was George Jacob Holyoake, whom he portrayed as Owen's greatest disciple. Of all the many biographies he had written, McCabe was proud to record that only with Robert Owen and Holyoake had there been no parts of their lives that he felt some need to "explain away or dress in the veil of charity."[27] Holyoake had been born in deep poverty and emerged from the engineering workshops of the English midlands as an Owenite radical, having been appointed missionary to the Sheffield Diocese of Owen's Rational Religion in 1841. While on Owenite duty, making his way to Bristol from Birmingham—being poor Holyoake had to walk the ninety miles—he stopped at Cheltenham and addressed an audience on the impeccable Owenite topic of "Home Colonization As a Means of Superseding Poor Laws and Emigration." The Vicar of Cheltenham sent men to the meeting to check for any atheist sedition, and when they heard none, tried to coax some out of

Holyoake at question time. They got what they wanted, because Holyoake responded to a question about our duty to God by observing that if "poor men cost the State so much, they would be put, like our officers, on half-pay. I think that while our distress lasts it would be wise to do the same thing with the Deity."[28] For this terrible crime, Holyoake was sentenced to six months prison. Holyoake went on to devote his long life to the Cooperative Movement, Secularism, antislavery, and a variety of other significant causes. In both the Secularist and Cooperative movements, McCabe saw the practical application of the Owenite vision. In dedicating his life to workers' cooperation and trade unionism, better educational and industrial conditions, freedom of speech, and access to power, Holyoake had put that vision into as much of a reality as one person's life could be expected to do.[29]

Holyoake saw each of these great causes being taken up by specialist organizations, dedicated to that issue alone. This represented a failure for Holyoake in that he had hoped his Secularist movement would be the vehicle for these various programs of reform. Holyoake's vision of Secularism was bound to fail, McCabe thought, but the legacy of that failure was a clearer understanding by successor organizations, like the RPA, of their role as a vehicle for the criticism of "erroneous religious traditions, in a broad, cultured, refined way, and with a care to impart positive education while older views were being modified or removed."[30] With this in mind Holyoake became the first chairman of the RPA. The sociologist Colin Campbell credits Holyoake's Secularism with bringing together the two divergent freethought traditions represented on the one hand by Thomas Paine's republican, anticlerical radicalism, and on other by Robert Owen's naturalistic, ethical utopianism.[31]

What is interesting about Holyoake is that he is quite different from McCabe. Unlike McCabe, Holyoake did make an accommodation with society in order to gain acceptance by powerful opinion leaders. Soon after his imprisonment, for example, he ceased to describe himself as an atheist. Many people from the Rationalist movement felt Holyoake had sold out to his comfortable friends, who preferred the safer term "agnostic," coined by T. H. Huxley in 1869. This feeling was particularly strong among supporters of Charles Bradlaugh, who also thought Holyoake had behaved shabbily toward their mentor during his times of troubles. We followed aspects of that dispute in chapter 2. So McCabe, who certainly never compromised his opinions and in fact became more radical as he got older, was the most able and vociferous supporter of a person thought to have done precisely those things. But equally, this person who never compromised his opinions was most painfully estranged from the supporters of Bradlaugh, whose chief virtue was held to be that he never compromised his opinions in return for power or esteem!

The key to understanding this otherwise bizarre affair is that McCabe remained truer to the rationalist dictum that nothing is sacrosanct, not even the memory of a fallen hero. We have seen that McCabe was fully aware of the weaknesses of his mentors, and aired them appropriately in his biographies of them. But as he criticized them, he also criticized others, including Charles Bradlaugh, as and when he thought necessary. Bradlaugh's followers were less able to be as dispassionate about their mentor as McCabe had been of his. The first important biographical work on Bradlaugh, written by his daughter, Hypatia Bradlaugh Bonner, with help from J. M. Robertson, was more hagiographical in character. David Tribe noted this in his 1971 biography of Bradlaugh; by far the best study of the great man yet to have been published.

The third great influence on McCabe was Sir Leslie Stephen, whose encouragement and assistance for the young seceder we outlined in the previous chapter. McCabe described Stephen as the "incarnation of common sense."[32] Even more than Holyoake, Stephen seems an unlikely mentor for someone of McCabe's background and temperament. To begin with, Stephen came from an altogether more privileged background, having been educated at Eton; Kings College, London; and Cambridge. Stephen's life was spent among the leading thinkers and socialites of London during the second half of the nineteenth century. But despite widely differing backgrounds, the two men shared some important experiences. Both had been ordained churchmen who, having lost their faith, took the unusual and honest step of seceding. Both took the even more unusual step of publicly criticizing religion after their secession. And both men earned their money with the pen.

The features that Robert Owen, George Jacob Holyoake, and Sir Leslie Stephen had in common were moral autonomy, kindliness, and a sense of social duty. They are all examples of Paul Kurtz's term "eupraxophy," which means the dynamic fusion of wise thought and consistent and altruistic action that together make up a fulfilling humanist life. This is the foundation of humanist ethics.[33] Given this, it is not surprising to find McCabe also admired the two classical schools of thought that most resembled the eupraxophic ideal: Stoicism and Epicureanism. Gilbert Murray, one of the twentieth century's finest scholars of antiquity, described Stoicism as religious in its exalted passion and philosophical inasmuch "as it had no pretence to magical powers or supernatural knowledge."[34] The attraction of such a combination to McCabe is obvious. Zeno of Citium (334–262 B.C.E.) is usually credited with founding Stoicism as a distinct intellectual tradition, but it was Chrysippus (280–206 B.C.E.) who transformed Stoicism into a systematic philosophy.[35] McCabe, however, only ever mentions Zeno. This bald outline of Stoicism penned by Jonathan Barnes gives a clear picture of its appeal to McCabe: "In ethics they rejected hedonism and counseled a life of 'virtue'; in physics they accepted a form of materialism but denied atomism; in logic they were empiricists, but they assigned a major role to reason in the development of knowledge."[36]

Stoicism provided for McCabe the model of enlightenment. Monist in physics, altruist in ethics, rational in behavior, Stoicism was the guide to practical and unpretentious living, untrammeled by arrogant presumptions of cosmic purpose or significance, while strongly defined by a social conscience and a sense of duty. Zeno and the Stoics, McCabe wrote in one of his Little Blue Books, "spoke of 'God,' but he was a material entity, and he was not at all the author and vindicator of the moral law. The law was an eternal part of nature, and a man was urged to live in harmony with nature." But the best was still to come. "Let me repeat—let me emphasize—this most austere and (in its more sober Roman form) most effective of moral systems was a *dogmatic Materialism!* The Stoics ridiculed the very ideas of spirit and free will: which we are asked to regard as the indispensable bases of any moral conduct."[37]

McCabe spoke of Epicureanism less frequently than of Stoicism, but its attraction was no less profound. The appeal of Epicureanism was in its earthy humanism and its foundational role in creating a genuinely humane moral law. "The common notion," McCabe wrote in 1913, "that Epicurus and his followers set up pleasure as the supreme good, and may therefore be excluded from the high fraternity of the philosophers, is quite inaccurate. Happiness, not pleasure, was the ideal of Epicurus, and his life and personal standard were sober and elevated."[38] McCabe cited Edward Clodd as an example of "the good Epicurean." Like Epicurus, Clodd concluded

> that the most enriching thing in a man's life is warm and untroubled friendship, a quite brotherly contact with as large a group as possible of his fellows. If there was any reaction to the "bleak Calvinism" of his youth, it was in this transition from a self-centred concern about his soul to an exuberant sociality.[39]

But more fundamental still than his Stoicism and Epicureanism was a staunch Prometheanism. The two great works on the sacrifice of Prometheus, by Shelley and Goethe, were bedrock sources of inspiration. McCabe noted that Shelley finished *Prometheus Unbound* in Rome "while the restored Papacy rejoiced in its belief that the thrones and altars were now re-established forever." In those dark years of reaction, Shelley's poem "was a magnificent encouragement to the minority who, in silence and solitude, believed that the world would yet return to its momentary vision of peace, happiness, liberty, and enlightenment."[40] *Prometheus Unbound* remained a source of inspiration for McCabe throughout his life. Shelley's poem provided not only the program for McCabe's life, but also an explanation for the spirit in which his, McCabe's, life would be conducted.

> Evil minds change good to their own nature. I gave all
> He has; and in return he chains me here
> Years, ages, night and day; whether the Sun
> Split my parched skin, or in the moony night
> The crystal-winged snow cling round my hair:
> Whilst my beloved race is trampled down
> By his thought-executing ministers.[41]

The major feature of both Stoicism and Epicureanism that McCabe rejected was the counsel to accept what one cannot change. McCabe's life was devoted to changing things that he thought unjust, outmoded, or prejudicial to progress. It was his Prometheanism that provided the motivation to work so unceasingly to inform and persuade others. McCabe learned from Prometheus how to be a rebel. But equally, McCabe took from Stoicism the recognition that he was, after all, only one man, and that there was a limit to what even he could achieve.

ERNST HAECKEL

H. G. Wells was a contemporary whose skills McCabe admired. Robert Owen, George Jacob Holyoake, and Sir Leslie Stephen were all mentors, or heroes, who McCabe looked up to from a slightly greater distance. Stoicism and Epicureanism were philosophies from which McCabe derived strength. Prometheus provided something of a mythological archetype. There is one more person we need to consider, one who combined several of these features at once. Not as close a contemporary as Wells, yet more than Holyoake or Stephen, this man's views were clearly and fundamentally influential. This was Ernst Haeckel (1834–1919) who, at the turn of the century, was one of the best-known and most controversial evolutionists in the world.

As noted above, McCabe achieved a local celebrity following the publication of *Twelve Years in a Monastery* and *Modern Rationalism* in 1897. But the book that truly launched McCabe's career was not one of his own, but his translation of Ernst Haeckel's *Riddle of the Universe*. Professor of zoology at the University of Jena from 1862 until 1909, Haeckel was Germany's first and most prominent advocate of Darwinism. His role in Germany was similar to that of Thomas Henry Huxley in England—if Huxley was Darwin's bulldog, Haeckel was Darwin's Rottweiler.[42]

Haeckel had been well known among the scientific community and readers of intelligent periodicals, but McCabe's translation of *The Riddle of the Universe* in 1900 provided him overnight with a huge international audience. This was not apparent at the time, however, as McCabe told the RPA he thought it would sell about one thousand copies in England. On that basis, McCabe translated what has been described as "one of the most incredible publishing successes of all times."[43] Haeckel's title was *Die Welt-rätsel* (loosely: the world riddle), but it was McCabe's brilliant idea to alter it slightly to *The Riddle of the Universe*. Armed with such a tantalizing title, the first-edition print run of ten thousand sold out quickly, and one hundred thousand copies of a cheap edition produced soon after sold out within a year.[44] McCabe could have read the phrase "riddle of the universe" in any number of places, but I like to think he read it in Sir Leslie Stephen's essay *An Agnostic's Apology*. We will see in chapter 9 that this was an influential work for McCabe. In any case, *The Riddle* sold over a half million copies in Germany alone and a quarter of a million copies elsewhere. Translated into twenty-five languages, it was the book most frequently mentioned by members of the RPA as a book that influenced their path to rationalism.[45] McCabe also acquired an international notoriety and was soon embroiled in the maelstrom of spleen that followed publication of Haeckel's book. Thirty-one years after translating *The Riddle of the Universe*, McCabe declared that "no book in my lifetime has had a wider influence in liberating the modern mind from superstition."[46]

As *The Riddle* became ever more popular, it began to attract ever more hostile attention from the churches. It is not difficult to see why. Haeckel described the book as "the complete expression of the conviction that has come to me, after many years of ardent research into Nature and unceasing reflection, as to the true basis of its phenomena."[47] It represented, as he put it, the ripe fruit of the tree of knowledge. It is not too strong a statement to see *The Riddle of the Universe* as the prototype for all subsequent single-volume volumes of science designed for the general reader. There is, I am sure, a straight line from *The Riddle of the Universe* to Edward O. Wilson's single-volume book *Consilience*, published ninety-eight years later. Haeckel's book was the first truly popular scientific work to offer a theory of everything. A century later, Wilson's book is subtitled "The Unity of Knowledge." Wilson's is undoubtedly the better book, but Haeckel's was more widely read. We will see in later chapters that McCabe remained committed to providing nonspecialists with a holistic overview of the universe and its workings throughout his writing career.

The motivations of Haeckel's detractors were of the same stamp as contemporary creationist opponents of evolution: the old (and, in the end, legitimate) fear that evolution equates with atheism. As one opponent put it, Haeckel belongs,

> to an Association of Monists, whose chief objects are to prove that man has evolved gradually—developed, step by step, from lower animals; to refute the Bible; and to do away with the belief in the immortality of the individual soul; and in a personal anthropomorphic God as Creator.[48]

The Riddle attracted over a hundred reviews and a dozen printed responses, some of which were intemperate, even unchristian. Dr. Horton, a respected theologian, lamented portentously in the *Christian World Pulpit* the "depths of degradation and despair into which the teaching of Haeckel will plunge mankind."[49] Horton was confident of this because Haeckel is "an atrophied soul, a being that is blind on the spiritual side."[50] J. G. Tasker, a prominent Christian apologist, insisted on the continued validity of the argument from design, even if evolution proved to be correct.[51] Another apologist, Frank Ballard, assured his readers that Haeckel's treatment of Christianity is "disrespectful and contemptuous to the last degree."[52] The *Times Literary Supplement* was offended that it was "among the mass of untrained and half-educated readers" that *The Riddle of the Universe* enjoyed its greatest support.[53] Even *Nature* sneered at what it dismissed as "Monism for the Multitude."[54]

McCabe's reply, published in 1903 as *Haeckel's Critics Answered*, is a masterpiece of intelligent polemic. He was bound to notice that most of the calumny directed at Haeckel came from churchmen. But the days when churchmen could make a statement about cosmology or any other branch of science, and expect, *because they were churchmen*, to be taken seriously, was fast coming to an end. "The sad truth is that the majority are morally hampered by the conviction of the sacredness and the exclusive truth of certain speculations, about God and the soul, which they have a corporate charge to defend. Every man who opposes them is constructed into a hater of their religion and a menace to human progress."[55]

The Riddle of the Universe and *Haeckel's Critics Answered* attracted two weighty replies. Frank Ballard's six-hundred-page *Haeckel's Monism False* came from the point of view of the Christian apologist, while Sir Oliver Lodge wrote *Life and Matter* in the hope of refuting materialism from his position as an eminent man of science. Both books spend a great deal of energy attempting to debunk Haeckel's monism. Even reviewers supportive of Ballard's views criticized his "answering heat and bitterness which serve no purpose."[56] We will examine these works in chapter 5.

While McCabe was destined to spend many years defending Haeckel's name, he was not uncritical of his mentor. Late in 1914, for example, he condemned Haeckel's support of Germany's violation of Belgian neutrality.[57] On one issue, however, McCabe was steadfast. This was the frequently recurring slur that Haeckel had altered some illustrations for one of his books in order to support his argument. An example from New Zealand can represent the general attack. The Catholic paper the *New Zealand Tablet* declared in 1929 that Haeckel "had been convicted of forgery in his efforts to establish what he wanted his readers to believe."[58] McCabe had parried these accusations since 1910 when the scandal broke during his visit to Australia and New Zealand. Haeckel had in fact been accused not of forgery but of falsification of an illustration he had made in one of his books. His accuser, Dr. Brass, appealed to the Kepler-Bund, a prestigious body of German scientists, not dissimilar to the Royal Society, to condemn Haeckel. Forty-six of the leading Kepler-Bund scientists replied by expressing concern at Haeckel's procedure, but roundly rebuked Dr. Brass for bringing such a charge against Haeckel. It later transpired that Dr. Brass was notorious for plagiarizing the works of colleagues and passing it off as his own work. The Kepler-Bund declared their full support for Haeckel.[59]

On Haeckel's death McCabe wrote a eulogy of his mentor that reads like a manifesto for McCabe's own life. McCabe noted that Haeckel had, in the main, rejected Nietzsche, but he had one Nietzschean strain. It is expressed by Nietzsche in a maxim that is often mistranslated into "Live dangerously." It means "live in danger"—danger to yourself. Hail the fight when the cause is good. Smite untruth wherever you find it. Prize manliness above comfort. Contribute your mite to the growing wealth of the world before you go out of it. Love the lunge and the parry, the thrust and the ward, as long as there are criminals and reactionaries on the earth. So to live is highest enjoyment and use of life. As the sun sinks and the shadows lengthen there are no regrets that the hour of strength is over.[60]

McCABE AND THE LAST MAN

As we have seen, McCabe's mission was to write for the nonspecialist general reader. Individually, McCabe's works did not, as a rule, enjoy the circulation of contemporaries like Wells, but his influence was almost as great because of the sheer volume of material he produced. His Haldeman-Julius Big Blue Books alone sold 1,892,000 copies.[61] The main readers were working men and women without significant formal education, but the Haldeman-Julius works were also very popular among undergraduate students in the United States through the thirties, forties and early fifties, much to the chagrin of many academics of the time. Their common complaint was that McCabe writes on so many subjects that he can't be reliable in all of them. Haldeman-Julius felt sufficiently moved by this jibe to pen a short, pugnacious retort as an appendix to one of McCabe's publications in 1946. "Where," he asked, "are the lists of his errors? They would be worth real money in the clerical market. He has written over 200 books, many of half a million to a million words, but theological and other critics are remarkably shy of them."[62] There are, in fact, quite a few errors in McCabe's later works, usually trivial errors made by trusting his memory when he should have consulted a reference work, or forgetting about a review which had in fact been written. Of the very few clear errors in the writing from the first half of his career can be found in his biography of George Jacob Holyoake. Here McCabe repeats Holyoake's false accusation that Charles Southwell ended his life editing a Methodist newspaper in Auckland, New Zealand, until his death in 1860. This is not correct, and McCabe stands condemned for this mistake. It has to be said, of course, that this hardly counts as a grievous error.

It is not surprising, given McCabe's admiration for Robert Owen and George Jacob Holyoake, that he wrote principally for the general reader. In the tradition of those two reformers, McCabe sought, by his writing, to expose error and open people's minds to the possibilities of how beautiful life could be, if only we planned for it rationally and with proper social awareness of needs. And it was from the general reader that McCabe received the staunchest support. Among that readership he was almost revered. The office of the New Zealand Rationalist Association, as it was then known, proudly displayed a signed photograph of McCabe forty years after his death. Again, the example of New Zealand is illustrative of his influence. During McCabe's tour of New Zealand in 1910 he visited Timaru, a provincial center in the South Island. As was common through McCabe's touring life, the people preparing his visit were having problems getting a venue for his lectures. Eventually, a local Presbyterian minister, Rev. James Henry George Chapple agreed to chair the meeting. Only once the authority of a Christian minister was bestowed on the visit was a venue secured. Chapple's willingness to chair the meeting was to cost him his career in the Presbyterian Church. The story of Chapple's life was later told in an award-winning novel called *Plumb* by the New Zealand novelist Maurice Gee, with the Rev. Chapple becoming Rev. Plumb and Timaru becoming Thorpe. McCabe, strangely enough, kept his real name in the novel. Here is how Plumb responded when hearing McCabe was to visit Thorpe:

> I knew all about McCabe: his Catholic upbringing, his twelve years in a Franciscan monastery—Father Anthony—his struggle to shake superstition off: and then the books, the pamphlets, the lectures, the life lived with a purpose; the crusade, if you like, against the forces of religious obscurantism. I had read every word he had written. He was one of the shapers of my mind. And this man was coming to Thorpe. Yes, I was excited.[63]

Gee went on to describe McCabe's mind as "an instrument of strength and delicacy. He had the reasoning powers of a John Stuart Mill and the wit of an Oscar Wilde, if one can imagine a marriage between those minds."[64] McCabe certainly did have a mind of strength and delicacy, and he had extraordinary reasoning powers, but with the best will in the world, one can't claim for him the wit of Oscar Wilde. He wasn't exactly humorless; McCabe's occasional caustic depth charges reveal his low-key, laconic side. But not even his friends would have described McCabe as witty in the Oscar Wilde style. Life was too serious a matter for that. During his dispute with McCabe in 1908 G. W. Foote was cruelly accurate. "George Meredith calls light literature 'the garden of the soul.' Mr McCabe, I fancy, is more at home in the kitchen-garden, amongst the sober, respectable, and nutritious vegetables."[65] Pursuing a similar path, G. K. Chesterton chided McCabe for subscribing to the fallacy common to "men of the clerical type" of thinking that "funny is the opposite of serious."[66] Though unkind, this is not entirely untrue. McCabe acknowledged Chesterton's lightness of touch, and the lack of humor in his own writings. "I never read Mr Chesterton's articles without regretting that I have, apparently, no share of that happy virtue."[67] But while he admired humor, McCabe was impatient of frothiness or superficiality when dealing with important questions. McCabe, in the best rationalist tradition, was a barely reconstructed puritan.

Witty or not, McCabe was deeply admired, and Gee's book captures brilliantly the influence McCabe had on people. When he returned to New Zealand in 1923, his promoters advertised him as "famous author, translator, lecturer. The greatest living exponent of science and evolution. 'No man has done more to enlighten mankind.' An eloquent speaker and a master of the English tongue. Thoughtful men and women cannot afford to miss these educational lectures."[68] Promotion, one might reply, is designed to get results, not tell the truth. True, but the people who devoted their time to promoting this visit were not professionals, but people who believed this to be true. Judging by the packed audiences, many others thought that this was true as well. Among those who made their way to hear McCabe at this meeting was Sir Robert Stout, Chief Justice of New Zealand. The seventy-nine-year-old Stout took the day-long train trip from Wellington especially to chair McCabe's first Auckland lecture of that tour. The people involved in preparing for McCabe's tour also founded the Auckland Rationalist Association. This organization, now called the New Zealand Association of Rationalists and Humanists, is still flourishing. Thirty-two years after his death, it was the sheer bulk of McCabe's written legacy that first excited my curiosity about and admiration for this extraordinary man.

McCabe spent a lifetime writing for the "common man," the "general reader," or, to use the grandly metaphysical phrase, the "Last Man." This term was originally employed by Friedrich Nietzsche (1844–1900) to express his contempt for the very people McCabe was writing for. "Books for everybody," Nietzsche wrote, "are always malodorous books: the smell of petty people clings to them."[69] Few contrasts between McCabe's values and those of Nietzsche and his disciples could be more stark than this. But where Nietzsche's prescription for the Last Man was to become the plaything for the Overman in closed societies, McCabe sought to guide and inspire them to build a better world in the here and now. "The correct art of living," McCabe wrote in 1932, "must be based upon truths that a man can find in Main Street and must be capable of expression in the language of Main Street."[70] The correct art of living came to revolve around the consistent application of the Golden Rule, which he described as the ultimate moral principle. At one stage he lamented wistfully that "one spends four decades exploring and meditating all the philosophies and theologies, the theosophies and anthroposophies, and one finds in the end that the truth about life is so simple that you can teach it to children of ten."[71]

A year after his death a meeting was held to commemorate the memory of McCabe and his old foe, Chapman Cohen. Hector Hawton, the new editor of the Literary Guide (he was soon to rename it The Humanist) admired McCabe's ability to write simply and to resist the temptation to display his erudition with long words, foreign phrases, or other impediments to the general reader. He went on to outline McCabe's (and Cohen's) extraordinary career. "Really, when I see how the world has treated such men I wonder if we deserve them!"[72]

That is very difficult to judge, as is determining the extent of McCabe's influence among the general reader. After all, everyone who saw McCabe lecture and most who were inspired by his books is now dead. All we can do is to note the tributes paid to McCabe after his death. A letter to a zealous young New Zealand law student in 1923 is, I feel sure, representative of his personality. The letter reads:

My dear Mr Barrett

I am desperately busy, but I must send you a line of congratulations on your early and deserved success. Keep and develop your manliness and you will be glad to be alive. Some of the finest men I met in New Zealand were lawyers—Stout, MacGregor, and O'Dea. You cannot better them, but I hope you will be like them. And go canny with your heresies while you are young. There is plenty of time, and there are plenty of unobtrusive opportunities. You have my hearty good wishes and my confidence in your future.[73]

After McCabe's death, Barrett was one of many friends and supporters of McCabe who penned a short tribute. "Some day an historian will record the full measure of McCabe's life and work and this will amaze future generations, as to what *one* man can accomplish in a lifetime—given the wisdom and the courage to do it."[74] Barrett had been involved in McCabe's three trips to New Zealand, in 1910, 1913, and 1923.

Among the many other tributes, F. W. Garley recalled hearing McCabe speak in Northampton in the early years of the century:

He always drew large numbers—often 2000 in the open air, and I well remember his magnificent voice, most clear and distinct, the way he put over his denunciation of the Roman Catholic Church, and his detailed account of his monastic life. He left an indelible impression on my life, especially by his chats with my father and ourselves at home, exposing the basis of fear and superstition in all religions.[75]

Another person who remembered McCabe's inspiring lectures was the scientist Hyman Levy (1889–1975). Born in Edinburgh to a family of Jewish refugees from Russian pogroms, Levy was warned about McCabe in no uncertain terms.

When I was a boy Joseph McCabe was taboo. He was the Bad Man who spread the gospel of wickedness, using Science, the gift of the Almighty, for his nefarious ends. And so when the Bad man came to Edinburgh to lecture the young boy slipped into the meeting (without paying), and listened enraptured to a discourse on the Evolution of the Universe, illustrated with a series of marvellous lantern slides.[76]

Even in faraway New Zealand it was the physical presence of McCabe while lecturing that people remembered. The local Rationalist journal made a genuine tribute to his memory, when it stated:

We in New Zealand (as Rationalists the world over) salute his memory. Some of the older members heard him speak years ago during the course of his lecture tours and retain memories of his dynamic personality and brilliant oratory, but the abiding monument to McCabe will be his books and countless articles to be found in the pages of Freethought journals.[77]

Half a century after his death, McCabe's influence is still strong, and not just in the English-speaking world. Sanal Edamaruku, a prominent Indian Rationalist, told me that McCabe ranks equal with Robert Green Ingersoll (1833–1899) as the most widely read rationalist author in that country. McCabe's works have been translated into Hindi, Tamil, and Malayalam, with twenty-five titles translated into Malayalam alone, including his autobiography, *Rome's Syllabus of Condemned Errors*, and *History's Greatest Liars*. The Indian Rationalist Association has also followed Haldeman-Julius's example by printing small tracts, designed for the non-specialist reader, also known as Little Blue Books.[78]

Having seen how extensive McCabe's legacy is, we will now examine the nature of this legacy.

NOTES

1. Joseph McCabe, *Peter Abélard* (London: Duckworth/Putnams, 1901).
2. Letter from H. J. Blackham to Mike Lloyd-Jones, November 29, 1972. I am grateful to Mr. Lloyd-Jones for this insight.
3. *Rationalist Review* (March 1955): iii.
4. Joseph McCabe, *Getting the Most Out of Life* (Girard, Kan.: Haldeman-Julius, 1932), p. 23.
5. Ibid., pp. 18–20.
6. Ibid., p. 30.
7. Ibid.
8. Gordon Stein, ed., *An Anthology of Atheism and Rationalism* (Amherst, N.Y.: Prometheus Books, 1980) p. 76.
9. Joseph McCabe, *Eighty Years a Rebel* (Girard, Kan.: Haldeman-Julius, 1947), p. 45.
10. I owe this insight to Mike Lloyd-Jones.
11. McCabe, *Eighty Years a Rebel*, p. 76.
12. John Passmore, *Serious Art* (London: Duckworth, 1991), p. 125.
13. Richard Dawkins, "Postmodernism Disrobed," *Nature* 394 (July 9, 1998): 141.
14. Joseph McCabe, *Edward Clodd: A Memoir* (London: John Lane, 1932), pp. 128–29.
15. *Literary Guide* (January 1, 1900): 5.
16. Joseph McCabe, *The Logic and Virtue of Atheism* (Austin, Tex.: American Atheist Press, 1980), p. 1.
17. *Literary Guide* (August 1922): 114–15.
18. Ibid., p. 138.

19. *Times Literary Supplement*, July 27, 1914, p. 354.

20. Joseph McCabe, *The Bankruptcy of Religion* (London: Watts, 1917), p. 303.

21. *South Place Magazine* 7, no. 9 (June 1902): 134–36.

22. Joseph McCabe, *Robert Owen* (London: Watts, 1920), p. 43.

23. Ibid., p. 94.

24. Joseph McCabe, *The Church and the People* (London: Watts, 1919), p. 87.

25. Joseph McCabe, *The Life and Letters of George Jacob Holyoake* (London: Watts, 1908), vol. 1, p. 295.

26. McCabe, *Robert Owen*, pp. 99–100.

27. Joseph McCabe, *George Jacob Holyoake* (London: Watts, 1922), p. 14.

28. Ibid., p. 18.

29. McCabe, *The Life and Letters of George Jacob Holyoake*, vol. 2, pp. 323–34.

30. Ibid., pp. 263–64.

31. Colin Campbell, *Toward a Sociology of Irreligion* (London: Macmillan, 1971), p. 48.

32. McCabe, *The Bankruptcy of Religion*, p. 254.

33. See Paul Kurtz, *Eupraxophy: Living Without Religion* (Amherst, N.Y.: Prometheus Books, 1989). The term is made up of "eu" (good, well), "praxis" (conduct, practice), and "sophia" (scientific and philosophic wisdom).

34. Gilbert Murray, "The Stoic Philosophy," in *Humanist Essays* (London: Unwin Books, 1964), p. 139.

35. My account of Stoicism is indebted to Jonathan Barnes, "Hellenistic Philosophy and Science," and Anthony Meredith, "Later Philosophy," both in *The Oxford History of the Classical World*, ed. John Boardman, Jasper Griffin, and Oswyn Murray (London: Guild Publishing, 1986).

36. See Barnes, "Hellenistic Philosophy and Science," p. 369.

37. Joseph McCabe, *The Story of Religious Controversy* (Boston: Stratford, 1929), pp. 189–90.

38. Joseph McCabe, *The Existence of God*, Inquirer's Library, no. 1 (London: Watts, 1913), p. 43.

39. McCabe, *Edward Clodd*, pp. 86–87.

40. Joseph McCabe, *One Hundred Men Who Moved the World* (Girard, Kan.: Haldeman-Julius, 1931), vol. 14, p. 37.

41. "Prometheus Unbound," Act 1, *The Poetical Works of Percy Bysshe Shelley* (London: Ward, Lock, n.d.), p. 168.

42. For a good examination of Haeckel's influence, see Alfred Kelly, *The Descent of Darwin: The Popularization of Darwin in Germany, 1860–1914* (Chapel Hill: University of North Carolina Press, 1981). For a shorter summary see H. James Birx, "Ernst Haeckel," *New Zealand Rationalist and Humanist* (September 1994): 2–4.

43. See entry on Haeckel in Richard Milner, *The Encyclopedia of Evolution* (London/New York: Facts on File, 1990), p. 206.

44. Frank Ballard, *Haeckel's Monism False* (London: Charles H. Kelly, 1906), p. 4.

45. Susan Budd, *Varieties of Unbelief* (London: Heinemann, 1977), p. 186.

46. McCabe, *One Hundred Men Who Moved the World*, vol. 17, p. 34.

47. Ernst Haeckel, *The Riddle of the Universe* (London: Watts, 1900).

48. Robert Miller-Argue, *Evolution Exploded by Many Infallible Proofs* (Sydney: Commonwealth Christian Evidence Press Association, 1910), p. 62.

49. Joseph McCabe, *Haeckel's Critics Answered* (London: Watts, 1903), p. 10.

50. See McCabe's added final chapter to the revised edition of Bölsche's *Haeckel: His Life and Work* (London: Watts, 1909), p. 121.

51. J. G. Tasker, "Does Haeckel Solve the Riddles?" in *Is Christianity True?* (London: Charles H. Kelly, 1904), p. 327.

52. Frank Ballard, *The Miracles of Unbelief* (London: T. & T. Clark, 1905), p. 349.

53. *Times Literary Supplement* (February 9, 1906): 42–43.

54. *Nature* 63, no. 1631 (January 31, 1901): 320–21.

55. McCabe, *Haeckel's Critics Answered*, p. 15.

56. *Times Literary Supplement* (February 9, 1906): 42–43.

57. Joseph McCabe, *Treitschke and the Great War* (Toronto: T. Fisher Unwin/William Briggs, 1914), p. 266.

58. *New Zealand Tablet*, September 25 1929, p. 3.

59. See McCabe's letter to the *Evening Post*, Wellington, New Zealand, July 7, 1910. He went over some of this ground again in *The Triumph of Evolution* (London: Watts, 1925), p. 29.

60. *Literary Guide* (September 1919): 129–31.

61. E. Haldeman-Julius, *My Second 25 Years* (Girard, Kan.: Haldeman-Julius, 1949), p. 22. I am grateful to Timothy Binga for helping me get access to this work, and for a lot of other assistance with McCabe's body of work.

62. See Haldeman-Julius, appendix in McCabe, *How Atomic Energy Will Affect Your Life and Future* (Girard, Kan.: Haldeman-Julius, 1946), p. 32.

63. Maurice Gee, *Plumb* (London: Faber & Faber, 1978), p. 102.

64. Ibid., pp. 102–103.

65. *Freethinker* (March 29, 1908): 195.

66. G. K. Chesterton, *Heretics* (London: John Lane The Bodley Head, 1911), p. 220.

67. Joseph McCabe, "Christianity Defended by Sleight of Hand," in *Christianity and Rationalism on Trial* (London: Watts, 1904), p. 88.

68. *Auckland Star*, June 20, 1923, p. 16. For further treatment of this tour, see my *Heathen in Godzone: Seventy Years of Rationalism in New Zealand* (Auckland: NZARH, 1998), chap. 1.

69. Friedrich Nietzsche, *Beyond Good and Evil* (London: Penguin, 1988), p. 43.

70. McCabe, *Getting the Most Out of Life*, p. 5.

71. Joseph McCabe, *Can We Save Civilization?* (London: The Search, 1932), p. 248.

72. *Freethinker* (March 9, 1956): 77.

73. Letter to E. J. Barrett, 1923, in the possession of the New Zealand Association of Rationalists and Humanists.

74. *Freethinker* (February 25, 1955): 60.

75. Ibid. (February 11, 1955).

76. *Literary Guide* (September 1934): 167.

77. *New Zealand Rationalist* (March 1955): 4.

78. I am grateful to Sanal Edamaruku, general secretary of the Indian Rationalist Association, for this information, and for several copies of McCabe titles translated into Malayalam.

4

Past and Present

McCabe As Historian
and Social Commentator

Before anything else, McCabe was a historian. Whether writing a biography, a survey of a field of science or a polemic against some aspect of religion, McCabe's preferred methodology was historical. More than half of his book-length works were either direct works of history or works employing historical method. The same can be said for about half of his Big and Little Blue Book publications. McCabe considered a historical understanding of any contemporary question to be essential to a proper understanding of it. "Theoretically," McCabe wrote in 1920, "we moderns, with our strong sense of mastery and creativeness, make our own institutions. In practice we do not."[1] In other words, only by a sound historical knowledge could the theory become a reality. It is highly likely that McCabe knew of, and was inspired by, Goethe's counsel:

> He who cannot give to himself
> An account of the last three thousand years
> Must remain unacquainted with the things of darkness,
> Able to live only from day to day.[2]

S. K. Ratcliffe, an acquaintance of long standing wrote of McCabe soon after his death that, had he been able to choose his field of research, it would have been medieval history.[3] I am not convinced McCabe would have been satisfied with such a removed specialism for long, but there is no question of McCabe's love of and facility for history. And McCabe was no mere chronicler of facts. He combined the roles of polemicist, historian, and prophet. This would seem to be a bad start to establishing his credentials as a historian, but McCabe was in fact a very good historian, and one who had a far more sophisticated view of history than he is given credit for—when he is noticed at all. To take one example among many, the *Times Literary Supplement* review of his biography of Goethe concluded that it "must unquestionably be reckoned among the best and most important studies of Goethe yet offered to English readers."[4] And yet one searches in vain to find McCabe's book mentioned in the bibliography of any study of Goethe. The same is true of his equally well-received studies of Peter Abélard (1901), St. Augustine (1902), Talleyrand (1906), or the Jesuits (1913). The one constant theme in the reviews over the half century of his writing career, whether from friends or foes, is that his scholarship was of a high standard. Not only is McCabe not appreciated as he deserves to be, he was in some respects a pioneer.

Before looking at McCabe's approach to history, perhaps the first job is to defend his historical outlook from the charge of historicism. It is a common criticism that rationalist historians are incurable historicists. By "historicism," I mean the term developed by Karl Popper (1902–1994), which refers to the tendency to see history in terms of large-scale historical development that conforms to the tenets of some ideology. In Popper's own terms, it is the claim that "sociology is theoretical history."[5] A historicist, in Popper's view, "would hesitate to admit that man, by any effort, can alter the laws of historical destiny even after he has discovered them."[6] Despite the fact that it was Popper—an uncompromising rationalist—who drew the world's attention to historicism, it has become a commonplace for postmodernists to blithely accuse rationalists of historicism as if it were self-evidently true. This is only one of a long list of thoroughly disreputable isms that rationalists have been accused of. Perhaps this can be explained in part by the different understanding of historicism on either side of the Atlantic. The understanding I have of historicism seems largely confined to the analytic tradition in philosophy outside North America. In North America, by contrast, historicism is often understood as "a recognition of diversity in values and ideas over time."[7] This, of course, is quite different from Popper's understanding of the term. We will see that McCabe is vulnerable to the charge of historicism in the Popperian sense, but it requires a generous helping of hindsight before it can be made comfortably. Of historicism in the American sense, McCabe is cheerfully guilty, and no more will be said of it.[8]

Let us first do what we can to implicate McCabe as deeply as possible in this charge. In his autobiography, McCabe wrote that history is "the continuation, besides sociology, comparative religion, and ethics, of the story which science in the ordinary sense carries forward from the birth of the earth to the end of the Neolithic and the Bronze ages. It is science."[9] Or again, McCabe described indefinite progress as "now as certain as any scientific law."[10] Or again, McCabe could call a study of the century from 1825 to 1925 *A Century of Stupendous Progress* and declare that during that time "there has in the last one hundred years been more progress in every respect than had ever before been witnessed in five hundred years, if not a thousand years."[11] On the face of it, McCabe is guilty as charged.

But the story is not nearly that simple. To start with, credit should be given to the various historicist fallacies popular in his time that McCabe saw through. A prime example is the nation-age histories which were in vogue in his day. The most influential nation-age exponent was Oswald Spengler (1880–1936), whose classic work *The Decline of West*, published in 1918, was vastly influential between the two world wars. Spengler depicted history as a series of rhythmic rises and falls of civilizations, with nations coming of age and dying. In fact, McCabe was in advance of much opinion when he condemned cyclic nation-age theories even before Spengler published his work. McCabe was aware of Professor McDougall's *Revolutions of Civilization*, published in 1911, which had advanced a similar thesis. He had also written a book on the historiography of Heinrich von Treitschke, an historian whose nation-age views were influential in pre–World War I Germany. With Treitschke in mind, McCabe told his nonspecialist readers that this "supposed historical law has no serious foundation whatever. A civilization may last for 8000 years, like that of Ancient Egypt, or 4000 years, like that of China, or 400 years, like that of Athens or of Florence. It depends entirely upon the circumstances and upon the neighbours of a particular state."[12]

McCabe's grounding in basic historical knowledge was too broad to be knocked off course by Spengler's superficial grandiosity. In 1931, McCabe described *The Decline of the West* as "one of the most confusing abuses of a large erudition that I know in modern literature."[13] Spengler's theory, he wrote, was simply false. "Its error is due largely to the European habit of ignoring Asiatic civilization. The theory obviously does not apply to China and still less to India." As another example, McCabe cited Japan, which has been "highly civilized far longer than any European people, yet is today is stronger than ever."[14] McCabe also reminded his nonspecialist readers that even assuming a nation "decays," this process is restricted, in most cases, to the tiny few at the top. "All that dies," McCabe wrote in 1932, "when a nation falls, is the political form, with the dynasty and aristocracy, and the accumulated wealth, with the industry and trade that created it and the art and culture which it had supported. The great body of the workers bow, as do the ears of corn when the storm blows, and then rise again to their unchanging tasks." I have quoted him from a passage written in 1932, but he repeated this sentiment several times.[15] He also criticized the notion of there being laws of history, which he described as "nonsense."[16] The last time McCabe bothered with Spengler was in the midthirties, when it was all too obvious how his history was being understood. "From the first his idea of 'decline' was that we were losing the fine military qualities of blind submission to authority, training for muscular work, bombastic arrogance, and readiness for occasional war."[17]

McCabe never subscribed to perhaps the most notorious historicist conception of them all, dialectical materialism, and was criticized by Marxists for this. McCabe saw dialectical materialism as "rather strained in its attempt to combine scientific Materialism, historical Materialism, and advanced economics, in one system."[18] Even in his last years, when his admiration of the Soviet Union was at its highest, McCabe thought dialectical materialism a pretentious and unnecessary addition to materialism proper. This contrasts favorably with recent attempts to reintroduce "the dialectic" into serious writing. For example, the Marxist postmodernist theorist Fredric Jameson is at his most lyrical when he speaks of the dialectic as " 'beyond good and evil' in the spirit of some easy taking of sides, whence the glacial and inhuman spirit of its historical vision. . . ."[19] One would struggle to find any rationalist popularizer as grandly historicist as Jameson. And it would be even more difficult to find historicism in as overbearing a form as that held by Martin Heidegger, the single most significant influence on postmodernism. According to one interpreter, Heidegger saw all Western intellectual history as *inevitable* following the Platonist "deflection" of the pre-Socratic thought.[20] Unlike these purveyors of the dialectic, McCabe was aware of the price he would need to pay for his disdain of historicist notions such as the dialectic. This is why we never find McCabe insisting that his histories were objective monuments that will remain permanently valid. He professed to be unconcerned about the reception his philosophy of history will receive from succeeding generations.[21]

McCABE AND PROGRESS

As we saw in the passage quoted from *1825–1925: A Century of Stupendous Progress*, McCabe did uphold and advocate the notion of progress. But for McCabe progress was not held up as an unconditional or absolute trend. He was always aware that history can move in several directions. Neither was McCabe's view of progress a strictly "linear" one—linear thinking being a high-level crime among postmodernist thinkers. Rather, his notion of progress is similar to the branching motion as understood by contemporary natural selection. "Progress is not a general rise simultaneously of large bodies of men and women. It is a growth outward from centers: from city to country, from one group in a city to others."[22] Neither was McCabe content with thinking in terms of "binary oppositions"—another grave crime among postmodernists. He deprecated the simple opposition of optimist/pessimist, preferring for himself the term "meliorist," which emphasizes the human effort that must be exerted before any improvement in the human condition is to be had.[23] His life's work can be seen as his contribution to that effort.

It is also important to remember that progressionism was certainly not an ailment specific to rationalists, another fondly held prejudice of many postmodernists and other critics of humanism. On the contrary, virtually all Europeans accepted the notion of progress, usually in forms a lot less acceptable now than McCabe's. For instance, Robert Miller-Argue, a lecturer for the Australian

Commonwealth Christian Evidence Press Association and opponent of McCabe, saw progress in this way:

> The Law of Progress is demonstrated clearly in one of the two sections of the human race, which we will now examine: The heathen nations, whose lands are habitations of cruelty, superstition and gross sensuality, and whose teeming millions are kept in curb by their mental superiors. In contradistinction to the heathen are the Anglo-Saxons, Latins and Teutonic races, more especially the peoples of England, Germany and America, who have placed the open Bible in the van of their onward march. . . .[24]

This was one of the most widely held notions of progress among thinking Europeans before the First World War. But while McCabe's views on progress avoid the racism and arrogance of Miller-Argue's conception, is he not vulnerable to charges of progression*ism*? In the example given at the beginning of this chapter, we see McCabe declaring that indefinite progress is now as certain as any scientific law; he goes on to make the point that "change is normal and stagnation abnormal."[25] Here McCabe can be charged with confusing a perfectly reasonable point about the human condition with a notion of progress. If he had simply said that "indefinite change is a basic fact of science," his point would have been uncontroversial. He stated his case most clearly in his 1914 book *The Sources of the Morality of the Gospels*, where he said that if "history has its lessons, the longer the stretch of history on which you look back, the wiser you should be; nor can the decay and crash of older civilizations be without a moral for the new."[26] It is difficult to detect an unsustainable progressionism in this observation.

Equally uncontroversial was his claim for "more progress" between 1825 and 1925 than had hitherto been the case. *A Century of Stupendous Progress* was a study of the developments in social legislation in England over that period that resulted in longer and more comfortable lives for millions of people. For McCabe, who had seen these changes firsthand, this was a simple, incontrovertible fact. In another work he listed the features of modernity he thought have changed the face of Europe. He mentioned compulsory mass education, mass dissemination of printing, the development of radio, and the proliferation of caring services.[27] Each of these had developed since his own childhood in the 1870s. McCabe came from a generation that had experienced firsthand the tremendous effects of these changes. What is more, McCabe was correct. A contemporary historian of Victorian society has concluded that life "for the great majority of Victorians was much better, materially, than it had been for their parents and grandparents."[28] It is easy to sneer at notions of progress, but taking its benefits for granted is an essential precondition for such an attitude. What McCabe would make of people who use high-powered computers and e-mail to lament the brutalizing effects of technology and the emptiness of progress can only be left to the imagination.

McCabe saw history as a science. In the current climate, this would be another reason for dismissing McCabe as being of no further interest. The idea of seeing history as a science was made popular after J. B. Bury (1861–1927) linked the two in his inaugural lecture as Regius Professor of Modern History at Cambridge. Bury became known as the leading theoretician of the concept of progress. But we have already seen that McCabe was more circumspect on the question of progress than many of his contemporaries. The same is true with his equation of history with science. All McCabe meant by this is that the historian needs to approach the materials at hand in a skeptical and dispassionate manner, and to realize that historical sources themselves have a history. While his description of sound scholarship has changed, the method has not. It is useful to recall that McCabe was well trained in German language and thought and that his conception of science resembled the German term *Wissenschaft*. This word, used by Kant, meant science in its broader meaning of "disciplined examination."

E. P. Thompson is only one of many recent theorists to argue against seeing history as a science. Thompson saw this linkage as "unhelpful and confusing" because it can allow us to forget that historical knowledge is provisional and limited and defined by the questions asked by the historian.[29] Thompson's point is perfectly sound, but as we have seen, McCabe was aware of these dangers and, by and large, avoided committing them. And of course Thompson did not have "disciplined examination" in mind when he was criticizing history being seen as a science.

McCabe illustrated his point by saying that historians need to take account of the environment in which they live. "A visitor to our planet," he wrote in 1928, "opening one of our older historical books would get the impression that the vast majority of the race had existed for the last five thousand years only to maintain and fight for political, military and religious institutions."[30] McCabe was not a supporter of the "great man" theory of history, particularly when the great men are taken only from the ranks of military leaders. It is not "the dictatorial strong men who did most for their nations and civilization but such men as Pericles, Hadrian, Ptolemy, Tai-Tsung, Abd-al Rahman III, Frederick II, and Frederick the Great. The work of the Caesars, Charlemagnes, and Napoleons was apt to be costly and impermanent."[31] In the main, McCabe placed little emphasis on great men.

History proper, as McCabe understood the term, was the study of the people, not of a few leaders or institutions. He expressed this preference throughout his career, but this example will suffice. Here McCabe is describing the history taught in Robert Owen's schools:

> History was taught, not in crabbed text-books which bristled with useless dates and unpronounceable names and such trivialities as the births and marriages of kings, but from colored charts which showed the nations blending and separating like the streams of Lanarkshire. The peoples of the world were described

in their surroundings, so that the defects of each could be charitably explained and the feeling of brotherhood encouraged.[32]

None of this was new to McCabe, of course; a point he fully acknowledged. He saw Winwood Reade's classic, *The Martyrdom of Man*, written originally in 1872, as the pioneering work of what he called the new history. McCabe was heir to the history of the Victorians, which one scholar characterizes as being concerned to "present the relation of the past and present as a steady growth, a chain of cause and effect related in accordance with discoverable natural laws."[33] In rejecting the great man theory of history, the Victorian historians were paralleling the geologists' rejection of catastrophism, the biologists' rejection of special creation, or the social scientists' rejection of the Social Contract. McCabe's philosophy of history was shaped fundamentally within this tradition. But where he parted from the Victorian historians was precisely in his loosening the bonds of historical inevitability. He was aware of the problems associated with notions of history as a process of slow and steady evolution, with its connotations of inevitability.[34] Whereas his Victorian predecessors were merely appraising their readers of the true situation, McCabe was trying to persuade his readers to actively contribute to directing history in that direction, lest it doesn't happen at all. He always wrote with this pedagogical aim in mind, and with a greater emphasis on the dangers to progress as he got older. In other words, McCabe's meliorism became more provisional as he got older. He was more than aware that other writers, with goals opposed to his own, were writing in order to persuade people as well. With the partial exception of his views on the Roman Catholic Church, which we will examine in chapter 8, McCabe never took for granted the comfortable notion that history was on his side.

Is it possible that McCabe is guilty of being a historical Whig? The classic definition of the Whig historian comes from Herbert Butterfield, the coiner of the term. This type of historian seeks to "emphasize certain principles of progress in the past and to produce a story which is the ratification if not the glorification of the present."[35] To the charge of historical Whiggism, McCabe could reasonably plead guilty and not guilty. He was guilty of historical Whiggism in two senses. First, in the years prior to the First World War, McCabe shared the confidence of most thinkers of his generation that the prospects for civilization were good, and his histories reflected that confidence. And while after 1918 McCabe came to doubt the level of confidence he had shown in prewar European civilization, he never lost his admiration for the achievements of modernity, and for the simple humanism that underlay them. But McCabe was not a Whig in the sense of repeating the errors of Dr. Pangloss, and insisting that this was the best of all possible worlds. In fact, McCabe began his short work *The Evolution of Civilization*, written in 1921, with a very un-Panglossian question of what civilization actually is, adding that no "earlier age in history ever asked the question, or would have tolerated the suspicion that it was not civilized."[36] Elsewhere he lamented that we are still blundering and fumbling toward "blending the love of culture and the love of life, the love of sensual pleasure and wisdom and philanthropy" achieved by the Moorish caliph Abd-al Rahman III one thousand years previous.[37] While the errors and follies of the modern world were obvious to all, McCabe was always prepared to defend modernity against the doomsayers. He is not guilty of the worst excesses of historicism, but would strongly defend nondeterministic notions of progress from their accusers.

WHAT KIND OF HISTORIAN WAS McCABE?

Having defended McCabe from the usual array of accusations thrown at rationalist historians, we can move on to examine what his histories were actually like. McCabe's approach to history can best be illustrated by examining the layout of a representative sample of his historical works. Here McCabe was certainly ahead of his time. Despite seeing history as a science, he never sought to accord his histories the status of "scientific" and therefore "objective." On the contrary, he would usually state his position clearly. As an example, he began a history of church attitudes to questions of marriage and divorce with the following preamble.

> I do not press any detailed solution of the problem of marriage, or any definite scheme of divorce legislation. I do not mean that I leave the problem entirely suspended between the three conflicting theories which I have described. The very grave human interests which are involved—the happiness or unhappiness of millions of men, women, and children—forbid one to discuss the subject in an entirely academic manner, and the facts I set forth make it ludicrous to affect an attitude of complete detachment.[38]

In other words, McCabe would lay his cards on the table, and then go on to present as objective an account as he was able to do, given his transparent and honestly divulged position. This was the approach he took to most of his historical works. He would begin by stating the issue under consideration or the point he wished to argue in the first one or two chapters, then go on to illustrate the issue from a survey of historical periods in the middle chapters of the book, and conclude by restating the issue, or suggesting his preferred solution, in the final chapter.

McCabe was frequently responding to claims made by apologists, and was critical of what he saw as the low level of scholarship in apologetic literature. Indeed, he began one historical survey by quoting *The Christian World*, an apologist periodical, making the same complaint.[39] One example of the sort of apologetic material McCabe was confronted with can be seen in a series of lectures, organized by Rev. Collier, superintendent of the Manchester and Salford

Wesleyan Mission. The lectures, later published as *Is Christianity True?* aimed to respond to the rising tide of unbelief Collier detected in his city. One such speaker was Miss Burstall, B.A., who spoke on "Christianity and Womanhood." Miss Burstall made it clear to her listeners that it

> is only within His kingdom, set up on earth nineteen hundred years ago, that woman, strengthened in her own heart by Christian faith, and protected and elevated in the world by the moral standards of Christianity, can be her best self, can rise to the height of devotion, benevolence, purity, and dignity of which her nature is capable, and can consequently take her right place in the social life of the community.[40]

I have no evidence that McCabe was responding to this precise claim, but it is certainly very close to the claims that he set out to refute in his 1905 book *The Religion of Woman.* "There is a vague feeling abroad that woman's greater attachment to religion has both utility and dignity. I propose in this little work to examine carefully these and other apologies for woman's position in the Churches."[41] After an introductory chapter outlining current opinions on the issue, a series of chapters examined the position of women in pre-Christian times, early Christendom, the Dark and Middle Ages, the Reformation, and on to the nineteenth century. He then dealt with the current situation and finished with some recommendations for the future. In each chapter he would contrast the received opinion he was criticizing with his own findings. He finished with the appeal for women to "rise and shake from their sex once and for all this stigma of indifference to intellectual movements, this honied insinuation of mental inferiority, this suspicion that they care not whether the basic ideas their spiritual belief are true or untrue."[42] At no time was McCabe saying that the changes he desired for women would happen by an inexorable law of history. These things would have to be fought for. The final chapter of this book was titled "An Appeal." McCabe noted that, at the time of writing, a prominent Roman Catholic female writer was assisting a group of conservative lawyers to show that women were incapable of serving on a jury. There was never anything metaphysical about McCabe's progress. Each new phase of the struggle needed to be fought for, with no guarantee of success. McCabe saw his books as contributions toward the struggle.

Twenty-five years later, despite significant differences in layout, we can see a similar general approach in *The Rise and Fall of the Gods.* This book, written for Haldeman-Julius, was produced in six monograph-length volumes, which could, at a pinch, be sold as stand-alone volumes. To say this extraordinary series has been neglected would be an understatement. It is a remarkable piece of scholarship. This work differs from many of its predecessors in that it was not primarily a reply to the claims of apologetic literature. It is more of a statement of the position McCabe had come to hold on an important issue; in this case, atheism. In

The Rise and Fall of the Gods McCabe's goal was to show that "every period of high intellectual development has, when and in proportion as men were free to express themselves, led to a growth of atheism."[43] The six volumes sought to prove the point by surveying prehistoric times (volume 1), the axial age (volume 2), Greece to the fall of Rome (volume 3), the Middle Ages (volume 4), the Enlightenment and nineteenth century (volume 5), and finally, the twentieth century and on to the future (volume 6). Again, in each chapter, he took relevant historians to task and illustrated his points by use of historical examples. "The two chief illusions, which I trust I have sufficiently exposed," McCabe concluded, "are that religion has done far more good than evil, and that irreligion, especially if allied with sensuality, has led to the downfall of nations."[44] McCabe ends his sixth volume with one of his more extravagant promises of a future made better by science. He says, "For my part, at least, I do believe that there is going to dawn an era as bright and sunny and cheerful as is a summer day in comparison with the lamplit night."[45] His attempt at a Wellsian flourish, which he never did as well as his mentor, can be criticized here, in an age when optimism is seen as a crime. There is no reason, however, why the nobility of the vision need be ridiculed. And again, at no point does McCabe claim transcendental status for his vision, which he insisted was his own belief. And neither can the reader have failed to appreciate the amount of work that will be required for such a vision to eventuate.

One of the many temptations with McCabe's approach to history is that inconvenient facts can be ignored so as not to disturb the flow of one's main argument. We have seen that even McCabe's opponents granted he did not do that. What his opponents did criticize, however, was the way his pedagogical themes dominated his history. A critical review of a history McCabe wrote of the recently deposed Romanov dynasty noted that "it is as easy to write a dynasty down as up. Neither branch of anecdote, however, has much interest for the serious student. . . ."[46] This approach to history certainly does have its limitations when seeking a balanced overview, but it is sheer snobbery to suggest that having such an objective is the only motivation of serious students. It also rests on an elevated notion of total objectivity to which McCabe did not subscribe. McCabe was constantly up against this sort of sniffy condescension from academics. It also ignores McCabe's purpose as an historian. He had no interest in writing finely balanced, narrative histories. As happened to Bertrand Russell during the First World War, McCabe decided it was more important to write works that were credible intellectually while being accessible to the general reader.

In a strange irony, parallels can be drawn between McCabe's attitude to history and the general approach of the gospel writers. It is now generally acknowledged that the gospels were not written as historical narratives, but as theological tracts that sought to impress upon the reader one particular interpretation of the life and career of Jesus Christ.[47] Obviously, this analogy can be pushed too far, not least because McCabe was a conscientious historian and the gospel writers were not. Nonetheless, the similarities are instructive. McCabe's histories were designed to be exhortations to the reader to learn whatever lesson of history McCabe was devoting the book to, to avoid the false counsels of the apologists, and to take action accordingly. The first task of the well-wisher of mankind, he wrote at the beginning of the First World War, is "to distinguish truth from untruth in our traditions. The story of man is a long story of the tyranny of consecrated shams, with occasional intervals of rebellion and advance to a higher stage. Rebellion is the salt of the earth."[48] And very late in his life, McCabe made a similar point when complaining about the prominent academic historians of the day. "The chief defect of the writing of both science and history is that a vast amount of unnecessary detail is included. This tires and repels a reader and he is less able to appreciate the (educationally) more important general truths."[49] McCabe was trying to provide his nonspecialist readers with, to use Mary Midgley's phrase, a teleological map, and his gospel was an informed, Stoic, meliorism. We will return to the question of teleological maps later on.

But does McCabe avoid the obvious pitfalls of writing like a gospel writer? Clearly, another example is needed. One of his later works, *The Testament of Christian Civilization*, published in 1946, set out to illustrate the point that the morally improving nature of Christian belief was not at all apparent in the behavior of the rather squalid gallery of popes, monks, soldiers, and statesmen he writes about. He finishes his preface noting that the "pleasant work of describing such virtue as there was in each century has been repeated until it wearies us. It is the turn of the *advocatus diaboli*."[50] McCabe made it quite clear that he was not writing a "balanced" account, any more than all the previous accounts he criticized had been balanced. The hostile reviewer of the *Times Literary Supplement* struggled manfully to admit that the "claims of accurate scholarship have on the whole not, in any obvious way, been subordinated to McCabe's prejudices." For reasons he didn't explain, the reviewer remained sure that McCabe's approach "does not constitute an argument."[51] The more appreciative reviewer in the *Literary Guide* thought that McCabe's book was the answer to the Christian criticism "that humanism fails because it has no higher sanction for ethics than man's own nature."[52]

McCabe's approach with *The Testament of Christian Civilization* was only a continuation of what he had begun over forty years before. In 1905, he noted that it "has long been the custom to judge pre-Christian civilizations by the lowest depths they ever touched, while the application of such a test to Christianity itself was bitterly resented."[53] So long as Christian historians continued to paint glowing pictures of the magnificent contribution their religion had made to European civilization, McCabe felt it his job to complete the picture by drawing the readers' attention to its less pleasing consequences. This was his principal aim as a historian. McCabe had employed this approach since 1907, with his book *The Bible in Europe*. He described his purpose in this way:

The following essay is a study in detail of the social effect of the adoption of the Christian religion in Europe. The beneficent results of some of the Christian ideas and emotions have been enlarged upon so fully at all times that it only remained for me to dwell, at any length, on the less familiar disadvantages of the new doctrines.[54]

In many ways, McCabe was ahead of his time in that he was writing intellectual history before people were ready for the concept. The notion of the history of ideas took modern form in the twenties and thirties, chiefly under the guidance of the American scholar Arthur Lovejoy, author of *The Great Chain of Being* (1936) and founder of the influential periodical *Journal of the History of Ideas* in 1940. But while the *term* history of ideas was only coming into circulation then, the *practice* of this variety of history was a lot older. McCabe's old mentor, Sir Leslie Stephen, is often mentioned as a pioneer of this type of history. For reasons beyond the scope of this study, the term "history of ideas" has given way to the term "intellectual history." But when Lovejoy coined the term "history of ideas," we find that McCabe was working in that genre for more than a decade. Needless to say, this debt to McCabe has not been acknowledged, much less celebrated.

HOW McCABE UNDERSTOOD HISTORY

McCabe's understanding of history was fairly conventional by the standards of his time and he worked according to the generally accepted periodizing of eras. Equally, his picture of each epoch was fairly constant throughout his writing career. Of antiquity, for example, he had a high opinion. Being a pioneering historian of ideas, he usually visited each era as and when was needed to make a point in the development of the topic he was considering at the time. Very often, as we have seen, McCabe was responding to disputable claims made by religious apologists. As with the case of Miss Burstall, mentioned above, the following passage is nowhere alluded to specifically in McCabe's writings, but is so pertinent that it is worth repeating. It comes from *Christianity: Its Nature and Truth*, written in 1909 by Arthur Peake, D.D., then professor of Biblical Exegesis at the University of Manchester. Peake, a well-known apologist, acknowledged that much of

Christian history has been of the most painful and disappointing character. Largely, this must be accounted for by a very obvious consideration. The level of morality in the heathen world at the time when the Gospel first touched it was indescribably low. The new religion planted in an uncongenial paganism, like leaven in the large mass of unleavened meal. Its external progress far outstripped the internal. The world became nominally Christian while it was heathen at its heart.[55]

This goes in many ways to the heart of what McCabe was protesting against. Peake's explanation is a deceitful sleight of hand that permits all that is good to be appropriated as evidence of Christian advance, while that which is wicked to be denounced as a pagan survival. McCabe was energetic in his defense of the ancient world from charges such as this. And Peake's account was avant-garde, in that he was prepared to concede that the Christian victory was largely nominal. The more common line of the apologists was the simpler claim that the sensual vice of antiquity was tamed and purified by the incomparable superiority of Christianity. Neither claim was (or is) historically sound and McCabe set himself the task to smite this variety of humbug.

To take one example of McCabe's account of antiquity, we can look briefly at his various discussions of the influence of the Stoics in the Roman Empire. We have already noted McCabe's high opinion of Stoic thought and practice, so it is not surprising to see him rally to the defense of these and other ancient moral and reform movements. This was necessary, because the vices of Rome were often an important weapon in the armory of Christian apologists. For example, during McCabe's debate with W. T. Lee in 1911, Lee's very first major piece of evidence for the superiority of Christianity over Secularism was that it rescued Rome from an unfathomable morass of vice. "I am not particularly anxious to take you back two thousand years to the Roman world, already burdened with accumulating miseries; mastered by abominations which, like an ever-present and active leprosy, ate into the life alike of patrician and plebeian."[56] Lee then spent a significant proportion of his speech doing precisely that; outlining in graphic detail Rome's accumulated miseries. McCabe began his reply by saying "I challenge every single word that Mr. Lee said in regard to ancient Rome." He was to defend Roman civilization for the rest of his life.

McCabe followed authorities of his day, notably Samuel Dill, Ludwig Friedlaender and W. E. H. Lecky, in extolling the reigns of Vespasian and those of Trajan to Marcus Aurelius, and hailing these years as the Stoic Age. He did not, of course, claim all these emperors were themselves Stoics. Rather, it was the age that deserves the label for the influence Stoic doctrines of brotherhood and philanthropy had on society, which was as much marked by the redressing of legal injustices as it was for the better-known sexual peccadilloes of the emperors. While the smart set of Rome's tiny elite were out for a good time, he asked whether things had changed that much. "There is no reason whatever to think that this set was more numerous, proportionately, than the corresponding set which patronizes actresses and chorus-girls today, and sets up mistresses in luxurious apartments."[57] By way of an aside, McCabe's attitude here suggests a greater tolerance among humanists toward marginal voices, to use currently fashionable language, than postmodernist thinkers have been prepared to acknowledge. Discussing the Roman example, McCabe concluded that "we are once more reminded how a people can attain a very high moral ideal, in regard to all conduct that is social, yet be uncertain or heterodox in regard to sex."[58]

Apologists in McCabe's day, keen to maximize the impact of Christianity, were sometimes prone to minimizing the efforts of the reformist Stoic lawyers who preceded them. This was guaranteed to rouse McCabe's fighting spirit. Typical was Charles Loring Brace, whose book *Gesta Christi: A History of Humane Progress Under Christianity* was hugely successful, going through at least four editions. Brace set out to highlight what he claimed was the unique record of Christianity as an agent of humane progress. Particular attention is given to the record of Christianity with regard to slavery and the status of women. McCabe frequently referred to this book as an example of the poor scholarship of a lot of Christian apologetics. His 1907 work *The Bible in Europe* is largely devoted to countering the claims made in Brace's work. After several pages surveying the measures adopted in the first three centuries of the common era, McCabe lamented that it is "unfortunate that I have been compelled to trace the steps in the emancipation of the slave in this polemical fashion, but the extreme inaccuracy of even the best apologetic work on the subject has compelled me to do so."[59]

While McCabe defended the Stoics stoutly, he was well aware of their faults and was not afraid to include them in his historical surveys. He noted, for example, the inability of Stoicism, Epictetus notwithstanding, to reach the poor and dispossessed.[60] But while mindful of these failings, McCabe held Stoicism responsible for much of the benevolence and public-spiritedness of Roman society during the first three centuries of the common era. "Philosophers and emperors proclaimed, in impassioned language, the universal brotherhood of men. Seneca, Epictetus, and Marcus Aurelius declared, in almost modern phrases, that all men were their brothers and the whole world their country."[61] Elsewhere he claimed that Europe was not to experience a humanitarian movement of such power and effectiveness until the nineteenth century.[62] McCabe summed up the fruits of the ancient world as "the independent scientific investigation of reality, the vastness of the universe, evolution, progress, a humanist ethic, and the brotherhood of men. They culminated in the philosophy of Epicurus, the ethic of Zeno, and the science of Alexandria."[63]

Of the Dark and Middle Ages, McCabe had an altogether grimmer view, although this was not always the case. Early in his career, when writing his biography of St. Augustine, McCabe was prepared allow that Christianity was morally and intellectually far superior to paganism.[64] Five years later, he was less prepared to concede this point. It was probably continued pressure from Christian apologists which stimulated this change. Brace, for example, had no difficulty in seeing Christianity as the savior of civilization in Europe. "The lamp of science and literature," he wrote, "was kept burning during the 'dark ages' in the monks' cell."[65] This remains a popular item of folk memory.

McCabe saw the Dark Ages in a much more sophisticated and critical way than that. One of the chief criteria for human progress, he wrote in 1907, is the attitude to mental development and free inquiry.[66] It didn't take McCabe long to gather evidence of the poor record of the Christian fathers in that regard. For instance, he quoted Tertullian (160–225 C.E.) who insisted that "after Jesus Christ all curiosity, after the Gospel all inquiry, were unnecessary." By this time we are unsurprised to read Pope Gregory I (590–604) rebuke one of the Gallic subordinates for the terrible crime of "teaching grammar to some," for "the praise of Jove must never be heard from the mouth that praises Christ."[67] The consequences of this anti-intellectualism and hostility to any unconducive thoughts from antiquity were appalling, McCabe concluded, leaving the next several centuries to thoroughly deserve their appellation of the Dark Ages. "It is a large part of our reasons for speaking of a Dark Age that all the works in which these ideas were expounded, except the famous poem of Lucretius, were destroyed by the early Christians, and the ideas were lost to the race for 1,500 years."[68] McCabe was scornful of the trend among historians to disown the title Dark Ages but he freely acknowledged that the darkness was not universal across Europe. In this regard, he mentioned southwestern France in the fifth and sixth centuries, Gothic and Lombard Italy, aspects of Celtic Christianity, and Ottonian Germany as examples of areas of relative prosperity and cultural attainment.[69]

As always, the heart of McCabe's argument came down to how the mass of the people lived. He summarized his case for retaining the phrase Dark Ages in these terms:

> In the Rome of the fourth century there were three entirely free workers to one slave, and even the slaves (of the cities), Dill says, "corresponded to our free laboring class" and were protected by law from cruelty; but from AD 500 to 1100 the vast majority of the workers of Europe were serfs—a distinction from "slave" which Vinogrador [sic] says, "late and artificial." The urban workers had had free education, princely free entertainments, free bread, magnificent baths (almost free) and gymnasia, and a splendid free supply of good water, free medical treatment, easy hours and holidays on 200 out of 365 days; from AD 500 to 1100 the workers had none of these things, no freedom, and no protection from cruelty. In the empire, women had been on the same legal and social footing as men; from 500 to 1100 they were treated as cattle. In the empire a large number of fine cities had half a million to a million citizens; from AD 500 to 1100 no towns had more than 40,000 and very few that much. In Roman law torture was very restricted; after the year AD 500 horrible tortures and mutilations were sanctified in law, the ordeal replaced trial, and in daily life the loss of eyes, ears, tongue, feet, or testicles was appallingly common. The Romans had produced a fine literature, had raised splendid buildings in the provincial towns and aqueducts, bridges, good roads, theatres, etc, all over the empire; from 500 to 1100 hardly a book was written that we now read, hardly a picture painted, a statue carved, or a building raised (except after 1000 in Germany) that we go to see. The Romans had had libraries up to 500,000 volumes; there was not one of more than 600 volumes in Christian Europe from 500 to 1100. That is why we speak of the Dark Age.[70]

While many would want to challenge McCabe's peremptory dismissal of the art of this age, and some may question his reading of this or that, McCabe's priorities are clear. The Dark Ages deserve the title because human suffering rose.

Just as calculated to raise McCabe's blood pressure were claims made about the Middle Ages. He quoted what for him was a representative example from the work of Professor H. S. Lucas's 1943 *Short History of Civilization*: "The Roman Catholic Church became the parent of culture, philosophy, theology, art, literature, and learning flourished under its protective wing."[71] McCabe tired of the Chesterbellocian jollification of happy peasants, prosperous guilds, and sublime art, all safe and warm in the embrace of Aquinas and the true church.

> What else is there besides the art? The guilds of craftsmen? These affected only a tiny minority of the workers, were pagan in origin, and were fiercely resisted by the Church until it found them irrepressible. What else is there? Nothing. The rest is misery, suffering, exploitation by priest and noble, appalling superstition, utter lawlessness, dense ignorance.[72]

In a short work devoted to the question of the church's record of service to working people, McCabe restated his position. "No one suggests that from the fifth to the fifteenth century Europe had no men of human feeling. What one dislikes is the tendency of historians to pay the Church a high compliment and then offer no evidence, or very unsatisfactory evidence."[73] But after all the facts, lists, and comparisons, it was, again, the miserable poverty of the people that was, for McCabe, the chief reproach of that age. The following passage is worth repeating in full, in order to convey McCabe's feeling.

> Try to picture to yourself the life of nine out of ten in Christendom at that time. Cut out those pictures of occasional saints or scholars, or silk-robed merchants and gay tournaments. Follow the life of the man working from dawn to sunset, then returning to a sty, the floor unpaved, the cesspool and mudheap at the door, the filthy interior without the cheapest comfort or adornment. Imagine the woman bearing her seven or eight children in it, doing twice the work of the poorest modern woman, brutally treated by most husbands; a cow. . . . And the same gossipy and crassly superstitious little village round her from cradle to grave, the scold's bridle or the ducking stool if she dare assert herself, the suspicion of witchcraft if she wondered if the gentle Jesus did really arrange all this, the sudden departure of the man for war, the famine drawing on with fiendish slowness, the plague spreading over the countryside. And there you have the true picture of the thirteenth century.[74]

The attitude of Christian apologists to the Middle Ages depended on their denomination. Whereas Catholics liked to talk up the era, Protestants were more prone to agree with McCabe's low estimate. One of the most militant Catholic apologists of the time, Hilaire Belloc, said to McCabe, "I don't care what you say, McCabe, but the intellect of Europe has been warped since the six-teenth century."[75] Belloc's friend Father Vincent McNabb expressed the same sentiment in a short work called *The Catholic Church and Philosophy*, designed for the nonspecialist reader. After a seventy-page panegyric of Thomas Aquinas (in a 123-page book) McNabb lamented the slide since the thirteenth century.

> But if ignorance has now become a world-wide disease and intellectual anarchy a permanent state in our seats of learning, it is because the trium-virate [Bacon, Descartes, Kant] were intellectually diseased and anarchic. They had cut them-selves off from the Latin civilization which was at once Roman in its civic structure and Greek in its thought. Intellectual anarchy and ignorance were the inevitable wages of death.[76]

In stark contrast, W. T. Lee, McCabe's Protestant antagonist in the 1911 debate on "Christianity or Secularism," was prepared to write the Middle Ages off, declaring rhetorically that "these abominations were not the outcome of the pure teaching of New Testament religion." Lee went on to "dispute absolutely" any identification of Roman Catholic Europe with Christian Europe.[77] As with Peake's example, mentioned above, this is nothing else than special pleading, in order that history should conform to the needs of one's denomination. McCabe was a better historian that that. Any Protestant, he wrote in 1919, "who imag-ines that the dreadful era of Popery, the Middle Ages, was succeeded by a period of human brotherhood when the Bible was restored to honor, labors under a very singular delusion."[78]

More recently, it has become fashionable among postmodernists and others to lament the spiritual poverty of modernity in a way reminiscent of Chester-belloc. But these lamentations are as nonsensical as those of their predecessors, and happily an increasing number of people are following in McCabe's footsteps in countering them. Raymond Tallis has written a particularly fine critique of postmodernism called *Enemies of Hope: A Critique of Contemporary Pessimism*. Tallis ends a discussion of this tendency insisting that there is "little evidence that being deprived of cold, hunger, unrelieved pain associated with chronic ill health, of petty and major oppression by unaccountable, unelected political masters and the casual and unpunished brutality of anyone in power over has, has resulted in a loss of happiness."[79] How true, and how like McCabe.

THE NINETEENTH CENTURY

Without question the major turning point in recent history, so far as McCabe was concerned, was the nineteenth century. In one book, he described the half cen-tury between 1820 and 1870 as "one of the greatest in European history," and likened it to Periclean Athens in its contribution to the general betterment of people.[80] In his view, this was the era when a purely disinterested social conscience developed. We have already seen that McCabe's three heroes, Robert Owen, George Jacob Holyoake, and Sir Leslie Stephen represented different faces of that social conscience, or as he put it elsewhere, humane spirit. We will discuss the nature of this humanism later, but now we need only list the fruits of these mighty labors, and the villains McCabe discerned trying to nip them in the bud.

The first point worth mentioning is that McCabe's views about the nineteenth century were not unusual at the time. It was common for Edwardian works, particularly those dealing with social policy, to record the tremendous achievements of the previous century. For example, Havelock Ellis (1859–1939), a prominent psychologist who specialized in questions of sexuality, predicated his work on the social improvements made in the nineteenth century. His proposed reforms could only be suggested, let alone acted upon, in the light of the nineteenth-century improvements in hygiene, industrial legislation, universal education, and so on.[81] Other thinkers, such as H. G. Wells, were given to writing visionary works about future possibilities because they shared the general optimism that the reforms of the nineteenth century had engendered. In the light of the extraordinary benefits the haphazard legislation of the nineteenth century had achieved, imagine what could be done if we actually planned ahead and worked for the betterment of all humanity? It was in this vein that Wells wrote prophetic works like *Anticipations* and *The Discovery of the Future*. So, up until the end of the First World War, McCabe's attitude toward the nineteenth century would have been unremarkable, but in the new mood after the war, particularly once Lytton Strachey's highly influential *Eminent Victorians* had been published in 1918, McCabe's championing of what was now disparaged as "the Victorian era" suddenly looked peculiar. The obituary notice that the *Times* ran on McCabe described him as "the last Victorian."

The other point about McCabe's elevated view of the nineteenth century is that it is not seen as unsound history now, almost a century later. Kenneth Clark, in his hugely successful popularization of cultural history called *Civilization*, described humanitarianism as the "greatest civilizing achievement of the nineteenth century."[82] While contemporary historians of the nineteenth century are less rhetorical than McCabe and Clark, their basic conclusions are similar. In the run-up to the British General Election of 1987, James Walvin, then Reader in History at the University of York, wrote a short work called *Victorian Values*. Walvin's book was a reply to the claims made by Margaret Thatcher that the Victorian era was one of thrift, sobriety, piety, and above all, laissez-faire. Walvin demonstrated that the spirit that made the Victorian era notable was the large raft of social reforms made possible largely through the intervention of the state. Walvin noted that a "new humanitarianism" was the driving force behind these reforms and was a major intellectual and social theme of the century. "Much of it grew from the evangelical movement, but it also derived from a secular attachment to social rights which created a new sensitivity in a broad range of people."[83]

When itemizing the achievements of the nineteenth century in 1908, McCabe assumed most people knew what he was talking about, and that they agreed with the value of the reforms. Consequently, he presented them in the form of a rhetorical question. In his biography of Holyoake, McCabe asked:

Who can measure the revolution that has taken place in the life of the worker since 1830? Shorter hours and better conditions of labour: free palatial schools for his children, with a fair opportunity for secondary education: magnificent collections of art and books and scientific objects wide open to him in his leisure hours: a literature of unbounded prodigality and of whatever quality he cares to demand it: cheap and comfortable travel: cheaper and better food, with higher wages and better homes: full freedom to discuss his political, religious, or industrial conditions, to enter into trade-combinations, to say what he pleases of Church and State, to put his hand on the very regulators of the civil and national machinery.[84]

But twenty-three years later, in his *History of Human Morals*, McCabe's approach was slightly different. Again, it is important to quote a lengthy passage, so as to get the sense of his different approach. It is interesting, by the way, to see these lengthy passages when summarizing a particular epoch. Nowhere else in McCabe's body of work are there such long sentences. It suggests, I think, the importance he put on a correct understanding of these periods, and of the prevalence of erroneous understandings of them. As he was writing for the general reader, he didn't have the luxury of going into excessive detail, so in these matters, he tended to merely itemize the factors he thought important. This technique is particularly noticeable in his writings for Haldeman-Julius.

McCabe listed the three main triumphs of the nineteenth century humane spirit as the dramatic growth in universal education for all people, without regard to social position; the first steps taken toward providing adult education; and that the nineteenth century "at least gave birth to the movement for the emancipation of women."[85] Having listed these cardinal features, he went on:

It gave birth to a movement for the prevention of cruelty to animals, which had never occurred to the obtuse moral sense of the religious earlier centuries. It wrought a revolution in the treatment of the insane, which as late as one hundred years ago was, at least in the case of pauper lunatics, barbarously inhuman. It provided orphanages on a scale that was unknown even to the Romans of the Stoic period or the Arabs and Moors. It in many centuries provided pensions for the aged and the widow and compelled employers to contribute to sick and unemployment insurance; and made employers liable for accidents. It inspired in most countries organizations for the employment and care of the blind and the deaf and dumb. It raised holiday funds for poor children, Christmas funds, Community Chests, funds for supplying cripples with apparatus, etc.[86]

It is interesting to see McCabe feeling the need to give the basic information, and then to persuade his readers of their value. He would not have had to
do either in the Edwardian years. It is also interesting to note how McCabe's
nineteenth century looks a lot like applied Stoicism—a more popular, philan-
thropic Stoicism.

The flip side of the nineteenth century coin was the efforts of reactionaries
to frustrate the growing fruits of this disinterested humanism. In 1935, a year
after his return to the RPA, McCabe wrote a book for the successful Thinker's
Library series called *The Social Record of Christianity*. This short work was largely
a summary for British readers of his *History of Human Morals*, which had been
written for Haldeman-Julius four years before. It was also an updating of his *The
Bible in Europe*, written in 1907. *The Social Record of Christianity* was one of the
advocatus diaboli works we discussed earlier. The theme of this book was Christianity's unimpressive role regarding its support for reform movements in Europe.
He quoted the Church of England modernist Canon B. H. Streeter, who
admitted the church's poor record. Streeter lamented that:

> the greatest blot on the history of the Church in modern times is the fact that,
> with the glaring exception of the campaign to abolish slavery, the leaders of the
> social, political, and humanitarian reforms of the last century and a half in Europe
> have rarely been professing Christians, while the authorized representatives of
> organised Christianity have, as often as not, been on the wrong side.[87]

McCabe illustrated Streeter's point by outlining some of the votes by the
bloc of bishops against various reform measures of the nineteenth century. No
fewer than twenty-one of the twenty-three bishops in the House of Lords
opposed the Reform Bill when it got to them in 1831. Only two bishops supported the Prevention of Cruelty to Animals Bill of 1809, only three bishops
supported the Prevention of British Capital in the Slave Trade Bill, and only two
bishops supported the Suppression of Slavery Bill. McCabe quoted Bishop
Horsley as saying "I do not know what the mass of the people in any country
have to do with the laws but to obey them."[88] McCabe had used much of this
material for a short work designed for working people, called *The Church and the
People*, published by the RPA in 1919. McCabe's view was plain:

> It would be a poor type of man or woman who, knowing all the facts of which
> I have given a selection and a summary, did not feel some warmth of resent-
> ment when he reflects that those vices and cruelties from which the nineteenth
> century partially revealed our civilization might, but for Christian tyranny and
> misdirection, have been removed centuries ago.[89]

Canon Streeter and McCabe were both deeply impressed by the great tide
of progressive and emancipatory legislation that had been so prominent in the
nineteenth century. And they both saw the essentially humanist motivation

behind it. This was very important for McCabe's worldview, and had important consequences for his thoughts on the humane spirit. We will examine the philosophical aspects of this conception in the final chapter, but we need here to look at the historical features of this idea.

Inextricably linked with McCabe's notions of the humane spirit was his understanding of the historical and temporal grounding of the moral law. The idea of a moral law is very ancient, but the most recent visitation of the idea was by Immanuel Kant (1724–1804). McCabe was closer on this issue to David Hume and Arthur Schopenhauer (not usually bracketed together), who both thought it a grave error to conceive of morality as a form of law. The basis of McCabe's conviction of the importance of the nineteenth century lay in what he saw as a fundamental shift in the axis of the moral law. "The chief reason for a change that can be found in the religious conditions of the time is that in the increasing struggle against heresy the emphasis tended to fall more and more upon character."[90] He saw the Deist revolt of the eighteenth century as a rejection of the Bible and Christianity accompanied by a strong profession of belief in God and immortality. As long as this theism remained intact, there was little challenge to the moral law. "But when the belief in God began to be assailed, the question of the moral law became more acute."[91] This became more acute with the onset of the French Revolution, and particularly in the reaction after 1815. During these decades,

> when the orthodox powers were bent on exterminating every rootlet of what they called revolution, it was easy to persuade them that the irreligion of the thinkers who preceded the outbreak in France and of their sympathizers in England was one of the great causes. Irreligion, it was said, led to a comprehensive degradation of character: to the free love of the Directorate as well as the bloodshed, confiscation, and rebellion against all authority of the preceding period.[92]

Character, in other words, became associated with conservatism and soundness, leaving innovation and the advocacy of reform to refractory types and heretics. "It has always seemed to me that this controversy about the consequences between Christians and skeptics, which developed out of the cry that irreligion cause the French Revolution, was an important cause of such growth of puritanism as there was in the nineteenth century."[93] This was an important matter for McCabe, as it explained why the nineteenth century was so productive of beneficent social legislation, while also being strongly puritanical in moral questions. "There was a sort of conspiracy of Christians and non-Christians to set up the fiction that, whatever was open to dispute and inquiry, the code of sex-ethic was not."[94] It was McCabe's task to liberate the notion of character from the puritanical notions that had been attached to it in the conservative reaction after 1815. This is why he argued that a crucial feature of the modern revolt against tradition is "the conviction that moralists and priests had usurped an illegitimate authority in matters of sex."[95] This blip notwithstanding, the transformation of transcendental conceptions of a moral law into humanist notions of character was one of the features of the nineteenth century that excited McCabe's admiration the most. We will follow McCabe's thinking in this area in chapter 6.

GERMANY

Before we leave this study of McCabe's philosophy of history, let us change tack somewhat and examine his historical understanding of what were for him current events, but are now history. We can take as an example the case of McCabe's treatment of Germany over his long career. In an interesting study of English intellectual life during the First World War, Stuart Wallace paints a depressing picture of academics failing to resist the temptations of war fever and anti-German hysteria.[96] The only outstanding exception, Wallace found, was Bertrand Russell. That is correct, and is one of the many features of Russell's life that make him so exceptional. However, Russell was certainly not alone in taking his principled stand. It is sad, but not surprising, that Wallace did not examine McCabe, whose works on the war show his steady judgment and ability to rise above fierce passions. In three different books, an article in the *Rationalist Annual*, and in several articles in journals, McCabe took the brave and unpopular stand of defending the German people from the avalanche of anti-German feeling ignited by the war. He was not a pacifist; he supported the war, but he campaigned against making it a war driven by national hatred. A good example would be McCabe's study of Kaiser Wilhelm II, written in 1915. Written shortly after the sinking of the *Lusitania*, and at the height of atrocity-in-Belgium stories in England, he is commendably dispassionate. In *The Kaiser: His Personality and Career*, McCabe rejects the more hysterical claims then in circulation that Wilhelm was insane, disagrees that he singlehandedly led his country into war, and is skeptical about the grosser accusations of anti-Semitism and anti-Catholicism. He does, however, attack Wilhelm's yellow peril speech and the broader racism that was the background to that speech.[97] This was an aspect of the kaiser's outlook that was the focus of less attention from his critics. McCabe concluded that the kaiser had been an evil influence on Germany insofar as he had imposed a militaristic education system on the country and had tirelessly pushed for a stronger navy. But he exonerated the kaiser of responsibility for singlehandedly instilling a mood for war among the German people.

McCabe was also alive to a common temptation Wallace finds British academics succumbing to at the time: blaming Prussia for everything that had gone wrong in order to deflect blame from all Germans. While critical of Prussia and "Prussianism," McCabe also reminded his readers—only two months after the battle of the Marne—that since "the rise of Prussia, Germany has not only contributed more original philosophy to the world than any other three countries of modern times, but in every branch of science she has sustained her high position."[98]

Elsewhere, he criticized a trend among some Allied publicists to trace the Prussians back to the rude, Slavic tribespeople, in an attempt to belittle the German pretensions to national greatness.[99] His book *The Soul of Europe*, written in 1915, was specifically designed to clear the air of such easy characterizations. He feared that "for some years to come, it is to be feared, the Englishman will be content with a single simple formula, 'the brutal Hun,' as an expression of that complex issue of traditions, impulses, and interests which we have recognized as the soul of Germany."[100]

Who, then, *did* McCabe see as responsible for the war? McCabe was too astute an historian and observer to be satisfied with simple scapegoating of the kaiser or Prussianism. The other popular targets of the time were a fearsome triad of thinkers: General Friedrich von Bernhardi, Heinrich von Treitschke, and Friedrich Nietzsche.[101] When writing about Nietzsche in 1931, McCabe acknowledged that Nietzsche seemed to be very popular among the German frontline soldiers, but then, so was the Bible, and yet only Nietzsche was saddled with blame for the war. McCabe lamented the "prejudice against Nietzsche in the superficial press and the mind of the general public which it reflects. . . ."[102] Treitschke (1834–1896) presented an easier target, and, early in the war McCabe dashed off a quick work devoted to this man's influence. McCabe gave more than enough examples of Treitschke's bloodthirsty militarism for him to be held to account. But he also provided some context to his ideas, which made easy condemnation less easy. He dismissed claims of one prominent academic that Treitschke's influence in Germany equaled that of Thomas Babington Macaulay and Thomas Carlyle in England put together.[103] How could such claims possibly be measured? In fact, McCabe noted, Treitschke's influence had been on the wane before his death in 1906, and the Young Germany movement had sneered at Treitschke.

McCabe saw a combination of factors as being responsible of the war. A climate of militarism and nationalism had been taken advantage of by the German government, and ultimately the kaiser. Treitschke's teachings, he reminded his readers, came with the full authority of the state, given he held one of the most learned chairs in Germany. But then the influence of Nietzsche can hardly be blamed on the state, as he was an exile, and then a lunatic.

Even more pointedly, McCabe warned that when "we smile at the language of German writers, we have only to turn back a few pages in English history to find precisely similar language used by Englishmen."[104] McCabe also protested against the widely held view that the entire German people were somehow responsible for the brutalities of the war. It is thoroughly absurd to say, McCabe wrote in 1916, "that the German people, as a body, are corrupt and brutal."[105] He did think that German people were in favor of the war when it began, but he argued strongly against then inferring that they were in favor of how the war was prosecuted.

McCabe also devoted time to a commonly laid charge that the outrages (real and imagined) in occupied Belgium and France were due to the pervasive influence of rationalism in that country. It was one of the more bizarre accusations made by the English clergy during the war that the German militarism and brutality was the inevitable consequence of that country having embraced rationalism and materialism. McCabe's survey of German intellectual history in *The Soul of Europe* demonstrated clearly the mystical, quasi-religious basis of German romanticism. Neither did it take him long to show that it was precisely a fear of materialism that inspired many of the German romantics and militarists. Far from leading to an aggressive militarism, the work of the German rationalists "led to a strict Puritanism in the narrower aspects of morals, and to a humanitarian glow which far outshone that of Christianity and helped to bring about that advanced social legislation and philanthropy which have distinguished modern Germany."[106]

McCabe's feel for German history was excellent. He was, in many ways, pro-German. His survey of German intellectual history in *The Soul of Europe* is as good as can be found, particularly as it was written during the heat of the conflict. His understanding of German history was sound enough to enable him to make some remarkably shrewd predictions on Germany's future. He didn't foresee the fall of the Kaiser, but he was quite clear, in 1915, that a defeated Germany would spend all its "vitality on a stupendous, subtle, utterly unscrupulous effort to secure revenge. They have been ruined by jealous enemies, they will say." He predicted that "the gospel of self-sacrifice and energy and child-getting will be preached with a fervor beyond anything in the annals of Prussia."[107] As events were to unfold, McCabe was shown to be correct on many of these counts. He continued to accurately call events in his 1932 book *Can We Save Civilization?* Here he predicted the imminent victory in Germany of the Nazis and, a far riskier call, an alliance between Germany and Russia. McCabe foresaw Germany making war on France as soon as she had rearmed adequately, and that neither France, nor Poland, nor Czeckoslovakia would be able to withstand a Russo-German alliance for long.[108]

So, to end this section, McCabe can be cleared, with a warning, from charges of incurable historicism. He held none of the more virulent strains of that malady, save for his commitment to the conception of progress. At this point I am sure that McCabe would vehemently object to being apologized for. He was a man of his time and was writing for people in his time. And as Peter Munz, a contemporary philosopher and follower of Popper, has observed, whatever the faults of historicism, "it was a net gain over history inspired by theology."[109] McCabe couldn't have agreed more. McCabe had experienced progress directly in his life and would be entirely bemused that, despite so many extraordinary advances since his day, the term is out of fashion. We have seen that, particularly with regard to dialectical materialism, McCabe demonstrated "incredulity toward metanarratives," which is Jean-Francois Lyotard's conception of postmodernism. Where McCabe accepted a concept, such as progress, he did so in a provisional way. He most certainly was incredulous to all metanarratives, both those that he accepted and those he rejected. McCabe's history was a means by which he could show to others the way to safeguard the benefits of progress and expand it to include all of humanity.

NOTES

1. [Joseph McCabe], *The Taint in Politics* (New York: Dodd Mead, 1920), p. 68.

2. Quoted from Raymond Tallis, *Enemies of Hope: A Critique of Contemporary Pessimism* (New York: St. Martin's Press, 1997), p. 86.

3. S. K. Ratcliffe, "Joseph McCabe: An Appreciation," *Rationalist Review* 1, no. 12 (March 1955): iv.

4. *Times Literary Supplement*, May 16, 1912, p. 205.

5. K. R. Popper, *The Poverty of Historicism* (London: Routledge & Kegan Paul, 1957), p. 39.

6. K. R. Popper, *The Open Society and Its Enemies* (London: Routledge & Kegan Paul, 1963), vol 1, p. 21.

7. I take this definition from Peter Levine's fine defense of humanist learning and method in *Nietzsche and the Modern Crisis of the Humanities* (Albany: State University of New York Press, 1995), p. xiv.

8. Edward O. Wilson is equally dismissive of these "sins made official by the hissing suffix." See his excellent book *Consilience: The Unity of Knowledge* (London: Little, Brown & Co, 1998), p. 9.

9. Joseph McCabe, *Eighty Years a Rebel* (Girard, Kan.: Haldeman-Julius, 1947), p. 46.

10. Joseph McCabe, *Can We Save Civilization?* (London: The Search, 1932), p. 106.

11. Joseph McCabe, *1825–1925: A Century of Stupendous Progress* (London: Watts, 1925), p. v.

12. Joseph McCabe, *Treitschke and the Great War* (Toronto: T. Fisher Unwin/Dodd Mead, 1914), p. 106.

13. Joseph McCabe, *A History of Human Morals* (Girard, Kan.: Haldeman-Julius, 1931), vol. 12, p. 9.

14. Ibid., pp. 34–35.

15. See McCabe, *Can We Save Civilization?* p. 23; *The Riddle of the Universe Today* (London: Watts, 1934), p. 245; or *The Origin and Meaning of Ideas* (Girard, Kan.: Haldeman-Julius, 1951), p. 36.

16. Joseph McCabe, *The Tyranny of Shams* (London: Eveleigh Nash/Dodd Mead, 1916), p. 5.

17. Joseph McCabe, *The Logic and Virtue of Atheism* (Austin, Tex.: American Atheist Press, 1980), p. 34.

18. Joseph McCabe, *A Rationalist Encyclopedia* (London: Watts, 1948), p. 157.

19. Fredric Jameson, *Postmodernism or, the Cultural Logic of Late Capitalism* (London: Verso, 1993), p. 62.

20. See Gregory Bruce Smith, *Nietzsche, Heidegger and the Transition to Postmodernity* (Chicago & London: University of Chicago Press, 1996), p. 197.

21. McCabe, *Eighty Years a Rebel*, p. 51.

22. McCabe, *Can We Save Civilization?*, p. 196.

23. McCabe, *1825–1925*, p. 160.

24. Robert Miller-Argue, *Evolution Exploded by Many Infallible Proofs* (Sydney: Commonwealth Christian Evidence Press Association, 1910), p. 50.

25. McCabe, *Can We Save Civilization?*, p. 106.

26. Joseph McCabe, *The Sources of the Morality of the Gospels* (London: Watts, 1914), p. 98.

27. Joseph McCabe, *The Social Record of Christianity*, The Thinker's Library, no. 51 (London: Watts, 1935), pp. 4–5.

28. James Walvin, *Victorian Values* (London: Cardinal, 1986), p. 162.

29. E. P. Thompson, *The Poverty of Theory* (London: Merlin Press, 1978), p. 231.

30. Joseph McCabe, *Key to Culture* (Girard, Kan.: Haldeman-Julius, 1927–29), vol. 15, p. 9.

31. McCabe, *Can We Save Civilization?*, p. 101.

32. Joseph McCabe, *Robert Owen* (London: Watts, 1920), p. 26.

33. J. W. Burrow, *Evolution and Society* (Cambridge: Cambridge University Press, 1970), p. 111.

34. McCabe, *Can We Save Civilization?*, p. 232.

35. Herbert Butterfield, *The Whig Interpretation of History* (London: Penguin, 1973), p. 9.

36. Joseph McCabe, *The Evolution of Civilization* (London: Watts, 1921), p. 1.

37. McCabe, *Can We Save Civilization?*, pp. 235–36.

38. Joseph McCabe, *The Influence of the Church on Marriage and Divorce* (London: Watts, 1916), p. xi.

39. Joseph McCabe, *The Bible in Europe* (London: Watts, 1907), p. 26.

40. Miss Burstall, "Christianity and Womanhood," in *Is Christianity True?* (London: Charles H. Kelly, 1904), p. 381.

41. Joseph McCabe, *The Religion of Woman: An Historical Study* (London: Watts, 1905), p. 15.

42. Ibid., p. 94.

43. Joseph McCabe, *The Rise and Fall of the Gods* (Girard, Kan.: Haldeman-Julius, 1931), vol. 1, p. 7.

44. Ibid., vol. 6, p. 51.

45. Ibid., p. 64.

46. *Times Literary Supplement*, December 4, 1918, p. 601.

47. Recent books outlining this for the general reader include E. P. Sanders, *The Historical Figure of Jesus* (London: Allen Lane/Penguin Press, 1993), and John Shelby Spong, *Liberating the Gospels* (New York: HarperSanFrancisco, 1996).

48. McCabe, *The Tyranny of Shams*, p. 21.

49. Joseph McCabe, *The Columbia Encyclopedia's Crimes against the Truth* (Girard, Kan.: Haldeman-Julius, 1951), p. 24.

50. Joseph McCabe, *The Testament of Christian Civilization* (London: Watts, 1946), p. vi.

51. *Times Literary Supplement* (December 21, 1946): 633.

52. *Literary Guide* (December 1946): 194.

53. McCabe, *The Religion of Woman*, p. 17.

54. McCabe, *The Bible in Europe*, p. viii.

55. Arthur S Peake, *Christianity: Its Nature and Truth* (London: Duckworth, 1909), pp. 16–17.

56. *Christianity or Secularism: Which is the Better for Mankind? Verbatim Report of Two Nights' Debate* (London: Watts & Hunter & Longhurst, 1911), p. 7.

57. Joseph McCabe, *The Story of Religious Controversy* (Boston: Stratford, 1929), p. 199.

58. McCabe, *A History of Human Morals*, vol. 4, p. 56.

59. McCabe, *The Bible in Europe*, p. 127.

60. Ibid., p. 14.

61. Ibid., p. 11.

62. McCabe, *The Sources of the Morality of the Gospels*, p. 135.

63. Joseph McCabe, *History's Greatest Liars* (Girard, Kan.: Haldeman-Julius, 1951), p. 6.

64. Joseph McCabe, *St. Augustine and His Age* (London: Duckworth, 1902), pp. 99–100.

65. Charles Loring Brace, *Gesta Christi* (New York: Hodder & Stoughton, 1884), p. 218.

66. McCabe, *The Bible in Europe*, p. 26.

67. Ibid., pp. 29–32.

68. McCabe, *History's Greatest Liars*, p. 6.

69. Ibid., pp. 26–27.

70. Ibid., p. 27.

71. Ibid., p. 17.

72. McCabe, *The Story of Religious Controversy*, p. 346.

73. Joseph McCabe, *The Church and the People* (London: Watts, 1919), p. 43.

74. McCabe, *The Story of Religious Controversy*, p. 354.

75. Joseph McCabe, *One Hundred Men Who Moved the World* (Girard, Kan.: Haldeman-Julius, 1931), vol. 9, p. 14.

76. Vincent McNabb, *The Catholic Church and Philosophy* (New York: Macmillan, 1927), p. 104.

77. *Christianity or Secularism*, pp. 22, 44.

78. McCabe, *The Church and the People*, p. 54.

79. Tallis, *Enemies of Hope*, p. 52.

80. Joseph McCabe, *The True Story of the Roman Catholic Church* (Girard, Kan.: Haldeman-Julius, 1930), vol. 11, p. 14.

81. See his *The Task of Social Hygiene* (London: Constable, 1927), pp. 10–11.

82. Kenneth Clark, *Civilization* (London: BBC/John Murray, 1971), p. 329.

83. Walvin, *Victorian Values*, p. 98.

84. Joseph McCabe, *The Life and Letters of George Jacob Holyoake* (London: Watts, 1908), vol. 2, p. 324.

85. McCabe, *A History of Human Morals*, vol. 11, p. 62.

86. Ibid., pp. 62–63.

87. McCabe, *The Social Record of Christianity*, p. 43.

88. Ibid., p. 125.

89. McCabe, *The Social Record of Christianity*, p. 140.

90. McCabe, *A History of Human Morals*, vol. 11, p. 50.

91. Ibid.

92. Ibid.

93. Ibid., p. 51.

94. Ibid., pp. 51–52.

95. Ibid., p. 55.

96. Stuart Wallace, *War and the Image of Germany: British Academics 1914–1918* (Edinburgh: John Donald, 1988).

97. McCabe, *The Kaiser: His Personality and Career*, (London: T. Fisher Unwin, 1915), pp. 13, 129–39. If anything, McCabe's assessment is too generous. For a contemporary view of Wilhelm in a book for the general reader, see Giles MacDonagh, *Prussia: The Perversion of an Idea* (London: Mandarin, 1995).

98. McCabe, *Treitschke and the Great War*, pp. 87–88.

99. Joseph McCabe, *The Soul of Europe* (London: T. Fisher Unwin, 1915), p. 31.

100. Ibid., p. 377.

101. For a fuller discussion of this see R. Hinton Thomas, *Nietzsche in German Politics and Society 1890–1918* (Manchester: Manchester University Press, 1983), introduction.

102. Joseph McCabe, *One Hundred Men Who Moved the World*, vol. 17, p. 7.

103. McCabe, *Treitschke and the Great War*, p. 261.

104. Ibid., p. 92.

105. Joseph McCabe, "Has Rationalism Corrupted Germany?" *RPA Annual for 1916*, p. 61.

106. Ibid., pp. 64–65.

107. Joseph McCabe, *The Kaiser: His Personality and Career* (London: T. Fisher Unwin, 1915), pp. 285–86.

108. McCabe, *Can We Save Civilization?*, p. 177.

109. Peter Munz, *Philosophical Darwinism* (London: Routledge, 1993), p. 93.

5

"A Future More Splendid Than Any Poet Can Imagine"
McCabe and Science

IS McCABE GUILTY OF SCIENTISM?

I f McCabe can be acquitted with a warning on charges of historicism, surely he is guilty of the equally heinous charge of scientism, or placing faith in science as an agency of salvation? This is the most common accusation against rationalist and humanist thinkers. The most comprehensive attack on science in recent years that I am familiar with comes from the English journalist Bryan Appleyard, who sees science as "spiritually corrosive, burning away ancient authorities and traditions. It cannot really co-exist with anything."[1] Appleyard accuses most contemporary popular science writing of scientism, singling out Carl Sagan, Jacob Bronowski, and Stephen Hawking.

As we began the previous chapter defending McCabe from the charge of historicism, so we need to defend him from the charge of scientism in this chapter, if we are to demonstrate the continuing relevance and reliability of the rationalist view of the world. No attempt will be made to defend Bronowski, Sagan, and Hawking directly, but if we can acquit McCabe of the charge, then the burden will fall back on Appleyard to demonstrate that his accusations against the others remain valid. Let us try to implicate McCabe as deeply as possible in this charge. One example will suffice. It comes from the end of his *Century of Stupendous Progress*, which we referred to in the previous chapter. McCabe finished this book with a clarion call for scientism in almost textbook terms: "A future more splendid than any poet can imagine is as certain as tomorrow's sun. It will be created by science; and the obscurantists who assail science are, or would be if their influence were great enough, the friends of pain and sorrow and tyranny, the enemies of light and freedom and happiness."[2] Surely this is evidence enough to lock McCabe up and throw away the key?

Not yet. McCabe was alive to the charge of scientism but was also critical of the assumptions he thought lurked behind such an accusation. He was unprepared to accept the charge of scientism solely on the terms of the accuser. He wrote in 1905 of the

> mockery of Humanism for its faith in the saving power of Science. It must be understood that this phrase chiefly means that we are going to substitute a most careful study of the conditions of happiness for the haphazard appeals and transcendent preaching of the past. Science is not a new goddess, nor a patent medicine for life's disorders.[3]

Then, as now, protesting the dangers of scientism often serves as a mask behind which essentialist notions of a soul and of the special status of human beings are advanced. McCabe, by contrast, sought to place *Homo sapiens* squarely on earth and in the realm of nature, alongside all other living things. But, as we also saw in the previous chapter, he was conscious of the majesty of the story of evolution, and used it as a visionary narrative. But even when doing this, he took care not to simply replace the laws of God with the laws of science.

Raymond Tallis has characterized scientism as an ignoring of subjective experience and regarding that methodological decision as also being ontologically binding.[4] This, we will find, McCabe did not do. The best way to illustrate this is to examine his views on the notion of laws of nature. It is under the guise of "laws of nature" that some of the more preposterous and wicked misuses of science have made their way. McCabe was critical of the notion of "laws of nature" as commonly understood at the time. Most of McCabe's religious opponents represented "laws of nature" as a guarantee for the continuing necessity of God in the universe. Frank Ballard, one of McCabe's more aggressive opponents, recommended a law to be "the permanent expression of the will of a creative principle."[5] Quite the most overblown use of the notion of a law was made by one of McCabe's Christian disputants in 1923. Obviously very keen on the Toreador song in *Carmen*, Reverend Shebbeare insisted, apparently in all seriousness, that it "is a 'law'—an observed uniformity such as may be made the basis of prediction—that men educated in the West of Europe in modern times are delighted by this song at a first hearing."[6]

McCabe's theory of laws was altogether more conventional. Laws "are not modes of behavior drawn up in advance for things to follow. They are merely the modes of behavior which we do observe in nature."[7] He also applied this to the term "scientific law." Such a law, he wrote in 1903, "only means 'a summing-up of experience,' a uniform mode of action of this or that force. . . ."[8] He expanded on this in his *Key to Culture* at the end of the twenties when he postulated that a scientific law is trustworthy "only insofar as [the scientist] knows it to have been based on extensive observations. He keeps an open mind until repeated observations all the world over have brought the same result."[9] Five years later again, McCabe made the simple observation that we "do not want to substitute the word science for the word God."[10] It would be entirely wrong, therefore, to see McCabe's understanding of scientific law or scientific method as "hegemonic," "marginalizing," or any of the other currently fashionable buzzwords.

On the other hand, McCabe would plead guilty with pride—as Karl Popper did—to the scientism that recognizes a similarity of method between the natural and social sciences.[11] We saw this when we examined McCabe's philosophy of history. McCabe would also plead guilty with pride to the accusation of believing that we need more rather than less science if we are to solve the planet's problems. That is really all McCabe was saying in the florid passage we quoted while trying to present the case for the prosecution. McCabe's points were, and remain, valid. They are repeated by commentators of our time who call for more rather than less science when dealing with the problems we now face. Few better examples exist than Carl Sagan's classics of popular science, from *Cosmos* (1980) to *Billions and Billions* (1997). Sagan's approach to popular science is very similar to McCabe's. If anything, McCabe was the more circumspect of the two. He was aware, for instance, of the pitfalls associated with scientific speculation, commenting in 1931 that "it is, perhaps, inevitable that when the speculations of scientific men are very novel or impressive, they should be broadcast in too positive a form."[12] He also lamented the tendency to oversell each new theory by portentously declaring its predecessors or rivals out of date.[13] McCabe, in other words, was conscious of the temptations of uncritical scientism.

So what were McCabe's views on science? Not inappropriately, McCabe used a technological metaphor to describe the progress of science. He likened it to the development of a photographic plate. "Certain features begin to stand out quite clearly while the greater part of the picture is still obscure. In succession, other parts of the picture emerge quite clearly and finally, and we may have a very good idea of the whole while a large amount of detail still lies buried under the obscuring chemical film."[14] In other words, science helps us get a clearer picture of things, but this can take time, and some areas may well be clearer than others. It would not be easy to detect unhealthy quantities of scientism in that metaphor.

McCabe's rendition of the scientific method is just as responsible and contemporary as his notion of science itself. Here is how he described the scientific method in one of his shorter popular works:

> In a word, a theory in modern science is based upon a colossal amount of actual observation, all the world over, by tens of thousands of trained and devoted observers. It has to face a fierce fire of criticism from scientific men themselves when it is launched. . . . Then, even when the theory is generally accepted, it is only "provisional" for a long time. It fits the facts at the moment, but new facts may disturb it.[15]

McCabe's conception of science and the scientific method was realistic, informed, and appropriately tentative.

But if this is the case, why did McCabe equate science with knowledge? Late in his life, McCabe thought of science being "as the word literally means, just knowledge. You might say that the real distinction between it and other operations of the intellect is that it is knowledge obtained by the observation of tens of thousands of men who are specially trained to observe with utmost care and check and cross-check their observations."[16] We saw that McCabe had this in mind when he described history as a science. All he meant was that history, or any discipline, is conducted more systematically and with greater care, if conducted in a way that conforms with scientific method. It is not fashionable to equate science with knowledge any more, as McCabe did, but that does make the equation unsound.

McCabe would win no plaudits from postmodernists of our day for his insistence that science is essentially materialistic. These critics, from the comfort of an air-conditioned office and with the help of a high-speed computer, bewail the spiritual price we are alleged to be paying for the success of science. McCabe's approach was much more down-to-earth. Unlike these comfortable critics, McCabe knew full well about the conditions science had done so much to alleviate: hunger, cold, malnutrition, poor hygiene, ignorance, and superstition.[17] Neither would McCabe be welcomed by revisionist historians, keen to play down notions of a conflict between religion and science. Far more important than these predictable criticisms, however, is the fact that many of the points McCabe campaigned for so bravely have become standard material of contemporary science. McCabe can be seen as a philosophical naturalist before philosophical naturalism. He saw nature as an indivisible whole which permitted no metaphysical intrusion or idealist schematizing.

In fact, McCabe's role in science was largely conservative. It was his misfortune to be active at a time when some strong antiscience trends were then at their peak. It was McCabe's aim to preserve the materialist conclusions of evolution, philosophy of mind, and, to a lesser extent, physics and astronomy from the vitalism and spiritualism then in vogue. Speaking of the demise of the dinosaurs, for example, McCabe noted acidly that "any man who tries to tell us that a 'vital principle' was working out the course of evolution on a definite plan is playing with words. At every step this course of evolution is conditioned by changes in the physical world which cannot reasonably be connected with any sort of plan."[18] McCabe's warning against vitalism read very much like those of Richard Dawkins, Lewis Wolpert, Raymond Tallis, or Alan Sokal several decades later. "While philosophers dispute about 'vital principles' and teleological aspects of life, the physiologist is moving slowly and disdainfully forward. His theory works."[19] In waging this campaign, a lonely one indeed, McCabe has been vindicated.

THE CONFLICT BETWEEN SCIENCE AND RELIGION

In waging war against vitalists and spiritualists, McCabe was bound to have some opinion of the hotly contested question of a conflict between science and religion. The thesis of a conflict between science and religion was made popular by two late-nineteenth-century theists, John William Draper (1811–1882) and Andrew Dickson White (1832–1918), and ever since then other theists have been insisting that no such conflict exists. One of the more recent and able criticisms has been by the English scholar John Hedley Brooke in his book *Science and Religion*. Brooke's aim was to show that the popular antithesis between science and religion was a great deal more complex than had been appreciated. He admits that the conflict model is "not without support," but that it tends to see science and religion as entities in themselves. Nonetheless, Brooke's point about the complexity of the conflict does not expunge it entirely, as Brooke acknowledges. He admits that there were violent attacks on evolution by Catholic and Protestant communities but sees the evolution issue as something that militants from both camps "still like to dwell" upon.[20]

Brooke's dismissal of the conflict that raged at street level is a serious flaw in his argument for one simple reason: how does one then explain what is going on? McCabe was critical of the elitism implicit in such a charge, because saying the conflict between religion and science is over merely indicates "a profound contempt for any who still hold the old religious view."[21] Elsewhere he described as absurd the claim of no conflict when "nine-tenths of the Christian controversial literature heatedly assails the evolution of life and the evolution of mind. . . ."[22] When the Church of England capitulated on the issues of a conflict between evolution and Genesis in their report on doctrine, which was released in 1938, they had to acknowledge that it "is generally agreed among *educated* Christians that these [the Genesis creation narratives] are mythological in origin, and that their value for us is symbolic rather than historical."[23] McCabe constantly defended the right of religious believers to a genuine hearing, contrary to the oft-repeated prejudice that rationalists never do this. Brooke's claim fails to explain the constant stream of declarations from theistic scientists or modernist theologians that there is real conflict. If this is the case, why do they keep on reminding us of this apparently obvious fact?

If the conflict thesis is more complex than earlier theorists such as Draper appreciated, then McCabe's view of the conflict is also more sophisticated than he has been given credit for—not that anyone has seriously examined his views in this area. The first and most important point is that McCabe was alive to the dangers of too simplistic an approach to the problem. In 1917, for example, McCabe denied that science was responsible for the drift away from religion. People's wider knowledge of history was also responsible for this drift.[24] He was also careful to limit his discussion of the conflict to the questions of evolution versus creation and varying theories of cosmology. In these two areas, McCabe told his readers, science was in direct conflict with religion, so long as religion continued to insist on a personal God and a created and purposive universe. With regard to cosmology, McCabe wrote that "if science regards the cosmos as self-sufficing, and religion regards the cosmos as not self-sufficing, one does not see that they are bound to be reconciled."[25]

In the area of evolution, McCabe was so sure of this that he made a rare recourse to italics to emphasize his point. "The basis of the religious argument from design in nature is that there is no other possible explanation of the organs and instincts of animals except a divine plan drawn up in advance. No plea for the supernatural origin of anything is valid as long *as there is a possibility of a natural explanation of its origin.*"[26] Forty years later Antony Flew revisited this theme with his advocacy of what he called the Stratonician Presumption. This philosophical gambit is named after Strato of Lampsacus (d. 269 B.C.E.), and insists that the burden of proof lies with the theist rather than with the atheist, for the simple reason that it is the theist who is making the larger claim.[27]

McCabe was also alive to the contradictory attitude taken by antiscience jeremiahs, both in his day and in our own. He noted in 1934 that we read

> on one page that science is bankrupt, that the superb knowledge of which the last generation boasted was but a mirage hovering above an ocean of mystery, that the newest hope of the race has vanished; and from the next page they learn that science has in our time developed so rapidly that it has dangerously outstripped the general intelligence and the more slowly advancing institutions of the human family.[28]

McCabe also noticed another popular habit of crossing disciplines in order to find harmony in nature. "Sir Oliver Lodge is a physicist, and finds evidence in biology; Professor J A Thomson and Principal Lloyd Morgan are biologists, yet they advise us to look to metaphysics; and religious metaphysicians refer us to psychology."[29] While the names are now different, this practice remains popular. The most common perpetrators of this practice at the end of the twentieth century have been creationists, but also postmodernists, who, safe from their haven in literary criticism, assure all who will listen that science is little more than one form of language among others.[30]

McCabe did not see the conflict as one of competing creeds. For McCabe, the question "is not whether science officially *denies* religious statements but whether what science teaches conflicts with what religion teaches."[31] McCabe even absolved Roman Catholicism of having a necessarily hostile attitude toward science. Speaking of the seventeenth century, McCabe observed simply that the church "resented and hampered departures from the stock of traditional learning."[32] But, so long as the spheres of science and religion overlap, and the conclusions they reach differ, conflict is inevitable.

McCabe frequently debated fundamentalists on evolution and was familiar with their fears and misunderstandings on the issue. It is all very well for Brooke to sneer that militants on either side "still like to dwell" on the question of evolution versus creation. The fact remains that this was a question of huge importance in McCabe's day, as it still is today. Keith Clements, an English church historian, has recently acknowledged that, while the theological cognoscenti might, by the twenties, have come to think that Genesis versus evolution was a burnt-out issue, for the majority of churchgoers and commentators on religious issues the question was far from settled.[33] McCabe recognized this point as well—in 1917. After a shrewd summary of the three main schools of thought within the churches regarding science and evolution, McCabe noted that most clergy and churchgoers "still regard the doctrine of evolution as an irreligious speculation and cling in a hazy way, to the doctrine of special creation."[34]

So long as many tens of thousands of people continue to find meaning in the notion of a conflict between religion and science, it will continue to have explanatory power. And contrary to the oft-repeated declarations to the contrary, many leading thinkers and scientists today share McCabe's views. Paul Kurtz, the leading self-confessed secular humanist scholar in the United States today, has described the conflicting claims to truth by religion and science as the "chief controversy in the modern era. . . ."[35] H. James Birx, author of *Interpreting Evolution*, agrees that the naturalist and supernaturalist approaches to the origin of life are "diametrically opposed."[36]

Carl Sagan made a point in 1996 very similar to McCabe's of seventy years earlier when he noted that religious pronouncements, even if testable only in principle, "enter the arena of science."[37] Sagan the cosmologist's point is made equally by Antony Flew, the philosopher. Flew is sure that the menace of Darwinism "is to assumptions about the peculiar and special status of man. . . . What is threatened is the basic and essential Christian assumption that man is not, or is not wholly, a creature of flesh and blood. . . ." He also asserts that Darwinism offers "massive support for materialism" and makes almost impossible "any even halfway plausible defence of a Platonic-Cartesian view of the nature of man. . . ."[38] McCabe was ridiculed seventy years ago for making that point. Going one step further again, Richard Dawkins has said that while it was logically tenable to be an atheist before Darwin, it is now possible to be "an intellectually fulfilled atheist."[39] McCabe's thoughts on evolution, and on religion for that matter, are remarkably similar to those of Dawkins. Other examples could be taken from Daniel Dennett, Ernst Mayr, Lewis Wolpert, Peter Munz, and many others, but the point has been made. McCabe's understanding of science was a lot more sophisticated than he was given credit for in his own day; so much so, in fact, that he can be described as ahead of his time.

The current derision of those who hold science in high esteem is nothing more than a fashion, one we hope will pass quickly. It is a far greater error than the scientism it despises. One American historian has noted that popular science "has always borne the mark of its Enlightenment heritage. It has always tended to glorify reason and progress, while ridiculing the forces of reaction and superstition."[40] We have seen that McCabe took his opponents too seriously to be satisfied by ridicule and we will see below that McCabe never glorified reason. This notwithstanding, McCabe was proud to write about the power that science can have to better the lives of millions of people. Indeed, a very good case could be made that McCabe's scientific writing provided just the sort of wider picture, or teleological map, that Mary Midgley has advocated as an antidote to the artificial isolating of science from the rest of our mental life.[41] Certainly, McCabe did not see science as isolated from other aspects of our mental life. In conflict sometimes, but never isolated.

McCABE AND EVOLUTION

When McCabe spoke of science, it was frequently evolution he had in mind. Nothing, in fact, determined the shape of McCabe's mind more than evolution. He declared in his autobiography that evolution "put a vertebral column and a spinal cord into what has hitherto been my loose connection of scientific facts. . . ."[42] He also thought evolution to be "the most revolutionary discovery science ever made." Here again McCabe has anticipated contemporary thinkers. Michael Ruse, a philosopher of biology, has stated recently that our biological origins "can and should be a starting point for philosophy today."[43]

What did McCabe understand by evolution? As is to be expected, some aspects of his evolutionary thinking are outdated and can now be seen to be incorrect. He had no idea about continental drift, for instance, and so spent much time dragging continents up and then sinking them down again in order to get the general effect the fossil record indicated. The point about this, of course, is that this is an error all scientists were making, until well after McCabe's death. Like everyone else, McCabe was following the cyclic uniformitarianism of Charles Lyell (1797–1875), the pioneer of modern geology. But the outstanding feature of McCabe's understanding of evolution, looked at eight decades later, is its breadth and accuracy. He had an admirable ability to distinguish a genuine intellectual development from a passing fad. And on most of the occasions when he departed from the conventional wisdom of the time, it was to assert a strictly Darwinian reading of the issue at hand. In doing this, of course, events have largely proved him correct. But what makes this achievement even more admirable is that, as we must always remember, McCabe was a popularizer, writing for the general reader, and was frequently despised by the academic professionals in the field.

Before examining McCabe's ideas about evolution, we need to get a general picture of the conditions in which he was active. Peter Bowler notes that Darwinism was at its lowest ebb during the first three decades of the century.[44] And these, of course, were the years McCabe was most active as an exponent and popularizer of evolution. While evolution in the broader sense was generally accepted, there was very keen competition between Darwinians, Lamarckians, and the school developing around the recently rediscovered works of Gregor Mendel. And the Darwinians were themselves divided into those who supported the rigid selectionism of August Weismann (1834–1914) and those who did not. The argument was not about evolution, but about which mechanism best explained the evolutionary process.

But of course the battle was not simply between rival brands of evolutionists. There were then, as there still are today, large bodies of people opposed to any form of naturalistic evolution at all. Typical of the sort of opponent McCabe faced was Frank Ballard, author of several works of Christian apologetics in the early decades of the twentieth century. Ballard's approach remains popular to this day. Unable to actually find any reason why natural selection is inoperative, he resorted to making rhetorical declarations: "Does natural selection, without intelligence of guidance anywhere, give us a rational explanation of our powers of vision? This is the real and plain question. And to that, common sense and science alike answer with an overwhelming negative."[45] But perhaps the best known example is Hilaire Belloc who conducted a pugnacious controversy with H. G. Wells over Wells's hugely popular *Outline of History*. Belloc insisted in 1926 that natural selection was "quite dead," leaving a saccharined evolution driven by "Design" in control of the field.[46]

The subsequent triumph of Darwinism must not blind us to the fact that the Darwinian school looked, at least until the twenties, like the least likely school to survive; the Mendelians remained adversaries of Darwinism until then. Bowler also notes that it was when Darwinism was in *eclipse* that the more bizarre, pseudoscientific and metaphysical offshoots of evolution thrived. Social Darwinism and its extension into eugenics was more compatible with the linear progressionism within Lamarckism than with natural selection, which sees the variation of species in not a linear fashion, but as a process of branching.[47]

So it was during this volatile and confused period that McCabe wrote on evolution. His first forays into this difficult area were his translations of several works by his mentor, Ernst Haeckel, and his defense of Haeckel's monism. These were followed by his own major works: *The Evolution of Mind* (1910), *The Story of Evolution* (1912), *The New Science and the Story of Evolution* (1931), and *The Riddle of the Universe Today* (1934). McCabe also wrote several shorter surveys in 1909, 1910, 1913, 1920, and 1922, plus a large number of pamphlets, debates, and articles.

The most important point about McCabe's evolutionism was his consistent Darwinism. Contrary to much of the metaphysical evolutionism of the time, and to many antiscience jeremiahs today, McCabe insisted that there "is no 'law of evolution.' Living things do not go on evolving if you leave them alone. They change little as long as they remain happily adapted to their environment."[48] "Many people," McCabe lamented, "imagine that when we speak of a law of evolution we mean that there is some principle within the living organism which impels it onward to a higher level of organization." This, he assured his readers, is "quite erroneous." There is no law of evolution in that things *must* act in such a way, but merely a "general expression of the fact that they *do* act in such a way." This point formed an important aspect to several of his works on evolution.[49] On the odd occasion when he did talk of a law of evolution, he did so in context of it being factual and beyond serious dispute.[50] Usually, he preferred to avoid talk of laws, and said simply that evolution is a fact.[51] In doing this, he anticipated the approach of popularizers of evolution sixty years hence such as Ernst Mayr.[52]

McCabe had a clear, nonmetaphysical understanding of evolution. In one of his most successful books of the thirties, McCabe wrote that evolution would be "unintelligible except as the inexorable action and reaction of the unconscious agencies of nature."[53] In another book he described evolution as the ability of organisms to adapt to their changing environment.[54] McCabe was, in other words, a straightforward Darwinian. There is, he told his readers in 1912

> no consciousness of law and no idea of evading danger. There is not even some mysterious instinct "telling" the animal, as it used to be said, to do certain things. It is, in fact, not strictly accurate to say that a certain change in the environment stimulates animals to advance. Generally speaking, it does not act on the advancing at all, but on the non-advancing, which it exterminates. The procedure is simple, tangible, and unconscious.[55]

It is not a case of the natural selection of the fittest, he went on, but the natural destruction of the less fit. By describing evolution in these terms, McCabe's understanding was far more compatible with contemporary understandings of evolution than most popular writers and, indeed, many of the specialists of his time. One would only need drop words like "advance" and this could fit comfortably into a sound work of popular evolution today.

While McCabe was a thoroughgoing Darwinian, that does not mean he was dismissive of evolutionary theories that predated natural selection, or that he was uncritical of Darwin. Among the bewildering array of crimes Darwinians have been accused of is that of assuming there was no credible evolutionary theory before Darwin. The contrary was true for McCabe. For example, he spoke of Johann Wolfgang von Goethe as a "convinced evolutionist at least twenty years before Lamarck published his great work."[56] McCabe was quite clear that both Goethe and Jean-Baptiste de Lamarck's evolutionary theories were incorrect, but that did not stop him appreciating the work they did in the field and their contributions to the growing body of knowledge. Neither was McCabe uncritical of Darwin. In one of his shorter popular works, he noted that Darwin's thinking included two beliefs that have subsequently been "sternly challenged." The first was the notion of the inheritance of acquired characteristics that Darwin had learned from Lamarck, and the second was the idea that all change must be very slow and gradual. This had been challenged by the Mutationist evolutionists.[57]

Perhaps the easiest way to illustrate McCabe's evolutionism is to outline some of the theories he did *not* subscribe to, or at least not fully. We will see that his understanding was sufficiently good to avoid many of the errors of progressionism, emergent evolution, eugenics, and social Darwinism, all of which captivated prominent sections of the academic community, often the same people who scorned McCabe as an amateur and generalist. Social Darwinism is the idea that the principles of evolution, in particular the "nature red in tooth and claw" variety, could be applied to human society. McCabe described social Darwinism in 1913 as a "pseudo-scientific application of evolutionary views to social problems," insisting that there is no scientific justification for a doctrine of eternal struggle.[58] This was when the prestige of social Darwinism was at its highest. He returned to the theme in 1921 when he dismissed as "quite stupid" the idea that conflict "in the muscular and sanguinary sense is necessary."[59] On another occasion, he criticized Nietzsche's Darwinism directly, although he did not describe his beliefs as social Darwinist. Nietzsche, in McCabe's view, "misunderstood Darwinism. He thought that natural selection was definitively proved to be the main agency of progress, and that it meant the selection of the strong and sacrifice of the weak. This misapprehension of natural selection," McCabe added rather hopefully, "is now understood by everybody. . . ."[60] McCabe's observations of Nietzsche are astute, although his belief that this misconception has been cleared up is, sadly, less so.

Another example of McCabe's attitude toward social Darwinism was his response to a controversial claim made by Sir Arthur Keith, FRCS, FRS. Like McCabe, Keith (1866–1955) was an honorary associate of the Rationalist Press Association, but unlike McCabe, Keith was a highly respected establishment figure, and one of the world's leading comparative anatomists. Keith's reputation was made on his work on the Piltdown skull. While being himself a kindly man, Keith espoused an evolutionism redolent of Tennyson's nature—red in tooth and claw. Keith shocked Britain in 1931 when he declared at a Rectoral Address at the University of Aberdeen that war is "nature's pruning hook." The following year McCabe devoted several pages in *Can We Save Civilization?* to a criticism of this claim. He began with a discussion of the role of war throughout the historical period and concluded that far from being a pruning hook, war "has been the vampire of the race. . . . The broad truth is that war develops only the characteristics which success in war requires, and their decay would not matter if war is abolished."[61] McCabe also noted that "nature" was being used by Keith in a deterministic manner, and was, in many important ways, open to change and adaptation by humans.

But despite having condemned social Darwinism as he understood the term, McCabe did hold a couple of opinions that would justify the label social Darwinist as understood today. There is reason to believe, McCabe wrote in 1916,

that "a race loses its educability if it remains unprogressive for too long a period."
As an example, he cited the Tasmanians, who were "one of the oldest and least
cultured branches of the human family, and [they] died out within a century
after contact with the whites."[62] This statement is foolish from at least two
points of view. First, it ignores the active part the Europeans played in the exter-
mination of the Tasmanians, and secondly, it assumes that ineducability is the
sole, or even the chief, reason for their extinction. Moreover, this is foolish in
McCabe's own terms; hindsight is not required for this to be seen as foolish. On
the very same page where he wrote off the Tasmanians, McCabe warned his
readers not to become dogmatic about which races are irredeemably unprogressive. "Nothing but candid and careful experience will show which races are educable and which ineducable."[63] We will examine this issue further when we discuss McCabe's views on race. This is as close as McCabe gets to espousing social
Darwinist views. Were one to take many contemporary antiscience and danger-
of-science jeremiahs too seriously, we could be forgiven for supposing that social
Darwinism was the major evolutionary theme of the early twentieth century.

McCabe was also scornful of the fad among some evolutionists between the
wars known as "emergent evolution." The term, made known by the psychologist C. Lloyd Morgan, sought to emphasize a vitalist creativity in each new evolutionary development. McCabe understood this all too clearly, and dismissed
emergence as nothing more than "mystic machinery."[64] He noted that it was
emergent evolution that the Church of England had in mind when it declared
that evolution was taking up views more favorable to religion.[65] It was also
favored by evolutionists with a theistic bent as it helped them reconcile religion
with science.[66] Even other freethinkers were taken in by emergent evolution for
a while. Chapman Cohen, McCabe's old rival, criticized his handling of emergent evolution in an otherwise positive review of The Riddle of the Universe
Today. Cohen insisted that emergent evolution is "strictly scientific in character" and is in fact "the only account which accurately fits the fact."[67]
Chapman Cohen was a capable writer and a useful popularizer of science and
religion to the general reader. Joseph McCabe, however, was significantly more
capable. Very recently the notion of emergence has made something of a comeback, but with the notable addendum that any suggestion of mysticism is
strongly denied.[68]

The story of McCabe and eugenics is more complicated. Until the last few
years of his life, he was as dismissive of the eugenics movement as he was of other
pseudoscientific fads. Eugenics was essentially a continuation of the social Darwinist worry about the potential of lower-quality types outbreeding better-
quality types, and thus somehow lowering the tone of the evolutionary neighborhood. McCabe warned his readers in one of his popular science works that
no eugenic scheme "has yet been formulated which quite satisfies the unbiased
mind."[69] He was always critical of the assumptions made by many eugenicists,
such as the physical and mental superiority of the middle and upper classes. Pos-

sibly with his own experience in mind, McCabe remarked on the "striking differences between any four children of the same parents warn us that breeding human beings is a very different matter from breeding sheep, cattle or hens."[70] He went on to make the obvious point that higher breeding among the lower classes bore no necessary correlation to a lowering of the mental and moral stock of the race. And neither are the mediocre children from able parents a source of encouragement. He noted acidly that the "inheritance of wealth or advantages is much clearer than the inheritance of talent."[71] Far more beneficial than pleading for more births among the middle class and professionals, McCabe scolded, was to make public the knowledge of methods of contraception.[72] He was also aware of the essential opposition between eugenics and natural selection. In doing this, he recognized Peter Bowler's important point, which we noted earlier in this chapter, that it was during the period of the greatest eclipse of Darwinism that these pseudo-Darwinian theories flourished.[73]

McCabe also disputed the existence of the huge increase in crime, lunacy, and diseases that eugenicists liked to see as the result of the scandalous permissiveness of unrestrained breeding from the lower orders. Heredity, McCabe wrote in 1916, "is still a mystery: and the relative importance of heredity and environment (or nature and nurture) is not yet determined." And besides, McCabe added, we "do not yet know the points to breed for, and there is no constancy of result."[74] That warning remains valid at the beginning of the twenty-first century as it did during the First World War. And, as if to further distance himself from social Darwinist views he had toyed with earlier in the same book, McCabe criticized Karl Pearson (1857–1936), a leading eugenicist, who insisted on the impossibility of altering the innate qualities of a child by education. Eleven years later, in his *Key to Culture*, McCabe labeled eugenics the new Calvinism, in which "every man's character is inexorably decreed in his embryo, is as unscientific as it is discouraging. It is a theory, and there are millions of facts of life and history against it."[75] At heart, McCabe always retained his Owenite belief in the educability of all people.

McCabe's attitude began to change after the neo-Darwinian synthesis. Accepting the importance of genetics, and thus heredity, in evolution, involved McCabe in a gradual shift from his basic contention that the environment was the deciding factor is in individual's behavior. Until the synthesis, McCabe had doubted the existence of what the eugenicists called "tainted stocks." Their idea of "tainted stock" rested on the Lamarckian notion that a family can pass on its antisocial behavior genetically to its offspring. McCabe, very rightly, had criticized this error, pointing out that most antisocial behavior or depravity is a result of a harmful and dangerous environment. But by the late forties, when he was compiling his *Rationalist Encyclopedia*, he thought that it was "generally agreed that there are tainted stocks or families with hereditary defects, and that these should not be allowed to propagate."[76]

In effect, McCabe had accepted the findings of recent science, but expressed it in terms of an outmoded social prejudice. He had not accepted the Lamarckian notion of tainted stock, but the genetic version, which posits families passing on *hereditary* defects. Our knowledge of genetics now makes this conclusion uncontroversial. McCabe's mistake was to then draw an unsound conclusion, drawn from eugenics, from a sound recognition of a new scientific consensus.

McCABE AND PROGRESSIONISM

If McCabe was a genuine and consistent Darwinian and avoided most the errors of the day, at the time when they were most fashionable, then surely he is guilty of confusing evolution with progress. Along with scientism, the crime most commonly imputed to rationalist evolutionists is that of progressionism, or the notion that evolution is purposive and directional. And McCabe cannot entirely escape these charges, but the story is not nearly so simple as his accusers would wish. Richard Dawkins has called progressionism the legacy of the old "great chain of being," which should have been demolished by evolutionary thinking.[77] In a revealing passage in his largest work devoted to evolution, McCabe employed a great chain of being idea, but with interesting results. He began *The Story of Evolution* with two chapters surveying the current thoughts on cosmological matters, and then began the third chapter with this caveat:

> The greater part of this volume will be occupied with the things that have happened on one small globe in the universe during a certain number of millions of years. It cannot be denied that this has a somewhat narrow and parochial aspect. The earth is, you remember, a million times smaller than the sun, and the sun itself is a very modest citizen of the stellar universe. Our procedure is justified, however, both on the ground of personal interest, and because our knowledge of the earth's story is so much more ample and confident.[78]

In other words, McCabe prefaced his study of evolution with a warning against cosmic presumption on the part of his readers. McCabe repeated this warning in his popular books when he criticized introducing anthropocentric notions into talk of higher and lower forms, noting that "it is not the place of science to set up such a standard."[79] Passages such as this are ignored by commentators wanting to lament the arrogance of humanism. McCabe's thought contrasts favorably against his longtime opponent Father Vincent McNabb, who in *The Catholic Church and Philosophy* employed the most anthropocentric form of the great chain of being. McNabb began this passage by giving it the authority of what he took to be a scientific law: "the higher the organism the wider is its area of assimilation."

> Lower organisms have such a specialized area of assimilation that they are fixed to one spot. Placed in another spot they find nothing they can assimilate.

Death is the result. But the highest visible organism, man, has a vast area of assimilation. He has the mineral, vegetable and animal kingdoms for his food. Even the highest mammals are not so catholic in what they can eat and live on as is man. If they attempted to do as man does, they would die.[80]

And to make this passage more eccentric still, McNabb is actually using it as a pseudoscientific illustration of the superiority of the Roman Catholic Church. He declared that by the church's "vast powers of assimilation it proved itself to be an organism of the highest type." Unlike McNabb's extravagant attempt to employ the great chain of being to place not only man but the Catholic Church at the apex, McCabe, in effect, turned the great chain of being on its head, so as to remind his readers that they—we—are not so indispensable to the universe after all.

But, if this is the case, why does McCabe frequently use the phraseology of an upward movement of evolution? After all, he did write that everything "known to us has evolved. From distant suns to our social and religious institutions, from diamonds or oceans to the human struggles of today and the ideals of tomorrow, the whole contents of the known universe fall into one grand and intelligible scheme."[81] All McCabe meant by "grand and intelligible scheme," was evolution itself. In another book he announced that "the universe has the word evolution written, literally, in letters of fire across it."[82] This passage could be accused of being purple, perhaps, but not anthropocentric. McCabe was saying what Richard Dawkins said more than sixty years later, when he announced to his readers that he wanted to persuade them "not just that the Darwinian world-view *happens* to be true, but that it is the only known theory that could, in principle, solve the mystery of our existence."[83] The important point is that McCabe never portrayed that movement as cosmologically *necessary*.

So, if McCabe is not guilty of cosmological progressionism, the same cannot be said as clearly with regard to human evolution. But before examining McCabe's views, let us again contrast him with his contemporaries. J. Arthur Thomson was a prominent Spencerian evolutionist, and theist, based at the University of Aberdeen. Thomson was a prolific popularizer of a vitalist evolutionism. He ended one such book, revealingly called *The Gospel of Evolution*, published in 1926, with the assurance that evolution contained the three great trends that are congruent with man's highest ideals of the good, the beautiful, and the true. This is because the "strengthening and complexifying of inter-relations is one of the ways of *securing progress*."[84] More typical is the Spencerian notion of evolution as evermore complex improvement, but without the overt Platonism. McCabe's early opponent, Frank Ballard is an example of this approach.[85]

McCabe's views are certainly less progressionist than these. In the larger context of evolution, he wrote quite bluntly, as we have seen, that there "is no 'law of progress.' If an animal is fitted to secure its livelihood and breed posterity in certain surroundings, it may remain unchanged indefinitely if these surroundings do not materially change."[86] McCabe specifically warned against seeing an evolutionary pedigree in the form of a simple linear descent. An excellent example is his treatment of the evolution of the horse.

> It must not, of course, be supposed that these fossil remains all represent "ancestors of the horse." In some cases they may very well do so; in others, as we saw, they represent side-branches of the family which have become extinct. But even successive forms of the *Eohippus, Mesohippus, Miohippus,* and *Pliohippus* must not be arranged in a direct line as the pedigree of the horse.[87]

George Gaylord Simpson is usually credited with demonstrating the fallacies and errors in positing a straight linear devolution of the horse, in his book *Horses*, which was published in 1951. Until then it was pretty much standard fare to present the evolution of the horse in this way. Indeed, its simplicity made it a popular example to use in nonspecialist works on evolution, for instance in the influential work *The Science of Life*, cowritten by H. G. Wells, Julian Huxley, and G. P. Wells.[88] But as we see Joseph McCabe, the popularizer, had warned his readers of this error twenty years before Wells and forty years before Simpson. It also goes a long way to showing how little McCabe allowed progressionism to color his scientific understanding.

It was, as we have said, when writing specifically of human evolution that McCabe was more likely to be of a kind with his contemporaries. Like Thomson, he maintained that humanity will "continue to make progress, at a constantly accelerated pace."[89] Where McCabe departed from Thomson and the others was to refuse to posit any transcendental standard of progress. In *The Story of Evolution* (1912), McCabe's main work devoted to the subject, the story of humanity was confined to the last forty pages of a 340-page book. He assured his readers that the "evolution of man is guided by the same laws as the evolution of any other species."[90] He also warned against assuming that "because there is a 'law of evolution' civilization is bound to advance from height to height."[91] He reminded his readers of how wasteful the evolution process is.

> The machinery of evolution has been ghastly. And the issue of hundreds of millions of years (as geologists now count) of this was a "man" so stupid and bestial that it took him two million years to reach a civilization in which seven out of ten still live in poverty and meanness, and wars are possible which will blast ten million out of existence for four years.[92]

McCabe was a long way from insisting evolution harbored within its bosom a cache of Platonist notions, as Thomson did. All we can say, McCabe insisted, is that history gives us good ground to suppose a continuous advance, but that this is by no means a certain and effortless process.

At this point it is time to turn back to his accusers and confess McCabe's mitigated progressionism proudly. As with McCabe's view of history, he can be excused this lapse—as it would be seen today—simply because he had experienced "progress" for ordinary people, and it was not unreasonable for him to see that as a permanent condition. Unlike Thomson, McCabe's understanding of human progress was thoroughly practical. It involved "the reduction of suffering, the increase of health and happiness, the wider extension of an appreciation of art and good literature, as well as in the multiplication of wealth. . . ."[93] It is time to recognize the nihilism inherent in those who would abandon notions of reason and progress, simply because of the misdirections or exaggerations of some—McCabe not among them—who have spoken in these terms.

McCabe was offering evolution as the central feature of a teleological map (Mary Midgley's phrase), or metanarrative (the postmodernists' favorite) by which to understand the world and the place of humans in it. Decades later, some scholars are beginning to appreciate the need for what McCabe was trying to do. Almost a century after McCabe began writing, E. O. Wilson echoed his forgotten predecessor.

> If the sacred narrative cannot be in the form of a religious cosmology, it will be taken from the material history of the universe and the human species. That trend is in no way debasing. The true evolutionary epic, retold as poetry, is as intrinsically ennobling as any religious epic.[94]

Wilson replaces "teleological map" and "metanarrative" with "sacred narrative," but essentially he is referring to the same thing. Science in general, and evolution in particular, has the explanatory power and capacity to inspire that is required in any large-scale intellectual framework. In an age that can no longer accept prescientific anthropomorphic gods, evolution can provide us with an intellectually satisfying account of who we are and why we are here. As we saw in the previous chapter, and again in this one, McCabe was ahead of his time in providing the general reader with a teleological map that was free of anthropomorphic pretensions and mysticism, and that captured the extraordinary capacity of real-world science to inspire.

MATERIALISM

Probably the only body of thought to have been vilified more than evolution would be the philosophy of materialism. There have been more confident predictions of the bankruptcy of materialism than of atheism—a strong claim. And yet materialism has now replaced idealism and dualism from their hitherto privileged places in academic philosophy.[95] Richard C. Vitzhum recently brought materialism to the attention of the general reader in his excellent book *Materialism: An Affirmative History and Definition*. He began the book by lamenting that no one in the twentieth century even tried to explain materialism with anything approaching the passion and depth of Titus Lucretius, Baron Paul-Henri Thiry d'Holbach, or Ludwig Büchner, the three great materialist thinkers of the past. Doubtless the reader will no longer be surprised that I should intercede at this point. Joseph McCabe was courageously advocating materialism when most scholars were quite sure that materialism was nothing more than a relic of nineteenth-century thought, long abandoned by all serious thinkers. What *is* true and, given McCabe's written output, extraordinary, is that he never brought his thoughts on materialism together in one work.

McCabe's philosophy of materialism derived very largely from Haeckel, whose influence we have followed, but also from Ludwig Büchner (1824–1899). Büchner's *Force and Matter*, published originally in 1855, but better known from its expanded fifteenth edition in 1884 and after, is the classic of nineteenth-century materialism. Neither Haeckel nor Büchner used the term to describe their own philosophy, and neither, for many years, did McCabe. Haeckel claimed allegiance instead to a Spinozistic monism that united matter and spirit in "the all-embracing divine essence of the world, the universal substance."[96] As we saw in chapter 3, McCabe loyally defended Haeckel's monism against all comers for many years, although it is interesting to see his progressive abandonment of the term monism in favor of materialism. Haeckel acknowledged that his monism was not far removed from scientific materialism, but was anxious to avoid the opprobrium connected with the notion of materialism. The view that Haeckel opposes, McCabe wrote, "is that there is another element in existence, totally distinct from this matter-force reality: that the mind of man cannot be an evolution from the matter-force substance, and that this substance itself could not have evolved into the orderly universe about us except under the guidance of a still higher intelligent principle, God."[97]

But as the years went on, McCabe became increasingly uncomfortable defending monism. This was because he found himself more and more in the company of vitalists such as Sir Oliver Lodge and George Bernard Shaw. Early on, McCabe was happy to endorse Haeckel's claim that, by claiming "substance" as a deeper reality than either spirit or matter, monism was acting as "a system that could unite harmoniously the finest ethical truths of the Christian religion with the unshakeable truths of modern science."[98] In his controversy with Lodge, McCabe denied Haeckel equated mind with matter. Rather, it was a "place or 'mode' of the fundamental cosmic energy. . . ."[99] The problem with this, of course, is that it was looking more like the vitalism he was at pains to oppose. Inevitably, McCabe's emphasis changed, so that by 1914, he was trying to distinguish Haeckel's materialist monism from the vitalist monism of Lodge and Shaw. But even then he was not prepared to deny the existence of spirit and rejected claims that materialism entailed such a denial.[100] Instead, McCabe portrayed spiritualism and materialism as competing dogmatisms, with the sensible attitude being described as agnosticism. It was in the face of the continuing onslaught of the Shaw/Lodge brands of vitalism that McCabe gradually ceased emphasizing the essential unity of matter and energy as substance in favor of a stricter, more classically recognizable materialist cosmology. But as late as 1923, he was agnostic on the question. "I do not think that our knowledge of reality is yet ample enough to enable us to put a label on the universe. Is matter evolved from ether? We are not sure. Is there anything beyond ether and electrons? We do not know."[101] But by 1945 McCabe knew enough to abandon the term monism for that of materialism, if only as a means to avoid vitalist interpretations of materialism. In the *Rationalist Encyclopedia*, McCabe defined a materialist simply as one "who either denies or disbelieves (lacks belief in) the existence of spirits. . . ."[102]

The concept of materialism, despite the almost overwhelming obloquy attached to it, was preferable to McCabe to being linked with a monism tainted with vitalism, Haeckel's preferences notwithstanding. More than half a century later we find that monism, a materialist monism completely shorn of any suggestion of vitalism, is making a comeback. In 1992 Nicholas Humphrey described monism as "that there is in reality only one sort of stuff, of which both minds and brains are ultimately made."[103] And in her celebrated study of cyberspace, Margaret Wertheim wrote of the "complete misnomer to call the modern scientific world picture *dualistic*, as is so often done. This world picture is entirely *monistic*, admitting the reality of the physical world alone."[104] McCabe would be well satisfied.

We can also learn something about McCabe's developing views on materialism by examining his changing views about ether. This is especially interesting, because it illustrates McCabe's handling of a subject in which events proved him to be mistaken. Ether is a very old idea, coming originally from the Greeks, and was revived by Newton as a possible solution to the problem of how the force of gravity could operate through space. Ether enjoyed a brief vogue in the last decades of the nineteenth century and up until the First World War. What is more, the vogue for ether was driven, in part, by the service it performed in the conflict between science and religion. Theists were proclaiming the death of materialism as it dissolved into nonmaterial ether. The main champion of ether in Britain was the ubiquitous Sir Oliver Lodge, but McCabe's views on ether were influenced by his lifelong loyalty to Ernst Haeckel. Contrary to the theists, McCabe was also a stalwart champion of ether, but he saw it as vindicating materialism. McCabe insisted that the burden of proof lay with the theist. "Ether exists; if any man supposes that there was a time when it did not exist, it is his place to prove that it had a beginning."[105] Expanding on this, McCabe asserted that nothing exists "beyond matter and ether."[106] Furthermore, materialists had "always recognised ether, and had generally felt that it would prove to be the stuff from which atoms were formed."[107] This reflects an essential tenet of Haeckel's monism, which distinguished between the ponderable and imponderable constituents of the universe. The ponderable side of the monistic universe was matter, while ether was the imponderable.[108]

Until the midtwenties, McCabe was prepared to defend ether against all comers. As late as 1923, he was insisting on the two fundamental realities of the universe: ether and electrons.[109] But between 1923 and 1925, when he wrote *The Marvels of Modern Physics*, McCabe's position shifted, albeit grudgingly and hesitantly. In this work McCabe defined ether as "a very elastic solid which 'shivered,' as it were, under the motion of particles of matter, and transmitted the shudder very rapidly across space."[110] But, in the same book, McCabe could see, in a way that Lodge could not, that the writing was on the wall for ether. "Sir Oliver Lodge is still convinced that ether is the fundamental reality; that the electrons are some kind of special centres in ether. Most physicists, as we shall see, ignore or reject ether, but even followers of Einstein admit some 'material substratum of the universe.' "[111]

So while McCabe was grudgingly willing to abandon Haeckel's ether, he was not prepared to abandon the monism-materialism that underpinned his concept of ether in the first place. He denied that Einstein's theories rejected ether altogether, arguing that it admitted a different kind of ether. Many physicists, McCabe told his readers, "maintain that there must be some material substratum of the universe. Why this cannot be called 'ether,' if we make it plain that the properties formerly ascribed to ether are disputable or inadmissible, one does not see. Possibly the name will return."[112]

Notwithstanding his concern to retain a material substratum, McCabe came to accept relativity theory. Whereas in 1920 he was dubious that relativity would ever be proved true, in 1925 he was telling his readers of the famous vindication of relativity at the solar eclipse in 1919.[113] An expedition of scientists, led by Sir Arthur Eddington, watched an eclipse with a view to testing the path of light coming near the surface of the sun. Consistent with Einstein's predictions, the path of light was bent. This vindicated the General Theory of Relativity. McCabe told his readers that the "new physics" has "deepened and expanded the old knowledge in a way every thoughtful physicist desired. . . ."[114]

The point McCabe was struggling toward was that twentieth-century physics was far from contradicting materialism, as was regularly being proclaimed by theists such as Sir Oliver Lodge, Sir James Jeans, and Sir Arthur Eddington. This point had to wait until J. J. C. Smart was able to put the case forcefully enough in his *Philosophy and Scientific Realism*, which appeared in 1963. Today, writers on materialism can declare that "the essential interactiveness of space, time, matter, energy, the reductionist program of modern physics has in fact much increased the likelihood that materialism's monistic view of the universe is correct."[115] McCabe defended this theory of a fundamental material reality, which he thought might as well be called ether as anything else, for the rest of his life. He saw this as merely a revision of Haeckel's theory of substance.[116] McCabe also recognized that it would make no difference to the validity of materialism if it transpires that there is no such thing as ether.[117]

McCabe's record on a subject like ether is honorable, in that he adapted his views to the developing scientific view of the day. He was certainly a long way ahead of Sir Oliver Lodge, who sneered that McCabe was an "amateur materialist" while at the same time insisting that ether is the physical medium for mental telepathy.[118] McCabe's steady retreat on the question of ether was informed by his growing appreciation of the importance and soundness of relativity theory. He was conscious of holding an unpopular line of materialism, as it was the standard wisdom that the new physics had finally smashed all materialism. But, as Vitzhum has pointed out, while relativity and quantum theory have both disproved claims by Büchner that space, matter, and time are independent, they have confirmed his basic tenet of an endless materiality.[119] And while twentieth-century physics has invalidated the classical materialist notion of the indivisible atom, the essential unit of reality is now seen as the "quantizeable force field."[120] McCabe, I think, was groping towards this point.

If McCabe struggled to grasp the consequences for materialism from the new physics, he was thoroughly consistent in applying materialism to the mind-body question. Joseph McCabe was an eliminative materialist before Daniel Dennett or Paul and Patricia Churchland were born. "The essence of materialism," McCabe wrote in 1934, "is the belief that man, body and 'mind,' is no more than an animal with an exceptionally developed brain, and that an animal is a structure of mechanisms, mainly chemical, which we can trace back, through fifteen millennia of unplanned and unguided development, to certain chemical combinations in the slime of primeval earth."[121] This materialism regarding mind was McCabe's most lasting legacy from Haeckel. And while Haeckel can be, and has been, criticized for many things, he deserves praise for popping the "mind" bubble for tens of thousands of nonspecialist readers.

This, of course, was not how Haeckel and McCabe's opponents saw it. It was precisely this materialism regarding notions of mind that most appalled these people. One of the most persistent critics of rationalism in the first years of the twentieth century was Frank Ballard, M.A., B.D., FRMS. Unlike Sir Oliver Lodge, Ballard defended a conventional Protestant orthodoxy. Ballard's six-hundred-page tome, *Haeckel's Monism False*, was the largest and most comprehensive response to *The Riddle of the Universe*. Ballard was better at exposing some of the contradictions and dogmatisms in Haeckel's thinking than in positing a clear alternative. Indeed, he tended to rely on equally sweeping assertions. At one point Ballard simply declared that it "matters not how 'intimate and exact' the correspondences between mind and brain, it remains for ever true that 'the two cannot be identified.' "[122] Ballard did little more than insist on the mystery of relations between mind and matter, in the hope that this left traditional religious explanations undisturbed.

McCabe also anticipated concerns held by some neurophilosophers today about "folk psychology," the phrase used to label traditional terms like "mind," "consciousness," or "instinct." Such terms are seen by these scholars to be barriers to further understanding of the brain, mainly because of the vitalist or spiritual associations many people make with such terms. "I said years ago," McCabe wrote in 1918, "that the word 'instinct' ought to be erased from the dictionary. Had that been done in time, our younger students of philosophy might have been spared the temporary epidemic of Bergsonism."[123] In one of his Big Blue Books, written in 1941, McCabe thought the words to be excised should be "soul, mind (except as a collective name for the functions of the brain), psyche, libido, will, instinct, and intuition."[124] Since McCabe's day, most of these terms have been discredited as naming any specific scientific process. Yet again, McCabe is vindicated. Instinct is the most important of those terms that has recovered a respectable scientific understanding. McCabe was reacting against the classical idea of instinct which was still current of a fixed stimulus leading to an equally fixed response. That notion of instinct came under attack in an article by K. Dunlap in 1919, called "Are There Any Instincts?" and was progressively undermined until it was replaced by the contemporary understanding of instinct as a function of genetic ordering.[125]

McCabe's most sustained treatment of this question was his work *The Evolution of Mind*, originally published in 1910. Despite the material for this book having come from his 1910 lecture program, *The Evolution of Mind* is the least accessible work for the general reader of any in his entire corpus. This is because McCabe's aim was essentially the technical one of ascribing a strictly materialist understanding to questions of physiology, anatomy, and zoology. He criticized, for instance, Dr. Russel Wallace's contention of the human mind having been "suddenly engrafted on the powers of the ape."[126] Wallace was one of many theistically inclined scientists of the time who was anxious to retain some shred of divinity for the human animal. McCabe criticized other scholars for attributing "faint glimmers of consciousness," "primitive reasoning," or "dim intelligence" to the behavior of animals. McCabe saw these attempts as "preposterously anthropomorphic." With admirable restraint, McCabe kept strictly to the facts as he understood science of the time to know them. "Nothing is gained by hiding with sonorous phrases the fact that consciousness is still a profound mystery: a fact that does not surprise those who know what exploration has still to be made in the region of the human cortex."[127] McCabe never dropped his suspicion of terms liable to idealist reinterpretations. As late as 1951, in one of his last works, McCabe regretted the continued use of words like "mind."[128] Would that all popularizers of science were so restrained.

RACE

Yet another feature of McCabe's thought that can be described as being ahead of its time was his genuine admiration for aspects of non-Western cultures. Going against much received wisdom of his day, when racism was usually accepted without question, McCabe specifically repudiated the idea of a scientifically arrived-at theory of race. Again, we can take as an example of contemporary opinion on race the views of Sir Arthur Keith. Keith was a facile writer, and produced several works of popular science on various aspects of evolution. Race was an important feature in Keith's understanding of evolution. In 1948, influenced by the American physical anthropologist Carleton Coon, Keith wrote a 430-page account of evolution in which race played the paramount role. Racial struggle was seen in social Darwinist terms as a necessary stimulus to improvement.[129] McCabe was aware of Keith's error well before this book came out, however. In 1939, McCabe told an American correspondent that "Keith made the one mistake of his life in taking up that racial superstition. . . ."[130] Ironically, it was not to be Keith's one mistake. Keith's reputation was built on his strong advocacy of Piltdown Man.

Another contemporary with whom McCabe can be favorably compared is C. E. M. Joad. Hugely popular and widely read in his day, Joad was a popularizer of current philosophical and social ideas. Like McCabe, though with more reason, Joad has been largely forgotten today. Joad was characteristically simple in his treatment of race, holding the inferiority of blacks to be "self-evident."[131] Joad was also prepared to use the term "nigger" in his writings. And this was not unusual; Joad was in the company of Edmund Gosse, Joseph Conrad, and Virginia Woolf, among many others. McCabe was one of the very few men of his time who not only did not use this derogatory term, but specifically condemned its use. He described the word "nigger" as a "contemptuous expression" that was also inaccurate.[132] McCabe attributed the backwardness of Africa not to racial inferiority, but to the relative isolation of African peoples to large-scale contact with other civilizations.[133] Eight decades later, this hypothesis has been put forward by Jared Diamond in his brilliant work *Guns, Germs and Steel.*

These are not unrepresentative examples against which McCabe can be compared: Sir Arthur Keith, the establishment eminence, and Cyril Joad, the pugnacious outsider. But the most pertinent comparison can be made with Ernst Haeckel, McCabe's mentor. Haeckel's entire evolutionary theory was saturated with explicit racism, so much so that one recent critic has charged Haeckel (rather extravagantly) with being the principal agent for making racism academically respectable in Germany in the late nineteenth century.[134] This was one area of Haeckel's worldview that McCabe never accepted. McCabe was not entirely without racist views, as we will see, but they were put in a provisional way and not accorded the status of a scientific fact, as Haeckel's racism was.

To begin with, McCabe criticized "superficial theories about the innate superiority of the white-skinned men." He condemned the presumption of a white man's burden, declaring it "superfluous mysticism for us to imagine that our 'white race' has some special genius for civilization."[135] Seven decades before Edward Said, McCabe wrote that the Europeans have "set up a fictitious 'Oriental imagination,' and try to make Orientals live down to it."[136] He thought it an insolence to see Chinese, Burmese, or Japanese as lower races.[137] "Until about 700 BC the philosophers of the world would have said that white men seemed incapable of civilization."[138] And yet, decades later, with McCabe now dead and forgotten, postmodernists feel able to declare that rationalist humanism is inherently "eurocentric."

But in talking of this sort of racism we have gone ahead of ourselves. The first exploration McCabe undertook in this area was not in what has become the more familiar field of white racism about nonwhites, but of racial prejudice among Europeans about other Europeans. In chapter 4 we examined his book *The Soul of Europe*, written in 1915. McCabe was invited to write this following the publication the previous year of Stanton Coit's book *The Soul of America*. These books were conceived as intelligent travelogues, with some historical and sociological observations thrown in. McCabe's book still makes brilliant reading as a travelogue, and as a series of observations about the peoples of Europe. It is amusing to see McCabe shuffling somewhat uncomfortably around the journal-istic device of a continent having a soul. He made it clear to his readers that the traditional national stereotypes were little more than misapplied poetry. He fin-ished the book concluding that "we may discard as foolish and mischievous superstitions all the claims of particular races to innate superiority over others. It will be found in every case that a series of definitely assignable circumstances have permitted or impelled certain races to advance more than others."[139] While there are broad national characteristics in a people, there is nothing metaphysical about them, and they are invariably unjust when applied to indi-viduals. The *Times Literary Supplement's* review of *The Soul of Europe* praised it as "an effective exposure of some prevalent racial fallacies which have done much to pervert the judgment of the public."[140] A decade and a half later, in the *Key to Culture*, McCabe enlarged on the question of national character, and con-cluded that "all our inferences from our typical judgments of the Frenchman, the German, the Irishman, etc, are most likely to be unjust to individuals."[141] It was not until 1940 that the next popular criticism of notions of national character was made available to English-speaking readers. The book, *The Illusion of National Character*, by a left-wing British journalist, Hamilton Fyfe, was a crit-ical success. McCabe is not mentioned in it.

It was one thing to smite humbug about national character of fellow Euro-peans, but, as we have seen, McCabe also praised the moral condition of Chi-nese and Japanese cultures. This was during the heyday of the yellow peril fear. He noted in 1905 that while Europeans "are timidly discussing the feasibility of training our boys and girls on a purely human basis, we find that it has been done successfully in China for 2,500 years and in Japan for several centuries." McCabe warmly admired that the notion of the *chun tzu*, or gentleman, is "a practical standard, and has been realized by millions, not by a few ascetic saints."[142] We saw that in 1910 McCabe recommended the morality and honesty of the Chi-nese to an unreceptive New Zealand audience. He constantly attacked racial stereotypes such as the "unprogressive Chinese."[143] In 1932 he made what would then have been the startling prediction that China would be one of the most formidable economies by the end of the century.[144]

McCabe also did much to share his admiration for much of Arabic culture. For instance, he once described Abd al Rahman III as the "greatest maker of civilization since Pericles." He thought the century from 661 to 750 C.E. to be a period when Arabic leaders made "almost unrivalled progress in civilization."[145] His most sustained treatment of this theme came in *The Splendor of Moorish Spain*, published by Watts in 1935. McCabe described with real admiration the paved streets and sewerage facilities, the higher level of religious tolerance, education, and social idealism than anywhere in Europe at the time. In one of his popular books, he concluded that the Moors were the "chief source of inspiration in directing the use of the new wealth and resources of Europe."[146]

But, as we have already acknowledged, it would be inaccurate to claim McCabe was not without any racist views. He was not *that* far ahead of his time. McCabe thought in terms of higher and lower races, but continually insisted that "higher" and "lower" were measured by the state of a people's culture, which in turn was determined by the sorts of contacts with other cultures a people enjoyed, which in turn was determined by their physical environment. The clue to understanding the stagnation of the "lower types" was their physical isolation. "Isolation," McCabe wrote, "is therefore the clue to lack of progress—not inferiority of race, or blood, or germ-plasm, or religion, or climate, etc—and we look for our lowest peoples in isolated spots."[147] In another context, while writing about the evolution of religion, McCabe made the same point. "Our lowest people—that is to say, our least progressive peoples—were found in islands and central forests, or at the tips of continents."[148]

What this isolation produced was varying levels of "ineducability." He was more openly racist when discussing races who "prove entirely ineducable," as he suspected was the case with the Australian aborigines. The degree of educability was in direct proportion to the level of stagnation and isolation a people had suffered from. It is important to emphasize that in none of his writings did he declare any race to be incorrigibly ineducable, which would be tantamount to a declaration of inferiority. In the case of the aborigines, McCabe was specific in *suspecting* them to prove ineducable. He never went further than that. He specifically excluded Africans from such a suspicion of ineducability. And recall that he sympathized with his ancient philosopher, who he imagined suspecting the same was true of white-skinned peoples. He warned against dogmatism in this area. "Nothing but candid and careful experience will show which races are educable and which ineducable."[149]

This notion of "educability" was not peculiar either to McCabe or to rationalists in general. What was unusual in his treatment was the absence of apocalyptic fervor in his dealing with the subject. Writing in the *Outline of Christianity*, Basil Mathews, a prominent Anglican theologian, described the "race problem" as fundamental, "and it is fundamental simultaneously in the fields of ethnology, sociology, biology, psychology, economics, ethics, and religion. Geographically world-wide in its range, if affects the future of the life of men in every continent." Like McCabe, Mathews saw education as an important part of the solution, but his notion of education sounds more like indoctrination. Mathews wanted religious education, by which he insisted he did *not* mean education about religion but education with a religious aim. "To this end the co-operation of the scholarship, experience, and executive leadership of Christendom is essential."[150] So while theologians like Mathews saw the race problem only being solved by the systematic imposition of Christianity among subject peoples, McCabe counseled a cautious wait-and-see approach, leaving the initiative to the peoples in question.

Even when making an observation that would not now pass muster, he had a habit of ironically subverting its intention. He was aware of the injustice of claims to superiority—even when he was making them. For instance, in 1929 he noted that a visitor to an Eskimo village "tried to explain to them that there was a war amongst the superior white folk. He did not succeed in getting them to understand what a war is."[151] Twenty-two years later, and even more cryptically, McCabe noted that those "we call our 'savages'—many of them find it difficult to understand our wars, atom bombs, and poison sprays—are prehistoric men."[152]

So, while McCabe did think in terms of higher and lower levels of civilization, he was far ahead of many of his contemporaries in not ascribing these differences to congenital differences. For races, as with classes, education and uninhibited contact between peoples was the key to progress. McCabe's views contrast very favorably with the attitudes of many of his contemporaries, particularly when one remembers that McCabe was writing for, and depended for his living from, the general reader. He shared with H. G. Wells a sense of shared humanity. McCabe was a man of his time in that he continually spoke of "the race," but he was ahead of his time in that he always meant the human race.

POPULARIZER OF SCIENCE

It is important to recognize just how skilful a reader of scientific trends McCabe was. We have seen him avoid pitfalls that ensnared the established academics of the time—many of whom also were not above sneering at popularizers like McCabe. We have already mentioned the case of McCabe's handling of the evolution of the horse, but there is more evidence of McCabe's shrewd eye. Two examples will suffice. Regarding Piltdown Man, for example, McCabe was admirably circumspect. It is a standard jibe at rationalists that they were uncritically keen to press-gang this controversial discovery into the service of evolution. And it was not until the very last months of McCabe's life that the skull found at Piltdown in Sussex was proved conclusively to have been a fraud. The Piltdown skull was found in fact to be a relatively recent human skull and the jaw of an even more recent orangutan, the teeth of which had been filed down by hand.

McCabe was always skeptical about Piltdown Man, and he conveyed his skepticism to his readers in his works. For instance, in 1922, he thought it "difficult to believe that such a jaw was associated with a 'modern' type of brain." "I do not think," he wrote prophetically, "that the last word of science has yet been said on the subject of Piltdown man."[153] McCabe came to relax his guard on Piltdown Man a little, under the influence of Sir E. Ray Lankester and Sir Arthur Keith. Lankester (1847–1929), a distinguished zoologist and honorary associate of the RPA, had originally been skeptical, but became an enthusiastic advocate of Piltdown Man. Even so, as late as 1948 McCabe's gut skepticism is still evident. In his entry on Piltdown Man in the *Rationalist Encyclopedia* he noted that the Piltdown skull "is in some respects very ape-like, and in others akin to the modern type. Sir Arthur Keith thinks that the race may have been ancestral to Modern Man."[154] Hardly a ringing endorsement.

Another example of McCabe's skill as a popularizer is his treatment of the celebrated neo-Darwinian synthesis. Richard Dawkins has emphasized the central role of R. A. Fisher in effecting what is now known as the neo-Darwinian synthesis of Darwinian natural selection with Mendelian particulate heredity.[155] And Julian Huxley is usually given credit for taking the lead in bringing this synthesis to the world's attention in his 1942 landmark *Evolution: The Modern Synthesis*. While Huxley's work was an important milestone, it is only fair to note that McCabe recognized the importance of Fisher's synthesis in 1934, only four years after Fisher himself had made it known. In fact, he had recognized the complementarity of Mendelism and Darwinism in 1931.[156]

In *The Riddle of the Universe Today* McCabe told his nonspecialist readers that the new position Fisher's work had created was that "the principles of the science of genetics are to be associated with Darwin's principle of explaining evolution." McCabe explained that "while Darwin attributed the modification of species to the accumulation of very small changes, it was really due to larger changes or 'mutations.' It has been found, Dr Fisher says, that these are of very little importance, and that evolution rests upon 'exceedingly minute' variations due to changes in the genes."[157] This is popular science at its very best.

McCabe also comes across as remarkably ahead of his time in his recognition of the need to expose the underhand tricks of opponents of evolution, people now known as creationists. In a short pamphlet put out by Watts in 1925, McCabe noted that creationists "invariably represent to their readers that Evolution is *disputed in science*."[158] This, McCabe correctly pointed out, is not the case. To illustrate his point, he listed twenty-two men commonly cited by creationists of his day as scientists opposed to evolution. It transpired that (a) of the scientists who were so identified, most had died many years previously, before current levels of evidence were to hand; (b) they were not scientists at all, and had degrees from unaccredited American theological colleges; or (c) they were evolutionists who had concerns about aspects of Darwinism as the best explanation of evolution.[159] How little creationist tactics have changed! One of the authorities most frequently named by opponents of evolution was William Bateson, a strong anti-Darwinian but nonetheless a convinced Mendelian evolutionist. Sixty years later Richard Dawkins had to make the very same complaint about misrepresentation of Bateson's views.[160]

McCabe came up against this tactic in a debate on evolution with the American creationist George McCready Price in September 1925. Price was a Seventh Day Adventist lecturer at a sectarian college in the United States. The debate was held in London, only days before McCabe left for the United States, where he gave more than forty lectures. In the wake of the infamous Scopes monkey trial, this was the topic of the hour on both sides of the Atlantic. Price also anticipated another notorious creationist tactic; that of making the most of various difficulties in evolutionary theory without at any time demonstrating his beliefs were any more sound. Showing more honesty that his creationist successors, Price at least acknowledged that this is what he was doing. He was reduced to making the (unfulfilled) promise that "within two years at the most you will see a very great change in public opinion here in England, as there is in America at the present time."[161]

A couple of years later, McCabe commented that when "you read that some professor or other has said that Darwinism or Natural Selection is 'dead,' you simply have one of those dogmatic and quite improper statements of which I have complained. No popularizer of science has even done half of the harm that some of the experts have done in recent years."[162] That observation also rings true beyond McCabe's time.

We can finish this chapter with the conclusion that McCabe was a gifted and responsible popularizer of evolution to nonspecialist readers. Despite being entirely self-taught, he avoided nearly all the fashionable errors of his day and gave his readers sensible, balanced, and reliable overviews on evolution. His books anticipated current ideas on evolution by two generations. And with one exception, McCabe never claimed to be anything more than a "camp follower" of science. The exception was his claim (made rather half-heartedly) that the ice ages exercised a stimulating effect on human evolution.[163]

Without doubt he towers above most contemporary postmodernists who have ventured to make comment on scientific affairs. Alan Sokal and Jean Bricmont have studied the scientific and mathematical understanding of leading French postmodernists and fellow-travelers and found that these people did not really know what they were talking about. Their use of scientific terminology was either incorrect or, more often, meaningless in the context, or they had simply invented new, entirely meaningless pseudoscientific terms, presumably to lend their work some of the credibility it would otherwise not enjoy.[164] The contrast with McCabe is stark. He employed virtually no jargon at all, and certainly didn't invent pseudoscientific terms. He was making absolutely no attempt to obfuscate or muddy otherwise clear waters. He wanted the general reader to understand science and to appreciate its majestic beauty. "I am going to try to tell the story," he said at the beginning of *The Marvels of Modern Physics*, "in such language that you can sit by the fire, or lie by the river, and read it."[165] McCabe deserves to be linked with Isaac Asimov and Carl Sagan as among the most intelligent, acute, and lucid popularizers of science of the twentieth century.

NOTES

1. Bryan Appleyard, *Understanding the Present: Science and the Soul of Modern Man* (London: QPD, 1992), p. 9. Interestingly, Appleyard employs the *advocatus diaboli* approach to science that the later McCabe did against the Catholic Church. Appleyard makes no apologies that his history will be seen by many as biased, given the number of works opposing his views.

2. Joseph McCabe, *1825–1925: A Century of Stupendous Progress* (London: Watts, 1925), p. 194.

3. Joseph McCabe, *The Religion of Woman: An Historical Study* (London: Watts, 1905), p. 90.

4. Raymond Tallis, *Enemies of Hope: A Critique of Contemporary Pessimism* (New York: St. Martin's Press, 1997), p. 224. Tallis's book also provides a thorough critique of Appleyard.

5. Frank Ballard, *Haeckel's Monism False* (London: Charles H. Kelly, 1905), p. 428.

6. Joseph McCabe and Rev. C. J. Shebbeare, *The Design Argument Reconsidered* (London: Watts, 1923), p. 14.

7. Joseph McCabe, *The Twilight of the Gods* (London: Watts, 1923), p. 56.

8. Joseph McCabe, *Haeckel's Critics Answered* (London: Watts, 1903), p. 28.

9. Joseph McCabe, *Key to Culture* (Girard, Kan.: Haldeman-Julius, 1927–29), vol. 35, p. 44.

10. Joseph McCabe, *Can We Save Civilization?* (London: The Search, 1932), p. 138.

11. K. R. Popper, *The Open Society and its Enemies*, (London & New York: Routledge & Kegan Paul, 1963), vol. 1, p. 286.

12. Joseph McCabe, *The New Science and the Story of Evolution* (London: Hutchinson, 1931), p. 44.

13. Joseph McCabe, *The Wonders of the Stars* (London: Watts/Putnams, 1923), pp. 75–76.

14. Joseph McCabe, *The Riddle of the Universe Today* (London: Watts, 1934), p. 7.

15. Joseph McCabe, *Ice Ages: The Story of the Earth's Revolutions* (London: Watts/Putnams, 1922), pp. 46–47.

16. Joseph McCabe, *The Next Fifty Years* (Girard, Kan.: Haldeman-Julius, 1950), p. 88.

17. I owe this insight to Raymond Tallis's excellent and doughty defense of science, *Enemies of Hope*, p. 134.

18. McCabe, *Ice Ages*, p. 78.

19. *Literary Guide* (June 1918): 82.

20. John Hedley Brooke, *Science and Religion* (Cambridge: Cambridge University Press, 1993), pp. 4–5, 35–45, 282.

21. Joseph McCabe, *The Religion of Sir Oliver Lodge* (London: Watts, 1914), p. 2.

22. Joseph McCabe, *The Bankruptcy of Religion* (London: Watts, 1917), p. 100.

23. *Doctrine in the Church of England*, quoted in McCabe, *The Passing of Heaven and Hell* (London: Watts, 1938), p. 36. McCabe italicized the word "educated" for effect.

24. McCabe, *The Bankruptcy of Religion*, p. 40.

25. McCabe, *The Religion of Sir Oliver Lodge*, p. 11.

26. Joseph McCabe, *The Story of Religious Controversy* (Boston: Stratford, 1929), p. 86.

27. Antony Flew, *An Introduction to Western Philosophy* (London: Thames & Hudson, 1971), pp. 180–81.

28. McCabe, *The Riddle of the Universe Today*, p. 3.

29. Joseph McCabe, *The Existence of God*, Inquirer's Library, no. 1 (London: Watts, 1913), p. 71.

30. See Alan Sokal and Jean Bricmont, *Fashionable Nonsense: Postmodern Intellectuals' Abuse of Science* (New York: Picador, 1998), for a brilliant critique of this practice.

31. McCabe, *The Story of Religious Controversy*, p. 553.

32. Joseph McCabe, *Crises in the History of the Papacy* (London: Putnams/Watts, 1916), p. 352.

33. Keith Clements, *Lovers of Discord: Twentieth Century Theological Controversies in England* (London: SCM, 1988), p. 132.

34. McCabe, *The Bankruptcy of Religion*, pp. 70–76.

35. Paul Kurtz, *In Defense of Secular Humanism* (Amherst, N.Y.: Prometheus Books, 1983), p. 122.

36. H. James Birx, *Interpreting Evolution* (Amherst, N.Y.: Prometheus Books, 1991), p. 24.

37. Carl Sagan, *The Demon-Haunted World* (London: Headline, 1996), p. 264.

38. Antony Flew, *Darwinian Evolution* (London: Paladin, 1984), pp. 67, 97.

39. Richard Dawkins, *The Blind Watchmaker* (London: Longman, 1986), p. 6.

40. Alfred Kelly, *The Descent of Darwin* (Chapel Hill: University of North Carolina Press, 1981), p. 11.

41. See Mary Midgley, *Science as Salvation* (London: Routledge, 1994).

42. Joseph McCabe, *Eighty Years a Rebel* (Girard, Kan.: Haldeman-Julius, 1947), p. 40.

43. Michael Ruse, *Taking Darwin Seriously* (Oxford: Basil Blackwell, 1989), p. xiii.

44. Peter Bowler, *Evolution: The History of an Idea* (Berkeley: University of California Press, 1989), especially chap. 9.

45. Frank Ballard, *Haeckel's Monism False*, p. 268.

46. Hilaire Belloc, *A Companion to Mr. Wells's "Outline of History"* (London: Sheed & Ward, 1929), p. 26.

47. Bowler, *Evolution*, p. 285. This is ignored by contemporary "creationists," who prefer to lay these and many other demons at the feet of Darwinism.

48. McCabe, *The Story of Religious Controversy*, p. 98.

49. This passage is quoted from McCabe, *The New Science and the Story of Evolu-*

tion (London: Hutchinson, 1931), p. 63, but could equally have come from *The Story of Evolution*, p. 60.

50. McCabe, *Key to Culture*, vol. 35, p. 22.

51. McCabe, *The New Science and the Story of Evolution*, p. 247.

52. Ernst Mayr, *One Long Argument: Charles Darwin and the Genesis of Modern Evolutionary* Thought (London: Penguin, 1993), p. 162.

53. McCabe, *The Riddle of the Universe Today*, pp. 18, 110.

54. McCabe, *The New Science and the Story of Evolution*, p. 63.

55. McCabe, *The Story of Evolution*, pp. 104–105.

56. Joseph McCabe, *Goethe: The Man and His Character* (London: Eveleigh Nash, 1912), p. 268.

57. McCabe, *Ice Ages*, pp. 9–10.

58. Joseph McCabe, *The Principles of Evolution* (London & Glasgow: Collins, 1913), pp. 207–208.

59. Joseph McCabe, *The Evolution of Civilization* (London: Watts, 1921), pp. 22, 23.

60. Joseph McCabe, *A History of Human Morals* (Girard, Kan.: Haldeman-Julius, 1931), vol. 12, p. 39.

61. McCabe, *Can We Save Civilization?*, 164–65.

62. Joseph McCabe, *The Tyranny of Shams* (London: Eveleigh Nash/Dodd Mead, 1916), p. 69.

63. Ibid.

64. McCabe, *The New Science and the Story of Evolution*, p. 247.

65. McCabe, *The Passing of Heaven and Hell*, p. 7.

66. Joseph McCabe, "Emergent Evolution," in *A Rationalist Encyclopedia* (London: Watts, 1948), p. 183.

67. *Freethinker* (May 27, 1934): 329–30. This is one of the only books by McCabe that the *Freethinker* reviewed after the Edwardian years.

68. See, for example, E. O. Wilson talking about emergence minus the mysticism in Roger Lewin, *Complexity: Life on the Edge of Chaos* (London: Phoenix, 1995), p. 177.

69. Joseph McCabe, *Science Yesterday, Today, and Tomorrow* (London: Herbert Jenkins, 1927), p. 76.

70. Ibid., p. 77.

71. McCabe, *Can We Save Civilization?*, p. 131.

72. McCabe, *A History of Human Morals*, vol. 12, p. 40.

73. See McCabe, *A History of Human Morals*, vol. 12, p. 39; Peter Bowler, *The Non-Darwinian Revolution* (Baltimore, Md./London: Johns Hopkins University Press, 1992), p. 169.

74. McCabe, *The Tyranny of Shams*, pp. 176–77.

75. McCabe, *Key to Culture*, vol. 12, p. 40.

76. McCabe, "Eugenics" in *The Rationalist Encyclopedia*, p. 196.

77. Dawkins, *The Blind Watchmaker*, p. 261.

78. McCabe, *The Story of Evolution*, p. 25. This is the first McCabe title to be included on the Gutenberg program of books available on the Internet.

79. McCabe, *The Principles of Evolution*, p. 53.

80. Vincent McNabb, *The Catholic Church and Philosophy* (New York: Macmillan, 1927), p. 11.

81. Joseph McCabe, *The ABC of Evolution* (London: Watts, 1920), pp. 5–6.

82. McCabe, *The Story of Evolution*, p. 28.

83. Dawkins, *The Blind Watchmaker*, p. xiv.

84. J. Arthur Thomson, *The Gospel of Evolution* (London: George Newnes, 1926), p. 198.

85. Ballard, *Haeckel's Monism False*, p. 250. Ballard specifically invokes Spencer as his authority for this definition.

86. McCabe, *The Story of Evolution*, p. 61.

87. Ibid., p. 250.

88. See H. G. Wells, Julian Huxley, and G. P. Wells, *The Science of Life* (London: Cassell, 1931), pp. 207–208.

89. McCabe, *The New Science and the Story of Evolution*, p. 300.

90. McCabe, *The Story of Evolution*, p. 307.

91. McCabe, *The Principles of Evolution*, p. 229.

92. McCabe, *The Twilight of the Gods*, p. 73.

93. McCabe, *The New Science and the Story of Evolution*, p. 299.

94. E. O. Wilson, *Consilience: The Unity of Knowledge* (London: Little, Brown, 1998), p. 295.

95. Richard C. Vitzhum, *Materialism: An Affirmative History and Definition* (Amherst, N.Y.: Prometheus Books, 1995), p. 19.

96. Ernst Haeckel, *The Riddle of the Universe* (London: Watts, 1900), p. 21.

97. McCabe, *Haeckel's Critics Answered*, p. 20.

98. Ibid., p. 93.

99. Joseph McCabe, "Sir Oliver Lodge on Haeckel," *Hibbert Journal* 3 (1905): 753.

100. McCabe, *The Bankruptcy of Religion*, p. 205.

101. McCabe, *The Twilight of the Gods*, p. 88.

102. McCabe, *A Rationalist Encyclopedia*, pp. 381–82.

103. Nicholas Humphrey, *The Natural History of the Mind* (London: Chatto & Windus, 1992), p. 4.

104. Margaret Wertheim, *The Pearly Gates of Cyberspace* (Auckland: Doubleday, 1999), p. 37.

105. McCabe, *The Existence of God*, p. 75.

106. McCabe, *The Religion of Sir Oliver Lodge*, p. 85.

107. McCabe, *The Existence of God*, p. 74; *The Wonders of the Stars*, p. 106.

108. Haeckel, *The Riddle of the Universe*, pp. 230–34.

109. McCabe, *The Wonders of the Stars*, p. 105.

110. McCabe, *The Marvels of Modern Physics*, pp. 58–59.

111. Ibid., p. 37.

112. Ibid., p. 110.

113. McCabe, *The ABC of Evolution*, p. 18; and *The Marvels of Modern Physics* (London: Watts/Putnams, 1925), p. 114.

114. McCabe, *The Marvels of Modern Physics*, p. 11.

115. Vitzhum, *Materialism*, p. 206.

116. Joseph McCabe, *How Atomic Energy Will Affect Your Life and Future* (Girard, Kan.: Haldeman-Julius, 1946), p. 12.

117. McCabe, *The Story of Religious Controversy*, p. 593.

118. McCabe, *The Religion of Sir Oliver Lodge*, p. 55.

119. Vitzhum, *Materialism*, p. 106.

120. Ibid., p. 206.

121. McCabe, *The Riddle of the Universe Today*, p. 122.

122. Ballard, *Haeckel's Monism False*, p. 247.

123. *Literary Guide* (June 1918): 82. McCabe is referring to the French philosopher Henri Bergson (1859–1941) whose influential book *Creative Evolution* (1911) introduced the vitalist principle to the world. McCabe had originally raised this objection in *The Evolution of Mind* (London: Adam & Charles Black, 1910), p. 152.

124. Joseph McCabe, *The Inferiority Complex Eliminated* (Girard, Kan.: Haldeman-Julius, 1940), p. 106.

125. For further treatment of this issue, see Donald B. Calne, *Within Reason: Rationality and Human Behaviour* (New York: Pantheon, 1999), pp. 231–32.

126. McCabe, *The Evolution of Mind*, p. 234.

127. Ibid., pp. 197–98.

128. Joseph McCabe, *The Origin and Meaning of Ideas* (Girard, Kan.: Haldeman-Julius, 1951), p. 19.

129. See Sir Arthur Keith, *A New Theory of Human Evolution* (London: Watts, 1950).

130. Letter from McCabe to Jack Benjamin, March 10, 1939. I am grateful to Mike Lloyd-Jones—again—for this insight.

131. C. E. M Joad, *Shaw* (London: Victor Gollancz, 1949), pp. 167–68.

132. McCabe, *Key to Culture*, vol. 11, p. 26.

133. McCabe, *The Evolution of Civilization*, p. 72.

134. Daniel Gasman, *The Scientific Origins of National Socialism* (London/New York: Macdonald & American Elsevier, 1971), p. 40.

135. McCabe, *The Principles of Evolution*, p. 204; *Ice Ages*, p. 99.

136. McCabe, *The Tyranny of Shams*, p. 107.

137. Ibid., pp. 69–70.

138. McCabe, *The New Science and the Story of Evolution*, p. 292.

139. McCabe, *The Story of Evolution*, p. 382.

140. *Times Literary Supplement* (August 19, 1915): 274.

141. McCabe, *Key to Culture*, vol. 35, p. 53.

142. McCabe, *The Religion of Woman*, p. 72.

143. McCabe, *The New Science and the Story of Evolution*, p. 291.

144. McCabe, *Can We Save Civilization?*, p. 55.

145. Joseph McCabe, *The Rise and Fall of the Gods* (Girard, Kan.: Haldeman-Julius, 1931), vol. 4, pp. 21–24.

146. Joseph McCabe, *The Social Record of Christianity*, The Thinker's Library, no. 51 (London: Watts, 1935), p. 80.

147. McCabe, *Key to Culture*, vol 11, p. 13. See also *The Evolution of Mind*, p. xi.

148. Joseph McCabe, *The Growth of Religion* (London: Watts, 1918), p. 167.

149. McCabe, *The Tyranny of Shams*, p. 69.

150. Basil Mathews, "The Race Problem," in *The Outline of Christianity*, ed. A. S. Peake and R. G. Parsons (London: Waverley, 1930), vol. 5, pp. 214–22.

151. McCabe, *Key to Culture*, vol. 11, p. 44.

152. McCabe, *The Origin and Meaning of Ideas*, p. 24.

153. McCabe, *Ice Ages*, p. 98.

154. McCabe, *A Rationalist Encyclopedia*, p. 452.

155. Dawkins, *The Blind Watchmaker*, p. 305.

156. McCabe, *The New Science and the Story of Evolution*, p. 104.

157. McCabe, *The Riddle of the Universe Today*, p. 114.

158. McCabe, *The Triumph of Evolution*, p. 9. See also *The Story of Religious Contro-versy*, pp. 554–55.

159. McCabe, *The Triumph of Evolution*, pp. 10–15.

160. Dawkins, *The Blind Watchmaker*, p. 305.

161. Frank Harris et al., *Debates on the Meaning of Life, Evolution, and Spiritualism* (Amherst, NY: Prometheus Books, 1993), p. 139.

162. McCabe, *Key to Culture*, vol. 5, p. 50.

163. McCabe, *Eighty Years a Rebel*, p. 41.

164. See Sokal and Bricmont, *Fashionable Nonsense: Postmodern Intellectuals' Abuse of Science*.

165. McCabe, *The Marvels of Modern Physics*, p. 3.

6

Edwardian Feminist
Gender, Politics, and Sex

Having followed McCabe through several chapters of grueling hard work and severe scholarship, all driven by an overwhelming sense of duty, one could be forgiven for thinking this man somewhat one-dimensional. Indeed, I have called him a barely reconstructed puritan. This is true, but not in the popular sense of puritanism being a misanthropic loathing of pleasure, particularly sexual pleasure. McCabe was puritanical in his sense of duty and his respect for learning, which manifested itself in the form of his unquenchable desire to educate, enlighten, and smite humbug. But by no means was McCabe puritanical in the sense of being hostile to all forms of sensuality. Far from it. On matters of gender, relationships, and sexuality, McCabe was an Epicurean.

We followed in chapter 2 his conflict with the RPA over his advanced views on sexuality. McCabe was proud to be one of the very first male supporters of women's suffrage. Early on in his career, when such moves were risky, he donated his pen to the cause by writing two books on the question of the rights and status of women: *The Religion of Woman* (1905) and *Woman in Political Evolution* (1909). He then summarized his views in his *The Tyranny of Shams* (1916). He campaigned actively for the women's movement while sojourned in New York in 1917. McCabe quarreled with some of the more radical members of the movement in England and was not invited to take part in the victory celebrations in 1918 when women finally won the franchise. He continued to advocate the rights of women for the rest of his life.

As always, it is important to be familiar with the sort of views that were common in McCabe's day, in order to appreciate fully the significance of what today seem like relatively commonplace observations. Even the progressive circles in which McCabe moved were reticent, and occasionally downright hostile, to the idea of the equality of women. We need not look far for examples. It would have irked McCabe that even among fellow rationalists could he find the most unconsidered nonsense. For example, one of the lesser rationalists, W. Nicol Reid, wrote a short work in 1924 called *The Supremacy of Reason*. Here we are told that women rarely make any intellectual advance except under male guidance; the reason for this being that women suffer from lower levels of initiative and sense of proportion that men enjoy.[1]

A more extreme example can be found in the influential book *Sex and Character*, written in 1903 by Otto Weininger, an unstable Austrian misogynist and anti-Semite. Weininger was convinced of the worthlessness of everything except the products of genius. Sexuality, in particular, was incompatible with the single-mindedness that genius requires. Weininger committed suicide in Vienna in 1903, aged twenty-three. *Sex and Character* was to become a lifelong source of inspiration for Ludwig Wittgenstein.[2] While Wittgenstein, thought by many to be the greatest mind of the twentieth century, was deeply influenced by Weininger, Joseph McCabe, forgotten and unlamented, dismissed Weininger's work as "drivel."[3]

Among the Christian apologists McCabe contended with, Charles Loring Brace (who we dealt with in chapter 4) had much to say on Christianity and the status of women. "Whatever position woman holds in civilized society is clearly a fruit of Christianity." Brace shuddered at the prospect of the "evil chance" of agnosticism becoming the creed of the world. Such an eventuality would see "woman become but as a weaker fellow-animal, with no especial respect encircling her, and perhaps will herself lose the purity and sanctity of so much reverence."[4] McCabe recognized that the cocoon of purity and sanctity was as much a shackle as a protection.

But perhaps no better example can be found than McCabe's old bête noire, G. K. Chesterton, the man who saw in McCabe all that he disliked most about modern society. Less extreme than Weininger, more whimsical than Reid, Chesterton contrasted the romantic heroine and the sensible wife. "The essence of the romantic heroine is that she asks herself an intense question; but the essence of the sensible wife is that she is much too sensible to ask herself any questions at all."[5] It may well have been McCabe who Chesterton had in mind when he noted that "it is a bad thing in sociology that men should deify domesticity in girls as something dainty and magical; but all men do. Personally, I do not think it a bad thing at all. . . ."[6] Chesterton carried the same glib superficiality of George Bernard Shaw, and few people got under McCabe's skin more than these two.

McCabe's attitudes toward women underwent a very rapid development after his secession from the church. In the year after his departure, his few references to women suggest a conventional stereotyping. Toward the end of *Twelve*

Years in a Monastery, McCabe laments the absence of "the sex which is, by instinct and education, more refined, and exercises a refining influence."[7] This sort of stereotyping disappears very quickly after that.

McCabe's first two works directly concerned with feminism, *The Religion of Woman* and *Woman in Political Evolution*, were principally historical accounts of the subjection of women, and were designed to counter the claims of apologists like Brace. Neither book suggests an unduly radical attitude toward sexuality itself, which first became apparent in his 1916 work, *The Tyranny of Shams*. This book earned him considerable notoriety, lost him friends, and was the turning point in McCabe's career as an up-and-coming intellectual sanctioned, or at least tolerated, by the establishment. It also confirmed the fears of some of McCabe's Rationalist colleagues that he was a liability. It is not difficult to see why. McCabe devoted relatively little space to the franchise. The arguments against it were so specious that victory here was only a matter of time. The cardinal issue, as he put it, was the economic position of women within marriage.[8] McCabe drew attention to the marriage vow "With all my worldly goods I thee endow," and insisted that this must mean something more than that the wife "shall have chocolates and pretty dresses *if* they humor the moods of a husband."[9] Too many marriages were run on the grossly unequal basis of the wife taking what the husband chooses to give her. McCabe's commonsense solution? See the wife's contribution as equal to the family welfare and pool all income as common income, managed in joint accounts. Many families already operated in this manner, he observed, with no noticeable moral decay ensuing as a result.

McCabe also took the next step, which was to recognize that many marriages are beyond rescuing, and that more liberal divorce laws would also be a boon to women. Divorce law reform was almost as significant and divisive an issue before the First World War as extending the franchise to women. As with most issues McCabe concerned himself with, his most lasting achievement was to produce a book on the subject. In *The Influence of the Church on Marriage and Divorce*, published in 1916, McCabe sought to provide a historical background to the notion of marriage as a sacrament and therefore indissoluble. He wanted his readers to see the tragic consequences of indissoluble marriage and to see divorce law reform as the humane alternative.

But McCabe went further than this when he predicted the day—he thought it would happen by the end of the twentieth century—when women could opt not to marry at all, if they chose, while remaining sexually active. There would be in every city "a growth of temporary unions and independent conduct. Woman will be mistress, morally and economically, of her own destiny; she will consult neither husband nor priest."[10] Far from bringing forth a moral apocalypse, as some Christian moralists predicted (then and now), it would, apart from being just in its own right, reduce significantly the many hypocrisies the old system required in order to function: the resort to prostitution, the pinched and lonely lives of countless thousand spinsters, and the tyranny of stupid men.

So vital was hypocrisy to the effective working of the old system that he at one stage he suggested we "call the Christian Era the Era of Hypocrisy."[11]

THE KEY TO LOVE AND SEX

The world of 1916 was almost ready to hear about unjust divorce laws, and injustices to women. But it certainly was *not* ready to hear the virtues of stable sexual relations between adults outside of marriage, let alone that this option might be a perfectly reasonable choice for a woman to make. Not surprisingly, McCabe's radicalism ended up pleasing nobody. His message didn't please conservatives and ecclesiastics for obvious reasons, and the socialist movement was divided and ambivalent on the question. Neither were some of McCabe's Rationalist colleagues pleased, because they were anxious about the negative effect these radical ideas would have on the broader program. Ever since the days of Bradlaugh and Holyoake, the Rationalist movement had been careful not to offend majority opinion on marriage. This is not surprising, given the puritan roots of rationalism. But neither did McCabe's radical message please the suffragists, many of whom had adopted an antisex puritanism as part of the language of liberation. And, as we have already noted, he had split with the radicals of the feminist movement because he disagreed on the trend toward violent protest.

It is characteristic of McCabe that, despite this subject having been nothing but trouble for him, he returned to it as soon as he got the opportunity. Within months of his break with the RPA, McCabe developed his views on gender and sexuality in his most comprehensive study of the subject. Within a little over a year of his rift with the RPA, he had written an eight-volume work for Haldeman-Julius, called *The Key to Love and Sex*. This extraordinary work was a compendium of current thinking on sexuality, a history of attitudes toward issues such as chastity and the proper role of women, a defense of sensuality, and a popular manual for the intelligent and curious. It is not unlikely that it was Haldeman-Julius, ever the shrewd purveyor of popular literature, who suggested the topic; the title was certainly his.[12] Either way, McCabe launched enthusiastically into the project. *The Key to Love and Sex*, like so many of McCabe's works, is similar to other, better-known books that appeared at the same time. In this case, the chief parallel example is, of course, Bertrand Russell's *Marriage and Morals* (1929). The two works are indeed similar, although McCabe began his work about a year before Russell's more famous work was published, and includes a lot more historical analysis. It is also more radical.

The main development in *The Key to Love and Sex* from his earlier works was the extra attention he devoted to sex itself. McCabe was enthusiastic about the role sex should play in a fully rounded life. *The Key to Love and Sex* was his most comprehensive attempt at outlining a modern view of Epicureanism. But before examining this remarkable publication, it is important to look again at

McCabe's views on marriage and divorce, because it is these opinions that constitute the main link between the *Key to Love and Sex* and his previous works. We have already seen that McCabe did not see marriage as the only legitimate place where sexual relations may be enjoyed. He was also alive to the repressive history of the marriage institution. As can be expected, he had no time for the Christian argument for marriage as a sacrament, noting that it was not officially made a sacrament until the Council of Trent. The only specifically Christian contributions to the idea of marriage were the notions that even within marriage, sexual intercourse was a distasteful practice, and the strict ban on divorce, except on grounds of adultery.[13] In McCabe's view, the only uniquely Christian contributions to the notion of marriage were the least helpful contributions.

However, McCabe was not opposed to marriage. He saw marriage, at its best, as "enriching life with generous and distinctive emotions."[14] His main point is that it should be one option among several for people to choose from. Marriage, McCabe stressed, is one option, and, when chosen freely, as good an option as any. But on no account is it the only option in which sexual relations are legitimate. Sex, in other words, was perfectly justifiable as a simple leisure pursuit. He looked forward to the day when we should all find "the thrill of sexual contact one of the most really ennobling and humanizing emotions in a rich and harmonious life . . . one in which every warm caress of sense and sex will be found consistent with the highest and wisest pursuit of thought."[15] He cited Goethe as his exemplar: "He was a great lover and a profound thinker, a great artist and a distinguished student of science, a sensualist and a statesman. He was, in other words, a beyond-man in the sense that he rose serenely above all the blunders and hypocrisies of modern times and equally enjoyed every pleasure of sense, sex, and intelligence."[16] Contrary to one of the most enduring prejudices about rationalists, McCabe eschewed notions of the inferiority of sex in relation to pleasures of the intellect. More shocking still, he declared "as one of the fundamental principles with which we approach the study of sex, that the pleasure associated with it does not need to be hallowed either by love or by the procreation of children."[17] It was entirely moral for sex to be a straightforward leisure pursuit.

McCabe devoted large parts of *The Key to Love and Sex* to the criticism of the many prejudices, misconceptions, and sentimentalisms then common currency about women, such as those we outlined above. It is wrong, for instance, that men have larger brains than women. He was also critical of current thinkers such as Havelock Ellis, who noted the lesser aptitude for science among females. McCabe pointed out that while psychologists were tabulating these apparent differences, "the young are themselves rapidly altering the situation. Sport, athletics, and new ideas are reducing all these differences. I have already pointed out that, while the girl is said to be poor at science, it is particularly in science (medicine, mathematics, economics, etc) that young women are now distinguishing themselves."[18]

There are few better examples of McCabe being ahead of his time than when he declared that it is "to a very great extent the male who has created what in our modern civilization we call the 'typical woman,' and we then call every woman unnatural and unwomanly who diverges from it."[19] McCabe made related points in other publications as well, such as *The Inferiority Complex Eliminated*, where he noted that the oft-repeated maxim that women are more intuitive than men was explained more readily by women "having been excluded for centuries from the mental interests of men. . . ."[20] He was even prepared to address the beloved popular prejudices about blondes, assuring his readers that there is no substance to such beliefs.

A related and equally popular fallacy of the time was the notion that women attend church more regularly than men because they are inherently more religious—and less rational. This goes back to McCabe's first book on gender issues, *The Religion of Woman*, and he added little to this question in his later works. It does, however, illustrate well my claim that McCabe was ahead of his time, and also helps explain why he has been so neglected. Ninety years after McCabe criticized notions of the irrationality and religiosity of women, we read Mary Midgley criticizing that same prejudice, but—not having read McCabe—ascribing it to "Enlightenment misogyny"![21] Worse still, Midgley's complaint came only a few pages after her lamenting the robust health of the Enlightenment-bashing industry. One has to feel sorry for McCabe at this point. In his own time he was criticized for unsettling the ordained bonds of society, while decades later the tradition he represents is criticized for not having done so enough! Truly, these are hard times for rationalists. It has been observed that postmodernism, or at least the French variety, is unconvincing because of its failure to engage seriously with Enlightenment ideas.[22] This is not a problem limited to postmodernists, as the example of Mary Midgley has shown.

Another issue McCabe devoted special attention to was the question of chastity, which he described as "a terrestrial Mussolini." Ever keen for a historical survey, he determined that the origins of chastity as an ideal lay in the supposed uncleanliness of woman, the gradual development of the male claim to ownership of women, and the idea that sacrifice is pleasing to the gods. "The law of chastity, in the double sense, virginity until marriage and fidelity to death after marriage," he concluded, "was imposed on the female."[23] But the very success of this law created a dilemma for men, and gave rise to prostitution, and with it a whole world of suffering and hypocrisy. Worse still was the Christian contempt for sex in any form, while retaining the injunction to increase and multiply. He attacked Christian theology's Eve as a prototype of the sex, seeing it as having brought "immeasurable tragedy on the race."[24] Late in his life, McCabe returned to this question, in a Big Blue Book written for Haldeman-Julius called *The Evolution of the Virtue of Chastity*. McCabe deserves, but of course has not received, recognition for his work over half a century on the question of chastity.

As against the tyranny of chastity, McCabe reiterated the praise of the modern woman he made in *The Tyranny of Shams*. This liberation has been brought about, in no small way, by the development of methods of contraception, which he described as "an important advance of modern times."[25] He derided the moralists' laments of the immorality of the times that contraception had spawned, observing that "the new freedom is not so much a violation of an accepted moral law as a claim that the law does not apply to acts which involve no injustice."[26] Moral law is no more exalted, and no less accessible to change, than any other type of law. He was particularly short with the portentous declarations about the laws of history, the wisdom of the race, the findings of sound science, or the eternal verities of religion. Showing remarkable prescience, McCabe predicted that in a "few more decades, when the battle is won, the Bishop of London of the time will be demonstrating that the reform was anticipated by the Fathers sixteen hundred years ago and was contained, in germ, in the New Testament." We have seen this happen over and over again.

McCabe's argument in *The Key to Love and Sex* is summarized in one sentence. "The revolt of woman against her social, political, and economic subjection on the one hand, and the discovery, on the other, that half of the traditions which have come down to us are false, have led our generation to confront the problem or problems of sex more seriously than they were ever confronted before."[27] This is classic McCabe. Few sentences sum up better McCabe's "project" better than this. After a long era of shams and half-truths, evasions and hypocrisies, largely engendered by false religious teaching and practice, it was time for new knowledge and new practices. McCabe saw his role as supplying that information to the new, freethinking public, keen to build a life for themselves free from misconceptions of the past. As with his views on evolution, some of McCabe's views are themselves now outdated. And no one would have been less surprised by that than McCabe. What is remarkable, though, is how much of his outlook on sexuality and relationships has stood the test of time. In an area that has developed out of all recognition, McCabe was years ahead of his time.

But having followed McCabe's views on the liberation of women, is he not in the danger of being identified as one of the selfish libertines who advocated free love simply in order to get a good time? The most notorious example of this type of man among McCabe's contemporaries is perhaps C. E. M. Joad. Like McCabe, Joad was chiefly a popularizer, although unlike McCabe, he had pretensions to higher things. Joad's longtime acquaintance Kingsley Martin remembered that Joad "made no secret of his success with women and said he was not interested in talking to any woman who wouldn't go to bed with him."[28] S. K. Ratcliffe, in his history of the South Place Ethical Society, commented on Joad's lack of success as a lecturer for that organization, not least because of his pronounced antifeminism.[29]

McCabe was assuredly not of this stamp. He disliked this type of boasting, selfish man.

We all know the type. They care not the toss of a coin about consequences to the woman. . . . Life is full of tragedies caused by selfishness of this sort. There are, therefore, very distinct limits to "free love." Where even the risk of children or of other distressing consequences to the woman is permitted there is very decidedly a moral law for the man, but it has nothing to do with chastity. Fortunately the knowledge of the use of contraceptive methods spreads and these tragedies are gradually becoming less numerous.[30]

Unlike several of the male champions of free love, McCabe was neither selfish, nor hypocritical in his relations with women. But might McCabe have remained a misogynist under the veneer of emancipation rhetoric? Ruth Branden, an English journalist and feminist, wrote a book called *The New Women and the Old Men*, first published in 1990, which examined the gap between the rhetoric and the actions of several men of McCabe's generation. They included H. G. Wells, Havelock Ellis, and Karl Pearson, all of whom we have come across at some stage in this study. Joseph McCabe, of course, was not mentioned. Brandon concluded that most of the men she studied were hypocrites. Each of them considered himself to be in the vanguard of social thinking. "Yet at the core of each of their philosophies the most old-fashioned thinking of all remained untouched. For each of them Woman the Mother reigned supreme." Brandon accused them all of seeing motherhood as the supreme and most fulfilling function a woman could have.[31]

Looking at the example of Havelock Ellis, who, as an authority on the psychology of sex at the time, is the most relevant example in this context, we find that Brandon's accusations are valid. Ellis did favor the emancipation of women, but not because it was a just cause in its own right. "The chief question that we have to ask when we consider the changing status of women is: How will it affect the reproduction of the race?" While Ellis was prepared to permit women the right of choosing not to bear children, he added that "in order to live a humanly complete life, every healthy woman should have, not sexual relationships only, but the exercise of those experiences which only maternity can give."[32] For Havelock Ellis, the woman question was fundamentally a question of eugenics.

Had Ruth Brandon extended her research to include McCabe, she would not have been so quick to sneer at the rationalist men and Darwinism. Had Brandon included McCabe in her studies, she would have been saved from making erroneous generalizations about the sexism she claims to find inherent in evolutionary theory. I think it is reasonable to say that the gap between McCabe's rhetoric and action was minimal. Brandon is also incorrect in her judgment of H. G. Wells, but that is another matter.

McCabe went further than almost all prominent men of his generation in exposing the self-interest inherent in a lot of male talk about women. What particularly attracted McCabe's scorn was the idea, popular among Christian thinkers, that Christianity had performed a great service by surrounding women with the halo of sanctity. A typical example of this is the American apologist C. Loring Brace, whose book *Gesta Christi: A History of Humane Progress Under Christianity* we have already come across a couple of times. As mentioned previously, Brace feared that if agnosticism were to prevail, woman "perhaps will herself lose herself the purity and sanctity which made her under Christianity the object of so much reverence."[33] *Gesta Christi* was a prime example of the superficial propaganda that passed for popular Christian apologetics and that so annoyed McCabe. It was a special target in his 1907 work *The Bible in Europe*. Far from being a great service to women, Christianity had in fact been more of a hindrance. Contrary to the conventional idea that these notions of purity and chastity ennobled women, "she lost, in so far as it was enforced, one of her chief opportunities of equality and became more exposed to the influences which tended to reduce her to submission."[34] McCabe had also visited this theme in *The Influence of the Church on Marriage and Divorce*. McCabe observed that, regarding indissoluble marriage, it

> was chiefly the women who suffered. When a man tired of a wife he could in most villages discover that his marriage was null; otherwise he might accuse her of witchcraft, or, if he were an easy-going man, put her out of doors or sell her in the tavern. Such was woman's lot in the palmy days of a religion which the Bishop of London calls "her best friend."[35]

Anticipating Karen Armstrong by more than seventy years, McCabe said that it was the "teaching of the Fathers that barred the way to the progress of woman's cause in Europe, and this was based on St Paul and the Old Testament."[36] Much of the sanctification and mystification of women was little more than subjection by saintliness.

McCabe was also scornful of another popular sentimentalism that of the "mystery of womanhood." "As to the men themselves, it is rather amusing to reflect that, while the poets have for two thousand years spoken about the impenetrable mystery of womanhood, in real life men have throughout that period insisted on their own superior knowledge of what she can or ought to do, and have arranged her life in every detail as if they understand her far better than she understood herself."[37] Rather than portentous talk of the mystery of womanhood, McCabe campaigned and wrote for the liberation of women from culturally contrived bonds of exploitation.

McCabe could so easily have undone much of his good work if, like so many men, his work betrayed little more than an obsession about sex, like the legions of Freudians who claimed to see sex as behind or explaining all sorts of things. For example, McCabe did not accept as a compete explanation the sexualized account of medieval nuns' dream fantasies. He didn't say such interpretations were inaccurate, merely that they had been overdone. He defended the reputations of several medieval ascetics.

It is rather piquant to read how the medieval saints had their Platonic friend-ships: Francis of Assisi and Clare, Francis of Sales and Mme. De Chantal, Peter of Alcantara and Theresa, etc. No one who knows their lives will attempt to accuse them of hypocrisy, and they were men and women who believed that their ecstasies would be ruined, perhaps for all life, if any thought of sex came into them.[38]

Had McCabe been half the hater of religion his enemies painted him as, this fashionable sexualizing of all motivations would have been too tempting to resist. Despite being a strong critic of religion, monasticism, and asceticism, McCabe never disparaged genuine religiosity. But equally, he never lost his horror of monasticism. Even in *Twelve Years in a Monastery*, written only a year after leaving the church, McCabe wrote, with evident relief, that even "in the hours of deepest faith I never found courage to send a girl to a nunnery: one girl, a penitent of mine, often solicited me about her vocation: I am thankful to say that I restrained her."[39]

Joseph McCabe was a feminist before his time. He was advocating the equality of women and the right of a woman to ownership of her own body decades before this became acceptable for males. McCabe was a feminist—he described himself in these terms in 1928.[40] In 1945 he defined feminism as "the feeling that women still suffer unjust disabilities or the general movement or agi-tation for removing them." He showed what would now be seen as too sanguine a confidence that few real barriers remained to women, when he declared the battle for emancipation almost won. But he also insisted that "so long as there are any barriers Feminism remains one of the just reform causes of our age."[41]

HISTORY OF HUMAN MORALS

But McCabe's heresies did not stop there. He also advocated a radical theory of history that saw a close and necessary relationship between sexual freedom and civilization. It was the purpose of his twelve-volume *History of Human Morals* to prove this point. It was one the most ubiquitous errors of history, McCabe argued, that sensuality and vice are given as reasons for periods of decline. "The idea that our civilization today depends, as regards the general character, upon the continuance of our minority of Christians to attend church services seem to most of us grotesque."[42] Having completed his exhaustive history of moral development, McCabe concluded that a general sense of "sensual pleasure and a large measure of sexual freedom never injured a civilization. . . ."[43] With man-ifest lack of sympathy, McCabe conceded that only in absolute monarchies could an exception to this rule be found, given the importance attached to the sexual outcomes, if not the behavior, of the monarch.

This radical view of history was tied in with his strongly held opinions on the human origins of morality, which we will discuss in chapter 9. It is important to make clear that McCabe did not mean that unrestricted sexual licence amounted to a golden age. What he meant was that periods popularly known as golden ages—Periclean Athens, Stoic Rome, Moorish Spain, Renaissance Italy, and so on—were also periods when the more puritanical and sexist taboos were significantly less powerful than at other times. What marked these periods off was that "sensual and sexual pleasure were refined and enlarged, and were vitally associated with intellectual pleasure."[44]

Thinking sociologically, we can see that McCabe was continuing to develop the concept of character, which we discussed in chapter 4. One of the features of nineteenth-century social thinking was the democratization of the concept of character. Whereas in the eighteenth century, respectability was still, in the main, related to one's social status, particularly as measured by property ownership, in the nineteenth century, respectability came to be something open to anyone possessed of the approved qualities of character. Such qualities usually involved self-reliance, self-discipline, thrift, and sobriety.[45] McCabe's contribution to this debate was to liberate the notion of sound character from the shackles of a puritanical sex ethic. In doing this, he was truly ahead of his time, particularly as it was not compromised by the suspicion of self-interest or hypocrisy, as has been argued for some of McCabe's contemporaries.

It is also worth noting that some opponents of rationalism accuse it of not permitting a sound and stable notion of character because of the ever-onward march toward novelty and newness.[46] McCabe's essentialist view of character and the (what would now be seen as conservative) traits he recommends rather undermine that claim. Elsewhere, postmodernists such as Fredric Jameson are assuring us that postmodernism means "not merely liberation from anxiety but a liberation from every kind of feeling as well, since there is no longer a self present to do feeling."[47] Michel Foucault and Gilles Deleuze went even further. Their goal has been described as the "liquidation of the principle of identity."[48] Rather than liquidating the principle of identity, McCabe wanted to expand simple identity with the more substantial notion of character. In fact McCabe's conception of character is infinitely more substantial to current image-centered notions of "personality" or, more worrying still, "performance."

And McCabe's conception is more egalitarian than that of rival postmodernists, such as the American political scientist Gregory Bruce Smith, who has attempted to restore notions of character, but linked with a Nietzschean will to power. "I do believe," Smith tells us, "that there is an unmistakable and unavoidable aristocratic element lurking within the essence of the genuinely postmodern."[49] Smith feels sure that this postmodern aristocratic element will open a path to and concern for, character. McCabe, by contrast, was convinced that "character" was available to anyone who was autonomous, informed, and active in the world.

While McCabe's point about an expressive sexuality as a feature of a mature character has become a truism, his wider claim of a link between permissive sexuality and periods of progress might seem less obvious. However, McCabe's argument has been echoed many decades later by the American humanist scholar Peter Levine. In a brilliant and doughty defense of the humanities from the current batch of irrationalist opponents, Levine notes that Karl Popper's notions of the open and closed society both function as something of an ideal type. However, he adds, "it does seem clear that societies become *relatively* more or less open in different periods, and that humanism plays a generally rationalizing and liberating role in any culture where it is allowed to operate."[50] This, of course, is the heart of McCabe's claims made in both the *Key to Love and Sex* and *The Rise and Fall of the Gods*.

McCabe's radical views on feminism, morality, and sexuality were more than enough to damn him in the eyes of just about everybody. Conservatives would have had all their suspicions about the moral laxity of atheists confirmed by McCabe's views on sexuality. However, libertarians of the Havelock Ellis stamp would have been equally suspicious of McCabe's criticisms of the selfish motivations behind much of the rhetoric about free love. McCabe was, in yet another area, years ahead of his time.

But while McCabe was a feminist, it would be inaccurate (quite apart from being bad history) to paint him in contemporary colors as a sensitive, New Age guy. With the advantage of hindsight, McCabe is vulnerable to criticism of his approach to gender issues. It is disconcerting for the contemporary reader to read of "woman" all the time. It is like reading about "society" or "space" or some sort of abstraction, when we are actually dealing with people. It does seem, though, to have been a normal practice of the time, and, disconcerting though it is, it would be unfair to quarrel with McCabe solely on this point.

McCabe was certainly not free of what would now be seen as sexist attitudes. For instance, he thought that women had until recently been "a much poorer judge of character than men."[51] This does not contradict his other protestations of the equality of women, however, because he said that this disability was characteristic of women *until recent times*. In other words, it was not intrinsic to women, but an historical by-product of forced inequality. More serious, perhaps, was his willingness to posit the "ideal woman" of the future. Such a woman would be one of "refinement and candor, tenderness and self-possession, delicacy of taste and disdain of prudery, pride in the beautiful body and its emotions and pride also in the mind and its powers, the emotional complement of man but an equal citizen of the universe."[52] This ideal, while not ignoble, undercuts the emphasis on pluralism and choice that he had argued so passionately for.

More serious still was McCabe's tendency to objectify women, or, as Simone de Beauvoir put it, seeing women as "other." One gets the impression he saw himself as writing exclusively for male readers.

One writer remarks that on the masculine side *we* get a larger proportion of such extremes of genius and idiocy. It seems to be true for idiocy, but in regard to genius, *we* have carefully to consider whether the historical record of genius does not rather reflect the fact that for more than two thousand years *we* have given no encouragement, and little opportunity, to female genius.[53]

So, in retrospect, McCabe was often guilty of thinking of women in terms of "other." As McCabe was writing before Beauvoir, and the idea of "other" had not yet been formulated, it requires a generous helping of hindsight to condemn McCabe too harshly on this point. These criticisms do little to detract from an otherwise honorable record as a feminist stalwart long before such things were acceptable from men wanting to taken seriously in intellectual circles.

McCABE AND MEN

Gender issues do not only involve speaking of women, of course, and McCabe also devoted attention to men's issues, although very significantly less than he did to issues relating to women. We have already seen McCabe condemn the self-centered boor, the man whose main boast is that of sexual conquests. In *The Tyranny of Shams*, he looked forward to the days when the norms of male behavior and identification would change. "There is something grotesque about the traditional idea that the human male must be distinguished by a greater capacity for taking alcohol and using meaningless expletives and telling sexual stories."[54] McCabe approved of the Victorian concept of manliness, but was adamant that this did not mean brutishness. He deprecated manliness that was mistaken as an overbearing disregard to the rights of other people in one's own household or in the wider society.[55] These are such commonplace observations now, that we must remember that McCabe was making them up to a hundred years ago. From the beginning of his career, McCabe denounced the less helpful sides of the male character. In his very first biography, McCabe condemned Peter Abélard's committal of Heloise into the nunnery when she had become a burden to him. Heloise, McCabe wrote, became "one more victim on the altar of masculine selfishness."[56] Neither was McCabe impressed by displays of male temper, even from people he otherwise admired. Speaking of Goethe's failure to secure the hand of young Kätchen Schönkopf, McCabe noted that he "loved, and lost, as many other young men have done, by bad temper; and it was well for him and for her that he did lose."[57]

As he had done with women, McCabe pictured the ideal man of the future. It is interesting that his vision of the ideal man had to be drawn as a sort of golden mean in between unsavory extremes.

Strength so often means selfishness, brutality, coarseness: refinement so often means a mawkish and anemic confinement to a world of illusion. Masculinity or virility is a fine quality. . . . This cobwebbed world of ours would soon be made clean and sweet to live in if our high-brows had more red blood in the veins and cultivated instead of foolishly despising sensuality, and if our low brows could but see that refinement of taste and cultivation of mind opened up additional sources of pleasure.[58]

While he was prepared to chastise Goethe for immature displays of temper, the German was for McCabe the outstanding example of the ideal man he described. Interestingly, McCabe's picture of Goethe matches very closely the ideal of masculinity that he penned twenty-one years later:

> Delicacy is as much a part of nature as robust vigor. But they are as a rule so sharply distributed in different persons that they present to us two hostile and mutually disdainful schools. The one flings the censure of "mawkish sentimentality"; the other retorts with a heavy charge of "animalism." In the rich personality of Goethe they were united in full development.[59]

Another aspect of masculinity that we can examine in some depth is McCabe's views on homosexuality. Doubtless influenced by the abuse he suffered as a child, McCabe was never able to approve of homosexuality. For many years he continued to use the Catholic description of it as "unnatural vice." But he slowly changed his position as he read more. In 1929 he explained to his readers that homosexuality is not simply a matter of a "hereditary taint," but rather "a structural bias impels the person sexually toward his own sex." More important was the reasonable and open-minded conclusion he drew when he admitted that not enough is known about homosexuality to allow a properly informed decision. From this he concluded that "perversities of taste do not concern the law, and we should have to inquire whether there is in the practice a social danger proportionate to the penalty which the law inflicts."[60]

This seems to be an object lesson to those who seek to devalue the power of reason to change one's outlook on life. McCabe's distaste for homosexuality was deeply ingrained from childhood. But this notwithstanding, McCabe was prepared to alter his views on homosexuality in the light of new evidence that became available. McCabe's reasoning led him to a more tolerant, open position toward the practices of others. He was also concerned to have his judgments remain in proportion to the known facts. This attitude is the very foundation material for the open society. McCabe's odyssey contrasts very favorably with the view of his old adversary, G. K. Chesterton, who was prepared to countenance the ideals of the Inquisition in preference over those of a society that lauded Oscar Wilde. "The age of the Inquisition has not at least the disgrace of having produced a society which made an idol of the very same man for preaching the very same things which it made him a convict for practicing."[61]

SOCIAL JUSTICE

Having seen how radical and forward-looking McCabe's views on gender were, we might expect his political views to be similarly avant-garde. However, this isn't the case, or at least, not in all cases. So what was McCabe's social program? What will *not* come as a surprise is that McCabe disdained to adopt one political philosophy and to advocate that as the panacea for all problems. McCabe's politics were an eccentric blend of socialism, liberalism and conservatism. By eccentric I mean off-center, rather than bizarre or laughable. This absence of a carefully worked-out theoretical program is hardly surprising. A. J. Davies noted the same practical-minded distrust of high-sounding manifestos among McCabe's contemporaries who founded the Labour Party. But, as Davies added, this "certainly didn't mean they had doubts as to what they were against."[62] McCabe's primary focus, as with his contemporaries whose careers were in politics, was that of opposition to the entrenched establishment, and offering a vision of a better future. Neither McCabe nor the early Labour politicians ever worked out a clear program of what would be done were power ever to be achieved. But McCabe had a superior understanding of the real workings of politics than many of his contemporaries in the early Labour movement. In fact it can be claimed that McCabe anticipated Karl Popper in preferring to couch his vision of a just society in the negative form.

> For my part I prefer always to conceive social progress in this negative form. . . . What our world wants is the removal of the evil and pain that still abound in it: the elimination of war and all forms of violence, the abolition of poverty and insecurity of employment, the end of the unjust distribution of the wealth we create, the scientific education of people out of the cruel, selfish, greedy, and generally unsocial impulses which centuries of religious education have done so little to eradicate.[63]

McCabe understood that conceiving of liberty in the negative form runs less risk of deteriorating into conformism or even totalitarianism. Rights conceived negatively permit greater individual freedom. Karl Popper was later to make this idea well known in his classic *The Open Society and Its Enemies*. McCabe's view of the role of the state was more interventionist than Popper's, but fell far short of the large-scale interventionism that was fashionable at the time. Like Popper after him, McCabe favored piecemeal social engineering to extravagant meta-narratives and grandiose promises.

> The essential thing in the life of a State is to promote the progress and happiness of the individual citizens to the utmost of its power; to educate the ignorant, to mitigate the burden of poverty, to organize or at least direct the industrial world, to care for the weak and powerless, to administer justice and to lay as little restriction on its people as these purposes will allow.[64]

This was written in November 1914, at a time when the role of the state loomed as large as it did at any time in the twentieth century.

As with much of his social history, McCabe generally confined his reformist political and social views to Britain. His most comprehensive treatments of these questions were in *The Taint in Politics*, published in 1920, and the 1932 work *Can We Save Civilization? The Taint in Politics*, originally published in the United States, was an anonymous work. McCabe acknowledged he was the author five years later. *Can We Save Civilization?* was published under his own name by an obscure company and is, in effect, a reworking of *The Tyranny of Shams*.

McCabe's social program consisted of working toward elimination of the ills and maladies he listed in the passage quoted above. He was at his most radical when writing on constitutional issues. The vital problem was gaining access to real power. It was essential to McCabe's worldview that the average elector—the sort of person he wrote for—was entirely capable of wielding power but was being denied the opportunity to do so. This is not to say that McCabe nursed some romantic notion of the incorruptibility of "the people." What he sought was a system so overwhelmingly run by the people that such corruption would become impossible. The party system as he saw it was

> corrupt, demoralizing, and intensely prejudicial to the interests of the country. . . . Men who are poor and independent may bruise their shins in vain. Men of no ability are promoted, even to peerages and the Cabinet, because their fathers contributed much to the party's purse or prestige, and they themselves will at least be loyal.[65]

So it was with a view to a radical rearrangement of power that he advocated sweeping changes to the constitution of Britain. He was a republican, and looked forward to the day when the monarch would be pensioned off on half-pay and his many hangers-on would be pensioned off on no pay. "A 'monarch' in the twentieth century is as anachronistic as a 'lord,' an hereditary monarch is an outrage to modern sentiments."[66] His republicanism very nearly got him into trouble at a soccer match in England. When, as usual, he had kept his hat firmly on his head while "God Save the King" was played before the game, someone from behind knocked his hat off. McCabe swung around in a great temper, demanding the man come forward. No one did, and McCabe confessed later on to being rather grateful for that, as his assailants were all a lot larger than he was.

Not surprisingly, the politicians McCabe had the least confidence in were the bishops, lackeys, and hereditary peers who comprised the House of Lords. As with the monarchy, McCabe saw these institutions as anachronisms and barriers to more equitable social legislation. We have seen him cite examples of this in his treatment of the nineteenth century. McCabe favored outright abolition of these institutions. Neither is it a surprise that McCabe favored disestablishment of the Church of England.

It would be wrong, however, to see all McCabe's opinions in black and white terms of retain/abolish or praiseworthy/blameworthy. Even with questions of aristocracy versus democracy, he saw ambiguities.

> It is ever a question of weighing the cultural demerits of Demos against the moral demerits of Ploutos: the imperfectly-grasped and erratic ideas of self-interest of the Many, and the very clear ideas of self-interest of the Few. An historical indictment of both forms of polity is quite easy. No democracy has had the long average life of monarchies; but no aristocracy ever used its gifts exclusively on behalf of the entire body or avoided corruption.[67]

Regarding the House of Commons, his views were similarly layered. *The Taint in Politics* was, in the main, a critique of the oligarchic tendencies of the Commons. He saw four main defects of the system: cronyism, rather than working disinterestedly in the national interest; the advantages accruing to politicians of independent means; the ability of powerful interest groups to scupper needed reforms; and the corrosive influence of self-interest affecting a politician's decision making.[68] McCabe saw the country being controlled by rival organizations, rather than rival sets of political principle. The solutions he offered were characteristically sensible and evolutionary. They included shorter parliamentary terms, adjustment of debating hours, shortening the time for speeches as a disincentive to rhetoric, and abolishing many of the more archaic protocols. But underlying all this was a crying need for more sophisticated education of the elector, so that he becomes immune to shallow electioneering, sectarian appeals, or rhetoric.[69]

For a while, McCabe included reform of the electoral system as a key item in his reformist platform. For many years, McCabe advocated replacing Britain's first-past-the-post system with a form of proportional representation, in the hope that it would permit a broader range of people access to parliament. His hope was that proportional representation would enable a new breed of politicians to operate more independently of the party whip. But, as happened so often, he could see potential pitfalls in any improvement he recommended and did not shy from mentioning them. His chief concern about proportional representation was that it would lead to a rise in sectarian groupings and narrow single-interest lobby groups. "We must hope," he wrote in 1916, "that the sterner education of the electorate will secure that these trivialities do not endanger grave national interests."[70] It is very interesting that he later renounced his support for this particular reform. By 1920 he seemed convinced that whatever sectional groups secured election, none would be able to put aside their narrow interests in the name of the national interest. "We should have an election, even in a grave and complex period like this," he wrote in 1919, "turning on a single and fantastic issue like the prevention of other people from consuming drinks which you yourself do not like."[71] No amount of education would prevent this sort of distortion to happen, he concluded.[72] Other electoral reforms he argued for included full female franchise, electorates of equal population, abolition of multiple voting and university and city seats, and strict control of election spending.

McCabe was less openly reformist on questions of economic policy. We have seen that McCabe was critical of unearned privilege retaining its hold on political power thanks to the vagaries of the political system. He also had little time for laissez-faire economics. Laissez-faire had "prolonged the horrors of the workers for two generations, planted the seeds of a terrible conflict, and is shown by the logic of events to have been from the first and academic superstition."[73] Many commentators would be repeating these criticisms seven decades later. But neither was McCabe a doctrinaire socialist. He was well aware of the limits to the state's ability to satisfy growing demands and was critical of politicians feeding unrealistic expectations. In fact his fears and warning sound familiar to those made eight decades later.

> Promise him [the elector] a fortnight's holiday with pay every year, and he will not dream of doing the very simple sum in arithmetic which is required to show that this would cost £150,000,000 a year. Tell him that all education ought to be free, all workers liberally pensioned at sixty, all houses provided at moderate rent for workers by a heavy subsidy, all medical treatment for the workers unpaid, and so on. He never works out the cost.[74]

The real blame for this lay not with the voter but with the unscrupulous politician who promised more than could reasonably be afforded. He was critical of the utopianism of a lot of socialist thinking in this regard.

> I see no moral principle which forbids that we should reward a man according to his inventiveness or other value to the community, although his fellows are not responsible for their lesser capacity; and it is idle to speculate on some imaginary phase of human development in which the more gifted and more useful to refuse to be more richly rewarded than the less useful.[75]

Even at the height of the Depression, McCabe supported the rights of private enterprise, and was critical of the socialism then being dogmatically offered as a panacea to the problems of the West. For instance, in 1932, he warned readers not to "make a fetish of the word 'socialisation' and imagine that it at once implies immense advantages. Certainly no national service such as we have at present would carry out the work of distribution as efficiently and cheaply as do certain private enterprises."[76] He cited the Soviet Union as a living example of the folly of what he called the "old socialist position" that "in the beautiful new State all would willingly contribute their talent for the common good."[77]

Indeed, McCabe went further when he observed gloomily, in 1932, that "the Russian regime approaches nearer every month to National Socialism." He noted that after the "confiscation of huge wealth and relying on a truculent repression of recalcitrants, it has in twelve years only reached a position which it is not eager to invite the world to inspect."[78] McCabe's position on Russia was practical and sensible. "I do not in the least accept the more sinister accounts of Russia's designs that are published; nor, for that matter, the prettier accounts of visitors who make conducted tours with an interpreter."[79] In 1940 he elaborated on these points when he criticized the Soviet regime for "its approval of the maxim that the end justifies the means," and accused it of adopting the "ethical and emotional outfit of the religion against which, as well as the social order, it rebelled a century ago. . . ."[80]

As in McCabe's willingness to praise Chinese civilization in a time of widespread perception of a "yellow peril," he was also prepared to criticize the Soviet Union at a time when that country was receiving a great deal of uncritical adulation. Had McCabe wanted to curry favor with his potential audiences in order to make a living from his unbelief, as he was accused of doing, in neither case was this a wise move. It is significant that McCabe never wrote for the Left Book Club, the readers of which would normally be thought to constitute a large section of his readership. It must always be remembered that McCabe was a popularizer writing for the general reader, and that the prejudices of these readers had a direct bearing on his income. But McCabe was an instinctive rationalist—not necessarily contradictory—because he genuinely believed that, when presented by facts, people will alter their beliefs accordingly. And he was prepared to sacrifice his income to this ideal.

Given McCabe's respect for individual effort and his suspicion of enforced collectivism, it will seem incongruous to many readers that McCabe described himself as a socialist. This depends on what one means when talking of socialism. Again, McCabe found it easier to state what he did not mean:

> If you press me for an opinion, though my experience is that most of the young who so press me generally retort, if I differ from them, that I know nothing about economics, I say that the world will never get rid of poverty, unemployment, irregular employment, and all the suffering they entail until it has discovered how to apply the Socialist principle without sacrificing or discouraging ability, without violence, and without entrusting power to conceited incompetence.[81]

Unlike most of his dogmatic socialist contemporaries, McCabe recognized that conventional conceptions of "the worker" were becoming increasingly anachronistic. The days of a straightforward division between capital and labor were long gone. Instead, as he wrote in 1932, "the operation of intelligence is now by far the most considerable factor in the production of wealth."[82]

The chief feature of McCabe's socialism is his confidence in the efficacy of planning. But by planning he did not simply mean a program of nationalization, mainly because he had very little confidence in the ability of politicians to oversee the planning process efficiently. What McCabe wanted was an independent Economic Council which would take over the functions of the Board of Trade, and consist of around fifty members composed of business leaders, industrialists, financiers, and scientists. Supporting the council would be a large number of advisors, again picked for their practical business expertise rather than their proficiency in passing civil service examinations. The council would be answerable to, although independent of, parliament, and would not have direct regulatory powers. In keeping with the priorities of the Depression, the primary aim of the council would not be the promotion of "growth" for its own sake, nor the nationalization of major industries, but the "co-ordination of consumption and production which has become the most pressing need of the world's economic life."[83] McCabe's ideas are unremarkable. The year before McCabe's book came out the influential *Weekend Review* published a National Plan for Britain, which argued for state intervention, five-year plans, and a Business University.[84] Pretty soon the press was awash with rival plans. McCabe's was just one more.

The vogue for planning in the thirties was largely inspired by the example of the Soviet Union, which was widely thought to have avoided the excesses of the Depression by virtue of its planning. But as we have seen, McCabe was not swept up with the wave of uncritical admiration of the Soviet Union until well into the war. Like many other people, McCabe was inspired by the scale of the Soviet war effort against Nazi Germany and came to see the United States as the greater threat to world peace. But even then he refused to call himself a communist and continued to be critical of the Soviet Union and of socialism as and when he thought appropriate. For example, in 1951 McCabe defended the Soviet Union from attacks by American historians. On the one hand he defended the veracity of the show trials, but equally he acknowledged that there had been a Red Terror between 1918 and 1920 in which huge numbers of people were murdered.[85] McCabe's defense of the show trials looks foolish in retrospect, but even here he offered evidence for his conclusions. He quoted the reports of an American engineer, John D. Littlepage, whose articles in the *Saturday Evening Post* over the end of 1937 and early 1938 argued for their genuineness. There had never been any shortage of material supportive of the trials in the British press, but it was only in the last decade of his life that McCabe's ability to distinguish credible from incredible evidence slackened. Even then, such an assessment is a lot easier with the advantage of six decades' worth of hindsight.

The best example of McCabe's later, rather uncritical pro-Sovietism can be found in a controversy he began in the *Literary Guide* in July of 1948. C. D. Darlington, FRS, a respected geneticist, had recently become president of the RPA, and had presented that year's Conway Memorial Lecture. In many ways Darlington's address should have delighted McCabe. It was scornful of the retarding effect of universities in promoting scientific research, critical of education systems that focused on the past rather than the future, and saw science as essential to the future of humanity. Where Darlington erred was in criticizing the Soviet Union. Darlington condemned the perversions being forced on Soviet biology at the hands of Trofim Lysenko (1898–1976).[86] McCabe responded by commenting on recent visitors to the Soviet Union who had praised the "happy position of scientific workers." He also misunderstood comments Darlington had made about equality in Russia, and ended up suggesting the lecture should never have taken place.[87]

It was not so much that he became an uncritical fellow-traveler of the Soviet Union. What let McCabe down in his later years was his failure to be sufficiently critical of his sources. We will come across this decline in critical ability again in chapter 8, when we examine McCabe's views on Catholicism.

INTERNATIONAL RELATIONS

McCabe had relatively little to say about international relations, but what he did say was consistently internationalist. McCabe was more concerned with the historical record. Once the record was accurate and shorn of its irrelevant emphasis on kings, battles, and trivial events, the interpretation of international affairs would follow as a matter of course. McCabe was an early advocate for the now-fashionable concept of globalization. In 1923, on a ship returning to England from Australia, McCabe declared that there is now only one worldwide civilization. "It is essentially the same in Tokyo and New York, London and Sydney, Paris and Buenos Aires, Warsaw and Mexico. The world now moves steadily on."[88] We saw in the previous chapter that McCabe saw the stimulating contacts between peoples as one of the principal agencies of progress in human evolution. "The condition of social and intellectual progress—free interchange of ideas in the social group and with other social groups—is now provided immeasurably more than ever before, and it is almost the most rapidly advancing change in the modern world."[89] Following on from this, he supported close international cooperation as necessary conditions of international peace and progress. He proposed a series of International Economic Councils, one per continent, as the vehicles best suited to achieve effective international planning. McCabe's International Council would have had powers similar to the International Monetary Fund (IMF), although I can't help thinking he would have been uneasy about the sort of influence the IMF has come to wield.

McCabe saw the problems caused by the Depression as exacerbated by the protectionist measures most countries had adopted. Whatever the future political development of Europe may be, he wrote in 1932, "it is certain that this removal of barriers to trade and intercourse will in time extend to the entire Continent."[90] McCabe had little faith in the League of Nations as a vehicle for the international cooperation and planing that he desired. He saw the league as irrevocably tainted by the conditions of its birth. The Treaty of Versailles had been grossly unjust and had guaranteed further trouble in Europe, and the league was in no position to change that, let alone undertake more radical reforms. McCabe could see, in a way that many of his contemporaries could not, that the economic future of the world may lie outside Europe. He posed the question: "Is it an unreasonable expectation that, as happened in England a century ago, capital and enterprise will increasingly use masses of cheap labour wherever they can be found? And for that they must quit England."[91]

As regards the British Empire, McCabe was unusually prescient. The various regions that make up the empire, he wrote in 1916,

> cling together on the understanding that we are quite insincere when we talk of them as our "possessions." It is a federation of free nations, bound together by thinning ties of blood and by the advantage of a collective defense. When the military system is abandoned, there will be a somewhat faded and amiable sentiment uniting the imperial fragments to each other more closely than to their nearer neighbors.[92]

Writing during the Depression, McCabe recognized the growing industrialization of the Dominions and colonies and wrote frankly about the ever-decreasing ability of England to maintain the advantage it had held in the nineteenth century. This was compounded by England's disadvantage in securing the new forms of energy, notably hydroelectricity and oil. Doubtless McCabe would have been dismissed as a crank for this suggestion. "Of two natural energies we have an abundance—wind and tidal water—and it is possible to conceive ways in which they might be utilized."[93] And now, of course, rationalists are dismissed as cranks for not, apparently, having made such a suggestion.

SOCIAL POLICY

Moving from economic to social policy, we tend to see the more punitive side of McCabe's character. Whereas some of his later intolerances regarding Catholicism or the Soviet Union can be put down to the mental rigidification of old age, his social opinions were held consistently throughout his life. Having said this, McCabe wrote relatively little on social policy, with the significant exception of gender and sexuality. He tended to see much social commentary as utopian and impracticable. But also, having the emphasis (one can't really call it a "Popperian" emphasis, given McCabe anticipated him) of outlining what one is against, it would have been inconsistent for McCabe to then itemize a long list of reforms he wanted implemented.

The more punitive side of McCabe came out on the few occasions he ventured to speak of penal policies; specifically on his views on penalties for "refractory types." He was, for instance, a lifelong supporter of capital punishment. In many ways, McCabe's penal policy anticipated the "three strikes and you're out" policy that has recently been employed in California and elsewhere. As we saw with his debt to Robert Owen, McCabe always stressed the importance of education as a vital means by which better, more civilized, socially aware thoughts and practices can be imbued. But what of the incurably refractory types, those who, despite all educational advantages, were incurably criminal? In *The Tyranny of Shams*, McCabe made several vague references to this problem, and suggested that repeated instances of criminal or antisocial behavior deserved sterilization, or even death. The only other time in his huge body of writing when he was in this mood was late in his life, when writing his projection into the future. There he proposed that recidivist rapists should be castrated.[94] Doubtless, the more rabid postmodernist, with Foucault in hand and deconstruction in mind, will delight in demonstrating the savagery and brutality inherent in "the Enlightenment project." Depending on one's views, McCabe is open to criticism and condemnation on this point. My own view is that McCabe's opinions here are a lapse from an otherwise honorable body of civilized liberal and humanist thought, which I am seeking to defend. And to seek to overthrow all of modernity of the basis of McCabe's opinions in one area would be a massive injustice.

EDUCATION

The concept of human nature is at a low ebb at the beginning of the twenty-first century, and it is yet another failing ascribed to rationalists that they hold dogmatically to notions of human nature. This prejudice is untrue in the case of Joseph McCabe, who specifically denied the idea of an unchangeable human nature. "The sage person who holds that we can't change human nature, which is really an historical statement, since it implies that there has been no change, does not know the social history of his own country." McCabe's example was the changes in England over the course of the nineteenth century.

> Law or no law, the great majority of us today do not want to get drunk whenever we can afford it, to beat our wives, to be cruel to animals, to see criminals hanged, to rear dogs or cocks for fighting; but the great majority of people certainly did a century ago. Our impulses, like our tastes, have changed; they are not merely better controlled.[95]

The key to changing human nature in McCabe's opinion was, of course, education, and we can end this chapter with an examination of his views in this all-important area. We need to remember that McCabe was brought up in the first years of universal education in Britain and schooling was not something he took for granted. On the contrary, education was the foundation of modernity.

> It is no longer simply a matter of justice, though the first educational reformers pleaded that every man had a right to enter this new world of knowledge. It is no longer simply a question of improving the character of our generation, though at least no social writer questions that the growth of education has been accompa-

nied by a marked refining of character in every country. The real question now is, whether in its own interests, the State is not bound to extend and deepen the work of education so that every man will be competent to exercise that share in the control of national affairs which will never again be taken from him.[96]

The main problem in McCabe's mind was what children were being taught. Were they being taught in such a way as to permit them to exercise that proprietary control? McCabe feared that education was neglecting its main purpose while concentrating on a mass of trivial detail.

To put it concretely, I find children in their early teens compelled to learn a mass of detail—about Elizabethan social life or literature, for instance, or about the geography of remote rivers or provinces—that in thirty years' experience as an all-round public educator or "popularizer" I have not found it of the least use to know.[97]

In place of an overcrowded and unnecessarily fussy curriculum, McCabe advocated for elementary school pupils a simple program centered around the "three R's" (his term) and an "easy, well-assimilated outline of the individual's place in the nation, the nation's place in the human family, and the relation of the whole to the universe. . . ."[98] Secondary education should also be purged of unnecessary detail, as teenagers, "their minds disturbed by the first onset of sexual maturity," cannot be expected to take in more than a "germinal knowledge."[99] He gave as an example the case of a fourteen-year-old, who "can rattle off the names of the wives of Henry VIII or the battles of Charles I, but has not an elementary idea of such things as diet, leucocytes, ductless glands etc, on which his health and happiness depend."[100] The job of the secondary school is in "laying the foundations of a philosophy of life, the general principles of psychology, anthropology, history, sociology, economics and international affairs."[101]

While McCabe was clear that education was to be identical for boys and girls, he was surprisingly uncertain about the appropriate level of sex instruction for the young. He admitted that he had not told his own boys the story of the birds and the bees. His wife had, but he remained uncertain of the value of this instruction. "The principle I have in mind is, of course, not the puritanical maxim that sex is malodorous, but simply the desirability of keeping children as much as possible from thinking about sex, for the sake of their health."[102] He had no fear of masturbation, which he viewed as entirely normal unless done to excess. What McCabe had in mind here is his notion of the whole person, for whom sex is a part of life, and not a focus of attention.

And few people this century have devoted themselves more wholeheartedly to the educating of the whole person. This is what motivated his lifetime of work as a popularizer. In the last chapter we saw just how good a popularizer McCabe was, and it is worthwhile to finish this chapter by looking quickly at his theory of education, which underlay his popularizing. Not surprisingly, McCabe scorned presenting large arrays of facts. Most manuals of astronomy, McCabe wrote in 1922, "tell everything about the contents of the universe and very little about the universe." What people want is "a sort of philosophy of the material universe, a mental picture of it as a whole, of its evolution, and of the relation of its various parts to each other."[103] This, of course, is another example of the teleological map that McCabe was anxious to give his readers.

> No man can master more than one branch of modern culture. Most of us have not the leisure even for a good knowledge of one. But it is a good thing to have *some* knowledge of many. The specialist is absolutely indispensable for the advancement of knowledge; but most of us nowadays want his details, or some of them, built into general views about the universe, the earth, life and man. I am trying to meet that want here by supplying a general view of the material universe and its evolution.[104]

Over the past two decades it has become fashionable to criticize rationalists of being reductionist, implying an inability to see the whole picture, which is then supplied by the critic. E. O. Wilson has demonstrated the lack of understanding this approach involves, given the central role reductionism plays in the scientific quest to gain precisely that wider picture.[105] Joseph McCabe's extraordinary career as an adult educator is a pioneering example of a scientifically respectable and suitably provisional, but nonetheless holistic, picture of the universe for the general citizen.

But while some people have accused rationalists of missing the whole picture by an overreliance on reductionism, others have criticized them for presuming to see any picture at all. Postmodernists insist that any such picture is little more than a trick of language, or a cultural construct. Another Wilson— not E. O., but A. N. this time—can be called in at this point. We should be happy, Wilson commented dryly, "to debate the essentially fictive nature of, let us say, Newton's Laws of Gravity unless and until someone threatened to throw us out of a top-storey window. Then the law of gravity would seem very real indeed."[106] Indeed.

The successfully educated person, in McCabe's view, is not stuffed full of irrelevant facts, but is equipped with a genuine wish and ability to learn, and to be critical of what facts are presented. The qualities to be cultivated in education should be "accuracy, persistence, (or perseverance), adaptability, enterprise, energy, responsibility, and sensitiveness (in the sense of awareness of and eagerness to understand and improve the world they live in)."[107] While one could quibble with aspects of McCabe's educational theory, few would question the end he had in mind.

NOTES

1. W. Nicol Reid, *The Supremacy of Reason* (London: Watts, 1924), p. 90.
2. For a fuller discussion of this see Ray Monk, *Wittgenstein: The Duty of Genius* (London: Vintage, 1991), especially pp. 19–25.
3. Joseph McCabe, *Key to Love and Sex* (Girard, Kan.: Haldeman-Julius, 1929), vol. 6, p. 60.
4. Charles Loring Brace, *Gesta Christi: A History of Humane Progress Under Christianity* (New York: Hodder & Stoughton, 1884), pp. 298–99.
5. G. K. Chesterton, *George Bernard Shaw* (London: Guild Books, 1949), p. 82.
6. Ibid., p. 55.
7. Joseph McCabe, *Twelve Years in a Monastery* (London: Smith Elder, 1897), p. 263.
8. Joseph McCabe, *The Tyranny of Shams* (London: Eveleigh Nash/Dodd Mead, 1916), p. 194.
9. Ibid., p. 196.
10. Ibid., p. 203.
11. Joseph McCabe, *A History of Human Morals* (Girard, Kan.: Haldeman-Julius, 1931), vol. 12, p. 63.
12. Joseph McCabe, *Eighty Years a Rebel* (Girard, Kan.: Haldeman-Julius, 1947), p. 85.
13. McCabe, *Key to Love and Sex*, vol. 8, pp. 16–17.
14. Ibid., vol. 8, pp. 16–17.
15. Ibid., vol. 8, p. 38.
16. Ibid., vol. 5, p. 5.
17. Ibid., vol. 1, p. 39.
18. Ibid., vol. 1, p. 44.
19. Ibid., vol. 1. p. 55.
20. Joseph McCabe, *The Inferiority Complex Eliminated* (Girard, Kan.: Haldeman-Julius, 1940), p. 37.
21. Mary Midgley, *Science as Salvation* (London/New York: Routledge, 1994), p. 103. I hasten to add that this criticism is limited to this single issue. In most other respects, Mary Midgley's book is admirable.
22. Paul Cliteur, "The Challenge of Postmodernism to Humanism," *New Humanist* 110 (August 1995): 4–9.
23. McCabe, *Key to Love and Sex*, vol. 3, p. 15.
24. Ibid., vol. 2, p. 29.
25. Ibid., vol. 2. p. 49.
26. Ibid., vol. 2, p. 51.
27. Ibid., vol. 1, p. 9.
28. Kingsley Martin, *Editor* (London: Hutchinson, 1968), p. 137.
29. S. K. Ratcliffe, *The Story of South Place* (London: Watts, 1955), p. 72.
30. McCabe, *Key to Love and Sex*, vol. 3, p. 61.
31. Ruth Brandon, *The New Women and the Old Men* (London: Flamingo, 1991), p. 251.
32. Havelock Ellis, *The Task of Social Hygiene* (London: Constable, 1927), pp. 58, 65–66.
33. Charles Loring Brace, *Gesta Christi*, p. 299.

34. McCabe, *Key to Love and Sex*, vol. 2, p. 24.

35. Joseph McCabe, *The Influence of the Church on Marriage and Divorce* (London: Watts, 1916), p. 140.

36. Joseph McCabe, *The Religion of Woman: An Historical Study* (London: Watts, 1905), p. 27.

37. McCabe, *Key to Love and Sex*, vol. 6, p. 54.

38. Ibid., vol. 6, p. 28.

39. McCabe, *Twelve Years in a Monastery*, p. 21.

40. McCabe, *Key to Love and Sex*, vol. 2, p. 58.

41. Joseph McCabe, *Outline of the World's Great 'Isms* (Girard, Kan.: Haldeman-Julius, 1945), pp. 39–40.

42. McCabe, *A History of Human Morals*, vol. 12, p. 43.

43. Ibid., vol. 12, p. 41.

44. McCabe, *Key to Love and Sex*, vol. 5, p. 42.

45. For a fuller discussion of this theme, see Hugh McLeod, *Religion and the People of Western Europe 1789–1970* (Oxford: Oxford University Press, 1981), pp. 109–10.

46. See for example, chap. 8 of Bryan Appleyard's *Understanding the Present* (London: QPD, 1992).

47. Fredric Jameson, *Postmodernism, or, the Cultural Logic of Late Capitalism* (London: Verso, 1993), p. 15.

48. David Macey, *The Lives of Michel Foucault* (London: Vintage, 1994), p. xv.

49. Gregory Bruce Smith, *Nietzsche, Heidegger, and the Transition to Postmodernity* (Chicago/London: University of Chicago Press, 1996), p. 329.

50. Peter Levine, *Nietzsche and the Modern Crisis of the Humanities* (Albany: State University of New York Press, 1995), p. 14.

51. McCabe, *The Inferiority Complex Eliminated*, p. 37.

52. McCabe, *Key to Love and Sex*, vol. 8, p. 63.

53. Ibid., vol. 1, pp. 46–47; emphasis added.

54. McCabe, *The Tyranny of Shams*, pp. 201–202.

55. McCabe, *The Influence of the Church on Marriage and Divorce*, p. 2.

56. Joseph McCabe, *Peter Abélard* (London: Duckworth/Putnams, 1901), p. 122.

57. Joseph McCabe, *Goethe: The Man and His Character* (London: Eveleigh Nash, 1912), p. 46.

58. McCabe, *Key to Love and Sex*, vol. 8, p. 63.

59. McCabe, *Goethe*, p. 108.

60. McCabe, *Key to Love and Sex*, vol. 4, pp. 38–40.

61. G. K. Chesterton, *Heretics* (London: John Lane The Bodley Head, 1911), p. 16.

62. A. J. Davies, *To Build a New Jerusalem* (London: Abacus, 1996), p. 41.

63. Joseph McCabe, *The Logic and Virtue of Atheism* (Austin, Tex.: American Atheist Press, 1980), pp. 38–39.

64. Joseph McCabe, *Treitschke and the Great War* (Toronto: T. Fisher Unwin/William Briggs, 1914), p. 234.

65. McCabe, *The Tyranny of Shams*, p. 94.

66. Ibid., pp. 105–106.

67. [Joseph McCabe], *The Taint in Politics* (New York: Dodd Mead, 1920), p. 208.

68. Ibid., pp. 16–22.

69. Ibid., pp. 272–76.

70. McCabe, *The Tyranny of Shams*, p. 101.

71. McCabe, *The Taint in Politics*, p. 273.

72. Joseph McCabe, *Can We Save Civilization?* (London: The Search, 1932), p. 113.

73. McCabe, *The Taint in Politics*, pp. 115–16.

74. Ibid., pp. 270–71.

75. McCabe, *The Tyranny of Shams*, pp. 133–34.

76. McCabe, *Can We Save Civilization?*, p. 92.

77. Ibid., p. 78.

78. Ibid., p. 74.

79. Ibid., pp. 177–78.

80. Joseph McCabe, *The God of War*, Thinker's Forum, no. 1 (London: Watts, 1940), pp. 41–42.

81. Joseph McCabe, *One Hundred Men Who Moved the World* (Girard, Kan.: Haldeman-Julius, 1931), vol. 15, p. 36.

82. McCabe, *Can We Save Civilization?*, p. 83.

83. Ibid., p. 88.

84. Davies, *To Build a New Jerusalem*, p. 182.

85. Joseph McCabe, *The Columbia Encyclopedia's Crimes against the Truth* (Girard, Kan.: Haldeman-Julius, 1951), pp. 46–47.

86. C. D. Darlington, *The Conflict of Science and Society* (London: Watts, 1948).

87. *Literary Guide* (July 1948): iii.

88. McCabe, *The Twilight of the Gods*, p. 12.

89. McCabe, *Can We Save Civilization?*, p. 137.

90. Ibid., p. 152.

91. Ibid., p. 58.

92. McCabe, *The Tyranny of Shams*, p. 106.

93. McCabe, *Can We Save Civilization?*, p. 59.

94. Joseph McCabe, *The Next Fifty Years* (Girard, Kan.: Haldeman-Julius, 1950), p. 12.

95. McCabe, *Can We Save Civilization?*, pp. 186–87.

96. Joseph McCabe, *Key to Culture* (Girard, Kan.: Haldeman-Julius, 1927–29), vol. 38, pp. 5–6.

97. McCabe, *Can We Save Civilization?*, p. 209.

98. Ibid., p. 212.

99. Ibid., p. 215.

100. Joseph McCabe, *Science Yesterday, Today, and Tomorrow* (London: Herbert Jenkins, 1927), p. 102.

101. Joseph McCabe, *The Origin and Meaning of Ideas* (Girard, Kan.: Haldeman-Julius, 1951), p. 88.

102. McCabe, *Key to Love and Sex*, vol. 7, pp. 36–37.

103. Joseph McCabe, *The Wonders of the Stars* (London: Watts/Putnams, 1923), p. 90.

104. Ibid., p. 91.

105. E. O. Wilson, *Consilience: The Unity of Knowledge* (London: Little, Brown, 1998), p. 58.

106. A. N. Wilson, *God's Funeral* (London: John Murray, 1999), p. 178.

107. McCabe, *The Origin and Meaning of Ideas*, p. 89.

7

The Apprehended Shadow
McCabe and Religion

W e have examined McCabe's attitude toward history, science, and evolution, and have, with difficulty, ignored his views on religion. It hardly needs be said that McCabe's views on religion are important to understanding his general *weltanschauung*. Having said this, it is interesting that, for someone who left the Catholic Church and spent the next six decades advocating rationalism, he wrote comparatively little on religion per se. After gaining an understanding of what he meant by religion, we can then see how that understanding developed in the various contacts he had with religious apologists.

Before we do that, however, we must be clear about McCabe's stance as a freethinker. The English sociologist Colin Campbell has posited two basic psychological types among nonreligious people. On the one hand there are those who seek to create a substitute for religion, while on the other hand there are those whose priority is not to build some substitute for religion, but to work toward its abolition. Both of these outlooks are determined by the nature of the individual's response to religion.[1] Using this approach, it is not hard to see McCabe as an abolitionist. He had abandoned religion after a long and difficult struggle and had no intention of setting up some sort of alternative. This is not, of course, to say that he had no coherent *weltanschauung* to offer in religion's place. It is to say that McCabe was not offering any substitute *to be accepted in the form of religion or in a religious way.*

A few years after Campbell, another English sociologist, Susan Budd, also suggested two central strands of freethought movements. There is the negative strand, which says "supernatural religion is erroneous, and that this error has important consequences." Then there is the positive strand, which emphasizes the perfectibility of humanity through education, an autonomous morality, and skepticism toward arguments from authority.[2] McCabe embodies both of these strands. Bringing Campbell and Budd together, McCabe can be defined as a negative abolitionist. However, this rather unpleasant-sounding label is far from a complete description of McCabe's variety of unbelief, or of his attitude toward religion. Putting the same thing more positively, we can say that McCabe built a positive program of humanism on a firm bedrock of criticism. That bedrock of criticism was composed of atheism (regarding metaphysics) and rationalism (regarding epistemology).

As with many freethinkers from the Western world, McCabe usually had Christianity in mind when he spoke about religion. But unlike many freethinkers, he was well acquainted with the beliefs and practices of the other major systems of belief. We will examine the nature of McCabe's positive *weltanschauung* in the final chapter, but first we need to study the nature of his response to religion in general, and, in the next chapter, Catholicism in particular.

The first thing to emphasize is the importance of religious questions that led to McCabe's loss of faith. While still a Franciscan monk, McCabe's doubts had involved the essentials of the philosophy of religion. It was his inability to resolve these questions that led to his loss of faith.

> My doubts were of a philosophical and fundamental nature. I had felt that, until the basic truths of religion were firmly assented to, the Anglican controversy had little interest for me, and even the Biblical question was of secondary importance. Accordingly, most of my time from my first introduction to philosophy was spent, directly or indirectly, in the invest-igation of the problems of the spirituality and immortality of the soul, the existence of and nature of God, and the divinity of Christ.[3]

This conforms very closely to Susan Budd's rendition of negative freethought: "supernatural religion is erroneous, and that this error has important consequences." McCabe takes this even further by noting that he had not been influenced by writers opposed to Christianity, both because he had had limited access to those works and because those he had read had not impressed him unduly. Two works he does mention as influential during his time in the Church were Goethe's *Faust* and Carlyle's *Sartor Resartus*.[4] Goethe, we know, remained an influence, but McCabe rarely missed an opportunity to criticize Carlyle, whose pessimism, fondness for hero worship, and hostility to science were not calculated to win McCabe's esteem. It was not that he found non-Christian literature to be correct so much, as that he found religious literature to be incorrect.

Once McCabe had answered the philosophical questions to his satisfaction, he spent little time reworking those arguments. He recognized that there was little value in sharing the methods by which he came to freethought. In discussing the existence of God, McCabe wrote that we "are, of course, investigating a question in which authority has no value; no man or woman can be deeply convinced of the existence of God because abler men are convinced of it."[5] The only work he devoted to one of his fundamental religious questions was *The Existence of God*, written in 1913 as the first volume of the RPA's Inquirer's Library. He rewrote the book twenty years later, and it was released as number 34 of the Thinker's Library.

McCabe began *The Existence of God* with the observation that there comes "a time in every civilization when men of keen intelligence arise and say that the whole process [the existence of God] has been only the development of a myth."[6] He was to develop this theme two decades later in some of his multi-volume works for Haldeman-Julius. As would be expected from reading this passage, McCabe placed profound importance of the origins of religion as the key to understanding it. We will examine his theory of the origin of religion in the next section. By religion, McCabe was content to use Professor Morris Jastrow's definition, from his book *The Study of Religion*, written in 1901. Jastrow, at the time professor of psychology at the University of Wisconsin, defined religion as "the natural belief in a Power or Powers beyond our control, and upon which we feel ourselves dependent." McCabe knew full well, however, that definitions of religion are as numerous as grains of sand, and a lot less useful. While he was content with Jastrow's conception, this does not mean he endorsed it completely. He objected to Jastrow's assumption that religion is something essential and universal to humanity, and that there is a natural tendency toward monotheism. These were both commonly asserted propositions at the time. The notion that religion is essential and universal has survived, although by and large the presumption of monotheism has not. Preference today is given to vacuous and, in the end, meaningless terms like a "spiritual dimension."

By God, McCabe meant "an infinite and intelligent God, personally and substantially distinct from man and the universe."[7] He recognized that, among theologians and advanced theists, there would be a degree of impatience with this sort of discussion. The God McCabe was questioning the existence of in 1913 was the relatively straightforward creator God, the "Father Almighty, Creator of Heaven and Earth." This had been dogma for the Roman Church since the early centuries and had recently been reaffirmed at the First Vatican Council in 1870. It had also been the belief of the Church of England until this time, but was increasingly under fire by the second decade of the twentieth century.

Among the new ideas, spiritualism, pragmatism, vitalism, and varieties of pantheism were all popular among some religious thinkers. McCabe defended his definition of God. "Their impatience is wholly unjustified. This is the belief of millions of people in England and every other civilized country."[8] The rest of *The Existence of God* was devoted to discussions on William James (1842–1910), Henri Bergson (1859–1940), and some other arguments for God. His conclusion looks good more than nine decades after it was written.

One conclusion we may confidently reach. The philosophers rely no longer on either the popular proofs of the existence of God, or the arguments of their philosophical predecessors. That whole apparatus of proof on which men have relied from the days of Socrates to the nineteenth century is condemned as unsound; in its place are put certain abstruse considerations which none but students of philosophy can appreciate, which have nothing approaching acceptance in philosophy itself, and which, even if they were admitted, would prove only the existence of an "Absolute," an "Absolute Spiritual Life," an "Ethical Individual," or an "Absolute Experience." Not before such august abstractions will Demos ever kneel, and he is told by these masters of thought that *his* arguments are valueless.[9]

Seven decades after McCabe wrote these words, Duncan Howlett, an eminent American religious liberal theologian made a similar observation in a powerful book called *The Fatal Flaw at the Heart of Religious Liberalism.* Howlett wrote:

Personally speaking, however, I find it difficult to distinguish between today's "Transcendent" and yesterday's "Wholly Other." The "Mysterium Tremendum" of Rudolf Otto, the "God Beyond God" and the "Ground of Being" of Paul Tillich, the "Unmoved Mover" of Aristotle—none of these solve the age old problem of the existence or the nature of Deity.[10]

McCabe spent little time after 1913 on the question of God's existence. His entries on these questions in the *Rationalist Encyclopedia* do not depart significantly from the views outlined here. He devoted one of his Little Blue Books to the question of "The Futility of Belief in God," which later became chapter 5 of *The Story of Religious Controversy.* There he commented pointedly that belief in God is "strongest where man has least to thank God for, and is weakest where men have most knowledge and most mental training."[11]

McCabe's last significant foray into the question of God's existence took place when Rev. C. J. Shebbeare, chaplain to His Majesty the King and author of several works of popular apologetics, invited McCabe to debate the argument to design.[12] Shebbeare had spoken to the Church Congress of 1921 on the subject and was confident that he had a new spin on an old argument. He recognized that the traditional argument to design, which infers a lawgiver from the existence of laws, is fallacious. However, his attempt to rescue the argument does not strike one as much of an improvement. Shebbeare's main point was that nature "seems always to produce schemes of color which, *at least negatively,* are in good taste."[13]

McCabe had little difficulty fending off this rather desperate restatement of the argument to design, and we won't spend much time on it. He thought it "doubtful if Mr Shebbeare's argument applies at all to Nature beyond his summer flowers."[14] The main reason for this, of course, was that Shebbeare had gotten things backward. The reason that the universe does not shock our standards is "because it made our standards."[15] While by no means a gifted thinker,

Shebbeare was a formidably cheerful disputant, and this controversy was conducted with a great deal of *bonhomie*.

THE ORIGINS OF RELIGION

McCabe was active when theories of religion stressed having a clear understanding of the origins of religion. The quest for origins dominated much nineteenth-century scholarship on religion, and eventually gave birth to a new discipline of religious studies. Given that God is a human construct, it behooves us to understand how and why this construct emerged. It is unfashionable to talk of origins now but it remains true that the quest for the origins of religion and of the idea of God has had profound effects on the Christian religion over the last century and a half. It is also worth noting that the emphasis on origins has not disappeared entirely. Many recent antirationalist thinkers, notably Joseph Campbell and Dudley Young, have employed a far more ambitious—and infinitely more problematic—theory of origins to buttress their various brands of primitivism. The theory goes that humanity has lost its essence since its rise from the primitive state, and that we need to somehow return to that state. Why one would want to do this is not explained. But as Raymond Tallis has noted, these scholars think that they can cure two maladies with one remedy: that "reconnecting ourselves with the primitive is also a way of reconnecting ourselves with the spiritual."[16] Tallis is correct when he points out that, among the many other problems with this approach, it involves at some stage a hostility to human consciousness, particularly abstract consciousness.

McCabe's theory of origins was etiological, which involves recognizing religion as a human institution and seeking knowledge as to how that institution evolved. McCabe saw the key to understanding the present predicament of religion in terms of the circumstances of its rise. He did not question the importance of understanding origins as a way to understand religion, but he did dissent from the procedure used by the scholars of origins. His most comprehensive study of this subject was *The Growth of Religion*, written in 1918. He described this work as "a compilation of facts from the best original authorities on each people; the author claims only the merit of arranging them in a more natural and more instructive order than is usually done."[17] Yet again, the general reader was presented with an intelligent yet critical account of the current thought on an important question. It is worth noting that my copy of *The Growth of Religion* is inscribed with name of T. A. Hunter. Professor Tommy Hunter, vice chancellor of Victoria University of Wellington between 1938 and 1946, was a very senior figure in the development of New Zealand tertiary education in the thirties and forties and was an outspoken rationalist. It is, of course, dangerous to speculate about the level of McCabe's influence from this, but it demonstrates, I think, the esteem in which McCabe was held by many important people in his day.

Even before he wrote *The Growth of Religion*, McCabe held to the importance of the origins of religion as the key to understanding it, and thought that most anthropological studies of primitive peoples made the error of not arranging peoples with due care as to their relative levels of culture. "The ideal scheme would be to classify peoples according to their level of culture, and then see how their religious ideas are graduated."[18] McCabe objected to one of the major conclusions most scholars (particularly those with a theistic bent) in this area reached: that religion is innate in human beings. McCabe isolated several peoples that he determined were the most primitive, and examined the various accounts of their religious views. His criteria for this division rested largely on the sophistication of tool making and language, domestication of animals and forms of abode.[19] Among the people in this group were the Veddahs of Ceylon, as it was then, the Andamanese Islanders, the Aetas of the Philippines, the Semang of the Malay Peninsula, the Bushmen, the Yaghans of Tierra del Fuego, and several Amazon tribes. His authority for this selection was Professor A. C. Haddon, D.Sc., FRS, (1855–1940), president of the Royal Anthropological Institute and University Reader in Ethnology at Cambridge.

In his summary of this question in *The Existence of God*, McCabe discerned four main theories of the origin of religion: those of Max Müller, Herbert Spencer via the adaptation of Grant Allen, Sir E. B. Tylor, and J. G. Frazer. After summarizing their views for his readers, McCabe concluded that there is "at present a growing tendency to believe that neither animism, nor magic, nor care for ancestors is the first stage [of religion], but that all three arise out of an earlier and vaguer phase of the primitive mind."[20] McCabe described his theory as an amalgamation and updating of the best of these theories. Four years later, when he came to write *The Growth of Religion*, he included the work of Emile Durkheim, whose important work *The Elementary Forms of the Religious Life* had appeared in 1915.

Having surveyed the various accounts of these peoples' religious beliefs, McCabe concluded that there was no clear evidence of either definite religion or definite magic. "It appears, then, that any theory of the origin of religion which would assign to it a single root, or make primitive peoples pass through definite and uniform phases is wrong."[21] Neither did McCabe assent to Durkheim's account of the elementary forms of religious life. "The distinction has been drawn that magic is individual and religion social. Whatever we may feel at later and higher levels, it is not true at this level. The roots of religion are in the individual mind, not in any social life or need."[22] He also noted that the absence of totems among the people McCabe selected constituted a problem for Durkheim's thesis. McCabe, in effect, was turning Durkheim on his head. While Durkheim argued that religion provided an essential social glue, and had studied the Australian aborigines—taken to be the most primitive people on earth—to demonstrate this, McCabe had examined the beliefs of yet more primitive peoples and found an absence of religion as a crucial factor in social organization.

McCabe also questioned other important conclusions of the day. For instance, he questioned the notion that fear is the central emotion that explains religion. He didn't dismiss the idea entirely, but he cautioned against laying undue stress on this one emotion. He noted that there was no necessary corollary between propitiatory religions and harsh environments, as one might expect were fear to be central. "Fear did not create gods; the gods created fear."[23] But if fear is not the central component in developing a religious understanding, still less can it be found in the gradual comprehension of an innate moral law, another favorite theory of theistically inclined anthropologists, and beloved by missionaries.

McCabe concluded that "religion is—in its simplest form at least—'the reaction of mankind to something apprehended but not comprehended,' and that the first 'apprehension' is (if one dare say so) emotional; though I cannot agree with Mr Shotwell that man begins with a sense of pervading, mysterious force."[24] James Thomson Shotwell (1874–1965), the coiner of the epigram McCabe quotes, was professor of history at Columbia University and author of a short work, *The Religious Revolution Today*, published in 1915. The English publication of the work by the RPA had an introduction by McCabe. Shotwell was one of McCabe's more important, and loyal, friends in the United States. Shotwell's book is itself worthy of study, not least for its theory of secularization, with that term specifically used.

Somewhat in opposition to his own claim that there is no single root to religion, McCabe argued that "religion begins chiefly with a belief in man's duality (generally founded upon his shadow) and survival of death."[25] It is this original apprehension that slowly develops into the comprehension of survival after death. Contrary to J. G. Frazer and others, McCabe saw magic as a later development that provided the mechanisms by which this important intuition was realized and, later still, propitiated. This led to the development of sorcerers and priests, who developed this function as a vocation. McCabe also noted that priests had an interest in the suppression of rival cults, and attributed this, and the natural attrition of defeated or merged deities, to what theologians like to call the instinct for monotheism.

Questions on the origins of religion were significant for rationalists in the first half of the twentieth century because they led to, and were seen to help answer, an important question: Are religions human creations that themselves have a history? If they are, then the supernatural origins claimed by each religion is false as history, which in turn has important consequences for the truth claims of that religion. Christian scholars had realized this in the nineteenth century, and had tried a variety of stratagems to protect the central core of Christianity from the consequences of this study. Rationalist scholars are among the few who continued the study on to include Christianity. Religion, McCabe wrote in 1923, "is not now conceived as beginning in any religious form, but as a slow evolution out of nebulous emotional material—so slow that you cannot say when it begins to be religion, any more than you can say, within half a million years, when man began to be human."[26] McCabe's point would now be seen as relatively uncontroversial, but it needed to be argued out in McCabe's day. And in an age of resurgent fundamentalism, the conclusions of the study of the origins of religion deserve greater understanding than they have. And without question McCabe's theory of origins is more constructive and less hopelessly romantic than those of contemporary primitivists who, in books written on computers in comfortable studies, would have us abandon rationality.

COMPARATIVE RELIGION

Just as significant for the study of religion at the end of the nineteenth century was the new discipline of comparative religion. In fact it is now clear that McCabe's views on the origins of religion were deeply influenced by the evolutionary approach to the study of religion that was standard in the early decades of comparative religion. As with studies of origins, there was a tendency in a lot of early comparative religion scholarship to exclude Christianity from the study altogether, or at least to undertake the comparative study in order to demonstrate the superiority of the Christian religion over all others. McCabe was not tempted, as most early theorists of comparative religion were, either to exclude Christianity from the conclusions of a comparative approach, or to argue that such study proved the essential superiority of Christianity to all other systems of belief. He had made this important point in his very first tract as a rationalist:

> To the impartial historian, whose views are subsequent, not antecedent, to his knowledge, Christianity is but one member of a large family of religions—Confucianism, Zoroastrianism, Buddhism, Mohammedanism etc; its birth and life are similar to theirs; its death will be like theirs: like man himself, it bears no peculiar marks to prove its supernatural origin and the immortality claimed for it.[27]

It is unnecessary to go into much detail illustrating McCabe's views regarding each and every religion. As our main interest is in his approach as much as his conclusions, one example should be representative enough. We have already noted McCabe's high opinion of Chinese culture and of the contribution of Confucianism to that culture. And yet he did not let his admiration of Confucianism blind him to its weaknesses. To take the discussion in his *History of Human Morals* as an example, McCabe wrote of Kung-fu-tzu and reverted to the Westernized "Confucius" only when making passing references to him in otherwise unrelated passages. McCabe's account was an unremarkable, contextual account of the Chinese sage's circumstances and ideas. In defending Confucianism against charges of aristocratic aloofness, McCabe's answer is characteristically multifaceted:

> In point of fact neither religion nor any other appeal has ever turned aside
> ambitious princes from their blood-spattered paths to greater power and wealth,
> and the appeal of Kung was as futile as any. He had a few thousand followers
> but to the end of his life he failed to secure a prince. But his appeal was demo-
> cratic and sentimental. "Within the four seas all men are brothers," he said, and
> benevolence is the first virtue. It was purely an emotional appeal, and under an
> autocracy the emotional appeal generally fails. Yet in the better conditions of a
> later dynasty the appeal succeeded and it has influenced more millions of lives
> than any creed.[28]

McCabe saw the real defects of Confucianism as an excessive asceticism,
although he recognized the Chinese literati did not follow Confucius too closely
in this area, and its contemplation of "an early and rather primitive social
order."[29] Not surprisingly, its greatest strength, in McCabe's opinion, is its intelligent, nonmystical humanism.

Yet again, the general reader was presented with an intelligent, clearly
written summary of an important issue. The contrast with many Christian views
of the time is stark and nowhere can this contrast be seen more clearly than in
the various views presented in *Outline of Christianity*. Subtitled "The Story of
Our Civilization," this five-volume, lavishly produced work was intended as a
Christian answer to H. G. Wells's fabulously successful *Outline of History*. Most
of the well-known names of English Christendom had articles in the *Outline of
Christianity*. The *Outline* is a particularly valuable comparative tool because it
was designed for the general reader, as most of McCabe's work was. In the
chapter on "The Christian Outlook on Other Religions," Professor J. N. Farquhar, M.A., D.Litt., assured his readers that all roads lead to monotheism.
Beginning with the "bare sheer rudiments of religion" among early primitives,
we gradually rose to a series of "crude polytheisms," some of which matured into
"cultured polytheisms" of Babylonia and most of Asia, but all leading, eventually, to "the spiritual religions, which make little of observances, insist on the
necessity of the transformation of the human spirit and train men not only for
this life but for immortality."[30] Elsewhere in the *Outline of Christianity*, we find
the Rev. Principal A. E. Garvie, D.D., insist in the article on immortality that
"the Chinese mind is not imaginative enough to present to itself the state of the
dead with any definiteness, except their need of the services of the living."[31]
Others, like Professor Edmund Soper, D.D., who contributed the article on comparative religion, were slightly more inclusive about non-Christian faiths, but
remained adamant that skeptics were beyond the pale. Soper declared that the
"only avenue of approach which will yield a fruitful understanding is that of personal appropriation through vital contact with spiritual reality, which we speak
of as religious experience. From this the skeptic is excluded by his own fundamental attitude."[32] Only a few lines later Soper exhorts us to take the attitude
toward other religions that we would want them to take toward our own! Such

high-minded reciprocity is not extended to those without religion. Soper also rather begs the question about whether such spiritual realities actually exist.

It would be misleading to picture these examples of religious arrogance as typical of Christian scholarship, but it does remain that they were selected by the editors, themselves senior theologians, to represent *the* Christian outlook on other religions to a mass audience. These approaches illustrate what McCabe had in mind when he commented that most religious thinkers are more than happy to concede that *other* peoples" religions have evolved, but prefer to insist that their *own* has faith has been revealed.[33] Rationalists like McCabe deserve recognition for being among the first scholars, certainly the first popularizers, to apply the tools of comparative religion to all religions without fear or favor.

There is no better example of this than his 1914 work *The Sources of the Morality of the Gospels*. This unjustly forgotten work sought to put the oft-repeated claim about the uniqueness of the Christian message to the test. As ever, McCabe included a historical survey, this time of the morals of Egypt, Babylonia, the Hebrews, Greeks, and Romans. He then presented a comparative list of ethical maxims from the New Testament and their parallels in Hebrew, Greek, and Roman literature. This list lasted more than eighty-six pages and was considered significant enough seven decades later to be anthologized in the 1980s by Gordon Stein, the editor of the *Encyclopedia of Unbelief*.[34]

McCabe concludes his study insisting that there is no significant ethical maxim that is original to the New Testament.

> That the flesh should be coerced; that the things of this world are little in comparison with the world to come; that the inner intention is as important as the outward act; that the violent should not be resisted; that one ought to love one's enemies; that impurity is one of the worst sins; that God is, alternately a merciful Father and a fierce punisher; that humility has great merit; that repentance disarms the divine anger—these, and every other maxim that has been thought distinctive of the Christian message, were commonplaces of the religions of Egypt, Mesopotamia and Persia.[35]

As ever, McCabe did not claim to have made any startling new discovery. He acknowledged that that liberal divine may well express impatience at this flogging a dead horse. McCabe recognized that this was common knowledge among liberal theologians. But, he added,

> it is far more urgent and useful to correct the errors of millions than to discuss the opinions of an enlightened few; nor does it entirely become a Christian minister to boast that Christ, unlike the Scribes and Pharisees, turned to the people, and that Christianity, unlike Stoicism, chose the market-place rather than the study, and then chide us for taking an interest in popular beliefs.[36]

Not only can rationalists take some credit for being among the first to employ the observations of comparative religion to Christianity, they also deserve credit for bringing these discussions to the general reader. In McCabe's case, this happened decades before liberal theologians brought similar material to their readers' attention. While these liberal theologians have been hailed as courageous radicals, the rationalists who preceded them, like Joseph McCabe, have been forgotten.

THE HISTORICITY OF JESUS

Another approach to understanding McCabe's views on religion is by following him on one particular topic, an interesting example being his views on the historicity of Jesus. This is yet another neglected area of intellectual history. Acres of paper have been devoted to the various Christian views of Jesus, and more recently attention has been directed at Jewish attitudes toward Jesus. But rationalists, too, have had a long debate on the nature of Jesus, and yet this story is still untold. As we saw at the start of this chapter, McCabe's changing view on the divinity of Christ was one of the crucial tests of his faith.

It has often been thought that the denial of the historicity of Jesus is almost one of the first axioms to look for while checking someone's Rationalist credentials. Even some rationalists themselves have made this mistake. As one lesser American writer said, "Orthodox Christians recognize him (Jesus) as a god, Unitarians as a man, and Rationalists as a myth."[37] As usual, the truth is more complicated than that. The question of the historicity of Jesus raged for four decades within the worldwide rationalist movement after the publication of J. M. Robertson's ponderous tome *Christianity and Mythology*, which was first published in 1900. Robertson argued that Jesus Christ was not a historical person but a synthesis of "two popular pagan myth-motives, with some Judaic elements as nucleus and some explicit ethical teaching added."[38] McCabe never believed this, but was as accommodating as possible to his more senior colleague's cherished view. For instance, in 1905, McCabe mentioned, but did not endorse, the fact that some non-Christian sources regard "Christ as a pure myth." His views were founded on more conventional scholarship. He wrote, also in 1905, that the "traditional figure of Christ is dissolving rapidly. Its most familiar and striking features are gone beyond recall. The Gospel story of his life is a late-written biography, full of contradictions and interpolations, or 'layers of tradition,' as these Christian authorities put it."[39] That thumbnail description still looks good more than ninety years later and would not be out of place when put aside contemporary sketches from scholarly books about Jesus aimed at the nonspecialist.

McCabe's most sustained treatment of the historicity question came in one of his Little Blue Books called *Did Jesus Ever Live?* It was later included as chapter 12 of *The Story of Religious Controversy*, the most comprehensive overview of McCabe's philosophy to be found in a single volume. *Did Jesus Ever Live?* was reprinted with two other former Little Blue Books as part of Prometheus Books's Freethought Library series in 1993. McCabe's scholarly caution frequently rewarded him well, not least by resisting the temptations to accept some of the more outlandish theories of possible dates of the Gospels that were circulating at the time, and which were an important feature of the case for the mythical Jesus. McCabe's own dating of the gospels was pretty conventional: he put Mark at between 65 and 70 C.E., Matthew and Luke in the nineties, and John in the second century. Like Robertson, McCabe thought the references to Jesus in the works of Josephus are interpolations, but, contrary to Robertson, he argued that the references in Tacitus and Suetonius are genuine. McCabe came to the euhemerist conclusion that it is "far more consonant with the facts of religious history which we know, to conclude that Jesus was a man who was gradually turned into a God."[40]

As usual, McCabe's stance won him no applause. Christian scholars ignored his work, preferring the stereotype that all rationalists are mythicists. But equally, many rationalists were as deeply wedded to this prejudice. On two occasions McCabe's thoughts on the historicity of Jesus came in for criticism from fellow rationalists. In a short 1937 work, L. Gordon Rylands, a minor myth scholar, accused McCabe of "unlimited assumption and imagination" in arguing for a historical Jesus.[41] McCabe was faulted for not considering a Gnostic tradition before Jesus, for seeing Paul's knowledge of a resurrection as proof of historicity, and for not accepting the late dating of the gospels advocated by the Dutch theologian Willem Christian van Manen (1842–1905). Van Manen's dates were important for the several of the myth theorists. McCabe's reaction to Rylands's attack can only be imagined. Three years later he could still only trust himself to call it—not unreasonably—a travesty of his views. He also defended the reputation of the biblical scholar Alfred Loisy (1857–1940), asking rather sniffily what heed one should pay to criticisms of a scholar of Loisy's caliber from someone "who reads about it in his leisure hours."[42]

Several years later, in one of his Little Blue Books, McCabe returned to the attack of the various mythicist scholars, relying on a series of ad hominem criticisms. Oddly, he drew attention to the fact that none of them were professional historians. This complaint is unfair, given that McCabe was not a professional historian either. A year later, in 1944, McCabe again came under attack from an American rationalist who wrote under the pseudonym "Historicus." This work added nothing to the debate and was little more than a posthumous defense of J. M. Robertson and a criticism of McCabe's controversial methods.[43]

This irrelevant little controversy was indicative of the fate of the historical Jesus position generally. By the time he was writing his autobiography in 1947, McCabe was able to dismiss the whole historicity question. He denounced the "hard dogmatism that pushes some eccentric opinion—as that Jesus was really a fish-god of ancient Palestine or the hero of a rustic passion play—because it has such a destructive air."[44] In 1951 he said simply that the mythical Jesus theory is "held by no writer of any consequence today."[45] The important point is that McCabe did not let his desire to impart a message override historical veracity. Robertson and Rylands, of course, thought they were operating in the same way, but it can be seen that they were thinking theologically rather than historically.

Having decided that Jesus lived, who did McCabe think Jesus was, and what did he think Jesus said? The first interesting point is that McCabe understood the process of secularization in a way that Robertson did not. "Not so long ago," McCabe wrote in 1923, "Christ dominated the lives, the beliefs if not the conduct, of nearly the whole of Europe and America. He has now passed out of the life of—to put it moderately and safely—at least a hundred million of them."[46] He went on to observe that the world may come to honor Christ for his zeal, but that you "cannot make a religion out of that. The figure of Christ, the great white Christ who has ruled Europe for a thousand years, will gradually pass away."[47] Liberal theologians have come to echo McCabe's words decades after he uttered them. The difference is that McCabe was written off as a foolish extremist, when he was noticed at all, but later on the liberal theologians are hailed as courageous pioneers for a new kind of faith.

A similar process can be seen when we examine what McCabe believed the message of Jesus to be. His views on Jesus evolve in an interesting, and not entirely unsurprising way. In his first publication as a nonbeliever, the pamphlet *From Rome to Rationalism*, written in 1897, McCabe asked what has, for rationalists, remained a pertinent question:

> Could anything be more credulous than to put faith in such a biography, especially when we see how every great religious teacher has been credited with supernatural powers by his followers in the course of a century or two after his death?

The answer seemed clear:

> The utmost we are justified in thinking of Christ is that he was a man of noble and generous life, with a singular influence over his fellow-men, which was counteracted by the intrigues of the priestcraft he so frequently denounced, and which ultimately brought about his death. In his character he will remain one of the heroes of humanity until the end of time; but more than this is unreasonable, amid the silence of contemporary writers.[48]

McCabe's historical evaluation of Jesus remained fundamentally the same through his long career. It was his moral and personal evaluation that changed. His later discussions of Jesus concentrated on placing in his correct historical context. And that meant placing him in his Jewish context. McCabe thought of Jesus as an Essene monk "who left his monastery by the Jordan to preach salvation to the erring townsmen."[49] He summarized the message of Jesus, as interpreted in Matthew, in these terms:

Jesus believes in God, and says that he must be worshipped in spirit only, not in temples and synagogues, not with the aid of priests or ministers. This God will punish sin with eternal torment—that is to say, *personal* sins; Jesus never mentions an inherited sin of Adam—and reward virtue with eternal bliss. Jesus believes in devils and angels, which the Jews had taken over from the Babylonians and Persians. He believes that the end of the world is near, and that God will then judge all men for their personal sins.[50]

Give or take the odd detail, it is McCabe's views that look good half a century further on, rather than those of his detractors. McCabe's views are all the more impressive, when we consider the strife the Church of England was going through at the same time on issues such as this. B. H. Streeter (1874–1937), a radical liberal, had written an article entitled "The Historic Christ," which had recognized the futility of attempting to write a Life of Jesus, as had been popular in the nineteenth century. Streeter concluded that a "Christ whom apologists have to 'save' is little likely to save mankind."[51] Other church leaders, such as Professor Soper, were happy to declare, even in his discussion on comparative religion, that there is "a certain inevitability about Him which makes Him in a very real sense the centre of the world's religious life."[52] The Church of England went through a long and quite bitter struggle over the extent to which modern scholarship can be allowed to alter the traditional theological dogmas about Christ. To this day many scholars lament the unwillingness of their New Testament colleagues to fully apply the historical method in their study of Jesus and the Gospels for fear of the consequences to the church.[53] Free from the constraint of theological dogmas, rationalist thinkers have been further ahead in their views on Jesus than most theologians, and, in the light of contemporary Jesus scholarship, more accurate as well. Yet again we find that rationalists were ignored and ridiculed for saying the same things that religious liberals were, decades later, lionized for.

CONTROVERSIES WITH RELIGIONISTS

Having grasped McCabe's views on religion, we can now follow the various controversies he had with religious apologists more clearly. We have already examined McCabe's debate about the argument to design with Rev. Shebbeare. Sadly, most other controversies with apologists were conducted as amiably as that. The first major controversy with Christian apologists McCabe was involved in was in 1903, and followed the publication that year of an influential book called *God and My Neighbour*. Written by Robert Blatchford (1851–1943), the editor of the *Clarion*, a highly popular and controversial socialist magazine, *God and My Neighbour* went through many editions and provoked a storm of controversy. The original inspiration for Blatchford's book was Haeckel's *The Riddle of the Universe*. McCabe later

Father Antony, OSF, taken in the second half of
1895, just months before his secession.
(*Rationalist Press Association*)

McCabe, aged about forty, taken from *The
Principles of Evolution.* (*Collins*)

Beatrice Lee, McCabe's wife for twenty-six
years. (*Stuart & Jenifer Blenard*)

Portrait of an outsider. Gathering at Highgate Cemetery, November 9, 1907, to commemorate the erection of the monument over George Jacob Holyoake's grave. McCabe strains for a view from the back, second from extreme right. (*Rationalist Press Association*)

Illustration for the cover of the second edition of *The Popes and Their Church*. (*Rationalist Press Association*)

Illustration for the cover of the second edition of *The Evolution of Civilization*. (*Rationalist Press Association*)

McCabe on the cover of *Woman in Political Evolution*, which argued for the political equality of women. (*Rationalist Press Association*)

McCabe at seventy. (*Stuart & Jenifer Blenard*)

Ernest McCabe (1909–1988), Joseph and Beatrice's youngest son. (*Stuart & Jenifer Blenard*)

Jenifer and Ernest McCabe, and their daughter, Jenifer Blenard. (*Stuart & Jenifer Blenard*)

acknowledged that Blatchford's recommendation of *The Riddle* was a not unimportant reason for its tremendous success. Following on the success of Blatchford's book, the *Clarion* opened its pages to objections from Christian apologists, and permitted several important rationalists to respond in turn, among them McCabe. Toward the end of the controversy, McCabe complained that it was difficult to oppose one apologist without backing into the arms of another.

> When we, for instance, point out to one of those stubborn apologists of the medieval type that the Old Testament is crude and inaccurate in most parts, another apologist hails this as a proof of its divine inspiration. When we say that the miraculous beginning and end of Christ's life do not concern us, but the life itself, one of the Liberal school at once says *this* is Christianity. One shrinks from Darwin as an emissary of Tophet, and another hails him as a fresh revelation; and so on.[54]

Rationalists are as familiar with this phenomenon at the beginning of the twenty-first century as they were at the beginning of the twentieth. One of the Christian apologists, George Haw, took the line of ascribing all that is best in Christianity to "impenetrable mystery," while G. K. Chesterton, on the other hand, insisted that Christianity was "too jolly" for sad-minded rationalists. This was the first time Chesterton and McCabe crossed swords, but it most assuredly was not the last.

The dispute in the *Clarion* had, by and large, been conducted in an amiable manner. But the next chapter of controversy was less civilized. One of the combatants in that controversy was a Protestant apologist, Frank Ballard. We noted his aggressive style in chapter 3. Ballard had taken particular umbrage to one passage from page 88 of McCabe's *Haeckel's Critics Answered* and sent it, shorn of its context, to a variety of leading English divines. The passage read:

> The truth is that the historical value of the New Testament is shattered, and Christian scholars are, as in the case of the Old Testament, retreating upon its ethical value.

This statement was to result in an avalanche of spleen descending on McCabe. Ballard printed the replies of the fifteen respondents. That they should all condemn McCabe's statement is not surprising, but the level of condescension and arrogance is. It is also noteworthy that most of the scholars condemned McCabe without actually disagreeing. The least convincing of the refutations came from the Rev. R. J. Knowling, D.D., canon of Durham Cathedral, formerly professor of New Testament Exegesis at King's College, London, who described McCabe's claim as "mischievous." He declared—apparently oblivious of the question-begging style of his declaration—that the ethical value of Christianity is being asserted more strongly because of the greater authority of the Divine Person doing the asserting.[55]

Another approach taken by McCabe's calumniators was to veil a tacit acknowledgement of the validity of the passage under a smokescreen of condemnation. For example, Dr. Rendel Harris M.A., reader in paleography in the University of Cambridge, accused McCabe of making hasty and extreme statements and wanting in humility. He then acknowledged that much in the Christian traditions need to be evaluated afresh, but implied that only Christians could honestly undertake this task. In a similar vein, Rev. V. H. Stanton, D.D., fellow of Trinity College, Ely Professor of Divinity in the University of Cambridge, declared that "the best-qualified students of the New Testament now, who approach it in the spirit of Christian faith, recognize far more readily than Christian believers generally were wont even a short while ago to do, that the New Testament writings must be studied with the same open-mindedness as other documents. . . ." That didn't prevent Dr. Stanton from accusing McCabe of misrepresenting grievously the opinion of New Testament scholarship.[56]

Another New Testament scholar, Dr. James Moffatt, attested to the authenticity of "at least three-fifths of the Synoptic stories of Jesus," but was still prepared to sneer that "it is only an amateur who would venture at this time of day upon the assertion that the frank recognition of inaccuracies, tender and heightened coloring, in certain portions of these stories, serves to shatter their historical validity."[57] Dr. Moffatt was soon to face a degree of persecution from his erstwhile (and nonamateur) colleagues for attempting to have his *Historical New Testament* published. Moffatt's New Testament had each book placed in the historical order in which it was written. This produces a remarkably different result than the traditional order.

And so on. Other descriptions include "unqualified and sweeping," "rash," and "reckless exaggeration." Two other scholars, not yet quoted, drew attention to McCabe's Catholic background to find the reason for his current folly. One of them, Rev. Professor J. Vernon Bartlett, D.D., professor of church history, Mansfield College, Oxford, had this to say:

> The fact is that Mr McCabe seems to think still in the all-or-nothing categories which he learnt as a Roman Catholic, and has not been able to adjust his mind and language to the more discriminating standards of the genuine historical method of estimating evidence.[58]

We will examine the other of those remarks in the next chapter. None of this abuse helped shed light on the issue or on Ballard's approach to apologetics. Neither was it good for McCabe. It suggested to him a certain cowardice and equivocation from the learned divines, and an unwillingness to contest the points openly and with respect for the integrity of the opponent. Repeated exposure to this sort of behavior made McCabe harder and more truculent as the years went by.

McCabe's opinion of Christianity was not improved by the standard of much Christian opinion. But he continued to take their claims seriously, and considered his time well spent in refuting them. A good example can be found in a review article, written in 1916, of a series of essays called *The Faith and the War*, edited by Canon F. J. Foakes-Jackson, D.D. The book was devoted to exploring various Christian responses to the war that was claiming an entire generation of Europeans. Foakes-Jackson's own suggestion was that Christianity was not to blame for the war because it has never been tried. McCabe was scornful. "The kind of person who could be rallied out of his doubts by such sophistry is really hardly worth writing for. The question is, of course: What have your churches to say for themselves when such a state of things exists after they have had enormous power in Europe for a millennium?"[59] Neither could McCabe see much virtue in the claim of other contributors. One of them maintained that the war was a God-sent opportunity to reinvigorate our spiritual life, though the incentive "be as it were by high explosives," while another contributor, Percy Gardner, saw the war as a just chastisement of Europe for its many sins. H. G. Wells, always more felicitous with the pen than McCabe, described *The Faith and the War* as "a volume in which the curious reader may contemplate deans and canons, divines and church dignitaries, men intelligent and inquiring and religiously disposed, all lying like overladen camels, panting under this load of obsolete theological responsibility, groaning great articles, outside the needle's eye that leads to God."[60]

McCabe could not match Wells for rhetorical dismissals of this sort, but neither was he as satisfied by them as an argument. So, McCabe put his thoughts on the state of religion together in a new book. The result was one of his most well-rounded and brilliant works, *The Bankruptcy of Religion*. This book's aim was to demonstrate the moral and intellectual bankruptcy of religion that the war had illustrated. Many of the examples McCabe discussed were reminiscent of the arguments employed by Canon Foakes-Jackson the year before. The book began strongly:

> The historical fact is, then, that the teaching of Christ has failed in Europe. I do not mean failed to produce any results. . . . When you say that the Christian writer begins a long list of the noble men and women it inspired, the schools and hospitals it created here and there, the efforts of our fathers to do justice and redeem iniquity . . . but why talk of founding a few schools when ninety-five percent of Europe remained illiterate until the nineteenth century? Why speak of hospitals and charitable institutions when the provision was miserably inadequate, and the roots of disease and poverty were never studied? Why single out a few good people when what we are discussing is the service of Christianity to the race generally? It remains true that, in proportion to the resources which pious folk have for ages put at the service of Christianity, the Gospel teaching has been a failure in Europe.[61]

McCabe went on:

> I have heard many men and women profess anxiety about the future if the
> Churches disappear. But I never heard a man or woman profess anxiety about
> *his* or *her* own future on that account; it is always the neighbor whose moral
> health gives them concern.[62]

McCabe denied nursing any hatred toward the church. Rather, his call was
in the form of an Owenite vision of building a paradise upon earth. "One feels
neither hatred nor bitterness," he wrote, "but such anger as Christ is said to have
felt when he drove the money changers from the temple. Away with the last
traces of this vanishing dream of heaven, which has too long drawn men's eyes
away from earth!"[63]

The Bankruptcy of Religion was written in the middle of a turbulent period in
the Church of England. The decade between 1912 and 1922 saw the Church of
England locked in a series of doctrinal disputes at a level unprecedented before
or since.[64] Central to these doctrinal disputes were the conflicting reactions to
the book *Foundations* (1912). It was the intention of the editor of *Foundations*,
B. H. Streeter, to reconcile Christianity with modern thought. We saw Streeter
admitting the poor record of Christianity as an agency of reform in chapter 4.
The "modern thought" they felt Christianity needed to be reconciled with was,
in no small way, the thought of men like McCabe.

Faced with intractable divisions, Archbishop Davidson instigated a commission to look into Church of England doctrine in 1923 with a brief to "demonstrating the extent of existing agreement within the Church of England and with
a view to investigating how far it is possible to remove or diminish existing differences."[65] The commission finally reported in 1938. Keith Clements, the church
historian I am following here, concludes his study of conflict within the Church
of England offering little hope that the divergent liberal and conservative versions
of the Christian faith can be reconciled.[66] Joseph McCabe had made the same
observations half a century earlier and was ignored. In a short and caustically incisive criticism of the Church of England report, written within weeks of its publication, McCabe came to the heart of the matter. We need only consider a couple
of examples. In the question of what constitutes divine inspiration, for instance,
McCabe quoted the relevant passage from the report:

> The truly inspired are those whose response to the Spirit of God has issued in
> a free surrender to His guidance. In this surrender all individual characteristics
> of mentality, temperament, knowledge, and the like remain, and when inspira-
> tion issues in writing these characteristics appear in what is written.[67]

McCabe concluded that "the authors of this Report have, in order to give
some satisfaction to the conservative, to reject the extreme liberal statement
that the Bible is 'inspired because it is inspiring,' but they dare not go so far in
pleasing them as to say that it is inspired because the Church says so."[68] The

result is that the formula "which is supposed to give unity to conflicting apprehensions is utterly futile, because it becomes impossible to distinguish the divine message from what is due to temperament or limitations of the writer."[69] Among the consequences of this approach is the surrendering of the infallibility of the Bible and the main foundation for the earlier hostility to science.

McCabe found similar problems with the report's attempt to reconcile the various notions of God then in circulation among Church of England thinkers. McCabe listed the contending notions as "the God of the Fundamentalists, the God of the Damnationists, the God of the Platonists, the God of the Aesthetes of the ritualist school, and the various Modernist conceptions of God."[70] McCabe had fun with the result, which attempted to allow for creation out of nothing *and* a universe without a beginning at the same time. He concluded: "I doubt if I have ever read a more evasive piece of apologetic in a serious book."[71]

In the end, McCabe offered the speculation that the report on doctrine was not so much about reconciling dissentient groups within the church, as to liberalize doctrines sufficiently to stem the flow of people out of the church.[72] Either way, he predicted that the "Church of England will continue to be rent by this acrid struggle, and the Report will not have the slightest influence on it."[73] Needless to say, no prominent churchman answered McCabe's criticisms.

McCabe understood the nature of the fatal flaw in liberal religion a long time before most religious liberals understood it. Or at least, McCabe was prepared to state the nature of this dilemma a long way before liberal Christians were.

> You surrender Adam and Eve, the garden of Eden, the fall, the flood. Very good, but then tell us in plain English what you mean by original sin and the atonement. If all men did not die in Adam, all men were not redeemed by Christ. If the New Testament was written decades after the death of Christ, we have no firm ground for belief in the resurrection.[74]

For McCabe, the fundamental dogmas of Christianity are the Atonement, the Incarnation, and the Resurrection.[75] He is asking, then, where does one draw the line? Where does one stop asking questions? Contemporary Christianity can be spread along a continuum, from fundamentalists who cease to ask questions and resort to dogma very early indeed, to Unitarians and religious humanists who have abandoned so many points of dogma it becomes problematic to see them as Christian in any meaningful sense. The most impressive recent statement of this fatal flaw is from Duncan Howlett, whose views we have already encountered. Howlett put the problem this way:

> The Liberals in religion never achieved the goal they sought. Always there came a point where they ceased asking questions, ceased reaching out for new concepts, and returned to the older pattern of belief. This was a fatal flaw, yet they left it untouched at the heart of their movement. The two approaches are mutually contradictory. If inquiry and exploration are appropriate, dogma

resting on revelation and the authority of the church has no place in our religious thought structure. If dogma is valid, inquiry is not merely unnecessary, it is impertinent, inappropriate, and not to be tolerated.[76]

The Church of England's time of troubles changed the sort of reception McCabe received. As a rule, they disengaged from the direct contact of earlier years. Churchmen had very often come away from these scrapes looking foolish, reactionary, out of touch, or a combination of the three. Other church thinkers were falling under the spell of the theologian Karl Barth (1886–1968) who was coming to prominence arguing for an antirationalist crisis theology that focused on faith. Disputing historical facts with rationalists therefore became unnecessary. Non-Barthian theologians fell silent at whatever point they found themselves trapped by the liberal dilemma and unable to concede anything more. So the solution was to disengage. This phenomenon is observable across the English-speaking world. Ceasing to engage in controversies with rationalists and other critics of the church does not mean, of course, that the criticisms will go away.

THE SPIRITUALISTS

It was not only the representatives of the established churches who did battle with McCabe. We saw in chapter 5 that one of the most prominent opponents of Haeckel from within the world of science was Sir Oliver Lodge, FRS (1851–1940), a leading physicist with pronounced leanings toward mysticism. The controversy between Lodge and McCabe had originally been over the merits of Haeckel's monism, but soon developed into a more general dispute between the mystical and rationalist worldviews. McCabe's controversy with Lodge, and later Sir Arthur Conan Doyle, entitles him to recognition as one of the century's leading sham-busters, the most prominent today being Martin Gardner and James Randi.

McCabe's battle with Sir Oliver Lodge began with Lodge responding to calls from church leaders for a scientist to defend the faith from Haeckel's attack. The controversy began in the *Hibbert Journal* with Lodge announcing the reconciliation of religion and what he called "a completer Science."[77] By that Lodge meant a science that conformed to his style of perennial philosophy mysticism. Lodge portrayed Haeckel as a lone materialist washed up on the farthest shores, far from the scientific mainstream. McCabe replied, denying that Haeckel was a materialist at all, insisting that Haeckel saw the spiritual universe subordinated in equal measure with the material universe as "aspects of a deeper reality."[78] Lodge, meantime, was consolidating his reply in a book-length treatment on the controversy entitled *Life and Matter: A Criticism of Professor Haeckel's "Riddle of the Universe,"* which appeared in 1905. He echoed more orthodox critics by lamenting the harmful influence Haeckel would have over "unbalanced and uncultured persons, with no sense of proportion and but little critical faculty. . . ."[79] He also insisted that it "behoves the man of science to put his hand upon his mouth, lest in his efforts to be true, in the absence of knowledge, he find himself uttering, in his ignorance, words of lamentable folly or blasphemy."[80] A few pages after this stern warning, Lodge noted, with disarming credulity, that our "highest thoughts are likely to be nearest to reality: they must be stages in the direction of truth, else they could not have come to us and been recognized as highest."[81]

McCabe replied in *The Origin of Life* the following year. Much of the debate in these books focused on the validity of Haeckel's monism and to what extent Haeckel's views were materialistic. McCabe's next major sally against Lodge came in 1914, and is just as successful a polemic as *Haeckel's Critics Answered*, although the focus of the debate had shifted from Haeckel's alleged materialism to the follies of Lodge's spiritualism. McCabe noted the incongruity of Lodge's accusation that Haeckel was stranded on the outer reaches of respectable science for advocating materialism, while Lodge himself claimed the harmony between science and spiritualism.[82] Certainly, Sir Oliver Lodge was on the periphery of both science and the conventional religion he was claiming to champion. In defending religion from the ravages of materialism, Lodge was prepared to abandon belief in almost all doctrines central to Christianity. McCabe illustrated this brilliantly by reworking the Apostle's Creed to include each of Sir Oliver Lodge's variations on doctrine. It is good enough to reprint:

I believe in God—a God who is one with Nature,
The Father Almighty—but not infinite and all-powerful,
Creator of heaven and Earth—which are, like him, eternal.
And in Jesus Christ—the loftiest spirit that ever lived,
His only Son, Our Lord—and brother, as we also are sons of God;
Who was conceived by the Holy Ghost—as an artist conceives his work,
Born of the Virgin Mary—and equally of the carpenter Joseph,
Suffered under Pontius Pilate—because his teaching was in advance of his age;
Was crucified, dead, and buried—with peculiar accompaniments;
He descended into hell—which does not exist;
The third day he rose again from the dead—or made a new body of ether.
He ascended into heaven—or made a final phantasmal appearance,
Sitteth on the right hand of God the Father Almighty—in a heaven which
    does not exist.
From thence he shall come to judge the living and the dead—or induce them
    to judge themselves.
I believe in the Holy Ghost—more or less,
The Holy Catholic Church—but certainly not the Roman or Anglican Church,
The communion of saints—by telepathy in space,
The forgiveness of sins—each for himself,
The resurrection of the body—which certainly will not rise again,
And life everlasting—which may not last forever.[83]

McCabe's satire would not have the same power today as it did in 1914, because significantly fewer people would regard failing to conform to the Apostle's Creed as any form of reproach.

One spiritualist even declared that McCabe was the reincarnation of St. Paul, on the grounds that both were insignificant in bodily presence though a power with the voice and pen, and who, moreover, were prepared to withstand other apostles to their face.[84] St. Paul or not, Sir Oliver Lodge obviously decided McCabe was beyond hope after this outrage, and the two men did not cross swords again, or at least, not directly.

The next champion of spiritualism to meet McCabe in controversy was Sir Arthur Conan Doyle (1859–1930). The two had crossed swords in several journals during the First World War. This phase of McCabe's career reached a climax in 1920 when he met Doyle in a debate at Queen's Hall in London on the question "Is Spiritualism Based on Fraud?" The debate attracted so much attention it was sold out weeks in advance. As well as a verbatim report of the debate, which was published jointly by the disputants, McCabe also wrote up his research for the debate in two books, one named after the debate and published by Watts, and *Spiritualism: A Popular History from 1847*, published by T. Fisher Unwin. McCabe later thought his debate with Conan Doyle to be the most interesting and important of his career.[85] Many people obviously agreed, as the proceedings of the debate sold all ten thousand copies within the year, and another edition was published independently in Australia, to coincide with Conan Doyle's trip to that country.[86]

It is a little-known fact, and one looks for it in vain in the various biographies about him, that Conan Doyle was a member of the Rationalist Press Association between 1908 and 1916. Conan Doyle resigned after his public declaration on behalf of spiritualism. Many theistic opponents have sought to portray the RPA (and rationalist bodies generally) as "just another religion," apparently oblivious of their using the notion of religion as a rebuke—while in the defense of religion. The fact that Conan Doyle should find the RPA a relatively congenial home for eight years speaks volumes for the commitment to toleration and heterodoxy in that organization—features not commonly observed in religions.

And here, at last, is an aspect of McCabe's career has been discussed in a recent work. Michael Coren's 1996 biography *Conan Doyle*, agrees that the Queen's Hall clash was "one of the most impressive debates of the era," not least for bringing together "two very able, very determined men."[87] Conan Doyle, while a gentleman, was not in any way a systematic thinker. For instance, part of the evidence he gave for spiritualism was an experience during the First World War, while on a tour of the Italian Front. One morning he awoke with the word "Piave" on his mind, not knowing what the word meant, only to hear some time later that the Austrian forces had broken the Italian line and pushed them back as far as the Piave River in a major offensive.[88] Knowing that Conan Doyle read the *Times*, McCabe had the simple job of looking through the previous month's issues to find frequent warning of the danger to the Italian front on the Piave sector. "Doyle was a man of complete honesty," McCabe later recalled, "but he had entirely forgotten and could not recall a reading experience of only a week or two weeks earlier. That is the real subconscious."[89]

Conan Doyle's final and presumably clinching argument was to stress the tremendous consolation that belief in spiritualism had brought many thousands of people.[90] Not surprisingly, McCabe's main argument centered on whether spiritualism is true. This goes to the heart of the rationalist/mystical divide on issues such as this. Conan Doyle had admitted that the Spiritualist movement had been beset by many frauds, but went on to insist that, making every allowance for fraud, "there was a great residuum which could not possibly be explained in such a way."[91] McCabe's response to this sort of special pleading was the commonsense objection that to invoke the supernormal after being unable to detect fraud was to make a very generous jump.[92]

Within weeks of the debate, McCabe responded to Conan Doyle's claims that he exaggerated the element of fraud in spiritualism and ignored its consoling power for the bereaved. He went patiently through the various examples hailed by spiritualists as beyond any shadow of suspicion, and found a marvellous rag-tag of charlatans and tricksters. Conan Doyle had admitted that many mediums were, as he put it, black or gray, but went on to name six "white" mediums, who could confidently be seen as entirely honest. They were Daniel Dunglas Home, Stainton Moses, Mrs. Piper, Mrs. Everett, Kathleen Goligher, and "Eva C." McCabe had little difficulty in demonstrating the decidedly gray-to-black aspects of these supposedly unimpeachable examples of the power of spiritualism.

One of Conan Doyle's "grays," an Australian named Bailey, had achieved a degree of fame by his apparent ability to "apport" birds straight from India at his seances. Bailey's fraud was exposed when it was realized he secreted the birds in what McCabe delicately described as "the unpleasant end of his alimentary canal."[93] Even Michael Coren acknowledges that Bailey had "probably" indulged in fraud in the past, and that Conan Doyle had allowed himself to be persuaded by friends that this had been committed under pressure.[94] Truly, anything is possible in the face of such credulity. Conan Doyle, in fact, would have to rival Paul Edwards's nominee as "probably the most uncritical person in the history of the world. . . ."[95] Edwards made this claim in an exposé of reincarnation and several strands of New Age thinking. While Edwards's nominee, Dr. Elisabeth Kübler-Ross, is, without doubt, a formidable candidate for this award, I must insist on Sir Arthur Conan Doyle's stronger claim.

It wasn't just Conan Doyle who expressed concern about McCabe's concentration on the element of fraud in spiritualism. Chapman Cohen, in his short work *The Other Side of Death*, written two years after the debate with Conan Doyle, thought this emphasis played "right into the hands of the Spiritualist." Cohen was concerned that this approach would let the spiritualists off the hook in that, if fraud couldn't be established, "there was nothing left but to accept the explanation which Spiritualists favor."[96] Cohen thought this approach betrayed a lack of knowledge of both religion in general and spiritualism in particular. Cohen's criticism is unfair, not least because it ignores the actual circumstances of the debate, and Conan Doyle's criticisms of McCabe afterward. It also takes no account of those aspects of McCabe's attack that did not focus on fraud. With regard to seances, for instance, McCabe acknowledged that some were very impressive, and recalled a "conversation" he had had with a departed German theologian, which he conducted in German and Latin. He noted, however, that communications with the "spirits" at seances never seem to rise above the intellectual level of the medium conducting it.

McCabe has been justified in emphasizing the role of fraud in the spiritualist movement. As recently as 1988, one could read the startling admission in the *Journal of the Society of Psychical Research* that psychic fraud had been "the single most important factor in damaging the reputation of parapsychology and retarding its growth."[97] Paul Kurtz, the United States's leading secular humanist thinker, came to the same conclusion in his book *The Transcendental Temptation*. After a survey of the history of spiritualism, very much in the style of McCabe's studies seventy years previous, Kurtz concluded that in almost every case the medium has been found to engage in fraud, or there are no reliable experimental conditions by which the claims of psychics may be verified.[98]

McCabe's reply to Conan Doyle's plea for the consolation value of spiritualism was characteristic. He ended *Is Spiritualism Based on Fraud?* with a characteristic piece of McCabean humanism:

> Do not listen to those who say that critics crush the voice of the heart in the name of reason. We want all the heart we can get in life, all the strength of emotion and devotion we can engender. But let it be expended on the plain, and plainly profitable, task of making this earth a Summerland. Do that, as your leisure and your powers permit, and, when your day is over, you will lie down with a smile, whether you are ever to awaken or are to sleep forever.[99]

The controversy with Conan Doyle rapidly deteriorated after the Queen's Hall debate. Conan Doyle, it seems, lost patience with McCabe's continuing accusations of fraud and lashed out. He had two types of opponents, he claimed: the theological types and the materialist "who clung obstinately to his putridity." "Very well," McCabe responded, "the gloves are off."[100] They soon were. Conan Doyle dashed off a short work entitled *Spiritualism and Rationalism*, which was largely devoted to a drastic attack on McCabe. McCabe does not seem to have answered it.

McCabe had, in fact, embraced one area of spiritualism for a while. Until at least 1916 he can be found describing the evidence for telepathy as satisfactory. In an article in the *Literary Guide* in 1910, McCabe defended telepathy as "no mere hypothesis, an interpretation of chance episodes, or a thing that rests on

music-hall performances," and urged it receive careful attention.[101] It was Sir
E. Ray Lankester who persuaded him that this was far from the case, so by late
1916 McCabe ceased to defend telepathy.[102] Lankester's opinion, as we saw with
the Piltdown question, was highly valued by McCabe. By the time of his debates
with Doyle, he was happy to dismiss telepathy as a "thin shade of mysticism."[103]
Apart from a couple of Haldeman-Julius pamphlets, McCabe ignored the question of spiritualism after 1920.

GOD AND MR. WELLS

Spiritualism enjoyed a massive recovery during the First World War, stimulated
by tens of thousands of grieving relatives, desperately hoping that making contact with slain brothers, sons, or husbands could allay their grief. Many others
who had not lost loved ones also felt a need for some spiritual solace during the
grim years of World War I, among them H. G. Wells. McCabe had reviewed and
commented upon Wells's works on many occasions since at least 1902, but it was
only during Wells's brief theological patch that the two men addressed each
other directly. As we have seen, McCabe admired few men as much as he
admired H. G. Wells. During the controversy with Wells in 1917, McCabe
described Wells was "one of the ablest and most usefully educative writers of our
generation" and a "man of exceptional gifts and fine courage."[104] You may dislike some features of his utopias, McCabe wrote in 1923, "but you will not fail
to recognize a fine conception of what human nature might be."[105] The background to the direct contact was laid early in 1917 when McCabe reviewed
Wells's *Mr. Britling Sees it Through* very warmly, and said that it "whets our
appetite for the book about religion which, I believe, Mr Wells is writing."[106] He
hoped Wells would reconsider his views on agnosticism.

Wells did indeed review his thoughts on agnosticism, but not as McCabe
would have wished. Wells was then in the middle of his mystic frenzy, advocating passionately what he later described as a sort of "deified humanism."[107] In
God the Invisible King, Wells devoted a chapter to the religion of atheists, commenting on their alleged predilection for "unwittingly reproducing the divine
likeness."[108] McCabe was the second example he gave to illustrate his point,
and, he said, "an extremely interesting case." After quoting extensive passages
of McCabe's *Tyranny of Shams*, Wells declared mockingly that McCabe's celebration of contemporary humanism was "half-way to 'Oh! Beulah Land!' and the
tambourine." McCabe "has but to realize fully that God is not necessarily the
Triune God of the Catholic Church, and banish his intense suspicion that he
may yet be lured back to the altar he abandoned, he has but to look up from that
preoccupation, and immediately he will begin to realize the presence of
Divinity."[109] Wells sent McCabe a copy of *God the Invisible King* wishing him a
speedy conversion.

The double irony, of course, is that McCabe was not strictly an atheist in 1917 and Wells ceased to be a theist reasonably soon after *God the Invisible King* came out. Wells lived to regret his lapse into theism and returned to the "sturdy atheism of my youthful days."[110] Indeed, McCabe noted this shift in a review of *Joan and Peter* at the end of 1918. He reviewed the novel very positively, expressing, with evident relief that Wells "is again a very secular moralist, a constructive humanitarian with a magical power of compelling an audience."[111] McCabe again pondered on Wells six years later when, on board ship bound for home after his third Australasian tour, he wrote the manuscript for *The Twilight of the Gods*. McCabe couldn't help noticing that, having accused him of unsupportable optimism, Wells went on to write his utopian romance *Men Like Gods*, which "far outsoars my poor flight!"[112]

McCabe can take credit not for Wells's climb down from his deified humanism, but for important aspects of Wells's subsequent return to a "sturdy atheism" later on in his life, particularly his hardening toward the Catholic Church. Late in his life McCabe wrote that H. G. Wells "twitted me for years about my seeing 'a Jesuit behind every bush.' In his later years he said harsher things about the Church of Rome than I have ever said."[113] It is true that Wells's attitude toward Roman Catholicism hardened in a similar manner to McCabe's, and at the same time. The first sequence of events that precipitated this hardening of attitudes was Wells' famous controversy with Hilaire Belloc, along with his friend G. K. Chesterton, the most famous English-speaking Catholic apologist in the English-speaking world. Belloc had taken offense at Wells's *Outline of History*, and published, in 1926, a *Companion to Mr. Wells's "Outline of History."* Wells responded later the same year with *Mr. Belloc Objects to "The Outline of History,"* where he began by disclaiming any animus toward the Roman Catholic Church, and noted all the praise he had heaped on the church in the *Outline*.[114] Wells had originally wanted to conduct the controversy in the pages of the Catholic journal the *Universe*, where Belloc was launching his attacks from. Despite being offered Wells's articles free of charge, the *Universe* wasn't prepared to let its readers read Wells's side of the story.[115] I suspect that Wells might well have concluded that perhaps McCabe had a point after all.

The worst suspicions of many people about the antidemocratic nature of Roman Catholicism were confirmed by the behavior of many Spanish Catholics, some in prominent positions, in the early years of the civil war in that country. The first evidence of it in Wells's writings is the searingly unflattering portrayal of Father Fayle, the lackey of fascism, in his 1938 novel, *The Brothers*.

A year later Wells publicly recommended McCabe's book *A History of the Popes*, commenting that the "Catholic reader will, I know, feel that my recommendation is in the worst possible taste. But let me nevertheless urge it upon his attention. It will trouble his mind, but it will purge it."[116] Wells recommended the book again in 1943 in his own short indictment of the Roman Catholic Church, calling McCabe's book "a classic which every student of religious history must study. . . ." Wells went further still, and warmly endorsed McCabe, describing him as "the ultimate Protestant, that is to say he has no scrap of religious belief left in him" and as "the most capable critic the papal system has ever had."[117]

Reaction to McCabe's works on Catholicism at this time usually came in tandem with comments on Wells's explosive little tract *Crux Ansata: An Indictment of the Roman Catholic Church*. While it was McCabe who was largely responsible for altering Wells's attitudes toward Roman Catholicism, it was Wells who had infinitely more ability to command press attention. Wells acknowledged his debt to McCabe in *Crux Ansata*, praising both *A History of the Popes* and McCabe himself. Characteristically, Wells noted of McCabe that, in controversy "a certain restraint falls from him" and he, Wells, wished to make his book as "unaggressive as possible"—before going on to make several far stronger claims than McCabe had ever made.

Typical of the reaction is that from Ivor Thomas, MP, who, in a magazine article, declared that "there is no fire left in the attack on religion" and that "Mr H. G. Wells and Mr Joseph McCabe . . . have discovered no new ideas since they first marshalled their forces." The *Literary Guide* responded that "Mr McCabe's *The Papacy in Politics To-day* and Mr Wells's *Crux Ansata* may not contain new ideas, but they contain what is more important—*facts* which tar the Catholic Church with the brush of treason to mankind."[118] This defense came from Archibald Robertson (1886–1961) and illustrates well the thin line between trenchant criticism of Catholicism (or, indeed, of anything) and emotive overstatement, which mars several of Mr. Robertson's works on Catholicism. As chapter 8 will demonstrate, McCabe was very largely successful in walking that thin line.

NOTES

1. Colin Campbell, *Toward a Sociology of Irreligion* (London: Macmillan, 1971), chap. 2.

2. Susan Budd, *Varieties of Unbelief* (London: Heinemann, 1977), pp. 8–9.

3. Joseph McCabe, *Twelve Years in a Monastery* (London: Smith Elder, 1897), pp. 226–27.

4. Joseph McCabe, *One Hundred Men Who Moved the World* (Girard, Kan.: Haldeman-Julius, 1931), vol. 15, p. 51.

5. Joseph McCabe, *The Existence of God*, Inquirer's Library, no. 1 (London: Watts, 1913), p. 33.

6. Ibid., p. 2.

7. Ibid., p. 7.

8. Ibid., pp. 11–12.

9. Ibid., pp. 142–43.

10. Duncan Howlett, *The Fatal Flaw at the Heart of Liberal Religion* (Amherst, N.Y.:

Prometheus Books, 1995), p. 167.

11. Joseph McCabe, *The Story of Religious Controversy* (Boston: Stratford, 1929), p. 76.

12. I am following Antony Flew, who makes the valid point that this argument should be called the argument *to* design (instead of *from*) because it is, after all, the point of this argument to lead to a designer. To call it an argument from design begs the question. For a fuller discussion of this, see his *An Introduction to Western Philosophy* (London: Thames & Hudson, 1971), p. 206.

13. Joseph McCabe and Rev. C. J. Shebbeare, *The Design Argument Reconsidered* (London: Watts, 1923), p. 9.

14. Ibid., p. 36.

15. Ibid., p. 50.

16. Raymond Tallis, *Enemies of Hope: A Critique of Contemporary Pessimism* (New York: St. Martin's Press, 1997), p. 73.

17. Joseph McCabe, *The Growth of Religion* (London: Watts, 1918), p. vi.

18. McCabe, *The Existence of God*, p. 17.

19. Ibid., pp. 17–18.

20. Ibid., p. 24.

21. McCabe, *The Growth of Religion*, p. 63.

22. Ibid., p. 74.

23. Joseph McCabe, *The Rise and Fall of the Gods* (Girard, Kan.: Haldeman-Julius, 1931), vol. 2, p. 18.

24. McCabe, *The Growth of Religion*, p. 76.

25. Ibid., p. 110.

26. McCabe and Shebbeare, *The Design Argument Reconsidered*, pp. 101–102.

27. Joseph McCabe, *From Rome to Rationalism* (London: Watts, 1897), p. 25.

28. Joseph McCabe, *A History of Human Morals* (Girard, Kan.: Haldeman-Julius, 1931), vol. 7, p. 16.

29. Ibid., vol. 7, p. 18.

30. J. N. Farquhar, "The Christian Outlook on Other Religions," in *An Outline of Christianity*, ed. A. S. Peake and R. G. Parsons (London: Waverley, 1930[?]), vol. 5, pp. 264–65.

31. A. E. Garvie, "Immortality," in ibid., vol. 4, pp. 353–54.

32. Edmund D. Soper, "The Comparative Study of Religion," in ibid., vol. 4, p. 308.

33. McCabe, *The Growth of Religion*, p. 11.

34. See Gordon Stein, *A Second Anthology of Atheism and Rationalism* (Amherst, N.Y.: Prometheus Books, 1987), pp. 97–139.

35. Joseph McCabe, *The Sources of the Morality of the Gospels* (London: Watts, 1914), p. 145.

36. Ibid., p. 7.

37. John G. Jackson, *Christianity before Christ* (Austin, Tex.: American Atheist Press, 1985), p. 185.

38. J. M. Robertson, *Christianity and Mythology* (London: Watts, 1900), p. 34.

39. Joseph McCabe, *The Religion of Woman: An Historical Study* (London: Watts, 1905), p. 78.

40. McCabe, *The Story of Religious Controversy*, pp. 218–28. He had moved on from his earlier opinion that it was unlikely any synoptic gospel was written between 70 and 90 C.E. See *The Bankruptcy of Religion* (London: Watts, 1917), p. 149.

41. L. G. Rylands, *The Christian Tradition* (London: Watts, 1937), p. 25.

42. *Literary Guide* (November 1940): 172.

43. I am grateful to Mike Lloyd-Jones for drawing my attention to this pamphlet, called *Did Jesus Ever Live, or, Is Christianity Founded Upon a Myth?* (New York: United Secularists of America, 1972). "Historicus" was actually Jack Benjamin.

44. Joseph McCabe, *Eighty Years a Rebel* (Girard, Kan.: Haldeman-Julius, 1947), p. 25.

45. Joseph McCabe, *The Origin and Meaning of Ideas* (Girard, Kan.: Haldeman-Julius, 1951), p. 48.

46. Joseph McCabe, *The Twilight of the Gods* (London: Watts, 1923), p. 33.

47. Ibid., p. 41.

48. McCabe, *From Rome to Rationalism*, p. 27.

49. McCabe, *The Bankruptcy of Religion*, pp. 148–49.

50. McCabe, *The Story of Religious Controversy*, p. 293.

51. Keith W. Clements, *Lovers of Discord: Twentieth Century Theological Controversies in England* (London: SPCK, 1988), p. 56.

52. E. D. Soper, "The Comparative Study of Religion," in *An Outline of Christianity*, ed. Peake and Parsons, p. 310.

53. I take one example from among many, again chosen because it comes from a short tract designed for the general reader. See James Veitch (a Presbyterian minister and religious studies academic), *The Birth of Jesus: History or Myth?* (Wellington: St. Andrew's Trust, 1997), p. 5.

54. Joseph McCabe, "Christianity Defended by Sleight of Hand," in *Christianity and Rationalism on Trial* (London: Watts, 1904), p. 86.

55. Frank Ballard, *Haeckel's Monism False* (London: Charles H. Kelly, 1905), p. 559.

56. Ibid., pp. 559–63.

57. Ibid., p. 562.

58. Ibid., p. 559.

59. *Literary Guide* (April 1, 1916): 57.

60. H. G. Wells, *God the Invisible King* (London: Cassell, 1917), p. 24.

61. McCabe, *The Bankruptcy of Religion*, pp. 20–21.

62. Ibid., p. 306.

63. Ibid., p. 295.

64. Clements, *Lovers of Discord*, p. 49.

65. Ibid., p. 103.

66. Ibid., p. 236.

67. Joseph McCabe, *The Passing of Heaven and Hell* (London: Watts, 1938), p. 14.

68. Ibid., p. 16.

69. Ibid., p. 14.

70. Ibid., pp. 31–32.

71. Ibid., p. 34.

72. Ibid., p. 51.

73. Ibid., p. 68.

74. Joseph McCabe, *The Social Record of Christianity*, The Thinker's Library, no. 34 (London: Watts, 1935), p. 19.

75. McCabe, *The Bankruptcy of Religion*, p. 194.

76. Howlett, *The Fatal Flaw*, p. 17.

77. Sir Oliver Lodge, "The Reconciliation between Science and Faith," *Hibbert Journal* 1 (1902): 227.

78. Joseph McCabe, "Sir Oliver Lodge on Haeckel," *Hibbert Journal* 3 (1905): 745.

79. Sir Oliver Lodge, *Life and Matter: A Criticism of Professor Haeckel's "Riddle of the Universe"* (London: Williams & Norgate, 1907), p. 6.

80. Ibid., pp. 87–88.

81. Ibid., p. 94.

82. Joseph McCabe, *The Religion of Sir Oliver Lodge* (London: Watts, 1914), p. 9.

83. Ibid., pp. 45–46.

84. McCabe, *Eighty Years a Rebel*, p. 32.

85. Ibid., p. 59.

86. *Twenty-Second Annual Report: 1920*, Rationalist Press Association Ltd., p. 8.

87. Michael Coren, *Conan Doyle* (London: Bloomsbury, 1996), p. 169. One searches in vain for any reference to this debate in the other biographical works on Conan Doyle. Indeed, they often seem apologetic about Conan Doyle's spiritualism in general. See, for example, John Dickson Carr, *The Life of Sir Arthur Conan Doyle* (London: Pan, 1953), pp. 259–60.

88. Sir Arthur Conan Doyle, *The New Revelation* (London: Hodder & Stoughton, 1918), p. 112. Carr also makes reference to this episode.

89. Joseph McCabe, *The Inferiority Complex Eliminated* (Girard, Kan.: Haldeman-Julius, 1940), p. 83.

90. Joseph McCabe and Sir Arthur Conan Doyle, *Debate on the Truth of Spiritualism* (London: Watts, 1920), p. 55.

91. Conan Doyle's "Introduction" to J. Arthur Hill's *Spiritualism: Its History, Phenomena and Doctrine* (London: Cassell, 1918), p. xviii.

92. Joseph McCabe, *Is Spiritualism Based on Fraud?* (London: Watts, 1920), p. 96.

93. Ibid., p. 90.

94. Coren, *Conan Doyle*, p. 173.

95. Paul Edwards, *Reincarnation: A Critical Study* (Amherst, N.Y.: Prometheus Books, 1996), p. 52.

96. Chapman Cohen, *The Other Side of Death* (London: Pioneer Press, 1922), p. 120.

97. *Journal of the Society of Psychical Research* 55 (1988): 107–109; quoted from Richard Wiseman and Robert L. Morris, *Guidelines for Testing Psychic Claimants* (Amherst, N.Y.: Prometheus Books, 1995), p. 15.

98. Paul Kurtz, *The Transcendental Temptation* (Amherst, N.Y.: Prometheus Books, 1991), p. 350.

99. McCabe, *Is Spiritualism Based on Fraud?*, p. 160.

100. *Literary Guide* (September 1920): 129.

101. Ibid. (March 1, 1910): 35–36.

102. Ibid. (December 1, 1916): 186.

103. McCabe, *Is Spiritualism Based on Fraud?*, p. 102.

104. *Literary Guide* (September 1917): 129.

105. McCabe, *The Twilight of the Gods*, p. 74.

106. *Literary Guide* (January 1, 1917): 6.

107. H. G. Wells, *Experiment in Autobiography* (London: Victor Gollancz/Cresset, 1934), p. 674.

108. Wells, *God the Invisible King*, p. 82.

109. Ibid., p. 97.

110. Wells, *Experiment in Autobiography*, p. 677.

111. *Literary Guide* (November 1918): 171.

112. McCabe, *The Twilight of the Gods*, p. 124.

113. McCabe, *Eighty Years a Rebel*, p. 22.

114. H. G. Wells, *Mr. Belloc Objects to "The Outline of History"* (London: Watts, 1926), p. 2.

115. See the entertaining study by Vincent Brome, *Six Studies in Quarrelling* (London: Cresset, 1958), p. 170. McCabe is not mentioned in this book, despite his famous quarrels with Sir Oliver Lodge, Sir Arthur Conan Doyle, and G. K. Chesterton.

116. *Literary Guide* (November 1939): 206.

117. H. G. Wells, *Crux Ansata: An Indictment of the Roman Catholic Church* (London: Penguin, 1943), pp. 63–65.

118. *Literary Guide* (June 1945): 70.

8

Was McCabe an Anti-Catholic Bigot?

W e can now, at last, turn to the subject McCabe is most remembered for: the Catholic Church. But before examining his changing attitudes toward the church he left, we need to address the question of bigotry. Was Joseph McCabe an anticlerical bigot? This would be an easy charge to make about someone who spent more than half a century criticizing the Roman Catholic Church. But that doesn't, of course, make the accusation correct. Significantly, this is not a charge that was leveled against him—except by Catholic apologists. He was more frequently accused of *retaining* distinctive features of Catholicism, as we shall see. But, despite the charge rarely having been laid, it is important to put the question.

For a charge of bigotry to stick, it needs to be shown that his work was motivated by a hatred that was permitted to cloud his judgment, resulting in extravagant accusations or improbable charges. By this standard, McCabe was most certainly not bigoted. He was a trenchant critic of Roman Catholicism, but only a couple of times, late in his life, could his opinions be said to be out of proportion to the evidence mustered. Even then, the problem was that of faulty scholarship rather than bigotry. "Catholics," McCabe wrote in 1924, "are no worse, and no better, than others."[1] Twice McCabe declared that he had no battle with the Catholic laity. In 1929 he acknowledged only friendly feelings for the laity, excepting only "a few contemptible journalists and paid officers of various organizations." [2] Even in an otherwise misanthropic autobiography McCabe insisted that hatred "is, in my code, one of those sentiments that belong to the same dark damned world as pugilism and war; and I have not the least prejudice against the Catholic laity, which would be stupid."[3]

211

If evidence of bigotry is wanted, it is to McCabe's enemies that we should turn. It is among these people where, not infrequently, bigotry and condescension mix happily. We saw enough examples of this in the previous chapter, particularly when Frank Ballard sent a fragment of McCabe's *Haeckel's Critics Answered* around to his friends for a response. One of the responses that I didn't mention in the previous chapter came from a senior and respected scholar, the Rev. R. F. Horton, M.A., D.D., fellow of New College, Oxford. Confident that he had right on his side, Horton assured his readers that McCabe's errors are not surprising. "It is only natural; he was brought up in the Roman Catholic Church, which, for the men of our time, is the halfway house to complete unbelief; but no instructed Protestant could fall into this error, nor will he when he carries his studies further."[4] Even when making an otherwise reasonable point, in this case challenging an overconfident assertion, McCabe's background became an issue. Nine years after McCabe had left the church, Frank Ballard sneered that a statement (about matter-force reality) was made with "all the self-complacency of Romish infallibility."[5] McCabe's criticism of Roman Catholicism was open, honest, and intelligent, and did his opponents the honor of taking their beliefs seriously. In return, he was disparaged, vilified, and slandered.

Consistent with McCabe's apparent inability to please anyone is the fact that anti-Catholic Protestants were ambivalent about his work. While some of them availed themselves of his writings, they were uncertain about using the work of an atheist to counter the claims of fellow Christians. And on McCabe's side, he never hid his disdain for the standard of Protestant anticlerical writing. For instance, he scorned the lurid accounts of misdeeds in the confessional or detention in monasteries, which was common fare among such writers. He also condemned the Protestant predilection to cast aspersions on the morals and greed of the Catholic clergy. "A simple exposition of the doctrines and the system of the Roman Church might convey an impression that the laity are all fools, and the priests all knaves. That," he wrote in 1918, "is very far from the truth."[6] McCabe even reminded his fellow rationalists that "the notion that Rome rebukes the imperious claims of reason is one of a number of strangely-enduring fallacies concerning that Church."[7]

For the vast majority of McCabe's writing career, he directed his attention to the *papacy*, and to leading Catholic apologists, not to the main body of Catholic believers. While, to state an obvious point, McCabe rejected Catholic *doctrines*, his main objection was to the political nature of the Catholic *institutions*, and the lengths they were prepared to go in order to maintain power, and hinder what McCabe considered to be progress.[8] To this extent, McCabe can be considered to be anticlerical. By anticlerical, I am following Hugh McLeod's understanding of the term as "suspicion of the power and pretensions of priests, and especially their association with reactionary politics."[9] McCabe's focus on the papacy as a political institution was a reasonable one, because during his long life the power of papacy over the church at large grew out of all recognition. The First Vatican Council of 1869–70 and the Code of Canon Law, which was completed in 1917, both had the effect on concentrating power in the hands of the papacy.

McCabe's anticlericalism was tinged with rationalism. Throughout his life McCabe took at face value the claims made by people or movements he was studying, and asked the simple, and now often dismissed as naive, question: Is this true? McCabe's histories of the Roman Catholic Church were concerned to show that, in the light of the historical evidence, Catholic claims to spiritual privilege do not accord with the facts. For rationalists like McCabe, demonstrating a dissonance between a claim and the relevant facts is held to be a decisive move. Since McCabe's death it has become fashionable to scorn this approach, preferring to concentrate on the function that a particular belief or practice may have in a person's life, or, more problematic still, to retreat into a nihilist relativism. The relativist is the person who asks "Whose truth?" or "Whose facts?" To ask *which* facts or even *which* truth is a relevant and sensible question, but *whose* facts or truth involves a collapse of any standard by which one person could be shown to be correct and another in error.

McCabe had no doubts there were such things as facts, and that facts are very useful things when seeking the truth. He had what also would seem now a naive confidence that, when faced with facts, people would change their opinions. After all, that is what he had done. So, for sixty years, McCabe presented the facts as he saw them. And for most of that sixty years he was vilified as a "traducer of the Holy See" or ignored as one whose mendacity was too far gone to bother answering.

McCabe took the claims of the Catholic Church so seriously, in fact, that his objection became a moral one. His approach was that, given that the facts were not in accordance with Catholic claims, *and given the extraordinary importance of those claims*, nothing less than a passionate and exhaustive search for the facts was a sufficient response to them. At the end of his twelve-volume history, *The True Story of the Roman Catholic Church*, written for Haldeman-Julius in 1929, McCabe told his readers that my "work in life is to purvey knowledge. I do not think that I ever purveyed a more useful supply of it that in writing this book."[10] This is why his greatest disdain was reserved for apologists who, in McCabe's opinion, evaded inconvenient issues, or simply resorted to ad hominem arguments rather than engaging with the issues raised.

As we have seen, McCabe originally came to notice with his autobiographical *exposé*, called *Twelve Years in a Monastery*. Originally published in 1897, this book proved to be immensely popular, going through three editions, and another three editions of a revised edition, which came out in 1930 for the RPA's Thinker's Library. *Twelve Years in a Monastery* was popular because it was interesting, well written, and forceful, not because it pandered to a prejudiced market. McCabe had every incentive to make this work a shilling shocker; it would have expanded sales, and made a name for himself as a controversial lecturer, which was an important source of income for him, and it would also have satisfied any craving for revenge he may have nurtured. But he didn't do that. Instead, as has been noted, he specifically dismissed as absurd and vulgar the common Protestant prejudices. He also spoke warmly of many of the individuals he had dealings with. The days are long gone, he insisted, "when the Catholic priesthood as a body could be accused of systematic and conscious immorality."[11] In the final chapter of *Twelve Years*, called "The Church of Rome," McCabe listed the weaknesses of the church. Not the iniquities, or even the failures—just the weaknesses. He saw the church's weaknesses as its vastness, providing a larger target for attack, the dogmatic nature of much of its teaching, and its being out of touch with contemporary thoughts about morality.[12]

Having neglected to provide any joy for eager Protestant-haters of Rome, McCabe also criticized the irrelevant nature of much of the rationalist-Catholic encounter.

> There is a curious misunderstanding on both sides; Roman theologians perversely represent Rationalists as men who reject mysteries, miracles, etc, on the mere ground that they are supra-rational, and without reference to their credentials; whereas many Rationalists are under the impression that the Church of Rome professes an irrational method, rebukes and demands the blind submission of reason, instead of offering it satisfactory evidence, and preaches authority from first to last.[13]

McCabe was prepared to criticize anybody if he thought their position unsound. He did so with no thought to temporary tactical advantage; he did so because he believed what he was saying to be true. The strongest criticism against the Catholic Church in *Twelve Years in a Monastery* was to become one of the dominant strands throughout the six decades of McCabe's anticlerical writing.

> Non-Catholics are gravely reminded that it is ethically imperative to study both sides of every religious question. Catholics are told in the same breath that it is sinful for them to read the works of opponents, because, naturally, they are already in possession of the truth and must not endanger its position.[14]

Few things excited McCabe's wrath more than systematic hypocrisy. But even this was tempered by the various strengths that he saw in the church. McCabe ended *Twelve Years* with a very genial inclusion of a Church of Rome into the new humane spirit he saw burgeoning throughout the world.

> But one result is even now detaching itself from the solemn struggle; a feeling of tolerance, a diminution of selfishness, a mutual trust and sympathy, a recognition that all are earnestly interpreting to the best of their power that shadow of a higher world that has somehow been cast upon the life of man.[15]

Twelve Years in a Monastery was a moving, well-written, sympathetic story of one man's odyssey away from Catholicism. Its only equals in the century that followed that I am familiar with are Anthony Kenny's *A Path from Rome* and Karen Armstrong's *Through the Narrow Gate*.

Much of McCabe's later writing on the Catholic Church can be understood in the face of his realization that his early optimism was misplaced. McCabe had come of age when the church was entering a period of sullen reaction against the modern world. McCabe's confident and naive wish that the Catholic Church would take part in the greater humanizing of humanity was to be rapidly and comprehensively disappointed as one reactionary pope succeeded another. Two decades later he began *The Popes and Their Church* with the observation that the "chief paradox of our age is the survival of the Church of Rome." The purpose of this book was to explain how it was that the church continued to survive in the twentieth century.[16] Indeed, much of McCabe's later writing on the Catholic Church was done to demonstrate to the world—and to himself—why this was not happening. As we follow McCabe's extensive writing on the Catholic Church, we can see his gradual disillusionment and growing anger.

An important milestone in McCabe's progressive disillusionment of the potential for reform with Catholicism came in 1901. We saw that McCabe's most serious objection to the church in *Twelve Years* was its refusal to acknowledge honest disbelief—the notion that error has no rights. He made reference on several occasions to the 1901 *Institutes of Public Ecclesiastical Law*, compiled by Father Marianus de Luca of the Papal University at Rome, issued from the Vatican Press, and endorsed by Pope Leo XIII, which supported the putting to death of "obstinate heretics and heresiarchs. . . ."[17] This exclusivism was maintained by apologists such as Father Vincent McNabb, who we have already encountered. McNabb saw the First Vatican Council, which sat over 1869 and 1870 as an "event unparalleled in the history of the world" and a "foregathering of the highest forces of mankind." He claimed that as a consequence of the council's various anathemas of aspects of modernity, "these denials of denials, philosophy began to breathe freely." This beneficent wisdom was to be expected, McNabb added, because no "other man has the Catholic bishop's experience of what is, and what is happening, in man."[18] The church did not relax this brand of exclusivism until the Second Vatican Council, which sat after McCabe's death. And that thaw has since been dissipated and frustrated by the conservative centralism of John Paul II. McCabe was angered by what he saw as the church's unwillingness to concede that someone could withdraw from the church in good faith. This he saw as "the antithesis of our most treasured social principles today. . . ."[19]

Another source of disillusionment for McCabe was the progressive freezing out of reformers and critics within the church. Not surprisingly, McCabe was an admirer of Alfred Loisy, the French historian and Catholic reformer. Loisy and his allies sought to reinterpret Catholic dogma in the light of modern historical and scientific thought while also defending Catholicism from Protestant charges that it was a distortion of the faith of the apostles. Loisy had already run into some trouble with Leo XIII, who had laid down rigid guidelines for biblical research that basically forbade any admission of error in scripture. In 1897, McCabe confidently predicted that Loisy "will simply wait patiently until Cardinal Vanutelli or some broader-minded man assumes the tiara; at present, as a matter of discipline and policy, they must keep silent."[20] But, of course, that did not happen. On the death of Leo, Cardinal Vanutelli was stalemated with the equally able Cardinal Rampolla, leaving the significantly less favored Giuseppe Sarto to sneak in as a compromise candidate on the seventh ballot. Sarto took the name Pius X and quickly proved himself to be "deeply hostile to intellectualism of every kind" and as ferociously opposed to any form of modernism as his most reactionary predecessors.[21] The writing was on the wall for Loisy. Significantly, Pius X is the only twentieth-century pope to have been canonized.

Typical of the responses to Loisy from within the church under Pius X was that of the Catholic Bishop of Newport. The bishop ended his lengthy denunciation of Loisy with as stern a declaration as Ignatius Loyola could have envisaged: "If the formulas of modern science contradict the science of Catholic dogma, it is the former that must be altered, not the latter."[22] Partly in response to Loisy's works, Pius issued in 1907 a decree against all Modernism, *Lamentabili*, following this up with a ninety-three-page encyclical *Pascendi*, which made it quite clear that "intellectual questions within the Catholic Church are not a matter for scholarly peer-group discussion but a moral matter to be resolved by papal authority."[23] A year later, Loisy was excommunicated. McCabe had been confident in 1897 that the church would soon embark on a more open-minded approach. He was to be disappointed time and again throughout his long life.

The unjust demise of another man further unsettled McCabe's sanguine confidence in the ability of the Roman Catholic Church to reform itself. It was also the occasion of one of his most successful polemics. His brief monograph *The Martyrdom of Ferrer* was written in 1909 to publicize the events leading up to the murder of the anticlerical education reformer and anarchist Francisco Ferrer (1859–1909). After the failure of an unsuccessful revolt in 1885, Ferrer spent sixteen years in exile in Paris. In 1901 he returned to his native Barcelona and founded a Modern School. He began that year with twelve girls and eighteen boys, and by 1906 had over fifty schools around Catalonia serving the needs of seventeen hundred students. Ferrer had long since abandoned violence, and sought instead to reform Spain by educating a new generation of clear thinkers. His educational philosophy was egalitarian, rationalist, and scientific. He educated girls and boys in the same way, was openly anticlerical, and was convinced of the need for an education inclusive of the physical, intellectual, and moral development of the child. Ferrer was part of the Spanish delegation at the Free Thought Congress in Rome in 1904, which McCabe, also attended, but it appears the two did not meet. E. S. P. Haynes, a friend of McCabe who attended the congress as a delegate representing the RPA, did remember them: "I must confess that when I saw my Spanish colleagues, of whom he was one, I felt a certain sense of insecurity; but this must have been my insular prejudice."[24] McCabe could think of no higher praise of the Spaniard when he declared, "Francisco Ferrer was the Robert Owen of Spain."[25]

Following unrest in Barcelona, Ferrer was arrested on trumped-up charges of fomenting revolution. He was tried by a military court, paraded in front of what would later come to be called a show trial, and shot by firing squad on October 12, 1909. McCabe concluded that Ferrer was "judicially murdered by Church and State."[26] The murder of Ferrer caused an international outcry, largely fueled by McCabe's book. This can be illustrated by returning to McCabe's successful 1910 tour of Australia. Much of the success of the tour can be attributed to the high level of interest in Ferrer's murder, and because McCabe's visit coincided with the bitter sectarian battle going on at the time. Two special editions of *The Martyrdom of Ferrer* were printed in Melbourne at the time of his visit, and much of his reception with Victoria's premier was taken up with questions about Ferrer. Similarly, McCabe was asked to add a lecture on Ferrer in Brisbane, after the Queensland premier was threatened with ejection for hosting an "ex-priest." Shortly after McCabe's visit the Australian government requested information about the death of Ferrer from the Spanish government. It got no reply.

Despite *The Martyrdom of Ferrer* being rushed into print, its principal conclusion has proved to be sound. As a result of the furor caused by McCabe's book, William Archer (1856–1925) a prominent London journalist, was commissioned to write a more lengthy and dispassionate account of the life and death of Ferrer. Published in 1911, Archer's book supported most of McCabe's contentions. Many years later Hugh Thomas, in his classic study, *The Spanish Civil War*, gave a slightly different account of the Ferrer episode, but arrived at the same principal conclusion McCabe had fifty years previously. Ferrer, Thomas wrote, "almost certainly had little to do with the preparation of the Tragic Week in Barcelona, though he was tried and shot for being 'the chief planner' of it, on the mendacious evidence of a few radicals anxious to destroy him."[27] Thomas emphasizes the role of the treacherous radicals, while McCabe emphasized the role of the Catholic/militarist/royalist establishment that oversaw the whole operation. Either way, the effect was the same. The closest conclusion to McCabe's comes from Edouard de Blaye, a journalist for Agence France-Presse and author of *Franco and the Politics of Spain*. De Blaye is adamant that Ferrer was "clearly innocent" of the charges he faced, and the "real reason for executing this first official martyr of the Spanish Anarchist movement was his militant anti-clericalism."[28]

THE CHURCH AND PROGRESS

The consequences for McCabe of his slow realization of his misplaced optimism in the reformist ability of the Catholic Church were manifold. Throughout the first twenty or so years of his career, McCabe nursed two potentially contradictory notions about the church, which go back to his juxtaposing Catholic doctrines and institutions. On the one hand he was sure that the church was in urgent need of reform and that either this reform would take place soon, or the church would perish. But on the other hand he saw the church in serious decline, which he often suspected to be terminal. He illustrated this in his historical works, which outlined the uneven record of the papacy, as well as by the more problematic method of speculating on the actual numbers of practicing Catholics relative to the rise in population. We will examine his historical works later, but first we need to look at McCabe's prognostications on Catholic numbers. This latter exercise held an inordinate interest for him, and he returned to it frequently. Given the scarcity of reliable figures, these exercises in number crunching are the least satisfactory aspect of his analysis of Catholicism. He indulged himself in this way most in *The Decay of the Church of Rome*, published by Methuen in 1909.

The Decay of the Church of Rome is one of the few books by McCabe that attracted a reply, a pamphlet called *The Rationalist as a Prophet* by Rev. J. Keating. Sadly, I have not been able to find this work anywhere. McCabe was later told by a fellow seceder that the general policy of the English hierarchy was not to mention him at all.[29] McCabe's speculations on numbers are among the more commonly quoted aspects of his work used by other critics of Catholicism, the most notable example being H. G. Wells.[30] There are also examples of Protestants using McCabe's figures. For example, in New Zealand, we see the Presbyterian anti-Catholic writer John Dickson using McCabe's research to justify his own accusations.[31] But while Dickson was prepared to use McCabe's speculations on numbers, he was not prepared to heed his other counsels. Dickson's anti-Catholicism is of precisely the bigoted type that McCabe had already demolished.

A typical example of the observations McCabe made regarding numbers can be found in his third edition of *The Papacy in Politics Today*, published in 1951, when he was eighty-three. He noted that the *Encyclopedia Americana* put the number of Catholics around the world at 294,000,000, the *Britannica* at 382,000,000, and the *Catholic Directory* at 423,000,000. "How," McCabe commented, "in view of this beautiful growth, the Pope and the bishops come to distress us so frequently with laments of the materialism of the age and the success of the devil in propagating Communism, it is not easy to understand."[32] McCabe went on to argue that 200,000,000 was more likely to be the correct figure.

McCabe continued speculations of this type until his death. One of his last monographs, published by the American freethought journal *Progressive World* in 1954, was called "How the Roman Church Counts Heads." It is not that his numerical prognostications are uninteresting, but rather that they can't easily be confirmed and therefore do little for his argument. Furthermore, if the Catholic method of counting heads was problematic, McCabe's speculations on those figures cannot be significantly more reliable.

THE HISTORICAL WORKS

However, the most substantial studies of Roman Catholicism from this first half of McCabe's writing career are sober works of historical scholarship. We followed McCabe's historical method exhaustively in chapter 4 and will try not to repeat ourselves unduly. However, it is important to look at the way McCabe handled the history of Catholic Church. We have already noted that he took Catholic claims very seriously indeed. So seriously, in fact, that his history sought to find the level of correspondence between papal claim and historical reality. Given the claim that the popes were the vicars of Christ himself, it is reasonable to expect a suitably pious standard of behavior from such people.

The best example of these works is his *Crises in the History of the Papacy*, published in 1916. The title is slightly misleading, in that McCabe was more intent on focusing on a selection of popes who had presided over the papacy at its various defining moments. He proposed to "make a selection neither of good Popes, nor bad Popes, but of the Popes who, in either direction, chiefly influenced the fortunes of the institution. . . ."[33] McCabe was fluent in Latin, Greek, German, French, Italian, and Spanish, and was able to read sources in the original. Readers got an intelligent and balanced survey of twenty defining moments in the development of the papacy in 460 pages. This history is free of both historicist notions of inevitability and dogmatic notions of inevitable error. And neither is it a parade of the various sexual peccadilloes of the popes. It is necessary to take one example, so as to show his approach. Let us examine Gregory the Great (590–604), to make an arbitrary choice. Gregory was "a great Pope: not great in intellect, nor perfect in character, but, in an age of confusion, corruption, and cowardice, a mighty protagonist of high ideals."[34] McCabe was quite effusive about Gregory.

> His palace was monastic in its severity. He discharged from his service, in Rome and abroad, the hosts of laymen his predecessors had employed, and replaced them with monks and clerics: incidentally turning into monks and clerics many men who did not adorn the holy state. He said mass daily, and used at times to go on horseback to some appointed chapel in the city, where the people gathered to hear his sermons on the gospels or on Ezekiel. Every shade of simony, every pretext for ordination, except religious zeal, he sternly suppressed.[35]

But, against these examples of piety, McCabe listed briefly Gregory's iniquities: his rebuke of Desiderius of Vienne for studying classical works; his prohibition on slaves entering monasteries, lest their vileness pollute the sacred orders; his prohibition against slaves marrying Christian women; and his support of torture as a legitimate tool against pagans and heretics.

In *The History of the Popes*, written twenty-three years and a mountain of abuse later, McCabe reversed his approach. He began the section of Gregory with a perfunctory nod to the genuineness of his religiosity, and then proceeded to relate other aspects of Gregory's reign that do the pope rather less credit. This time he devoted the detail to the list of Gregory's crimes. McCabe began his account of Gregory by noting how strange it is to regard Gregory as a restorer of social ideals and secular civilization when he himself was entirely convinced that the end of the world, and of course all its civilization as well, was near.[36] McCabe's list of Gregory's crimes include the unhappy story of Gregory's duplicitous relations with the Byzantine emperors, including his unseemly joy at the murder of Emperor Maurice; Gregory's ability to enrich the papacy by exploiting apocalyptic fears among landowners, and an extended look at his attitude toward slavery and discouraging classical learning. McCabe closed his account of Gregory almost with an apology. "In an age when most of our literature accepts the myth that the greater popes helped to rebuild civilization in Europe it is necessary to make these observations, but for the reader with any sense of historical proportion they ought to be superfluous."[37] This was the justification for *The History of the Popes* in particular and his *advocatus diaboli* methodology in general.

McCABE'S OPPONENTS

But perhaps the best evidence for the nature of McCabe's anticlericalism can be found from the opinions of his opponents. Twenty years after his secession, McCabe wrote that:

> People tell me constantly of meeting Catholics and trying the delicate experiment of mentioning my name. They at once, as a rule, adopt an expression of horror, lament my persistent libel of their beliefs, even tell quite ingenious romances about my career; and they have invariably never read a single line I have written.[38]

What such people did read were the works of various Catholic apologists. One example, D. A. Lord, wrote a short pamphlet for the Catholic Truth Society of Ireland called *I Can Read Anything*. Despite the title, Lord suggested his readers were far too sensible to pit themselves against the "trained, clever, brilliant minds" of the church's enemies:

And when they are utterly unscrupulous, as let's say, Joseph McCabe is, and will twist any little bit of history to make a case, and pile yarn on yarn to construct a proof, and use fable for fact and supposition for solid argument, what chance has the average reader against him?[39]

McCabe noted dryly that the English Catholic Truth Society dare not publish the pamphlet, for fear of legal action that he would certainly have brought.

Another Catholic apologist was Herbert Thurston, editor of the *Month*, a major Catholic journal, and author of *No Popery: Chapters on Anti-Papal Prejudice* (1930), a study of some histories of the Catholic Church. Like Lord, Thurston attacked the quality of McCabe's historical scholarship, but came up with very little against him, and indeed rather ruined his own cause, as we shall see. In a generally intelligent criticism over 311 pages, Thurston devotes only two pages to McCabe. Thurston's main grievance is that McCabe makes a relatively mild criticism of Pope Boniface VIII in his *Crises in the History of the Papacy*, which was published by the reputable firm of Putnam, "who are well aware that in the United States the Catholic Church is influential and cannot be outraged with impunity,"[40] but then goes on to make a much bolder criticism of Boniface in his more popular account, *The Popes and their Church*, which was published by the Rationalist Press Association. It is uncertain precisely what crime is being imputed to McCabe at this point, but presumably Thurston wants to accuse McCabe of dishonesty. Thurston is angry that McCabe accepted assessments of Boniface's character from the pontiff's "unscrupulous and bitter enemies."

Thurston is correct that McCabe devotes more attention to the medieval pope in his shorter, more popular account. It is equally true, however, that none of McCabe's claims are contradicted by contemporary accounts. Indeed, Eamon Duffy's recent history of the popes is similar in tone and content to McCabe in *The Popes and Their Church* and harsher than McCabe is in *Crises in the History of the Papacy*.[41] And Duffy identifies himself in his preface as a Catholic. Recall, also, that McCabe had vowed to write "something stronger" about the church following an attack on him and his family by Father McNabb in 1916. *The Popes and Their Church* was the result of that vow.

Thurston goes on to lambaste McCabe for trying to "court popularity or to take money by flinging dirt at the Church which he had quitted."[42] This is grossly unfair. If McCabe had wanted to court popularity he could so easily have repeated the frenzied accusations made against the Catholic Church by large numbers of Protestant critics. That Thurston could only find such trivial and contestable examples of historical wording to complain about in McCabe's books suggests that it is Thurston's accusations that are wide of the mark. Thurston's complaints leave vastly more important and damaging claims unchallenged. The fact is that *Crises in the History of the Papacy* and *The Popes and Their Church* are sound pieces of scholarship that offer significant and important criticisms of Catholic history and practice for the general reader.

Three decades after Thurston's study, a prominent Australian Catholic historian, P. J. O'Farrell, made a far more credible study of McCabe, in the context of the Australian sectarianism we have already had cause to mention. Writing about the situation during McCabe's 1910 visit to Australia, O'Farrell lamented the ignoble feuding and name-calling between Catholics and Protestants, describing the debate as being "at the level of Protestant thrust and Catholic parry." "From these continuing, bitter exchanges," O'Farrell wrote, "only the infidel—acknowledged to be generous, capable, intelligent—emerged with honor."[43] O'Farrell felt it worthwhile to repeat this statement fourteen years later, in a larger history of Australian Catholicism.[44] He also acknowledged that Protestants and Catholics were more interested in scoring points at each others' expense, than in combating the infidel. In this heated atmosphere, not all were prepared to acknowledge McCabe's integrity. He had to be given a police escort into a debate with Cardinal Moran in Sydney, having received a threat to his life—the second in his career so far.[45] Cardinal Moran even described McCabe as "the emissary of an international society for the propagation of atheism and anarchy [and that] no decent person would touch him with a pair of tongs."[46]

McCabe had to put up with abuse of this sort all his adult life. He observed wryly that no charge "is too gross to repeat, if it discredits an 'enemy of the faith.' "

> Dozens of times I have heard the wildest calumnies about myself which circulate throughout the English-speaking world, because I have occasionally written a critical work (always grossly misrepresented in the Catholic press) about the Catholic Church. I never belonged to the Catholic priesthood: I was discharged from it for a fraud: I left it in order to marry a nun I had seduced: and so on. Only the lighter of these things are put in print, and then always with the name omitted.[47]

This tactic of silent slander was not reserved only for McCabe—most former priests of his acquaintance related similar experiences. McCabe probably suffered more of this, if only because of his greater profile. The occasional example may still be found. One from his New Zealand tour in 1923 will suffice. Shortly after McCabe left the country, the *New Zealand Tablet*, the major Catholic journal of the country at the time, complained that it "is not fair to the sort of uneducated people who are willing to take at his own valuation a 'fourth-rate amateur' and a 'palpable outsider.' "[48] Six years later, the *Tablet* cited McCabe as the first in a list of examples demonstrating "the unclean spirit of rationalism."[49] McCabe bore this sort of harassment for the rest of his life. In his autobiography, he took great pleasure in scotching rumors of his imminent return to the church. Even after his death, the story circulated that he had died screaming for the absolution of a priest.[50] As he had been unconscious for a week prior to his death, this story seems unlikely. The tradition of ascribing to infidels an anguished deathbed repentance is an old one. I have had believers assure me of the deathbed repentance and conversion of both Darwin and Jean-Paul Sartre. Stories about Voltaire screaming for a priest are even more venerable

THE LATERAN TREATY, SPAIN, AND BEYOND

As we saw in chapter 2, McCabe's career underwent a sea-change around the midtwenties, when he was in his late fifties. Accompanying this change was a different slant and tone to McCabe's criticism of Roman Catholicism. For many people on the Left, the Concordats with Mussolini and Hitler, Mussolini's invasion of Abyssinia, and the Spanish Civil War were seen as successively more outrageous attacks on democracy and liberty. This hardening of attitudes reflected the greater authoritarianism of Pius XI, who became pope in 1922. But when writing *The True Story of the Roman Catholic Church* in 1929, McCabe felt the need to explain his actions. "Ten years ago there were many who assured me that my ideas of the Roman Church were out-of-date; that it had experienced very considerable changes in a liberal direction since I quitted it thirty-two years ago."[51] McCabe then spent some time explaining why books such as the one he was writing were still needed. His main argument was that world conditions had changed and that Vatican policies and priorities had also changed, and that these changes required criticism.

By 1936, many in the progressive sections of English-speaking countries were inclined to agree with McCabe, and his views gained a new audience. The hardening of attitudes toward the church can be traced in H. G. Wells, for example. Originally far less opposed to Catholicism than McCabe, he ended up far more outspoken in his opposition. Wells had actually criticized McCabe's attitude toward the church in an article. But by 1943 Wells would be accusing the Catholic populations as "an essentially alien body."[52]

McCabe's main works in this later period were *The Papacy in Politics Today*, which was published in 1937 (with rewritten versions appearing in 1943 and again in 1951); *A History of the Popes*, which came out in 1939; and a series of Big Blue Books, published by Haldeman-Julius in 1941 and 1942. This series of Big Blue Books, called the Black International, featured some blood-curdling titles like *How the Pope of Peace Traded in Blood* and *Fascist Rome Defies Civilization*. These titles, devised by Haldeman-Julius for marketing purposes, are unfortunate because they give the impression that the contents must be equally scurrilous. That, as we will see, is far from the case. The worst failing of the Black International series is that they ramble.

The reaction to these works illustrates the new climate of opinion. From being dismissed as an irrelevant Victorian obsession, the affairs of the Roman Catholic Church were again news. The Rationalist Press Association sent a copy of *The Papacy in Politics Today* to every member of British parliament. One consignment of his Black International series, containing the twentieth issue, was seized by the

American customs authorities, worried they might damage the war effort. In New Zealand a ban was placed for the duration of the war on a similar monograph written by Edith Moore and with a preface by McCabe. John A. Lee (1892–1980), a populist renegade from the ruling Labour Party, was later to issue cheap reprints of *The History of the Popes* and several of the Big Blue Books soon after the ban was lifted. The Rationalist Association in New Zealand defied the ban and printed the entire contents of Moore's work in its journal. As part of its complaint against the ban, it proclaimed that "the fact that 'No Friend of Democracy' is prefaced by Mr Joseph McCabe is sufficient recommendation of its worth."[53]

McCabe's later works are distinguished from their predecessors chiefly by his greater willingness to concentrate on the negative aspects of Catholic history. This is another example of the *advocatus diaboli* approach toward history we saw in chapter 4. In one of his Big Blue Books, McCabe declared,

> I really do not care two pins about the question how many children Innocent VIII, Alexander VI, Julius II or Paul III had or just how many popes were sodomists or murderers. I recall these things only when I find so many other writers, even professors, pretending that the Papacy promoted civilization in Europe. . . .[54]

There are two main reasons for this change in McCabe's approach: his frustration at the level and manner of response to his earlier works, and his greater sense of outrage at developments in the world at the time and the role he saw the papacy playing in them. Up until Spain, McCabe, as with many rationalists, was confident that history was on his side. Even in 1929, he was prepared to predict that the church would have abolished clerical celibacy before the close of the twentieth century.[55] After Spain, he was less complacent about the inevitability of peaceful reform. In many ways McCabe was the victim of his mildly historicist, sanguine confidence that the Catholic Church would either reform or perish. We saw him display this confidence in 1897. It was becoming increasingly apparent that the church was not going to wither gracefully in the face of history.

Even at this late stage in his life, McCabe preserved, in most cases, a high standard of scholarship. Only in the last few years of McCabe's writing career, and even then only a few times, did he depart from the high standard he had set himself for half a century. The quality of McCabe's work between 1929 and 1945 can best be illustrated by concentrating on the shorter books and pamphlets he wrote for the general readers. It is reasonable to suggest that if we are going to find extravagant accusations being thrown around, we will find them in these quickly written and cheaply produced works. A quick tour through some of these publications will be sufficient to make the point.

Another way to monitor McCabe's views is to contrast his judgments with those of contemporary Catholic historians. The obvious choices are Eamon

Duffy, whose superb history of the papacy, published in 1997, is called *Saints and Sinners: A History of the Popes*; and John Cornwell, whose 1999 work, *Hitler's Pope: The Secret History of Pius XII*, caused a storm of controversy in Britain. Duffy is a very fine historian who considers that, for "all its sins, and despite its recurring commitment to the repression of 'error,' the papacy does seem to me to have been on balance a force for human freedom, and largeness of spirit."[56] Cornwell's book is similarly well researched and written. Another work McCabe's views can be judged against is a 1973 work called *The Vatican in the Age of the Dictators 1922–45*, by Anthony Rhodes. This book, published by Hodder & Stoughton, is more straightforwardly apologetic: Rhodes finished this work concluding that the Vatican is "an institution of such unique value that without it the civilized world would be immeasurably poorer."[57] The overwhelming impression from comparing McCabe's writing about the interwar and wartime papacy with these more recent writers is of McCabe's accuracy and restraint.

Even at the height of the war, when things looked most bleak for England and the Allies, McCabe was careful with his accusations.

> Let it be understood that we are not attributing vileness of character to the Pope and his court of cardinals or to the hierarchy of archbishops and bishops through whom they act; and assuredly we are making no charge against the Catholic laity, beyond saying that they ought to know what to expect from the writers of their papers and literature who are aware that the reader is sternly forbidden to read any criticism of what they say. The gist of our accusation is that in all ages the outlook upon life of the Catholic hierarchy and its leader, the principle upon which they act, is regard for the interests of the Church alone, and this has led them to enter upon just such alliances whenever it was expedient.[58]

McCabe's argument in the years between 1929 and 1945 was that the papacy found it expedient to ally itself with, or at least tolerate, fascism, in order to fight off Bolshevism, and with a view to secure more favorable conditions at home. McCabe said of Pius XII that he "loathes democracy. He hates Socialism and Communism with all the intensity of a really pious soul."[59] None of these contentions are at odds with the views of Duffy, Cornwell, or Rhodes.

McCabe's new train of thought begins with the Lateran Treaty, signed in February 1929 between Pius XI and Mussolini. In first edition of *The Papacy in Politics Today*, the one that went to every British MP, McCabe described the treaty as "one of the most tainted bargains of modern times and a fit inauguration of a decade of increasing corruption."[60] He itemized the details of the treaty in these terms:

> The Pope got nearly $100,000,000, the independence and sovereignty of the Vatican City, the control of all Italian education except in the universities, and the enforcement of the Canon Law, the establishment of the Church and endowment of the priests. The Duce got a free hand for the complete destruction of democracy in Italy and the silence of the Pope while he murdered

democrats and set out on his glorious campaign to make an empire by selecting weak countries for aggression.[61]

The Concordat was followed by a series of events that shocked sections of progressive opinion. A good example is *Quadragesimo anno*, an Encyclical of 1931 that, in McCabe's words, "imposed Mussolini's Corporate State on the whole Catholic world."[62] *Quadragesimo anno* was, largely, a restatement of Leo XIII's 1891 Encyclical *Rerum Novarum*, which had aimed at stopping the spread of socialism among the poor of Europe. McCabe conceded that Leo's Encyclical was well meaning, but felt bound to add that it came far too late to help improve the condition of the workers, particularly in countries outside the pope's sphere of influence.[63] McCabe's discussion of these Encyclicals has been echoed very recently by John Ralston Saul, who described *Rerum Novarum* as a "modern version of the medieval Scholastic dream of the perfect social order. This was in reality a rejection of humanism, democracy and responsible individualism." Saul also comments on the growing predilection of Catholic elites in the thirties for what he calls "Corporativism."[64]

McCabe acknowledged fully the strained relations between Pius and the Fascist leadership. He wrote that, "the Pope remained, we will not say on cordial terms but at least in alliance with the treacherous warmonger [Mussolini], and the Italian hierarchy and priesthood acclaimed every step he took and every crude boast he made. . . ."[65] To illustrate the duplicitous relationship between pope and dictator McCabe gave the example of Pius XI's response to Mussolini's victory over the Abyssinians.

> Foxy to the end, the world's great moral oracle had the bells of St Peter's rung to call the people to the piazza for the final announcement of victory on October 1st, but St Peter's was not illuminated and every other church was. And the entire Italian hierarchy ordered prayers for God's blessing on "Italy's rulers and her glorious army, which once more is used in defence of the Christian civilization."[66]

McCabe noted that in England, Cardinal Hinsley was claiming the pope had condemned the invasion of Abyssinia, when Pius XI had in fact given the highest possible honor Catholic women could receive, the Golden Rose, to the Italian queen *in her capacity as Empress of Abyssinia*.[67] He also quoted Cardinal Hinsley justifying the relationship:

> As Cardinal Hinsley, head of the Church in Britain, said at a later date, Fascism was "in many respects unjust" but it "prevented worse injustice—if it goes under, God's cause goes with it." (*Catholic Times*, October 18 1935) God's cause is, in the mouth of a cardinal, the power of the Church; and the end justifies the means.[68]

Hinsley's opinion, we now know, mirrored that of Pius XI and Pius XII. As part of the post-Concordat relationship, McCabe recorded that, as part of the deal for the Concordat with Mussolini, Pius XI agreed that the papacy would withdraw support from the Catholic-led *Partito Populare*.[69] Father Don Luigi Sturzo had been given the blessing of Benedict XV in 1919 to create the party. But conditions had changed and Benedict's successor, Pius XI, ordered Father Sturzo to resign and withdraw support from the party he had created. As Eamon Duffy put it half a century later, Pius's action "thereby assisted at the deathbed of Italian democracy. It is unlikely that he shed many tears, for he was no democrat."[70] Rhodes also acknowledges the abandonment of the Catholic parties in exchange for the tenuous security of concordats with dictators to be mistaken.[71] Yet another historian agrees, adding that the Vatican was prepared to dump its support for the *Partito Populare* because a more extreme, and well-placed grouping of "clerico-fascists" enjoyed good relations with the fascists, and were more interested in seeking a resolution to the "Roman question."[72]

McCabe's main error in these accounts was a certain inconsistency in his understanding of the workings of the Italian hierarchy. On the one hand he appreciated that the hierarchy may act differently from the Vatican, as for instance in the hierarchy's generally positive response to Mussolini's invasion of Abyssinia, as opposed to the more reserved response from the Vatican. But on the other hand, he denied that the hierarchy could so act without prior authority from the Vatican.[73] While any senior Catholic could be reprimanded *after* committing some act held by the Vatican to be harmful to the church's interests, it is altogether too much to assert that all bishops seek clearances for their actions before making them. On most occasions McCabe was well aware of this, but once or twice, he let his denunciations get the better of him. This lapse aside, McCabe's account of the relations between Italian fascism and the Vatican is very substantially correct. This is a remarkable achievement, given that he was writing at the time these events were unfolding. It took two generations before apologetic scholarship caught up with him.

GERMANY

McCabe was just as incisive when analysing the situation in Germany. Far from claiming that the papacy was in league with Hitler as a willing coconspirator, McCabe suggested that Germany was using the papacy for its own ends and that once victorious would embark on a persecution of religion "such as the modern world has not seen."[74] He was scrupulous to record the deep personal hostility Cardinal Pacelli (who became Pius XII in 1939) felt toward Hitler and the Nazi leadership.

As with Italy, one of the conditions of the agreement with Germany also came under scrutiny. In that agreement, Pius XI recalled Ludwig Kaas, the priest leader of the Catholic Centre Party, to Rome, and Pacelli assured the Germans that they had no interest in the Centre Party, despite the Centre Party having been crucial to Hitler's victory.[75] Duffy concludes, as McCabe had done at the time, that, in "sacrificing the Catholic political parties Pius assisted in the destruction of mediating institutions capable of acting as restraints and protections against totalitarianism."[76] McCabe's claim was that Hitler had succeeded in duping Pius—among others. Hitler

> double-crossed everybody: Hugenberg, who was openly saying that the imperial family was now to be restored; Hindenburg, whom he assured that he would respect the Constitution; the pope, to whom he gave the Concordat which had had promised, but violated its most treasured clauses before the end of the year; and the German people, to whom he promised peace and a prosperity which has become a mockery.[77]

Another good example of McCabe's approach is his coverage of the plebiscite of the Saar in 1935. McCabe recorded the overwhelming vote for inclusion in Germany in the strongly Catholic province. After noting that the Catholic bishops of Germany bade their flock to vote for inclusion, he made it clear that "I have here no evidence to offer that they acted on instructions from the Vatican."[78] He suggested that this is what happened, but made it clear it was no more than a suggestion.

There was one area where McCabe's usually canny antennae let him down: the show trials of large numbers of monks, mostly Franciscans, over 1936 and 1937. The monks were arraigned on a variety of charges, from illegal currency transactions to sexual violation of minors and imbeciles under their care. While there was substance in some of the charges, there is little doubt that the campaign was engineered by Nazi authorities as part of its long-term program to dechristianize Germany.[79] McCabe was prepared to take the trials at face value, describing them as "this amazing exposure of a comprehensive and incredible corruption. . . ."[80] He even devoted one of his Big Blue Books to the subject: *Vice in German Monasteries* (1937). He was aware that the whole affair had been dismissed as a Nazi jack-up, but was persuaded it was legitimate. His reasoning for thinking this is interesting.

> I read the accounts of them in the *Kölnische Zeitung* and the *Westfalische Kurier*, papers which may be described as Catholic, since they have three or four Catholic readers to one non-Catholic. These reflected and emphasized the sentiments of the Catholics of Rhineland. . . .[81]

Without doubt McCabe's reasoning here is faulty, but it is a lot easier to see this now, with seven decades worth of hindsight. He also had the evidence of a letter by Count Preysing, the anti-Nazi Bishop of Berlin, who wrote to Hitler, admitting that some of the charges were justified, but deprecating the general persecution of the church the Nazis were widening the trials into.[82] In other words, McCabe gave evidence to justify his use of this material, and then proceeded to use it reasonably. McCabe can legitimately be accused of insufficient skepticism in handling this evidence, but he can hardly be accused of bigotry. The generally accepted interpretation of the vice trials is that they were a Nazi retaliation to a very strongly worded Vatican denunciation of Nazi mistreatment of Catholic interests in Germany.[83]

While McCabe saw more fault in the vice scandals than was sensible, he was more than aware that the German Catholic Church had suffered persecution. In *The God of War,* he acknowledged the losses the church sustained in Germany and the attacks on Nazism made by Cardinal Faulhaber.[84] However, he also went on to make the point that Cardinal Faulhaber does not constitute the whole church any more than the enthusiastic collaborators. McCabe commented that, as with Pacelli, Cardinal Faulhaber's complaints were not about the many barbarities the Nazi regime was committing, but the doctrinal unsoundness of the Nazi leadership and beliefs.[85] Faulhaber had been an outspoken opponent of the Weimar Republic and was anti-Semitic. As late as 1941, Faulhaber celebrated Hitler's escape from an assassination attempt with a solemn *Te Deum* Mass at Munich. McCabe's explanation for this difficult relationship was that, despite the huge differences between the Catholic and the Nazi aims and doctrines, there was sufficient common interest in essential areas to justify the continuance of the relationship. The most significant area of common interest was in their shared hatred of communism. The fact that Operation Barbarossa, the invasion of the Soviet Union in June 1941 drew "fulsome approval" from the churches is evidence of this.[86] Only seven days after Hitler launched Operation Barbarossa, Pius XII said in a radio speech "Certainly in the midst of surrounding darkness and storm, signs of light appear which lift up our hearts with great and holy expectations—these are those magnanimous acts of valor which defend the foundations of Christian culture, as well as the confident hope in victory."[87]

As we have seen, McCabe was well aware of the complex and layered nature of relations between the Nazis and the papacy. For instance, he aired, on several occasions, a suspicion that the pope had some idea of Nazi intentions to invade the West before it began. He referred to the meeting between Ribbentrop, the Nazi foreign minister, and the pope on March 11, 1940. This might explain, McCabe suggested, the flurry of allied war despatches the *Osservatore Romano,* the official Vatican newspaper, ran for a few weeks after the meeting.[88] McCabe suggested that an alarmed papacy was warning the allies as unobtrusively as possible. McCabe only ever speculates about this meeting; he made no declaration about it. As it turns out, though, McCabe was right that Pius XII knew about the invasion before it took place, but wrong to infer that he learned it from Ribbentrop. Both John Cornwell and Heinz Höhne confirm that the Vatican came to know about the date of the offensive from Lieutenant Josef Müller, a Catholic then working for the Munich Abwehr, the German High Command's intelligence service, who had informed the Belgian Legation in the Vatican. Müller was later arrested, along with Dietrich Bonhoeffer, but survived the war and went on to cofound the Christian Socialist Union.[89] Despite being wrong about the source of Pius's advance knowledge, McCabe interpreted these events shrewdly and responsibly, and was far from painting Pius as a simple scion of the Nazis.

A dominant theme throughout the Black International series was the absence of any papal condemnation of the Axis powers. In *The Totalitarian Church of Rome*, for example, published in 1942, McCabe made the straightforward point that the papacy had long been silent about the war.[90] The whole series was completed before the first papal condemnation finally took place. McCabe did *not* say that no condemnation would or could happen. He speculated, correctly as it turned out, that Pius XII may, "like Pius X in the last war, turn against Germany when its shadow lengthens."[91] And, nine years later, in his final revision of *The Papacy in Politics Today*, McCabe dutifully recorded that this had happened. But he couldn't help commenting that it wasn't until 1943 that the papacy could genuinely be said to be neutral about the war, and that it was not until June 1945 did it issue a stern condemnation of the brutality of Nazism.[92] Half a century later, Duffy confirmed McCabe's claim by pointing out that Pius XII returned to the policy of neutrality Benedict XV had maintained during the First World War, despite this being "a very different war." Duffy maintains that Pius did condemn the Axis powers at the end of 1942, but concedes that the Allies thought it "timid and oblique."[93] Cornwell is stronger than either McCabe or Duffy when he says that Pius XII's "failure to respond to the enormity of the Holocaust was more than a personal failure, it was a failure of the papal office itself and the prevailing culture of Catholicism."[94]

Duffy also goes on to say that Pius XII's three encyclicals in a space of ten days, denouncing the Soviet invasion of Hungary, present a striking contrast with the silence of the war years.[95] Indeed, this contrast could be found soon after the war itself, when Pius XII condemned the forcible repatriation of Russian renegades who had been captured in German uniform. The pope lost no time describing these actions as "a betrayal of the morality and ideals for which the Allies fought."[96] Pius's behavior can be understood because, as Duffy put it, "he saw Soviet Communism, not Nazism or Fascism, as public enemy number one."[97]

McCabe had recognized this at the time. He goes on to suggest that the Vatican could only hope to recover sufficient influence to protect the Catholic schools and institutions by lending a degree of assistance to Hitler's plans to smash Bolshevism, not by itself an aim the papacy would find uncongenial.[98] He mocked attempts to paint the pope as "a villain of melodrama, masking his evil intentions," but thought the pope was "as sincerely duped by Hitler, Mussolini, and Matsuoka into believing that they would promote his aim at least by destroying Socialism and Communism and signing favorable Concordats with the Vatican, as the Western statesmen were."[99] This is what Rhodes concluded two decades later. Pius XI's "belief that a series of concordats with the dictators would promote the Church's apostolic activity more effectively than would Catholic political parties appears to have been, on the whole, mistaken."[100]

The other main theme of the Black International series was the simple, almost banal, charge that the Fascists "had the co-operation and most valuable assistance of the clergy of the Church of Rome. . . . That, I am fully conscious, is an appalling charge."[101] It is a charge that Rhodes, Cornwell, and Duffy, among others, have vindicated. Many of these wartime pamphlets were devoted to substantiating aspects of that charge. However, McCabe was *not* saying that the Nazis rode to power on the backs of the church. The claim was that the church "had a material share in the destruction of German democracy."[102] This, I think, is a fair and reasonable assessment, and McCabe's ability to make it as the events were unfolding is remarkable.

The extent of McCabe's achievement can also be appreciated by looking at some of the Protestant writing on the Vatican at the time. As an example, there is Dr. L. H. Lehman, an Irish-born convert, who in 1942 was director of Christ's Mission in New York and editor of the *Converted Catholic Magazine*. In a monograph called *Behind the Dictators*, Lehman indulged in precisely the sort of nonsensical conspiracy theories that McCabe eschewed. Lehman described what he called Nazi-Fascism as "the spearhead of a hidden force which set out long ago to impose a new ideology upon the post-Reformation world."[103] Unlike McCabe, Lehman was prepared to speak of conspiracies, in his case, Jesuit ones.

McCabe was sternly critical of what he saw the self-interested nature of papal policies toward the Nazis. At the end of *The Vatican and the Nazis*, McCabe wrote: "You may say that he [Pius XII] looked only and always to the interests of the Church. But that is the very essence of this indictment."[104] Three decades later, Richard Grunberger, in his *A Social History of the Third Reich*, made a similar charge, though in more diplomatic language, when he said that the church shared "an indifference in matters of peripheral concern with a tenacious defence of essentials."[105] Rhodes also admits this. He acknowledges that personal courage of those German bishops who protested, but also observes that "these bishops appear not to have been aware of, or made reference to, the danger of National Socialism to humanity as a whole."[106]

Recent stirrings by the papacy suggest that even it is now prepared to accept in part the reading of events that McCabe outlined as they were occurring. The first outward sign of this change of heart included the French Church's decision, in September 1997, to stage a ceremony at Drancy deportation camp near Paris at which a statement was read that admitted Catholic inaction and collusion with Vichy authorities.[107] But at a Vatican symposium on "Christians and anti-Semitism," held in Rome the following month, Pope John Paul II stopped short of an apology for the Christian contribution to anti-Semitism over the centuries, and for its tragic denouement in the Holocaust. But the pope criticized what he called "wrong and unjust interpretations of the New Testament" which contributed to a lulling of Christian consciences.[108]

THE LAST YEARS

It was not until after the war that McCabe's hitherto high standards of scholarship began to slip. As the Cold War intensified, McCabe felt the fear of an imminent third world war. It is important to appreciate how widespread this pessimism was in the late forties and early fifties. Motivated by these fears, and under the spell of the extraordinary sacrifices the Soviet Union had made in defeating Nazism, McCabe let his suspicions run away with him on a few occasions. A couple of instances of this slippage can also be found in his wartime tracts, but they are not as common. McCabe was an old man by now, and with a fearsome reputation, even among other rationalists, many of whom saw him as an anachronism. On the occasion of the World Union of Freethinkers Conference in April 1946, McCabe chaired a session devoted to the subject of rationalism. He later accused his two fellow panellists of having "offensively snubbed" him after he accused the American Catholic hierarchy of fomenting war fever against the USSR. Times were changing, and McCabe no longer fitted them.

It was in some of his late publications that he came closest to positing conspiracy theories and making claims out of proportion to the evidence mustered in their support. For instance, in his rewritten 1943 version of *The Papacy in Politics Today*, after repeating several of the straightforward claims we surveyed earlier, McCabe went one step too far when he insinuated that Catholic populations generally could not be relied upon as staunch opponents of fascism.[109] Until then, McCabe had taken care to speak of the papacy rather than the Catholic people as a whole. In his final revision of *The Papacy in Politics Today*, he went on to claim that the Vatican had been "straining every nerve for the last four years to drive America into war" against the Soviet Union.[110] Contrary to the popular opinion of the time, that the Soviet Union was hell-bent on war, McCabe suspected that it was the papacy and the United States that had the larger dose of war fever. The problem is not that McCabe's contention was necessarily incorrect. After all, Pius XII left little room for compromise with his Cold War declaration of December 1946: "Either with Christ or against Christ, either with His Church or against His Church." McCabe's error was to clothe as facts what could only be suspicions.

Having said all this, not everything McCabe wrote about Catholicism in his final years was marred by extremism. McCabe's mistake in some of these late publications was to depart from standards he had set himself and had maintained conscientiously for over five decades—often in the face of grievous provocation. He never lowered himself to the levels reached by many Protestant-haters of Rome, because he was never motivated by hatred. It was the standard of his scholarship that he let slip. At the Seventh RPA Annual conference, held in Oadby, Leicestershire, in August 1952, McCabe was the opening speaker. The theme of the conference was "The Menace of Roman Catholicism." McCabe made a series of points from a study he had undertaken of the disproportionate rate of Catholics among criminals. "Roman Catholicism demoralizes its adherents, I suggest, because it chains them to arbitrary dogmas and prevents them from cultivating an attitude of mind which sees clearly its duty to the community before its duty to the priest."[111] McCabe developed that theme in the last publication he produced, a monograph-length study called *Crime and Religion*, published in 1954. McCabe's conclusions in these late studies are problematic and question-begging, not because of some undying hatred of the church, but precisely because he took the truth-claims of the church at face value. If the church claims to be incapable of error because of its exclusive possession of fundamental truths, how is it possible that any from among its flock could stray? McCabe's answer was that they stray because the church is *not* incapable of error or in exclusive possession of basic truths. That this conclusion doesn't get us very far is because people can now approach a question of this type with McCabe's conclusion already assumed, and proceed from there to ask more relevant, sociological questions. They can, to use the jargon, "bracket" the truth-claims, and proceed accordingly. It is not, however, part of the rationalist approach to bracket truth-claims.

In conclusion, then, Joseph McCabe deserves to be taken seriously as a scholar and critic who had something intelligent and worthwhile to say about the Roman Catholic Church. He was the most consistent and intellectually credible anticlerical of the twentieth century. McCabe deserves to be recognized as a forerunner to contemporary historians of the papacy, who are able to be sternly critical of that institution's history, while remaining within the Catholic faith tradition. Eamon Duffy's *Saints and Sinners* and John Cornwell's *Hitler's Pope* are both oblique tributes to McCabe's lifelong odyssey.

NOTES

1. Joseph McCabe, *The Popes and Their Church: A Candid Account* (London: Watts, 1918), p. 132.

2. Joseph McCabe, *The True Story of the Roman Catholic Church* (Girard, Kan.: Haldeman-Julius, 1930), vol. 12, p. 56.

3. Joseph McCabe, *Eighty Years a Rebel* (Girard, Kan.: Haldeman-Julius, 1947), p. 22.

4. Frank Ballard, *Haeckel's Monism False* (London: Charles H. Kelly, 1905), p. 557.

5. Ibid., p. 256.

6. McCabe, *The Popes and Their Church*, pp. 171, 220–21.

7. Joseph McCabe, *Peter Abélard* (London: Duckworth/Putnams, 1901), p. 330.

8. I owe this point to Professor John R. Burr of the University of Wisconsin at Oshkosh.

9. Hugh McLeod, *Religion and the People of Western Europe 1789–1970* (Oxford: Oxford University Press, 1981), pp. 103–104.

10. McCabe, *The True Story of the Roman Catholic Church*, vol. 12, p. 57.

11. Joseph McCabe, *Twelve Years in a Monastery* (London: Smith Elder, 1897), p. 116.

12. Ibid., pp. 279–86.

13. Ibid., p. 271.

14. Ibid., p. 275.

15. Ibid., p. 289–90.

16. McCabe, *The Popes and Their Church*, p. v.

17. Father Marianus de Luca, *Institutes of Public Ecclesiastical Law* (Rome: Papal University, 1901), vol. 1, p. 143; quoted from McCabe, *The Popes and Their Church*, p. 211–12. He mentioned this again in *The True Story of the Roman Catholic Church*, vol. 12, pp. 14–16.

18. Vincent McNabb, *The Catholic Church and Philosophy* (New York: Macmillan, 1927), pp. 113–19.

19. Joseph McCabe, *The Papacy in Politics Today* (London: Watts, 1951), p. 6.

20. McCabe, *Twelve Years in a Monastery*, p. 75.

21. Eamon Duffy, *Saints and Sinners: A History of the Popes* (New Haven, Conn.: Yale University Press, 1997), p. 249.

22. *New Zealand Tablet*, August 27, 1904, quoted from Oliver Lodge, *Life and Matter* (London: Williams & Norgate, 1907), p. 79.

23. John Cornwell, *Hitler's Pope: The Secret History of Pius XII* (London: Viking, 1999), p. 38.

24. E. S. P. Haynes, *Pages from a Lawyer's Notebooks* (London: Watts, 1939), p. 31.

25. Joseph McCabe, *The Martyrdom of Ferrer* (London: Watts, 1909), p. 54.

26. Joseph McCabe, *A Biographical Dictionary of Modern Rationalists* (London: Watts, 1920), p. 249.

27. See Hugh Thomas, *The Spanish Civil War* (London: Penguin, 1979), p. 64.

28. Edouard de Blaye, *Franco and the Politics of Spain* (London: Penguin, 1976), pp. 53–54.

29. McCabe, *The Papacy in Politics Today*, p. 128.

30. See H. G. Wells, *Crux Ansata: An Indictment of the Roman Catholic Church* (London: Penguin, 1943), p. 65.

31. See John Dickson, *Shall Ritualism and Romanism Capture NZ?* (Dunedin: Otago Daily Times and Witness Newspapers Ltd., 1912), p. 148.

32. McCabe, *The Papacy in Politics Today*, p. 82.

33. Joseph McCabe, *Crises in the History of the Papacy* (London: Putnams/Watts, 1916), p. vii.

34. Ibid,. p. 77.

35. Ibid., pp. 62–63.

36. Joseph McCabe, *A History of the Popes* (London: Watts, 1939), p. 134.

37. Ibid., p. 149.

38. McCabe, *The Popes and Their Church*, p. 206.

39. D. A. Lord, *I Can Read Anything*, Catholic Truth Society of Ireland pamphlet, p. 22; quoted from McCabe, *How the Pope of Peace Traded in Blood*, Black International, no. 2 (Girard, Kan.: Haldeman-Julius, 1941), p. 8.

40. Herbert Thurston, *No Popery: Chapters on Anti-Papal Prejudice* (London: Sheed & Ward, 1930), p. 263.

41. Duffy, *Saints and Sinners*, pp. 119–21.

42. Thurston, *No Popery*, pp. 264.

43. P. J. O'Farrell, "McCabe and Sectarianism," *Manna*, no. 6 (1963): 77.

44. See P. J. O'Farrell, *The Catholic Community and Church in Australia: A History* (Melbourne: Nelson, 1977), p. 292.

45. Joseph McCabe, *Vice in German Monasteries* (Girard, Kan.: Haldeman-Julius, 1937), p. 3.

46. *Literary Guide* (November 1, 1910):162.

47. Joseph McCabe, *The Tyranny of Shams* (London: Eveleigh Nash/Dodd Mead, 1916), p. 279.

48. *New Zealand Tablet*, July 26, 1923, p. 18.

49. Ibid., September 25, 1929, p. 3.

50. See Emmett McLoughlin, *Famous Ex-Priests* (New York: Lyle Stuart, 1968), p. 220. McLoughlin was also a seceder, and he had heard these rumors even about himself during two critical illnesses.

51. McCabe, *The True Story of the Roman Catholic Church*, vol. 12, p. 44.

52. Wells, *Crux Ansata*, p. 83.

53. *New Zealand Rationalist* (December/January 1942–43): 14. My Ph.D. thesis, *"The Best of Causes": A Critical History of the New Zealand Association of Rationalists and Humanists* (Wellington: Victoria University of Wellington, 1998), especially chap. 10, discusses this in much greater detail.

54. Joseph McCabe, *The Totalitarian Church of Rome*, Black International, no. 11 (Girard, Kan.: Haldeman-Julius, 1942), p. 12.

55. McCabe, *The True Story of the Roman Catholic Church*, vol. 12, p. 49.

56. Duffy, *Saints and Sinners*, preface.

57. Anthony Rhodes, *The Vatican in the Age of the Dictators 1922–45* (London: Hodder & Stoughton, 1973), p. 358. I do not know whether Rhodes is a Catholic.

58. Joseph McCabe, *The Vatican and the Nazis*, The Thinker's Forum, no. 26 (Girard, Kan.: Haldeman-Julius, 1942), p. 4.

59. Ibid., p. 6.

60. Joseph McCabe, *The Papacy in Politics Today* (London: Watts, 1937), p. 54.

61. Ibid., pp. 15–16.

62. Joseph McCabe, *The Testament of Christian Civilization* (London: Watts, 1946), p. 266.

63. Joseph McCabe, *The Church the Enemy of the Workers*, Black International, no. 14 (Girard, Kan.: Haldeman-Julius, 1942), pp. 10–11.

64. John Ralston Saul, *The Unconscious Civilisation* (London: Penguin, 1997 [1995]), pp. 17–29.

65. Joseph McCabe, *The Pope and the Italian Jackal*, Black International, no. 8 (Girard, Kan.: Haldeman-Julius, 1942), p. 4.

66. McCabe, *The Papacy in Politics Today* (1937), p. 63.

67. McCabe, *The Pope and the Italian Jackal*, p. 5.

68. McCabe, *How the Pope of Peace Traded in Blood*, p. 16.

69. Ibid., p. 15.

70. Duffy, *Saints and Sinners*, p. 258.

71. Rhodes, *The Vatican in the Age of Dictators*, p. 355.

72. John Pollard, "Conservative Catholics and Italian fascism: the Clerico-Fascists" in *Fascists and Conservatives*, ed. Martin Blinkhorn (London: Unwin Hyman, 1990), p. 41.

73. Joseph McCabe, *The Papacy in Politics Today* (London: Watts, 1943), p. 31.

74. Joseph McCabe, *The Pious Traitors of Belgium and France*, Black International, no. 7 (Girard, Kan.: Haldeman-Julius, 1942), pp. 31–32.

75. For a fuller discussion of this, see Richard Grunberger, *A Social History of the Third Reich* (London: Penguin, 1974); and Cornwell, *Hitler's Pope*, especially chap. 8.

76. Duffy, *Saints and Sinners*, p. 259.

77. McCabe, *The Papacy in Politics Today* (1937), p. 74.

78. McCabe, *The Vatican and the Nazis*, pp. 16–17.

79. Grunberger, *A Social History of the Third Reich*, pp. 557–58.

80. McCabe, *The Vatican and the Nazis*, p. 19.

81. Ibid.

82. Ibid., p. 23.

83. Rhodes, *The Vatican in the Age of Dictators*, pp. 207–209.

84. Joseph McCabe, *The God of War*, Thinker's Forum, no. 1 (London: Watts, 1940), p. 17.

85. McCabe, *The Vatican and the Nazis*, pp. 13–14.

86. See Grunberger, *A Social History of the Third Reich*, p. 566; and Rhodes, *The Vatican in the Age of Dictators*, pp. 257–58.

87. Rhodes, *The Vatican in the Age of Dictators*, pp. 257–58.

88. McCabe, *The Pious Traitors of Belgium and France*, p. 27.

89. See Cornwell, *Hitler's Pope*, pp. 238–39, 242; and Heinz Höhne, *The Order of the Death's Head: The Story of Hitler's SS* (London: Pan, 1981), pp. 447–48. It is also worth noting that Bonhoeffer's opposition to the Nazis was not as straightforward as has subsequently been made out. He had portrayed the *Kristalnacht* pogrom of 1938 as proof of God's curse on the Jews. See Grunberger, *A Social History of the Third Reich*, p. 570.

90. McCabe, *The Totalitarian Church of Rome*, p. 3.

91. McCabe, *The Vatican and the Nazis*, p. 30.

92. McCabe, *The Papacy in Politics Today* (1951), pp. 29–30.

93. Duffy, *Saints and Sinners*, p. 264.

94. Cornwell, *Hitler's Pope*, p. 295.

95. Duffy, *Saints and Sinners*, p. 267.

96. Nicholas Bethell, *The Last Secret* (London: Andre Deutsch, 1974), p. 192.

97. Duffy, *Saints and Sinners*, p. 263.

98. McCabe, *The Papacy in Politics Today* (1951), p. 49.

99. Ibid., p. 26.

100. Rhodes, *The Vatican in the Age of Dictators*, p. 355.

101. Joseph McCabe, *Fascist Romanism Defies Civilization*, Black International, no. 10 (Girard, Kan.: Haldeman-Julius, 1942), p. 6.

102. McCabe, *The Papacy in Politics Today* (1951), pp. 49–49.

103. L. H. Lehman, *Behind the Dictators* (Auckland: N. V. Douglas, 1946), p. 31.

104. McCabe, *The Vatican and the Nazis*, p. 30.

105. Grunberger, *A Social History of the Third Reich*, p. 565.

106. Rhodes, *The Vatican in the Age of Dictators*, pp. 297–98.

107. "French Bishops to Admit Collusion with Nazis," *Guardian Weekly*, September 28, 1997, p. 4.

108. "Christians Failed Jews, Pope Says," *Guardian Weekly*, November 9, 1997, p. 16.

109. McCabe, *The Papacy in Politics Today* (1943), pp. vi–vii.

110. McCabe, *The Papacy in Politics Today* (1951), p. 121.

111. *Literary Guide* 47 (October 1952): 153–54.

9

A Twentieth-Century Diderot

I n this final chapter, I would like to attempt several, possibly contradictory things. On the one hand, we need to follow McCabe's views on rationalism, humanism, and atheism, given the importance he attached to these concepts. From there it is important to give some sense of McCabe's philosophy of life. And to finish, we will examine McCabe's views on the Enlightenment, and how they cohere with his life philosophy. The purpose in doing this is to see whether McCabe's view of the world is still credible in the light of all the recent postmodernist criticism that suggests— or would suggest if it took any notice of McCabe—that it is not.

RATIONALISM

In the early days after his secession McCabe was content to describe his program as rationalist, humanist, and agnostic. But even in his earliest books, he was uncomfortable with problems and inconsistencies he saw with this approach. His earliest explorations into the nature of rationalism reveal the influence of nineteenth-century thinkers such as W. E. H. Lecky (1838–1903), whose book *History of the Rise and Influence of the Spirit of Rationalism in Europe* (1865) helped put the term on the intellectual map. While John Stuart Mill and Leslie Stephen were responsible for the backbone of late-nineteenth-century rationalist thought, it was Lecky who introduced the concept of rationalism to a wider public. Lecky saw reason as the "the elevation of conscience into a position of supreme authority as the religious organ, a verifying faculty discriminating between truth and error. . . ." McCabe dissented from this conception, observing that, far from being a faculty of *verification*, the principal legacy of rationalism had been destructive. Unless, "this activity of reason yields conspicuous destructive results, it does not attract the title of Rationalism."[1] He then amended Lecky's conception of the rationalist spirit by seeing it as "a critical action of reason on authoritative religious tradition, which leads to its partial or entire rejection, either from defect of satisfactory evidence to recommend it, or because it conflicts with known facts or evident moral or speculative principles. . . ."[2] Nevertheless, he acknowledged that rationalists do not necessarily reject suprarational theories, unless they are contrarational or there is insufficient evidence in their favor.

McCabe appreciated that rationalism was not the preserve of unbelievers. He was well aware that the main schools of thought in the churches that had been described as rationalist were reformist, or possibly heretical, but were there nonetheless. Indeed, his first biography, that of Peter Abélard, published in 1901, discussed this at length. One of Abélard's main purposes had been to reconcile reason and faith, and it was the spirit of Abélard that had survived in the church, rather than the mysticism of his accuser, Bernard of Clairvaux.[3] It is not unlikely that Abélard was a significant influence on McCabe's eventual secession. You will recall that McCabe listed the points in favor of church dogma in credit and debit columns during the last crisis of his faith. It is quite likely that he did this under the influence, not of Mancunian commercialism, but of Peter Abélard. Eight hundred years before McCabe was born Abélard juxtaposed the thoughts of church fathers on crucial questions of church dogma, which highlighted their inconsistencies. This work came to be known as *Sic et Non* (*Yes and No*) and helped ensure Abélard was convicted of heresy. This is only one of several remarkable parallels between Abélard and McCabe.

Despite all this, it has to be said that McCabe's early thought on rationalism was, in the light of hindsight, unstable. On the one hand it recognized rationalism's role as a criticism of Christian principles from within as well as from without, while on the other hand it seemed to prescribe a rejection of authoritative religious tradition. This tension in McCabe's early notion of rationalism mirrors the situation in the Rationalist movement generally, particularly the composition of the newly created Rationalist Press Committee, the predecessor to the RPA. In *Twelve Years in a Monastery* he describes rationalism as "not only 'naturalism,' but also that attenuated theism which rejects orthodox Christianity in virtue of the results of the Higher Criticism." McCabe listed materialism, agnosticism, positivism, pantheism, secularism, theism, and unitarianism as component parts of that alliance.[4] The RPC/RPA was made up of such an alliance. Atheism was not mentioned. McCabe was to become impatient of this notion of rationalism as he grew older.

The use of the word "rationalism" was changing during these critical years of McCabe's development, not least because of the RPA's success in branding the term in the public mind as irrevocably secularist. In philosophy, rationalism was losing the initiative to the newer school of Idealist neo-Hegelians, of whom F. H. Bradley (1846–1924) was the most prominent. In Christian circles reformers were no longer calling themselves rationalists, preferring the term "modernist." And a new cohort of thinkers came to prominence in the Edwardian years who were critical of all forms of rationalism or modernism. Many saw the Edwardian years as involved in a headlong flight from reason. McCabe, however, never tired of defending rationalism from the various prejudices that were held against it. One such prejudice, which continues to this day, is that rationalism is aridly cerebral and bloodless. McCabe attacked this prejudice throughout his career. The very first article he wrote for the *Literary Guide*, in March 1898, was called "Rationalism and Sentiment." "Truth," McCabe wrote,

> is not the only, though the primary, object of the Rationalist. Once the true relations of human life have been ascertained the real province of emotion is opened. Whether he be an Agnostic, an Idealist, or a Materialist, the Rationalist never for a moment loses sight of the value and the importance of feeling in the conduct of life.[5]

Six years later, during his controversy in Robert Blatchford's *Clarion*, McCabe returned to this theme.

> No Rationalist is so absurd as to suppose that reason is the whole of life. Emotion is the great driving force. The heart is the doer of great deeds. But what appalling waste, what havoc, we discover in the past through a wrong application of these forces! They must be directed by reason.[6]

McCabe's early insistence on what might now be called a holistic rationalism put him at odds with the RPA's definition of rationalism, which spoke of "the mental attitude which unreservedly accepts the supremacy of reason and aims at establishing a system of philosophy and ethics consistent with intellectual honesty, verifiable by experience and independent of all arbitrary assumptions of authority." McCabe preferred to see the supremacy of reason in practical terms. All the RPA definition means, he wrote in 1936, is "that we drastically check by every means in our power our inferences from what we have observed and our imaginative constructions to see whether they represent realities."[7] "Reason," he wrote in 1905, "we know from experience to be a serviceable and generally reliable instrument."[8] And this was during the period of his life when he was most at home in the Rationalist Press Association, and most prepared to use Rationalist nomenclature. McCabe gave his finest elaboration of rationalism during his debate with Conan Doyle in 1920:

> I represent Rationalism. That is to say, I want the whole world to use its reason, every man and every woman in the world. I will respect any man or woman, no

matter what their conclusions may be, if they have used their own personality, their own mind, and their own judgment, rigorously and conscientiously. I do not care what conclusions they come to.[9]

McCabe anticipated Bertrand Russell by thrity-four years in characterizing reason in this way. In *Human Society in Ethics and Politics*, Russell insisted that reason "has a perfectly clear and distinct meaning. It signifies the choice of the right means to an end that you wish to achieve. It has nothing whatever to do with the choice of ends."[10] Apart from a more terse rendering of the principle, the statements are the same.

We have seen that McCabe was not entirely successful in achieving that indifference to the conclusions people arrived at. Neither as a born teacher and communicator, nor as a man of passionately held opinions, *could* McCabe ever be successful in that area. It was, however, his goal, and one he honestly worked toward. This is hardly a rebuke specific to McCabe, of course, as it is an ideal that few of us manage to retain for long. However, that doesn't make it any less worth striving for.

In his later years, McCabe became less and less prepared to tolerate the notion of the supremacy of reason. In 1936, McCabe pointed out that "all we demand is a recognition of the supremacy of reason *in its own sphere*—the attainment of truth or a correct knowledge of realities."[11] Nine years later, when opening his account of rationalism in his *Outlines of the World's Great 'Isms*, he again dismissed the RPA definition of rationalism as comprehensible "only in regard to the circumstances of the nineteenth century."[12] He rejected it as vague and thought it had been preferred because it evaded the question of atheism. This is broadly accurate, as we have seen, because when the RPA was brought together in 1899, its founding directors consisted of a coalition of liberal theists, agnostics, and secularists and atheists.[13]

The problem for McCabe, and for many twentieth-century rationalists, lay in what constituted the legitimate sphere in which reason could be employed. Even though he always wanted to distinguish sentiment from reason, McCabe never wavered from one of the principal tenets of contemporary rationalism: that religious truth claims can legitimately be criticized by the use of reason, and that holding a false opinion, even a religious opinion, has important consequences. And as he was writing at a time before the concept of secularization was widely known, McCabe almost instinctively linked rationalism with rebellion. "Rationalism," he wrote in the introduction to his *Biographical Dictionary of Modern Rationalists*, "has, like every other idea or institution, evolved; and the earlier phases of its evolution still live, in some measure, side by side with more advanced stages of rebellion."[14] It was the products of this intellectual evolution that interested McCabe and constituted the basic principle of selection for the *Biographical Dictionary*.

The variety of types included in this work, and the principle of selection, thus become intelligible. It includes Theists (when they do not conform to the authority of any branch of the Christian Church), Pantheists, Agnostics, and the few who prefer to be called Atheists. It includes distinguished Secularists, Positivists, Monists, and Ethicists. But amid this variety there is a steady progression which is obscured by the need to arrange the names in alphabetical order. . . . The vast majority of the names in the work belong to this and the last generation, and they are predominantly the names of Agnostics, Positivists, Monists, and others who do not accept any fundamental religious beliefs. [15]

The problem here is a long-standing one for contemporary rationalism.[16] A few pages earlier in his introduction to the *Biographical Dictionary*, McCabe had dutifully described rationalism as a "mental attitude, not a creed or a definite body of negative conclusions." But the main criterion for inclusion in the dictionary seems to involve the conclusions arrived at, rather than the process used. That is because McCabe never fully recognized that he was on the one hand committing himself to seeing rationalism as a method, while on the other hand committing himself equally strongly to the conclusions reached by that method.

The anonymous reviewer of the dictionary in the *Times Literary Supplement* was close to making this point, but there was an important difference. The review was generally condescending in tone and cast McCabe as a Victorian throwback. The reviewer complained about the method of selection for inclusion in the dictionary.

The fact a man should have reached the wrong solution is of little importance: that he should have seen there was a problem matters a great deal. Our complaint against Mr McCabe and the Victorian attitude he represents is that he seems unconscious of the problem: the same may be said of his theological opponents.[17]

In fact, of course, it matters a great deal that we should reach the right conclusion. For that not to matter is to fall into the same uncritical relativism that is implied by contemporary postmodernism. The difficulty lies in ascertaining what constitutes the right conclusion, and here the rationalist tenets of exposing one's thoughts to criticism from informed people, using a transparent and repeatable methodology, being conscious of one's premises, and so on becomes very important indeed. While McCabe was not clear about the distinction between method and result, he upheld all the standard principles of rationalism, in the *Biographical Dictionary* and elsewhere.

And contrary to what a "Victorian rationalist" would be expected to do, McCabe kept in touch with the changing conceptions on the nature of reason and continued to keep his readers similarly informed. In a late work devoted to current thinking in psychology, McCabe wrote: "Reason is one of the words which psychologists are now disposed to abandon, but 'reasoning' is a distinct aspect of the human thought-process, a stage beyond the simple form of adjustment to a novel situation."[18] Despite his problems with the RPA and his (justified) difficulties with the supremacy of reason, McCabe remained a "common unconverted Rationalist" until his last breath.[19]

McCabe's rationalism anticipated the conceptions of Karl Popper and Ernest Gellner (1925–1995). Popper wrote *The Open Society and its Enemies* during the Second World War and intended it as his contribution to the antifascist struggle for democracy. Popper likened rationalism to an attitude of reasonableness and linked it to the scientific attitude. He also warned that we should be aware of our own limitations and of the limitations of reason. Suitably equipped "with the help of argument, we can in time attain something like objectivity."[20] Later still, Ernest Gellner, a polymath of similar breadth to McCabe, defended rationalism with a very similar style to McCabe. Gellner saw rationalism as essential to the development of an autonomous individualism. "Truth is acquired in a planned orderly manner by an individual, not slowly gathered by a herd."[21] Rationalism is not merely a choice for us to use or reject, as we see fit, Gellner argued: "Rationalism is our destiny. It is not our option, and still less our disease."[22] The rationalism of McCabe, Popper, and Gellner does not fit the preferred stereotype of contemporary postmodernist calumniators of "Reason." It is strange that the only people who capitalize "Reason" now are these postmodernist critics. Very rarely do they take the trouble to actually examine rationalist thinkers and see whether their victories are real or merely hollow victories over straw men of their own construction. Rationalist thinkers have, by contrast, gotten to the heart of postmodernism. Gellner has equated postmodernism as merely the currently fashionable exterior of relativism, which in turn entails nihilism.[23] The corrosive effects of this nihilism on early-twenty-first-century Western civilization are so pernicious that it constitutes the most pressing intellectual problem of our time. It is encouraging to see that, since Alan Sokal's celebrated exposure of the intellectual pretensions of the postmodernist journal *Social Text*, the tide may well be turning. That is to be hoped, and worked, for.

ATHEISM

As he grew older, McCabe became increasingly impatient with many of the reasons unbelievers gave for avoiding the term *atheist*. In line with his growing insistence on linking science with materialism, he became increasingly prepared to not just use the term atheist to describe himself, but to actively argue for atheism. In doing this, he was many years ahead of his time. McCabe underwent a long and difficult odyssey with regard to atheism. But he was, in all but name, a thoroughgoing atheist long before he started describing himself in these terms. We saw above that, when he listed the component parts of modern rationalism, he did not even mention atheism. His early attitude toward atheism was influenced by that of his mentors, George Jacob Holyoake and Sir Leslie Stephen. "Dogmatic Atheism," wrote Stephen, is, "to say the least, a rare phase of opinion." The agnostic, by contrast, "is one who asserts   what no one denies—that there are limits to the sphere of human intelligence."[24] Interestingly, though, Stephen's agnosticism is strongly, even aggressively, stated, and anticipates McCabe's later tone very closely indeed.

> If Agnosticism is the frame of mind which summarily rejects these imbecilities, and would restrain the human intellect from wasting its powers on the attempt to galvanize into sham activity this *caput mortuum* of old theology, nobody need be afraid of the name.[25]

How like McCabe this passage is! McCabe learned from Stephen an uncompromising agnosticism. But over the years, he became less prepared to describe himself as agnostic the more he came to believe that compromise and agnosticism were inseparable. It is a tribute to his loyalty to Stephen's memory that McCabe stuck with the title as long as he did.

McCabe, as I said, was also influenced by George Jacob Holyoake regarding the terms atheist and agnostic. McCabe explained that when Holyoake used the term "atheist," he did not mean "that he could disprove the existence of Deity. This is not the meaning of the word. His view was, he wrote at the time, the view of Pythagoras: 'I know nothing of Gods.' "[24] Holyoake was a "pure Agnostic, and thanked Huxley for the term. He resented the term Atheist, because most of those who would apply it to him understood it to involve a more or less dogmatic denial of the existence of a Supreme Being."[27]

These attitudes of Stephen and Holyoake overshadowed McCabe's thinking for many years. His reticence is understandable, given the opprobrium the term still attracted. However, McCabe would certainly have known that Holyoake's understanding of agnosticism was almost identical to what Charles Bradlaugh, Holyoake's old rival, called atheism. Late in the 1870's Bradlaugh wrote an essay called "A Plea for Atheism," where he wrote:

> The Atheist does not say "There is no God," but he says: "I know not what you mean by God; the word 'God' is to me a sound conveying no clear or distinct affirmation. I do not deny God, because I cannot deny that of which I have no conception, and the conception of which, by its affirmer, is so imperfect that he is unable to define it to me."[28]

Before we continue, we need to clear up some technical terms. Both McCabe and Bradlaugh's definitions here are examples of what is known as negative atheism. Michael Martin, in his classic study *Atheism: A Philosophical Justification*, sees negative atheism as considering there to be no justification for believing in

God. This is distinct from positive atheism, which is the stronger position of specifically holding the view that God does not exist.[29] McCabe's account is a more extreme expression of negative atheism than Bradlaugh's, because it stresses the agnostic position of not being able to know anything about God, rather than the more conventional stance of negative atheism, which is the view that there is no justification for believing in God. It is worth going into this, in order to understand properly the course of McCabe's later development.

What we see is McCabe's steady retreat from what he came to see as an unsatisfactory position. Five years after his biography of Holyoake, in his *The Existence of God*, McCabe is closer to Bradlaugh's firmer negative atheism. But he is still preferring the term agnostic. In a footnote late in the book, McCabe justifies his position:

> I prefer the term "Agnostic" to "Atheist," because there is a common tendency to conceive the Atheist as one who believes he can disprove the existence of God, and there are men who hold these lines. . . . At the same time, the word "Agnostic" is not free from ambiguity. . . . I mean only that no satisfactory evidence is offered to us of the existence of God (any God).[30]

In a few years, McCabe had moved a long way. Under the banner of agnosticism, he was now advocating what is clearly an atheist philosophy. He was critical of some of the foundational arguments of agnosticism. For example, he criticized Herbert Spencer's distinction between the knowable and the unknowable. This device was second in influence only to T. H. Huxley's own writings on agnosticism, and enabled Spencer to sideline theological questions and get on with what interested him more. McCabe thought Spencer's ploy "an arbitrary distinction which led to an unsatisfactory Agnosticism."[31] All that is missing is his continued reticence about common understanding of the term.

Four years later, in 1917, the question of McCabe's atheism again became a matter of public controversy. As we noted in chapter 3, H. G. Wells, in the middle of his war-induced theistic phase, described McCabe as an atheist in *God the Invisible King*. But it was no more correct then than it had been in 1908, although the nature of McCabe's excuses for avoiding the term changed. During that controversy, McCabe admitted that the only reason he avoided the term was the popular conception that it involved dogmatism.[32] As late as 1926, he was still avoiding the word. In one of his earliest Little Blue Books, written on a ship a thousand miles out from Cuba, on his way home to an uncertain future, McCabe still described himself as an agnostic. But the change is that he now seems anxious to justify his use of the word "agnostic." When we use the term "agnostic," he wrote, "we do not mean that it is quite an open question whether there is a God or not. There is no respectable evidence whatever for God, and there is a mass of evidence which disposes us to believe there is no God." He was also ready to make the case for atheism, assuring his readers that atheists "merely mean that they have no belief in God."[33] This, it will be noted, is a move to the center of the negative atheist position.

Five years later, in *The Rise and Fall of the Gods*, McCabe abandoned entirely his agnosticism, and became an indomitable advocate and campaigner for atheism. Intellectually, we can see that his transition from 1926 to 1931 was not great at all. The real gap was the psychological one of willingly describing himself in terms the majority of the population had been trained to fear and revile. Even then he was careful to define his terms. "A man may disbelieve in God, which cannot reasonably mean more than that he is without belief in God, without caring to make the dogmatic statement that there is no God."[34] But while McCabe acknowledged that people *may* adopt such a stand, his position was "I not only do not believe in God, but I am convinced that there is no God."[35] By 1931, McCabe was a positive atheist.

McCabe followed up *The Rise and Fall of the Gods* with a series of Big Blue Books on atheism in the midthirties. Here, he developed his positive atheism to a degree rarely seen before the sixties. The following passage illustrates both the psychological nature of the move to atheism, and the role of the RPA in providing the stimulus to make that change. In 1936 McCabe recalled that:

> Into this agnostic world I passed when I quit the church 40 years ago, and until some ten or more years ago it never even occurred to me to question the accuracy of my description of my position. Every non-theist I met called himself an Agnostic. I have now seen for many years that the distinction favors superstition, and I have done all in my power, in spite of the hostility of many prominent American and British Atheists, to induce skeptics to call themselves Atheists and Materialists.[36]

To McCabe, the atheist "emphatically rejects the proposal to transfer the name God to nature or any element of it, and he rejects the belief in any sort of deity that is supposed to be distinct from, however much it may be intermingled with, nature."[37] It is interesting to see Bertrand Russell going through the same process. In a short work, written for Haldeman-Julius in 1949 called *Am I an Atheist or an Agnostic?* Russell concluded that, before an audience of philosophers he would call himself an agnostic, bearing in mind the difficulties of proving that God or gods don't actually exist, but when speaking to non-philosophers, he would describe himself an atheist, so as to convey in practical terms, his satisfaction that, in fact, they don't exist.[38]

By the time he was compiling the *Rationalist Encyclopedia*, McCabe's mind was set. His entry on "atheism" began like this:

> **Atheism**. The absence of belief in God. The religious writer's usual definition of the Atheist as one who denies the existence of God, differently from "the reverent Agnostic," is a controversial device to maintain the odium which often attaches to the word.[39]

While this odyssey was undertaken entirely within the framework of English philosophical and social thinking, there is some evidence that McCabe had been influenced by Nietzsche. As early as 1931, McCabe was recommending Nietzsche as among the half dozen most influential people of the past half century.[40] McCabe recommended Nietzsche's works in a suitably cryptic way: "There is no need here to give the dates of the powerful prose works, expounding his ideas, which Nietzsche wrote in the next three years. The Nietzscheans know them, and others never will." McCabe recommended *The Antichrist* as "very sane."[41]

McCabe's advocacy of atheism amply demonstrates his courage to publicly take on a term that was still hugely unpopular, and even dangerous. There was little benefit to him by doing this; he stood only to lose readers, his main source of income, and friends. So why did he adopt the term atheist? We have noted that even his agnosticism was at the atheist end of the spectrum. As early as 1897 a perceptive reviewer of *Modern Rationalism* speculated that there was little real difference between his agnosticism and Bradlaugh's atheism.[42] Twenty-nine years later those differences were so trivial as to be worthless. But still McCabe demurred. What finally launched him into this uncomfortable new world was his desire, stimulated by his break with the RPA, to rid himself of any suggestion of what he saw as lukewarm advocacy of unbelief. A prime example is McCabe's criticism of Gerald Bullett in the midthirties. Bullett had argued that the real issue was not between theism and atheism but between those who could and those who could not "apprehend the mystery of the universe."[43] Bullett accompanied this appeal with a criticism of materialism. McCabe was severely critical of Bullett's obfuscation. "The radical fallacy of these pacifists of the world of unbelief is to persuade themselves that superstition is just ignorance, and that the spread of knowledge is bound to be fatal to it."[44] McCabe saw, as the more sanguine agnostics (and some later humanists) did not see, that religion and superstition will not simply fade away in the bright glare of progress. Events have shown that this lazy progressionism to be foolishly optimistic. Yet again McCabe proved to be correct. Even infidels, it seems, do not like Laodiceans.

McCabe's espousal of positive atheism in the midthirties marks him as a pioneer in a field that has been followed so illustriously since the war by J. J. C. Smart, Wallace Matson, Antony Flew, J. L. Mackie, Kai Nielsen, and, most recently, Michael Martin. McCabe also preempted Richard Dawkins by over fifty years when he conceded to fundamentalists the point that evolution does indeed lead to atheism because of evolution having answered problems that most branches of theism were unable to answer satisfactorily.[45] Dawkins, as we noted in chapter 5, made a similar point in 1986 when he declared that only since Darwin "has it been possible to be an intellectually fulfilled atheist."[46]

While hailing McCabe as a pioneer, I recognize fully that other people were espousing atheism before McCabe was. He acknowledged the priority of Bradlaugh, J. M. Robertson, G. W. Foote, and Chapman Cohen to him in this regard.[47] David Berman, in his historical study of atheism in Britain, describes

Chapman Cohen as the "last popular and popularist champion of atheism in Britain."[48] Strictly speaking, this is true, but it ignores McCabe's tremendous contribution. McCabe was *a* pioneer, rather than *the* pioneer. He still deserves to be called a pioneer, because of the quality of his thinking, both during his long road to atheism and once he went on to advocate atheism.

In one area of atheist theory, McCabe was most certainly ahead of his time and his rivals. This is in his appreciation of the antiquity of atheist thought among Asian systems of belief. In *The Rise and Fall of the Gods* McCabe was generous in his praise of the atheistic components of the Buddha's teaching, as well as of the Sankhya school of Hinduism, the Lokayata materialists, Lao Tzu, and Confucius.[49] Readers had to wait over sixty years before scholars like James Thrower and Finngeir Hiorth made similar points.[50]

HUMANISM

The Term

The term *humanism* shares with *existentialism* and *postmodernism* the dubious honor of being among the most indistinct terms of the twentieth century. In fact it can outdo those terms by claiming an indistinctness that goes back for centuries. As with rationalism and atheism, McCabe had a long and changeable relationship with the various understandings of humanism. At the everyday level, he identified with the term and used it regularly. But on a more academic level, he frequently found the term annoying. His first serious confrontation with the term came after the publication of Dr. F. C. S. Schiller's book *Humanism* in 1903. Schiller's study was heavily influenced by the American Pragmatists and was the first systematic attempt to employ the term humanism in a coherent body of philosophy.[51] Schiller was scornful of the "sterile pedantry" of purely intellectual traditions, which were being "flung aside with a contemptuous smile by the young, the strong, the virile."[52] For a while McCabe seemed content with Schiller's down-to-earth, practical humanism. He had spoken of the future of religion in similar terms to Schiller in an early work called *The Religion of the Twentieth Century*, only he hadn't used the term humanism to describe it. In *The Religion of Woman*, McCabe declared that "[i]n the solid facts of life and history, in the plain teaching of experience as to what is needed to bring gladness into our lives, we have a broad and massive foundation to build upon. This is Humanism."[53]

However, McCabe soon became uneasy with the relativism inherent in Schiller's humanism. In 1913 he expressed some of his concerns. "The fundamental objection to this theory is that it comes very near to defining truth as, in the old phrase, what each man troweth." Many people urgently desire immortality, for example, while others do not. But immortality cannot be both true and false. "Is it not better to say, in plain terms, that they may be equally valuable or helpful to their possessors, and still to regard truth as a statement of fact?"[54] Contemporary rationalists are fighting the same battle with Schiller's postmodernist heirs. Neither could McCabe help noticing that Schiller's exemplars of youth, strength, and virility were all either dead or in their dotage. Schiller's brand of humanism did not outlive its creator.

For the next thirty years, "humanism" was bandied about, mainly in the United States and mainly in the service of unitarian or mystical creeds on the fringes of organized religion. McCabe took little part in this process, but it did little for his opinion of the term. In 1945, he spoke of humanism as seeking "to promote all human interests except theology from what you might define as a moralist-individualist-liberal angle." But he also noted that its critics see the term as "too broad to be pointed and too literal to be critical."[55]

McCabe stopped speaking positively about humanism after 1949 when an American academic, Professor Oliver Reiser, published a pamphlet advocating "Scientific Humanism" and proposing an international forum with the same name. Reiser's scientific humanism was pantheistic, elitist, and idealistic, in the worst senses of those words, and McCabe saw (correctly) little chance that a group of university pantheists could succeed in being seen as genuinely international. Not surprisingly, he criticized Reiser's pantheism, seeing it as nothing more than "atheism in a silk hat." He attributed that saying to Schopenhauer, which seems to me unlikely, as the German thinker had been dead nine years before T. H. Huxley coined the phrase. This can join the very short list of McCabe errors. McCabe admitted there was "fine stuff" in Reiser's manifesto but decided to withhold support until it proved itself.[56] Reiser's trajectory continued upwards for another twenty years, ending up with an extravagant notion of cosmic humanism.

In some ways, McCabe's attitudes toward humanism are a foretaste of the arguments about rationalism and humanism which divided Freethought in the English-speaking world in the fifties and sixties. Many postwar humanists, such as Kathleen Nott, came to see rationalism's emphasis on the criticism of religion as sterile, whereas many rationalists feared that the new humanism was a mealymouthed collaboration with religion succeeding only in diffusing the movement's energy.

The Humane Spirit

But while McCabe's opinion of the *term* humanism became less positive as he got older, his vision of humanism remained much the same through his long career. McCabe's lifelong admiration for the Stoics can be understood in this regard. As Nicolas Walter noted, the Stoics were the first permanent tradition that preached the universal brotherhood of humanity. McCabe's humanist vision went by a variety of names over his long career: the humane (or modern) spirit, humanitarianism, or humanism. "Science," he wrote in 1916, "is not the greatest phenomenon of modern times. It is the vast, pervasive, all-conquering idealism of the modern spirit that makes our age great in the eye of the liberal historian."[57]

There are few better examples than his final rallying call at the end of his 1917 work *The Bankruptcy of Religion*.

> Let us make a science of the life and resources of humanity on this planet; let us organize it as men organize a great business. So that the work of the world will alternate happily with the play of the world; let us act as if there is no heaven, and the one chance of happiness we have is before the heart ceases to beat; let us each be apostles of the social spirit until a sound standard of conduct rules the world.[58]

The idea of a humane spirit originated with his early reading of Sir Leslie Stephen's *Science of Ethics*, and developed into several related themes in his work. On the one hand was the idea he espoused in the *Key to Love and Sex*, that sexual liberty was an essential component of the greatest periods in history. On the other hand was the contention of *The Rise and Fall of the Gods* that atheism, too, is a feature of the greatest ages of history. McCabe's humane spirit was a precursor to Karl Popper's notion of the open society. The humane spirit rose and prospered in proportion as religion, with its dogmas and exclusiveness, declined. It prospered in Greece and the Rome of the Stoics, and it withered in the Middle Ages. But the humane spirit was only enfeebled, and gained new heart in the eighteenth century.

At the heart of the humane spirit was a new recognition of an old humanism. The willingness to play some part in improving the time and place in which one lives is intrinsic to human beings. This idea developed from McCabe's philosophy of evolution. Among very primitive peoples, he argued, people are moral without knowing anything of morality. He often quoted Dr. A. C. Haddon, FRS, an anthropologist contemporary. Haddon said of these peoples that "they do not recognize virtue, but do not practice vice."[59] Morality arises "when the intelligence develops sufficiently to recognize the social value of these habits, and the elementary law of conduct is laid down."[60] Morality, in other words, is a sensible evolutionary development, one entirely compatible with natural selection. There is nothing grandly metaphysical about this humanism; it is simply a facility in each person to cooperate with others and deal with them as they would wish to be dealt with.

McCabe was expressing a humanist confidence in the essential goodness of people. We are, by nature, humane. This innate humanity was at last allowed to blossom in the nineteenth century, which was the first time, in Europe at least, that took seriously the idea of educating the mass of the people. We have noted elsewhere McCabe's admiration for the Chinese civilization and this confidence in the essential goodness of humanity is not the only resemblance between Confucianism (particularly as interpreted by Mencius) and McCabe's thought. One of the more influential Confucian works is *The Great Learning*, which outlines the Confucian educational, moral, and political program. Central are the "three items" of (in order) clear character, loving the people, and abiding in the highest good. These three items are achieved by "eight steps" of the investigation of things, the extension of knowledge, sincerity of the will, rectification of the mind, cultivating the personal life, regulation of the family, national order, and world peace.[61] McCabe gave his nonspecialist readers a positive account of Confucian humanism in volume 7 of his *History of Human Morals*. "Kung fu-tse, instead of searching for some mystic principle which should compel men to be just and honorable, as Lao-tse did and so many modern moralists do, pointed out the simple fact that the cost of selfishness and injustice was the misery of millions of people."[62] From the foundations of clear character and the investigation of things, the world can be made better. It will surely take Promethean effort, but if all work toward that goal to the best of their ability, it may yet happen. This was McCabe's creed. It could be called a Promethean humanism.

Predictably, McCabe had to fend off assertions of having reverted to an essentially Christian claim. He acknowledged the basic continuity of the creed of the humanism with that preached in parts of the New Testament. But he also pointed out that the basic message of the New Testament is fundamentally opposed to the message of humanism. The New Testament's

> fundamental principle was the belief, borrowed from the Persians, that the social order would very soon be swallowed up in the end of the world, and then there would be a general judgment and sorting out of those who were to burn for ever in a lake of fire. This belief was very well fitted to inspire a most intense zeal for individualistic virtue and asceticism, but not social enthusiasm.[63]

Reforming Christians such as Wilberforce were no "more Christian," as apologists liked to argue, than St. Thomas Aquinas or the crusaders; what was different was the age they lived in and the resurgent humanism that was in the air in the nineteenth century. And the characteristic of the nineteenth-century ethicists he admired was the holistic centering of ethical motivation. The ethicists he admired

> are convinced that morality will only be elevated when moral acts are no longer performed for the sake of supernatural rewards, or out of torment, and that men will be the more easily induced to lead consistently moral lives when they are taught to regard the moral law, not as an alien precept imposed by a tantalizing Deity, and in utter antagonism to self-interest, but as a rational adjustment of their own self-interests, the higher and the lower, and the individual impulses with the social obligations.[64]

McCabe's notion of the humanism stands as a direct rebuke to the prejudices of postmodernists, who have insisted that "the Enlightenment project" has desacralized life, analyzed the life-blood out of society, and so on (the rhetoric goes on). Here, of course, we find McCabe not doing this at all. On the contrary, he is holding before people a noble goal, one that is greater than the individual while retaining the individual's sense of self-worth. Many contemporary nihilists will reply by saying this is precisely McCabe's greatest crime. By positing a humanism in this way, these critics may argue, a metanarrative has been created, along with its awful consequences of a threatening hegemony, a likelihood of marginalization, and the inevitability of a resurgent historicism. This is a case of damned if you do and damned if you don't. On the one hand the humanist is vilified for envisioning a unified theory of society, and on the other hand, the humanist is vilified for not doing so. Perhaps the best course of action is to leave the last word here to McCabe himself. Let the reader judge the merit of his vision. "The end or purpose of life," McCabe wrote late in 1925, "is what we choose to make it. There is no end or purpose written upon the stars. We make our goal; and the only end upon which we can agree, the 'supreme good' to which all other ideals are subordinate, is general happiness—the greatest happiness of the greatest number."[65] But, as if to recognize the difficulties posed by this ideal, he asked on the very next page: "But what is happiness? I am not sure that I know."

McCABE AND THE LAST MAN

Joseph McCabe was part of the tradition of popular writers, from Diderot to Carl Sagan, who sought to broaden the horizon of the general citizen. Ever since the development of widespread literacy there has been a demand for intelligent popularizations of current thought. But as Bryan Magee (himself a popularizer of great skill) has noted, it was not until the 1960s that academics appreciated this audience. For the most part, Magee comments, this work had been undertaken by journalists.[66] I would claim that with Joseph McCabe, the general reader got the best of both worlds: the breadth of knowledge one expects from academics combined with the journalists' ability to put material across in an accessible manner. And as we have seen, he often avoided the errors the established academics fell into; the same academics who pooh-poohed McCabe's work.

At this point we need to digress in the direction of Friedrich Nietzsche, the single most important influence on postmodernism, and a man with very pronounced opinions about the general citizen. For Nietzsche the death of God happened when Christianity's chief virtue, truthfulness, was turned against itself. This new truthfulness had developed into skepticism, which in turn soured into the nihilism he was struggling against.[67] While McCabe never spoke of the death of God, he had observed a similar process. But he interpreted it very differently. Much of his early book *Modern Rationalism* is devoted to the phenomenon Nietzsche was talking about—that of Christianity fighting a defensive action against truthfulness. Whether in biblical criticism, science and religion, theology, mythology, ethics, or politics, the Christian religion had retreated constantly in the face of rationalist scholarship.

Nietzsche and McCabe saw the same problem, but it was their response to it that differed so markedly. Whereas Nietzsche fell into lamentation over the mastery of the Last Man, McCabe welcomed the dawn of a new age where rational, fully human citizens, building on the achievements of their predecessors, could indeed create a new secular, egalitarian civilization. More recently, postmodernists have preferred the aristocratic aloofness of Nietzsche and have sneered at the optimism of people like McCabe. In the light of the twentieth century, such optimism is, they say, at best misplaced. At worst, it is itself responsible for much of the carnage the century produced. Safely distant from the general citizen in their university sinecures, postmodernists shrug their shoulders and declare it impossible to educate, improve, reason, or believe. Frightened by the challenge of Prometheus, they prefer the company of Narcissus.

Throughout his life, McCabe defended the general citizen. And yet Nietzsche and Heidegger, the two most important influences on postmodernism, strove to insult the general citizen. To Nietzsche, the general citizen was "the superfluous," "the many-too-many," or the "Last Man." Less poetic but even more disparaging, Martin Heidegger wrote of the general citizen as *das Man*, or "the they," who are fallen beings, not by virtue of some primeval crime, but by virtue of their "undifferentiated primitive everydayness." Nietzsche yearned for a new nobility, lest time be handed over to the mob, in which case "drown all time in shallow waters."[68]

> To ordinary men, finally, the great majority, who exist for service and general utility and who *may* exist only for that purpose, religion gives an invaluable contentment with their nature and station, manifold peace of heart, an ennobling of obedience, one piece of joy and sorrow more to share with their fellows, and some transfiguration of the whole everydayness, the whole lowliness, the whole half-bestial poverty of their souls.[69]

For Heidegger, the chief crime of "the they" seems to have been its failure to recognize Heidegger as the intellectual redeemer of the age. But once the rhetoric of the beautiful prose (in Nietzsche's case) or the dismal verbal fog (Heidegger) has been blown away, we are left with simple snobbery. More prosaically put, but amounting to the same thing is this from McCabe's contemporary, Cyril Joad, who was also quick to scorn the general public.

> What do we talk about? Sport, generally, and politics occasionally. If, however, we are women, we talk about men and about other women. We prefer jazz and thrillers to Bach and Flaubert, bathing belles on the covers of magazines to the pictures of Picasso or Cezanne, watching the games to acquiring knowledge, going to the movies to reading by the fire. Our standards, in fact, are very low.[70]

While Joad liked to parade his disdain of the vulgar, even he continued to write books for them. But Nietzsche's greatest contempt was reserved for any attempts to relieve the lives of the Last Man, in particular, for the books directed toward them. "Books for everybody are always malodorous books: the smell of petty people cling to them."[71] Thus stand condemned the works of some of the greatest humanist educators this century: Joseph McCabe, H. G. Wells, Jacob Bronowski, Carl Sagan, and Isaac Asimov among others. The books of any of these men would certainly have been deeply offensive to Nietzsche's nose because they were written precisely for the Last Man.

Joseph McCabe's whole career was directed toward the Last Man. Toward the end of his career he wrote that he left the serene world of the academy "and went down to the market places of the world."[72] Again, a parallel can be drawn with Nietzsche. Zarathustra, in the final cycle of his wisdom, came to learn that he committed "the great folly: I appeared on the market-place." Zarathustra urged the Higher Men to learn from him. "In the market place no one believes in higher people. But if you will speak there, very well! The populace, however, blinks: 'We are all equal.' "[73] So, while for McCabe, having gone to the market-place to speak, and earn his living among ordinary people was a mark of pride, for Nietzsche, it is a mark of shame. More recently it has become fashionable to situate important thinkers in the stream of life outside the universities in order to build their antiestablishment credentials. In his biography of Michel Foucault, David Macey hailed him as a "traveler who is unwilling to be shut up in the academic 'ghetto.' "[74] This was true of McCabe before Foucault was born, and with the additional recommendation that he wrote in a way the general reader can understand.

And neither was McCabe embarrassed by the products bought at the market. On one occasion he wrote that "nearly 40 years' experience has shown me that a taste for beer and cowboy-stories is entirely consistent with a taste for perfect art and the highest intellectual exercises."[75] McCabe realized that there were problems, but was equally sure that retreating into an Olympian scorn was hardly a constructive solution. As part of a discussion of the pessimistic literature of the twenties and early thirties, however, McCabe admitted that:

> Yes, there is an increase of frivolity—thank heaven. Let us try to be serious. In what way have these four-fifths of any nation deteriorated in character? A larger number than ever before have their little libraries and gramophones or wireless and appreciate good music and art galleries. A far larger number even of young folk attend lectures and classes, debates, visit museums and art galleries, read serious literature. Not enough, you may say; but who gives a damn about them once they have left the primary or the high school? There is a certain amount of voluntary effort to help them—a novelty of modern times, remember—but it is totally inadequate. The work-conditions of most of them do not exactly leave them leisure, and the intellectual world must seem to such of them as do turn to it, without guidance, a bewildering and sterile confusion. So they dance or flirt or go to the movies. Terrible.[76]

McCabe was not saying that there are no such things as frivolity and vulgarity. What he was doing was reminding readers that frivolity, vulgarity, and coarseness are not the preserve of the general citizen, and neither does an enjoyment of simple pleasures, to rename them, irrevocably define one as base. And, of course, McCabe continually returned to his Owenite (and, to an extent, Confucian) belief that human beings are educable and willing, given the right circumstances, to be educated. No better illustration of this can be found than in his discussion of Nietzsche himself. Here McCabe is describing Nietzsche's discussion with Jacob Burckhardt about forming little monastic colonies in which men of culture could escape from the herd. Having described the project in these terms, McCabe added:

> Pardon my little ironies whenever I come to these anti-democrats. I have never been able to see why the blunders of an uneducated democracy, as ours still is (though many an artisan is a sounder politician than many a professor or property owner), recommend anything except a practical education of the people.[77]

And as we have seen throughout this book, fundamental to this belief is his conviction that education is the central pillar of any moral law, not only because education brings more knowledge, but because education is the key to happiness.

In defending the intelligence and humanity of the Last Man (we'll use Nietzsche's term for the sake of emphasis), McCabe anticipated by half a century the defense of pluralism and the Last Man undertaken by thinkers like John Rawls, Isaiah Berlin and Ernest Gellner. Peter Levine also echoes McCabe's views when he observes that the contemporary pluralist is no less committed to, or enriched by, a set of values, by understanding that their truth-claims are contingent. Indeed, modern pluralists are distinctive by the frequency with which they will defend the rights of others to enjoy values different from their own. The "contemporary pluralist hardly lacks values, therefore, and is far from a nihilist."[78] McCabe recognized all this before the Wall Street crash. Furthermore, he related this to the Last Man in accessible writing, and at a price they could afford.

TWENTIETH-CENTURY *PHILOSOPHE*

McCabe has been likened to Denis Diderot (1713–1784).[79] Diderot has been described as "the first modern atheist—both in the sense of making matter the ceaseless cause of things, and of rendering the question of God's existence a matter of little consequence."[80] This description fits McCabe very well indeed, particularly after 1925, when he labeled himself an atheist and materialist. The parallel between the two men can be seen in McCabe's own descriptions of his famous predecessor. In a short work, published in 1919, written for working people, McCabe described Diderot as an "Atheist and Encyclopaedist, and one of the most learned men of his time, [and] an ardent republican and champion of the people."[81] In his *Biographical Dictionary of Modern Rationalists* published the following year, Diderot was praised as a "generous and high-minded man, a passionate lover of truth, a scholar of marvellous range and power."[82] Well, McCabe was these things as well.

Both McCabe and Diderot were born into Catholic families and had early phases of piety turn into lifelong atheism at the hands of the intolerance and intellectual clumsiness of the church. Both were deeply skeptical of tradition. Both held genuinely radical opinions of sexuality, and both were very prolific writers. Neither Diderot nor McCabe were part of the formal education industry, and to that extent both could be considered outsiders, although Diderot came to enjoy a lot more official support than McCabe ever did. Most importantly, both men were polymaths. In practical terms, this made both men *encyclopédistes*. The contribution of Diderot to the *Encyclopédie* is well known, that of McCabe in this area, less so. Perhaps the best single example of McCabe's credentials as a twentieth-century *philosophe* is his extraordinary *Key to Culture*. In forty volumes, each of around sixty-four pages, McCabe provided his readers with a coherent overview of the universe and the place of humans in it. He'd been working on the idea for a few years but had not been able to find a publisher in Britain willing to run with the idea. It was Haldeman-Julius who had the foresight to publish the *Key*. The whole idea of the *Key to Culture* is rminiscent of Diderot's *Encyclopédie*, which has become a symbol of the confidence Enlightenment thinkers had in the improving power of learning. "No other single work," he wrote of the *Encyclopédie* in 1951, "has had so beneficent and massive a part in making a new world."[83] It was McCabe's wish that his *Key to Culture* would play a similar role in enlightening the nonspecialist working person in the spare time allotted to them. "In forty small and simply-written books I gave the whole of modern knowledge (except mathematics, which one would not include) in so far as it seemed necessary for a man to take the intelligent interest in life which I have defined."[84] The *Key to Culture* was essentially an enlargement of his *The Story of Evolution*, written in 1912. The first eleven volumes (later sold separately as *The Foundation of Science*) provided the universal framework, beginning with volumes on physics, astronomy, geology, biochemistry, and moving on to embryology and psychology. The next major section of the *Key*, which was later sold separately as *A Complete Outline of History*, traced world history in a manner similar to H. G. Wells's earlier work. There were then three further sections on economics, art, and literature, and finally education and philosophy. The final volume was called "The Progress of Science."

In fact, this parallel with Wells can be taken even further. The *Key to Culture* can be seen as an attempt to condense in a single volume the work of Wells's three important textbooks for the world. *The Outline of History* was his historical contribution, *The Science of Life* his scientific contribution, and *The Work, Wealth and Happiness of Mankind* was his economic and sociological contribution to the betterment and education of the general citizen. The *Key to Culture* covered a broader field of knowledge in fewer pages, and was designed for people with less money and leisure than those who would read Wells's works. McCabe's *Key to Culture* was his most ambitious attempt to articulate an holistic rationalism for the general reader. It alone is a sufficient monument to McCabe's greatness.

Five years after beginning the *Key to Culture* McCabe wrote an abbreviated version called *An Outline of Today's Knowledge*, and five years later he penned another series for Haldeman-Julius called the *ABC Library of Living Knowledge*. Each of the monographs that made up this series was more able to stand alone than those that constituted the *Key to Culture*.

> In each booklet I took a point or theme which was actually and widely dis-cussed (Germany, Fascism, Russia, the distribution of wealth, television etc), distilled the contents of half a dozen of the best and most recent works (with differing points of view) on the subject, and gave the reader the essential facts—the facts of real use for your adjustment to the social environment.[85]

McCabe thought this series "the most useful enterprise from the educational angle I ever set my pen to."[86]

An essential motivating force for McCabe's work in popular education was his belief that we have touched on a couple of times about the human origins of any moral law. Throughout his life McCabe insisted that there is no such thing as *a*, let alone *the*, moral law, in a transcendental sense. "The scientific conclu-sion," McCabe wrote, "is that man made his moral law and that, except where his superstitions distorted his ideas and conduct, he made it simply as a law of social life."[87] Moral law, he wrote elsewhere, "is social law: a series of checks upon the impulses of the individual when they were found to injure others and so provoke retaliation."[88] The moral law McCabe had in mind, he put like this:

> *Our* supreme law for men and women is: Thou shalt be happy. Our fundamental counsel is: do unto others as you would they should do unto you. Make no man or woman weep, as old Egypt said. Enjoy the sun, and cloud not the lives of others. Cultivate those qualities which, if generally cultivated, will make life a joy for all: virility, wisdom, tenderness, delicacy, justice, kindliness, truthful-ness, straightness. Then yours is the kingdom of earth, and it has no other laws.[89]

McCabe's objection to religious thinkers' claims of monopoly rights over the humane spirit is part of a long struggle, one that even some postmodernist scholars are continuing. Michael Luntley concluded his book *Reason, Truth and Self* with the declaration that the "moral world is ours. It is not leased by a divine landlord who will bale us out if we mess it up. We alone bear the responsibility if we fail to colonize our world and make it a place of value."[90] Quite correct, though let us remember we did not have to wait until postmodernism for this observation to be made.

McCabe was truly radical in this way. His nineteenth-century predecessors, such as Mill, Spencer, and Huxley, had sought to preserve Christian morality while abandoning Christian theology. As Nietzsche had done, McCabe sought to go the one step further by severing the links between Christianity and morality. But whereas Nietzsche sought to do this by the radical rejection of the entire corpus of morality, McCabe took the more sensible step of demonstrating to his readers that this morality was by no means an exclusively *Christian* morality. Whereas Nietzsche tried to show that Christian morality had reduced us to a herd, McCabe's emphasis was to show that the genuinely Christian additions to the moral code were the least helpful, but that the moral code was generally sound.

All this is testimony to McCabe's desire to present the general reader with a teleological map of the universe that is both intellectually and emotionally satisfying. And as such, it links with McCabe's outlook to his histories and to his popularizations of science. We have seen examples of this in previous chapters.

A century after McCabe began writing, E. O. Wilson concluded that we all need a sacred narrative, a sense of a larger purpose that can underpin our lives and provide it with meaning and purpose.[91] I do not agree that the narrative need be *sacred*, because we seem never to agree on what constitutes sacred. What is sacred to one people is profane, or worse, to another. The principal features sacred narratives seem to have in common are the least helpful ones: an outmoded and foolish anthropomorphism, and a strong sense of "other." But McCabe recognized the need for a narrative larger than oneself.

He articulated the vision best at the end of his short work *The Evolution of Civilization*, published in 1921. "What is the end of life? It is whatever we men may choose to make it; and since we live in social groups, and a man's actions depend upon and influence his neighbours, it is what we choose to make it *collectively*." But what is it that we would want to do collectively?

> There is no doubt today about our choice. We are going to develop what is most clearly worth developing in us: intelligence, refinement, character, health. We are going to eliminate pain, unhappiness, ignorance, coarseness, violence and poverty, as far as possible. We are going to have a hundred commonwealths, ten thousand cities, competing with each other in the realization of this ideal. So, when the war drums beat no longer and the strong have ceased to exploit the weak, the fundamental condition of progress, mutual stimulation, will be provided on a higher plane, and the close interconnection of the whole world will make it more effective than ever.[92]

McCabe's vision here is a metanarrative in the sense that it projects a vision of the future at the end of a book about the past. But at no point does he offer this as more than his vision. It is not a metanarrative in the sense of being etched unerringly into the fabric of history in the way dialectical materialism was supposed to be. McCabe's vision is something that needs to be worked for. And it is something that other people will, for one reason or another, oppose. These people will need to be reasoned with and engaged in public disputation. It is difficult to understand McCabe's life and work without appreciating that this is what he devoted his life to doing.

The next question also needs to be asked: Is McCabe's vision so bad? Post-modernists have been so concerned to deny people the chance of a vision of the future to which they may devote their lives that we have become afraid of seeing the future in any positive way at all. It is time that the postmodernist "incredulity to metanarratives" is exposed as the nihilism it really is. Incredulity to anything requires a sound base of knowledge and a healthy rational faculty in order to process the information and produce an informed incredulity. And yet postmodernists have sought to divest us of these essential tools as well. Rationalists like Bertrand Russell, H. G. Wells, and Joseph McCabe were incredulous of metanarratives before most postmodernists were born. And more than that, they preserved for us the tools by which we may become sensibly incredulous. And latterly, motivated by the ferocity of the postmodernist critique, some very important counterattacks by people such as E. O. Wilson and Raymond Tallis have reestablished the respectability of looking at the wider picture without the hitherto compulsory sneer. But it is worth recalling that these people walk in the footsteps of Joseph McCabe.

THE CURIOUS ENLIGHTENMENT
OF JOSEPH McCABE

An important conclusion of this book is that many of the central assertions made by postmodernists and other critics of rationalism fail to stand up when measured against the writings of Joseph McCabe. Paul Cliteur has made the valid observation that postmodernist theorists have failed to confront seriously the ideas of the Enlightenment.[93] We have found that there has been little serious confrontation with twentieth-century defenders of the Enlightenment tradition either. And, of course, the reason for this is fairly clear. A serious examination of thinkers like McCabe would take away the glow of victory over the caricatures that are postmodernists' preferred adversaries. Yet again, let us take an example: this time David Harvey's book *The Condition of Postmodernity*, published in 1990. Harvey's sole authority for "Enlightenment thought" is Ernst Cassirer's 1951 study *The Philosophy of the Enlightenment*. An excellent book, to be sure, but hardly a sufficient foundation for Harvey's sweeping generalization that the Enlightenment "took it as axiomatic that there was only one possible answer to any question."[94] A cursory glance at Diderot's novel, *Rameau's Nephew* should be enough to disabuse Harvey of this fallacy.

We need here, then, to examine McCabe's views on what has come to be seen as a pivotal period in the development of the modern world. To keep things simple, I will use the term "modernity" as a catchall phrase to cover the history of the world since the seventeenth century. I say seventeenth century, because McCabe dated the birth of modern skepticism not to the Enlightenment at all, but to 1677, the occasion of Edward Stillingfleet's *Letter to a Deist*. McCabe saw this as a suitable milestone because it is the first orthodox reply to a deist.[95] It is as good a milestone as any. Stillingfleet, as Bishop of Worcester, felt the case against orthodoxy was sufficiently strong to justify a published reply. This suggests Christianity on the defensive, and without its earlier recourse to persecution.

Those looking for an extravagant talking-up of the Enlightenment from McCabe will be disappointed. To begin with, he never used the term "Enlightenment," which, so far as I can tell, became popular only after the publication of Cassirer's book. More important, McCabe didn't have the inflated view of the Enlightenment that postmodernists and others like to believe rationalists have. As we saw in chapter 4, McCabe's golden age was the much-maligned nineteenth century. Certainly, McCabe admired the *philosophes* and their achievement, but in far from an uncritical way.

A quick examination of some of McCabe's relevant historical works will illustrate the point. In his twelve-volume *History of Human Morals*, the nineteenth century got a volume to itself, while the eighteenth century was merely tacked on the end of a volume on a volume examining "The Effect of the Reformation on Morals." And *A History of Human Morals*, remember, set out to demonstrate that morality has improved as it has become more secular. Similarly, in *The Rise and Fall of the Gods*, which was dedicated to linking the growth of atheism with periods of freedom and toleration, the eighteenth century is broken up into chapters examining national trends in thought since the Reformation. *The Story of Religious Controversy* barely mentions the eighteenth century at all.

McCabe admired the achievements of the eighteenth century but saw them as limited in the light of the tremendous progress in the following century. Of the *philosophes*, McCabe wrote that they "sought wisdom, not in the cloudland of metaphysics, but in regard to the nature of man and his practical problems."[96] In the area of Biblical criticism, for instance, he praised eighteenth-century thinkers for opening the subject up to scholarly criticism, but saw much of their work as rendered superficial in the light of subsequent developments.[97] McCabe praised the spirit of inquiry that was reignited in the seventeenth century and kept alive in the eighteenth. But he had no doubts that it was the nineteenth century that saw the most dramatic application of this spirit in the lives of ordinary people. Only at the very end of his career did McCabe come to see the achievements of the nineteenth century as rooted in those of the eighteenth century.[98]

McCabe's ideals were always at their best when they remained practical and human. Only once, in 1950, did he indulge himself by writing a utopia. This is, I think, the least successful of all McCabe's works. Reminiscent of H. G. Wells's

The Shape of Things to Come, McCabe's *The Next Fifty Years* illustrated most of the common objections against the construction of utopias. McCabe's projected world looked worthy, prudish, potentially totalitarian, and unspeakably dull. It bore a striking resemblance to Robert Owen's New Lanark experiment writ across the globe. It also highlights McCabe's weaknesses with imaginative writing, and compares unfavorably with Wells's work. It is possible McCabe himself recognized the inadequacies, because only the next year, he was writing skeptically about high-sounding plans and models.

The fact that McCabe's utopia had these unpleasant characteristics will delight many postmodernists, who will doubtless say, "Aha, the implicit totalitarianism of modernity that we have been talking about!" But it would require breathtaking duplicity to insist that McCabe's miserable utopia (the only one he wrote, at age eighty-three) discredits modernity while at the same time insisting that Heidegger's antidemocratic totalitarianism causes postmodernism no discomfort. Gregory Bruce Smith notes that National Socialism was seen by Heidegger as "better equipped to respond to the rootless nihilism of technological modernity than any other modern political dispensation."[99] Smith is quick to add that this does not mean that any genuinely postmodern elements in Heidegger's" thought are intrinsically fascist. Well, if that is good enough for Heidegger, it is good enough for McCabe. This is especially so when we consider that McCabe's utopia can be seen as an aberration in the general trends in his thought, in a way that totalitarian thought is not an aberration in Heidegger's thought. It will take more than one utopia in a corpus of two hundred works to make a totalitarian out of Joseph McCabe, and it constitutes no significant rebuke to "the Enlightenment project."

Apart from this aberration, McCabe took from the Enlightenment a simple and down-to-earth notion of what was needed. "In the eighteenth century," McCabe wrote,

> reformers just looked around them and said: let us reduce this appalling volume of pain, disease, poverty, ignorance, superstition, squalor, violence, and greed that brutalizes the life of the mass of the people. The dynamo of that proposal or ideal has vastly improved the life of the people, in spite of all the duping and lying that have been used in our generation. But there is still a mighty volume of all these evils and social sores around the world. That is enough for us.[100]

It is an important claim of the Enlightenment-bashing industry that it, and those who have been inspired by its program, should be given over to grandiose utopianism and even totalitarianism.[101] Desperate indeed would be the attempt to pin this accusation on McCabe on the strength of one dreary utopia and a few conservative social theories.

We can now return to another work inspired by the Enlightenment to help us complete our understanding of McCabe and his world. Steven Lukes's excellent satirical novel *The Curious Enlightenment of Professor Caritat* outlines a creed as close to McCabe's heart as any that could be found. Lukes's main character, a scholar of the Enlightenment, believed

> that partisanship should not predetermine analysis, that simple dichotomies should be viewed with caution, that there were different, non-convergent ways of being reasonable, that the ideas of one's bitterest enemies were worth taking seriously and that spending time interpreting world-transforming ideas was worthwhile.[102]

McCabe believed these things as well. I have shown that McCabe tried always to be a meticulous scholar, and was usually recognized to be so, even by his enemies. As late as 1951, when few scholars were taking any notice of his work, McCabe was still warning his readers to be as skeptical of congenial conclusions as of opposing ones. He was the first to admit that this is not easy. "It is hard to sacrifice a succulent piece of news that helps your cause because it is not sufficiently proved."[103] Where McCabe was writing partisan works, he clearly and honestly stated them to be so, and is not guilty of feigning objectivity or passing interpretation off as fact.

One of the outstanding features of McCabe's career was his caution over simple dichotomies. For example, he saw more difficulties than many of his rationalist colleagues with the mythical Jesus thesis. He also saw the conflict between science and religion in a much more complex and layered way than did his contemporaries, both the believers who insisted that science and religion were inevitably in harmony, and unbelievers who saw only total war. McCabe was also scrupulous not to make a simple pope = fascism equation. Neither did McCabe avail himself of reason/emotion, religion/rationalism, male/female, objective/subjective, or other binaries that rationalists are often claimed to be addicted to.

It must be conceded that McCabe scores poorly as one who recognized that there are different, nonconvergent ways of being reasonable. He was more aware than some of his fellow unbelievers that the "supremacy of reason" was a nonstarter. He saw as early as 1905 that reason was an instrument, and as such, something that could be ill-used. And McCabe rarely questioned the integrity of people with whom he conducted controversies—even when such doubts seemed justified, and even when his own was questioned. But McCabe never really came to terms with the fact that there are as many paths to a coherent, satisfying, intellectually sound, nontheistic worldview as there are to a theistic one. He knew this intellectually, but he always found it difficult to resolve with his temperament. This goes a long way toward explaining his tortured relations with people who should normally have been his closest allies.

And finally, nobody would question that McCabe paid his opponents the compliment of taking their views seriously, or that spending time interpreting world-transforming ideas was worthwhile. He devoted his life to interpreting world-transforming ideas. He tried to do this in down-to-earth language that the ordinary inquirer could comprehend. In short, he embodied many of the finest traits of what are now seen as Enlightenment values. It has now become fashionable to sneer at the Enlightenment and its core beliefs of reason, freedom, tolerance, and an informed skepticism. Worse still, this fashion is led by Western opinion leaders and intellectuals who are among the most privileged beneficiaries of the very system they deride. As the Canadian sociologist John O'Neill has observed, it is not the poor of the world who have abandoned the goals and values of the Enlightenment, but "those who already enjoy these things who have denounced them on behalf of others."[104] Against this narcissistic hand-wringing, O'Neill warns that too much "of the world still starves, dies young and is wasted by systematic greed and evil for anyone to write the obituaries of philosophy, ideology and humanism."[105]

While the obituary for McCabe has been written, it is to be hoped that it is too early to write the obituary of the things McCabe stood for. He wished for himself the simple epitaph: "He was a rebel to his last breath."

NOTES

1. Joseph McCabe, *Modern Rationalism* (London: Watts, 1897), pp. 6–7.

2. Ibid., p. 7.

3. Joseph McCabe, *Peter Abélard* (London: Duckworth/Putnams, 1901), p. 329.

4. Joseph McCabe, *Twelve Years in a Monastery* (London: Smith Elder, 1897), pp. 282–83.

5. *Literary Guide* (March 1, 1898): 33–34.

6. Joseph McCabe, "The Splendid Isolation of Mr. George Haw," in *Christianity and Rationalism on Trial* (London: Watts, 1904), p. 12.

7. Joseph McCabe, *The Logic and Virtue of Atheism* (Austin, Tex.: American Atheist Press, 1980), p. 40.

8. Joseph McCabe, *The Religion of Woman: An Historical Study* (London: Watts, 1905), p. 66.

9. Joseph McCabe and Sir Arthur Conan Doyle, *Debate on the Truth of Spiritualism* (London: Watts, 1920), pp. 47–48.

10. Bertrand Russell, *Human Society in Ethics and Politics* (London: George Allen & Unwin, 1954), p. 8.

11. McCabe, *The Logic and Virtue of Atheism*, p. 43.

12. Joseph McCabe, *Outlines of the World's Great 'Isms* (Girard, Kan.: Haldeman-Julius, 1945), p. 68.

13. See Adam Gowans Whyte, *The Story of the RPA: 1899–1949* (London: Watts, 1949); and F. J. Gould, *The Pioneers of Johnson's Court* (London: Watts, 1929).

14. Joseph McCabe, *A Biographical Dictionary of Modern Rationalists* (London: Watts, 1920), p. vi.

15. Ibid., p. viii.

16. I have dealt with it in relation to New Zealand in my earlier work, *Heathen in Godzone: Seventy Years of New Zealand Rationalism* (Auckland: NZARH, 1998), especially chap. 9.

17. *Times Literary Supplement* (May 12, 1921): 302.

18. Joseph McCabe, *The Inferiority Complex Eliminated* (Girard, Kan.: Haldeman-Julius, 1940), p. 52.

19. McCabe, *Outlines of the World's Great 'Isms*, p. 44.

20. Karl Popper, *The Open Society and Its Enemies* (London: Routledge & Kegan Paul, 1963), vol. 2, pp. 225–27.

21. Ernest Gellner, *Reason and Culture* (Oxford: Blackwell, 1992), p. 3.

22. Ibid., p. 159.

23. See Ernest Gellner, *Postmodernism, Reason and Religion* (London & New York: Routledge, 1992).

24. Sir Leslie Stephen, "An Agnostic's Apology," in *An Agnostic's Apology* (London: Watts, 1931), p. 1.

25. Ibid., p. 4.

26. Joseph McCabe, *The Life and Letters of George Jacob Holyoake* (London: Watts, 1908), vol. 1, pp. 56–57.

27. Ibid., vol. 2, p. 266.

28. Charles Bradlaugh, "A Plea for Atheism," in *Humanity's Gain from Unbelief*, ed. Hypatia Bradlaugh Bonner (London: Watts, 1932), p. 25.

29. Michael Martin, *Atheism: A Philosophical Justification* (Philadelphia: Temple University Press, 1990), especially p. 77.

30. Joseph McCabe, *The Existence of God*, Inquirer's Library, no. 1 (London: Watts, 1913), p. 144.

31. Ibid., p. 132.

32. *Literary Guide* (July 1, 1917): 98.

33. Joseph McCabe, *The Story of Religious Controversy* (Boston: Stratford, 1929), p. 97.

34. Joseph McCabe, *The Rise and Fall of the Gods* (Girard, Kan.: Haldeman-Julius, 1931), vol. 2, p. 53.

35. Ibid., vol. 5, p. 48.

36. McCabe, *The Logic and Virtue of Atheism*, p. 4.

37. Ibid., p. 6.

38. Bertrand Russell, "Am I an Atheist or an Agnostic?" in *Bertrand Russell on God and Religion*, ed. Al Seckel (Amherst, N.Y.: Prometheus Books, 1986), p. 85.

39. Joseph McCabe, *A Rationalist Encyclopedia* (London: Watts, 1948), p. 36.

40. Joseph McCabe, *One Hundred Men Who Moved the World* (Girard, Kan.: Haldeman-Julius, 1931), vol. 17, p. 5.

41. Ibid., vol. 17, p. 14.

42. *Literary Guide* (December 1, 1897): 279.

43. Ibid. (December 1938): 220.

44. McCabe, *The Logic and Virtue of Atheism*, p. 24.

45. McCabe, *The Rise and Fall of the Gods*, vol. 6, p. 33.

46. Richard Dawkins, *The Blind Watchmaker* (London: Longman, 1986), p. 6.

47. McCabe, A Rationalist Encyclopedia, p. 36.

48. David Berman, A History of Atheism in Britain (London & New York: Routledge, 1990), p. 220.

49. McCabe, The Rise and Fall of the Gods, vol. 2, pp. 55–60.

50. See James Thrower, The Alternative Tradition: A Study of Unbelief in the Ancient World (The Hague: Mouton, 1980); and Finngeir Hiorth, Introduction to Atheism (Pune: Indian Secular Society, 1995).

51. Nicolas Walter, Humanism: What's in the Word (London: RPA with the British Humanist Association and the Secular Society [G. W. Foote Ltd.], 1997), p. 34.

52. McCabe, The Existence of God, p. 55.

53. McCabe, The Religion of Woman, p. 90.

54. McCabe, The Existence of God, p. 56.

55. McCabe, Outlines of the World's Great 'Isms, p. 44.

56. Joseph McCabe, Comments on Professor Reiser's New Scientific Humanism, with Oliver L. Reiser's Scientific Humanism As Creative Philosophy (Girard, Kan.: Haldeman-Julius, 1949), p. 32.

57. Joseph McCabe, "The Humaner Spirit," in A Generation of Religious Progress, ed. Gustav Spiller (London: Watts, 1916), p. 78.

58. Joseph McCabe, The Bankruptcy of Religion (London: Watts, 1917), p. 308.

59. McCabe, The Existence of God, p. 101.

60. Ibid., p. 102.

61. For a fuller discussion, see Wing-tsit Chan, A Source Book in Chinese Philosophy (Princeton, N.J.: Princeton University Press, 1973), p. 84.

62. Joseph McCabe, A History of Human Morals (Girard, Kan.: Haldeman-Julius, 1931), vol. 7, p. 16.

63. Chan, A Source Book in Chinese Philosophy, p. 82.

64. McCabe, Modern Rationalism, pp. 159–60.

65. Joseph McCabe, 1825–1925: A Century of Stupendous Progress (London: Watts, 1925), p. 147.

66. Bryan Magee, Confessions of a Philosopher (London: Wiedenfeld & Nicolson, 1997), p. 337.

67. I owe these observations about Nietzsche to Peter Levine's superb study, Nietzsche and the Modern Crisis of the Humanities (Albany: State University of New York Press, 1995).

68. Friedrich Nietzsche, Thus Spake Zarathustra (Amherst, N.Y.: Prometheus Books, 1993), p. 222.

69. Friedrich Nietzsche, Beyond Good and Evil (London: Penguin, 1988), Part 3, No. 61.

70. C. E. M. Joad, The Testament of Joad (London: Faber & Faber, 1943), pp. 162–63.

71. Nietzsche, Beyond Good and Evil, part 2, no. 32.

72. McCabe, Comments on Professor Reiser's New Scientific Humanism, p. 27.

73. Nietzsche, Thus Spake Zarathustra, part 4, p. 73.

74. David Macey, The Lives of Michel Foucault (London: Vintage, 1994), p. 213.

75. Joseph McCabe, Getting the Most Out of Life (Girard, Kan.: Haldeman-Julius, 1932), p. 58.

76. McCabe, *A History of Human Morals*, vol. 12, p. 25.

77. McCabe, *One Hundred Men Who Moved the World*, vol. 17, p. 10.

78. Levine, *Nietzsche and the Modern Crisis of the Humanities*, p. 198.

79. This likening of McCabe with Diderot was originally made by Professor John R. Burr. I am indebted to him for this observation.

80. John Hedley Brooke, *Science and Religion* (Cambridge: Cambridge University Press, 1991), p. 174.

81. Joseph McCabe, *The Church and the People* (London: Watts, 1919), p. 64.

82. McCabe, *A Biographical Dictionary of Modern Rationalists*, p. 215.

83. Joseph McCabe, *The Columbia Encyclopedia's Crimes against the Truth* (Girard, Kan.: Haldeman-Julius, 1951), p. 27.

84. Joseph McCabe, *Can We Save Civilization?* (London: The Search, 1932), p. 217.

85. McCabe, *The Inferiority Complex Eliminated*, p. 77.

86. Ibid.

87. McCabe, *A History of Human Morals*, vol. 12, pp. 10–11.

88. Joseph McCabe, *Key to Love and Sex* (Girard, Kan.: Haldeman-Julius, 1929), vol. 3, p. 57.

89. Joseph McCabe, *The Twilight of the Gods* (London: Watts, 1923), pp. 125–26.

90. Michael Luntley, *Reason, Truth and Self* (London/New York: Routledge, 1995), p. 218.

91. Edward O. Wilson, *Consilience: The Unity of Knowledge* (London: Little, Brown, 1998), p. 295.

92. Joseph McCabe, *The Evolution of Civilization* (London: Watts, 1921), p. 120.

93. Paul Cliteur, "The Challenge of Postmodernism to Humanism," *New Humanist* 110, no. 3 (August 1995): 9.

94. David Harvey, *The Condition of Postmodernity* (Oxford: Blackwell 1990), p. 27.

95. McCabe, *The Story of Religious Controversy*, p. 7.

96. McCabe, *The Columbia Encyclopedia's Crimes against the Truth*, p. 25.

97. McCabe, *Modern Rationalism*, p. 46.

98. McCabe, *The Columbia Encyclopedia's Crimes against the Truth*, p. 25.

99. Gregory Bruce Smith, *Nietzsche, Heidegger, and the Transition to Postmodernity* (Chicago/London: University of Chicago Press, 1996), p. 177.

100. Joseph McCabe, *The Origin and Meaning of Ideas* (Girard, Kan.: Haldeman-Julius, 1951), p. 11.

101. See, for instance, Harvey, *The Condition of Postmodernity*, pp. 14–15.

102. Steven Lukes, *The Curious Enlightenment of Professor Caritat* (London: Verso, 1996), p. 19.

103. McCabe, *The Origin and Meaning of Ideas*, p. 92.

104. John O'Neill, *The Poverty of Postmodernism* (London/New York: Routledge, 1995), p. 1.

105. Ibid., pp. 195–96.

APPENDIX 1

A Bibliography of Works by Joseph McCabe

1897   *From Rome to Rationalism*. London: Watts. Reprint 1902, 1905, 1907.

        Why I Left the Church. London: Freethought Press/Watts. Reprint 1912, 1916, 1944.

        Modern Rationalism. London: Watts. Rev. ed. 1909.

        Twelve Years in a Monastery. London: Smith Elder. London: Smith Elder/New York: Putnams, 1903; London: Watts 1912, 1930, 1931, 1938, 1949. 1930, 1931, 1938 & 1949 were revised editions, published as Thinker's Library, no. 3.

1898   *Life in a Modern Monastery*. London: Grant Richards.

1899   *Religion in the Twentieth Century*. London: Watts.

1901   *Peter Abélard*. London: Duckworth/New York: Putnams. Reprint, New York: Burt Franklin, 1972; North Stratford, N.H.: Ayer, 2001.

1902   *St. Augustine and His Age*. London: Duckworth.

1903   *Haeckel's Critics Answered*. London: Watts. Reprint 1910.

        Church Discipline: An Ethical Study of the Church of Rome. London: Watts.

1905   *The Religion of Woman: An Historical Study*. London: Watts. Reprint 1912.

1906   *The Truth about Secular Education: Its History and Results*. London: Watts. Reprint 1908.

        The Origins of Life. London: Watts.

Talleyrand. London: Hutchinson. New York: D. Appleton, 1907.

1907 *A Hundred Years of Educational Controversy*. London: Watts. Reprint 1908.

The Bible in Europe. London: Watts.

1908 *The Life and Letters of George Jacob Holyoake*. 2 volumes. London: Watts.

[Arnold Wright]. *In the Shade of the Cloister*. London: Constable.

1909 *Woman in Political Evolution*. London: Watts.

The Martyrdom of Ferrer. London: Watts. Melbourne: W. E. Cole, 1910.

Evolution: A General Sketch from Nebula to Man. London: Milner/New York: Frederick A. Stokes.

The Iron Cardinal. London: Eveleigh Nash/New York: John McBride.

The Decay of the Church of Rome. London: Methuen. Reprint 1911.

1910 *Prehistoric Man*. London: Milner/New York: Frederick A. Stokes.

The Evolution of Mind. London: Adam & Charles Black. London: Watts, 1911, 1921.

1911 *Empresses of Rome*. London: Methuen/New York: Henry Holt.

1912 *The Story of Evolution*. London: Hutchinson/Boston: Small Maynard.

Goethe: The Man and his Character. London: Eveleigh Nash.

1913 *A Candid History of the Jesuits*. London: Eveleigh Nash.

Empresses of Constantinople. London: Methuen/Richard D. Badger.

The Existence of God. Inquirer's Library, no. 1. London: Watts.

The Principles of Evolution. London/Glasgow: Collins.

Shakespeare and Goethe. Melbourne: W. E. Cole.

1914 *The Sources of the Morality of the Gospels*. London: Watts.

The Religion of Sir Oliver Lodge. London: Watts.

George Bernard Shaw: A Critical Study. London: Kegan Paul.

Treitschke and the Great War. London: T. Fisher Unwin/Toronto: William Briggs.

1915 *The Soul of Europe*. London: T. Fisher Unwin/Dodd Mead.

The Kaiser: His Personality and Career. London: T. Fisher Unwin.

The War and the Churches. London: Watts.

1916 *Crises in the History of the Papacy*. New York: Putnams/London: Watts.

The Influence of the Church on Marriage and Divorce. London: Watts.

The Tyranny of Shams. London: Eveleigh Nash/New York: Dodd Mead.

1917   *The Pope's Favourite.* London: Hurst & Blackett.

        The Romance of the Romanoffs. New York: Dodd Mead. London: Allen & Unwin, 1918.

        The Bankruptcy of Religion. London: Watts.

1918   *The Popes and Their Church: A Candid Account.* London: Watts. Reprint 1924, 1933, 1936, 1947, 1950; New York: Freethought Press, 1953.

        The Growth of Religion. London: Watts.

1919   *Georges Clemenceau.* London: Watts.

        The Church and the People. London: Watts.

1920   *A Biographical Dictionary of Modern Rationalists.* London: Watts. Bristol, England: Thoemmes Press, 1998.

        Robert Owen. London: Watts.

        Does Democracy Need Religion? People's Platform Series. London: Watts.

        The ABC of Evolution. London: Watts. New York: Putnams, 1921.

        Is Spiritualism Based on Fraud? London: Watts.

        Spiritualism: A Popular History from 1847. London: T. Fisher Unwin/New York: Dodd Mead.

        The Taint in Politics. New York: Dodd Mead. Written anonymously.

1921   *The End of the World.* London: Routledge/New York: E. P. Dutton.

        The Evolution of Civilization. London: Watts; New York: Putnams, 1922.

1922   *George Jacob Holyoake.* London: Watts.

        Ice Ages: the Story of Earth's Revolutions. London: Watts/New York: Putnams.

1923   *The Twilight of the Gods.* London: Watts.

        A New Creed for a New World. London: Watts.

        The Wonders of the Stars. London: Watts/New York: Putnams.

1925   *The Marvels of Modern Physics.* London: Watts/New York: Putnams.

        The Lourdes Miracles. London: Watts.

        The Triumph of Evolution. London: Watts.

        1825–1925: A Century of Stupendous Progress. London: Watts. New York: Putnams, 1926.

1926   *The Truth about the Catholic Church.* Girard, Kan.: Haldeman-Julius.

1927   *Science Yesterday, Today, Tomorrow.* London: Herbert Jenkins.

        Key to Culture. 40 volumes. Girard, Kan.: Haldeman-Julius, 1927–29.

1928   *Debunking the Lourdes Miracles and Other Articles.* Girard, Kan.: Haldeman-Julius.

A Letter from Mr. Joseph McCabe to the Members of the RPA. Self-published.

1929   *The Story of Religious Controversy.* Boston: Stratford.

Key to Love and Sex. 8 volumes. Girard, Kan.: Haldeman-Julius.

1930   *The True Story of the Roman Catholic Church.* 6 volumes. Girard, Kan.: Haldeman-Julius.

The Ancient World. Girard, Kan.: Haldeman-Julius.

The Wonderful Greco-Roman World. Girard, Kan.: Haldeman-Julius.

Greco-Roman Civilization. Girard, Kan.: Haldeman-Julius.

The Joseph McCabe Magazine. Girard, Kan.: Haldeman-Julius, 1930–31.

1931   *A History of Human Morals.* 12 volumes. Girard, Kan.: Haldeman-Julius.

The Rise and Fall of the Gods. 6 volumes. Girard, Kan.: Haldeman-Julius.

The History and Meaning of the Catholic Index of Forbidden Books. Girard, Kan.: Haldeman-Julius.

One Hundred Men Who Moved the World. 17 volumes. Girard, Kan.: Haldeman-Julius. First three volumes later sold as *Ancient Great Men Series.*

The New Science and the Story of Evolution. London: Hutchinson.

Spain in Revolt. London: John Lane. New York: Appleton, 1932.

1932   *Edward Clodd: A Memoir.* London: John Lane.

Can We Save Civilization? London: The Search.

An Outline of Today's Knowledge. Girard, Kan.: Haldeman-Julius.

A Book of Popular Superstitions. Girard, Kan.: Haldeman-Julius.

The Story of the World's Oldest Profession. Girard, Kan.: Haldeman-Julius.

Getting the Most Out of Life. Girard, Kan.: Haldeman-Julius. Reprint 1941.

1933   *The Existence of God.* Rewritten, Thinker's Library, no. 34. London: Watts. Reprint 1934.

The Rhythm Method of Natural Birth Control. Girard, Kan.: Haldeman-Julius.

Great Ideas Made Simple. Girard, Kan.: Haldeman-Julius.

1934   *The Riddle of the Universe To-day.* London: Watts.

Mr. G. K. Chesterton as an Historical Oracle. London: Golden Eagle Publishing.

1935   *Appeal to Reason Library.* 3 volumes. Girard, Kan.: Haldeman-Julius.

The Splendor of Moorish Spain. London: Watts.

The Social Record of Christianity. Thinker's Library, no. 51. London: Watts. Reprint 1937; Escondido, Calif.: Book Tree, 1976.

1936   *Are the Latest Discoveries in Science Giving Support to the God Idea?* Girard, Kan.: Haldeman-Julius.

Upton Sinclair Finds God. Girard, Kan.: Haldeman-Julius.

Is the Philosophy of Dialectical Materialism Out of Date? Girard, Kan.: Haldeman-Julius. New Delhi: Indian Atheist Publishers, 1985, 1999.

A Critical Review of the Latest Claims that are Supposed to Give Validity to the God Idea. Girard, Kan.: Haldeman-Julius.

Is the Position of Atheism Growing Stronger? Girard, Kan.: Haldeman-Julius.

Absurdities of the Christian Religion. Girard, Kan.: Haldeman-Julius.

Reason or Faith—Which Shall Prevail? Girard, Kan.: Haldeman-Julius. Ridgefield, N.J.: Independent Publications, 1992.

Christianity's Social Record. Girard, Kan.: Haldeman-Julius. Ridgefield, N.J.: Independent Publications, 1992.

Does Atheism Rest Its Case on Logic? Girard, Kan.: Haldeman-Julius.

Would a Godless World Make for Social Progress or Decline? Girard, Kan.: Haldeman-Julius.

History of the World Since 1918. Girard, Kan.: Haldeman-Julius.

1937   *The Futility of Basic Religious Ideas.* Girard, Kan.: Haldeman-Julius.

Vice in German Monasteries. Girard, Kan.: Haldeman-Julius. Reprint 1949.

Newest Discoveries in Astronomy. The ABC Library of Living Knowledge, no. 1. Girard, Kan.: Haldeman-Julius.

The Failure of Fascism. The ABC Library of Living Knowledge, no. 2. Girard, Kan.: Haldeman-Julius.

Economic Gains of the Soviet Union. The ABC Library of Living Knowledge, no. 3. Girard, Kan.: Haldeman-Julius.

Nazism and the State of Germany. The ABC Library of Living Knowledge, no. 4. Girard, Kan.: Haldeman-Julius.

The Causes of the War in Spain. The ABC Library of Living Knowledge, no. 5. Girard, Kan.: Haldeman-Julius.

Imperialist Japan and Its Aims. The ABC Library of Living Knowledge, no. 6. Girard, Kan.: Haldeman-Julius.

The Emancipation of Modern Life and Letters. The ABC Library of Living Knowledge, no. 7. Girard, Kan.: Haldeman-Julius.

What America Could Produce and Consume. The ABC Library of Living Knowledge, no. 8. Girard, Kan.: Haldeman-Julius.

Television—What It Is and How It Works. The ABC Library of Living Knowledge, no. 9. Girard, Kan.: Haldeman-Julius.

Man a Million Years Ago. The ABC Library of Living Knowledge, no. 10. Girard, Kan.: Haldeman-Julius.

Economics: The Science of Getting and Conserving Wealth. The ABC Library of Living Knowledge, no. 11. Girard, Kan.: Haldeman-Julius.

The Papacy in Politics Today. London: Watts. Reprint 1939.

1938   *The Passing of Heaven and Hell.* London: Watts.

Women Who Become Men. Girard, Kan.: Haldeman-Julius.

How the Talkies Talk. The ABC Library of Living Knowledge, no. 12. Girard, Kan.: Haldeman-Julius.

Your Body and Its Functions. The ABC Library of Living Knowledge, no. 13. Girard, Kan.: Haldeman-Julius.

What Vitamins and Diet Will Do For You. The ABC Library of Living Knowledge, no. 14. Girard, Kan.: Haldeman-Julius.

The Earliest Man in America. The ABC Library of Living Knowledge, no. 15. Girard, Kan.: Haldeman-Julius.

Our Wonderful Glands. The ABC Library of Living Knowledge, no. 16. Girard, Kan.: Haldeman-Julius.

What War and Militarism Cost. The ABC Library of Living Knowledge, no. 17. Girard, Kan.: Haldeman-Julius.

The Wonders of the Atom. The ABC Library of Living Knowledge, no. 18. Girard, Kan.: Haldeman-Julius.

How Freethinkers Made Notable Contributions to Civilization. Girard, Kan.: Haldeman-Julius.

1939   *A History of the Popes.* London: Watts. Auckland: N. V. Douglas, 1945.

[Martin Abbotson]. *The Liberation of Germany.* London: Watts.

1940   [Martin Abbotson]. *Bureaucracy Run Mad.* London: Watts.

Golden Ages of History. London: Watts. Reprint 1944.

The God of War. Thinker's Forum, no. 1. London: Watts.

The Inferiority Complex Eliminated. Girard, Kan.: Haldeman-Julius.

1941   *Russia and the Roman Church.* Thinker's Forum, no. 16. London: Watts/Girard, Kan.: Haldeman-Julius. Auckland: N. V. Douglas, 1945.

The Vatican's Last Crime. Black International, no. 1. Girard, Kan.: Haldeman-Julius.

How the Pope of Peace Traded in Blood. Black International, no. 2. Girard, Kan.: Haldeman-Julius.

The Pope Helps Hitler to World Power. Black International, no. 3. Girard, Kan.: Haldeman-Julius.

The Vatican Buries International Law. Black International, no. 4. Girard, Kan.: Haldeman-Julius.

1942 *Hitler Dupes the Vatican.* Black International, no. 5. Girard, Kan.: Haldeman-Julius.

The War and Papal Intrigue. Black International, no. 6. Girard, Kan.: Haldeman-Julius.

The Pious Traitors of Belgium and France. Black International, no. 7. Girard, Kan.: Haldeman-Julius.

The Pope and the Italian Jackal. Black International, no. 8. London: Watts/Girard, Kan.: Haldeman-Julius. Auckland: N. V. Douglas, 1945.

Atheist Russia Shakes the World. Black International, no. 9. Girard, Kan.: Haldeman-Julius.

Fascist Romanism Defies Civilization. Black International, no. 10. Girard, Kan.: Haldeman-Julius.

The Totalitarian Church of Rome. Black International, no. 11. Girard, Kan.: Haldeman-Julius.

The Tyranny of the Clerical Gestapo. Black International, no. 12. Girard, Kan.: Haldeman-Julius.

Rome Puts a Blight on Culture. Black International, no. 13. Girard, Kan.: Haldeman-Julius.

The Church the Enemy of the Workers. Black International, no. 14. Girard, Kan.: Haldeman-Julius.

The Church Defies Modern Life. Black International, no. 15. Girard, Kan.: Haldeman-Julius.

The Holy Faith of the Romanists. Black International, no. 16. Girard, Kan.: Haldeman-Julius.

How the Faith is Protected. Black International, no. 17. Girard, Kan.: Haldeman-Julius.

The Artistic Sterility of the Church. Black International, no. 18. Girard, Kan.: Haldeman-Julius.

The Vatican and the Nazis. The Thinker's Forum, no. 26. London: Watts/Girard, Kan.: Haldeman-Julius. Auckland: N. V. Douglas, 1945.

The Fruits of Romanism. Black International, no. 19. Girard, Kan.: Haldeman-Julius.

1943   *The Papacy in France.* London: Watts. Auckland: N. V. Douglas, 1945.

The Papacy in Politics Today. Rewritten. London: Watts. Reprint 1944, 1945, 1947.

1944   *Religion and the Rights of Man.* London: Watts.

Life of Joseph Stalin. Girard, Kan.: Haldeman-Julius.

The Picturesque and Adventurous Career of Chiang Kai-shek. Girard, Kan.: Haldeman-Julius.

Life of Churchill. Girard, Kan.: Haldeman-Julius.

Hitler and His Gang. Girard, Kan.: Haldeman-Julius.

1945   *The Life of Roosevelt.* Girard, Kan.: Haldeman-Julius.

Outlines of the World's Great 'Isms. Girard, Kan.: Haldeman-Julius.

Biographical Dictionary of Ancient, Medieval, and Modern Freethinkers. Girard, Kan.: Haldeman-Julius.

1946   *A History of the Second World War.* Girard, Kan.: Haldeman-Julius.

Rome Irreconcilable with Democracy: The Goebellisms of American Catholic Writers. Girard, Kan.: Haldeman-Julius.

How Atomic Energy Will Affect Your Life and Future. Girard, Kan.: Haldeman-Julius.

The Testament of Christian Civilization. London: Watts.

The History of Flagellation. Girard, Kan.: Haldeman-Julius.

The Meaning of Existentialism. Girard, Kan.: Haldeman-Julius.

1947   *The Menace of Mysticism.* Girard, Kan.: Haldeman-Julius.

The Bloody Story of Anti-semitism Down the Ages. Girard, Kan.: Haldeman-Julius.

Eighty Years a Rebel. Girard, Kan.: Haldeman-Julius. New Delhi: Indian Atheist Publishers, 1991.

Lies and Fallacies of the Encyclopedia Britannica. Girard, Kan.: Haldeman-Julius.

1948   *The Life Story of Robert Owen.* Girard, Kan.: Haldeman-Julius.

The Dumbness of the Great. Girard, Kan.: Haldeman-Julius.

A Rationalist Encyclopedia. London: Watts. Reprint 1950.

The Encyclopedia of Essential Knowledge. 4 volumes. Girard, Kan.: Haldeman-Julius.

The Epic of Universal History. Girard, Kan.: Haldeman-Julius.

A History of Satanism. Girard, Kan.: Haldeman-Julius.

Evolution of the Virtue of Chastity. Girard, Kan.: Haldeman-Julius.

1949   *The History of Torture.* Girard, Kan.: Haldeman-Julius.

A History of Freemasonry. Girard, Kan.: Haldeman-Julius.

The Amazing Career of the Marquis de Sade. Girard, Kan.: Haldeman-Julius.

Sexual Rejuvenation as a Problem of Science. Girard, Kan.: Haldeman-Julius.

Comments on Professor Reiser's New Scientific Humanism, with Oliver L. Reiser's *Scientific Humanism as Creative Philosophy.* Girard, Kan.: Haldeman-Julius.

Masochism, and How It Manifests Itself. Girard, Kan.: Haldeman-Julius.

Judged. Girard, Kan.: Haldeman-Julius.

1950   *The Next Fifty Years.* Girard, Kan.: Haldeman-Julius.

The Myth of Catholic Scholarship. Girard, Kan.: Haldeman-Julius.

Rome's Syllabus of Condemned Opinions. Girard, Kan.: Haldeman-Julius.

Cybernetics—The New Science of the Electronic and the Human Brain. Girard, Kan.: Haldeman-Julius.

1951   *The Origin and Meaning of Ideas.* Girard, Kan.: Haldeman-Julius.

History's Greatest Liars. Girard, Kan.: Haldeman-Julius. Austin, Tex.: American Atheists Press, 1985.

The Papacy in Politics Today. Rewritten. London: Watts. Reprint 1953.

The Columbia Encyclopedia's Crimes Against the Truth. Girard, Kan.: Haldeman-Julius.

A Book of Popular Fallacies. Girard, Kan.: Haldeman-Julius.

1954   *Crime and Religion.* Clifton, N.J.: Progressive World.

TRANSLATIONS AND REVISIONS

1900   Ernst Haeckel. *The Riddle of the Universe.* London: Watts/Harper Brothers. Reprint 1905; London: Watts 1903, 1904, 1905, 1908, 1913, 1929, 1931, 1934, 1937, 1946; Amherst, N.Y.: Prometheus Books, 1992. 1929 and 1931 editions, Thinker's Library, no. 3.

1901   Ludwig Büchner. *Last Words on Materialism and Kindred Subjects.* London: Watts.

1904   Samuel Laing. *A Modern Zoroastrian.* Revised and updated. London: Watts.

Ernst Haeckel. *The Wonders of Life*. London: Watts. Reprint 1905, 1906, 1910.

1905   Ernst Haeckel. *Last Words on Evolution*. London: Watts. Reprint 1910, 1912; Peter Eckler, 1920.

Conrad Guenther. *Darwinism and the Problems of Life*. London: A. Owen/E. P. Dutton.

Samuel Laing. *The Future and Its Problems*. Revised and updated. London: Watts.

Ernst Haeckel. *The Evolution of Man*. London: Watts. Reprint 1906, 1908, 1910, 1911.

1906   Wilhelm Bölsche. *Haeckel: His Life and Work*. London: T. Fisher Unwin/Watts. Reprint 1909.

1907   Albert Kalthoff. *The Rise of Christianity*. London: Watts.

Alexander Kielland. *Napoleon's Men and Methods*. London: A. Owen.

Philip Fauth. *The Moon in Modern Astronomy*. London: A. Owen.

1911   Edouard Dujardin. *The Source of the Christian Tradition*. London: Watts.

Compilation of *Selected Works of Voltaire*. London: Watts. Reprint 1920, 1921, 1935, 1948. Published in the United States as *Toleration and Other Essays*. New York: Putnam, 1912; Amherst, N.Y.: Prometheus Books, 1994). 1935 and 1948 editions, Thinker's Library, no. 54.

1912   Arthur Drews. *Witnesses to the Historicity of the Jesus*. London: Watts.

1913   Francisco Ferrer. *Origins and Ideals of the Modern School*. London: Watts.

1920   Philip Fauth. *The Moon in Modern Astronomy*. London: A. Owen.

1921   Wilhelm Windelbrand. *Introduction to Philosophy*. London: T. Fisher Unwin.

Rudolf Eucken. *Socialism: An Analysis*. London: T. Fisher Unwin.

Rudolf Eucken. *Rudolf Eucken: His Life, Work and Travels*. London: T. Fisher Unwin. New York: Scribners, 1922.

S. Baring-Gould. *The Story of the Nations: Germany*. Revised and enlarged, with Arthur Gilman. London: T. Fisher Unwin.

Hermann Klaatsch. *The Evolution and Progress of Mankind*. London: T. Fisher Unwin/New York: Stokes.

1922   Jean Carrere. *Degeneration of the Great French Masters*. New York: Brentano's.

Charles Nordmann. *Einstein and the Universe, a Popular Exposition of the Famous Theory*. London: Allen & Unwin.

Pierre Denis. *The Argentine Republic: Its Development and Progress*. London: Allen & Unwin.

1923   Dr Edon Caesar Corti. *Leopold I of Belgium*. New York: Brentano's.

O. P. Gilbert. *The Prince de Ligne, A Gay Marshal of the Old Regime*. London: Allen & Unwin.

Gustav Cassel. *The Theory of Social Economy*. London: Allen & Unwin.

1925   Samuel Guyer. *My Journey Down the Tigris*. London: Allen & Unwin/Miami: Adelphi.

Nicolae Iorga. *A History of Roumania: Land, People, Civilization*. London: Allen & Unwin.

GHOSTWRITING

McCabe ghostwrote the following titles for William Montgomery Brown.

1928–32 William Montgomery Brown. *The Bankruptcy of Christian Supernaturalism*. Galion, Ohio: Bradford Brown. Eight volumes: Volume 1, "From the Viewpoint of the Trial" (1928, 1930, 1932); Volume 2, "From the Viewpoint of Science" (1929, 1930, 1932); Volume 3, "From the Viewpoint of History" (1931); Volume 4, "From the Viewpoint of Philosophy" (1932); Volume 5, "From the Viewpoint of the Bible" (1931); Volume 6, "From the Viewpoint of Sociology" (1931).

1932   *Science and History for Boys and Girls*. Galion, Ohio: Bradford Brown.

1935   *The Teachings of Karl Marx for Girls and Boys*. Galion, Ohio: Bradford Brown.

1937   *The Fascist and Communist Dictatorships*. Galion, Ohio: Bradford Brown.

COAUTHORSHIPS

1899   *Can We Disarm?* With George Darien. London: Heinemann/Chicago: Herbert S. Stone.

1908   *The Independence of Ethics*. With Rev. A. J. Waldron. London: Watts.

1911   *Christianity or Secularism: Which is Better for Mankind?* With W. T. Lee. London: Watts.

The Answer of Ernst Haeckel to the Falsehoods of the Jesuits. With Thaddeus Burr Wakeman. London: Truth Seeker.

1920   *Debate on the Truth of Spiritualism*. With Sir Arthur Conan Doyle. London: Watts; Amherst, N.Y.: Prometheus Books, 1993. Also released as Little Blue Book, no. 122.

1923   *The Design Argument Reconsidered.* With Rev. C. J. Shebbeare. London: Watts.

1924   *Revelation of God in Nature.* With Rev. C. J. Shebbeare. New York: Putnams.

1925   *Has the Universe a God?* With Carlyle Summerbell. Chicago: Chicago Rationalist University.

         Is Evolution True? With George M Price. London: Watts. Amherst, N.Y.: Prometheus Books, 1993. Also released as Little Blue Book, no. 1262.

1927   *A Book of American Shams.* With N. A. Crawford, Bertrand Russell, M. Fishbein, J. V. Nash, M. A. de Ford, and E. T. Brewster. Girard, Kan.: Haldeman-Julius. This appeared as Little Blue Book, no. 1125.

1942   *How Man Made God.* With E. Haldeman-Julius. Girard, Kan.: Haldeman-Julius. This appeared as Little Blue Book, no. 1730.

         Atheism in Russia. With E. Haldeman-Julius. Girard, Kan.: Haldeman-Julius. This appeared as Little Blue Book, no. 1731.

         What Gods Cost Man. With E. Haldeman-Julius. Girard, Kan.: Haldeman-Julius. This appeared as Little Blue Book, no. 1732.

         The Blood of the Martyrs. With E. Haldeman-Julius. Girard, Kan.: Haldeman-Julius. This appeared as Little Blue Book, no. 1733.

COLLECTIONS THAT INCLUDE McCABE CONTRIBUTIONS

1904   Charles Watts, ed. *Christianity and Rationalism on Trial.* London: Watts. Includes McCabe contributions "The Splendid Isolation of Mr. George Haw," "The Service of Man," and "Christianity Defended by Sleight of Hand."

1909   Wilhelm Bölsche. *Haeckel: His Life and Work.* London: Watts. Revised edition with an extra chapter written by McCabe.

1916   G. Spiller, ed. *A Generation of Religious Progress.* London: Watts. Includes McCabe contribution "The Humaner Spirit."

1934[?]   Sir J. A. Hamerton, ed. *Our Wonderful World.* London: Amalgamated Press. 4 volumes. Volume 1, "Meteors and Meteorites"; Volume 2, "The Rainbow and the Halo"; and Volume 4, "Decisive Discoveries in Astronomy."

1980   Joseph McCabe. *The Logic and Virtue of Atheism.* Austin, Tex.: American Atheist Press. This is an adapted abridgement by Richard G. Bozarth of McCabe's Big Blue Books *Does Atheism Rest Its Case on*

Logic? Girard, Kan.: Haldeman-Julius, 1936, and *Would a Godless World Make for Social Progress or Decline?* Girard, Kan.: Haldeman-Julius, 1936.

1980   Gordon Stein, ed. *An Anthology of Atheism and Rationalism.* Amherst, N.Y.: Prometheus Books. This includes a selection of passages from *The Existence of God.*

1983   Gordon Stein, ed. *A Second Anthology of Atheism and Rationalism.* Amherst, N.Y.: Prometheus Books. This includes a selection from *The Sources of the Morality in the Gospels.*

LITTLE BLUE BOOKS WRITTEN BY JOSEPH McCABE

Written between 1926 and 1947. Underlined numbers were later brought together as *The Story of Religious Controversy*

1926

<u>1008</u>   *The Origin of Religion*

<u>1007</u>   *The Revolt Against Religion*

<u>1059</u>   *The Myth of Immortality.* Reprinted in *The Forgery of the Old Testament and Other Essays.* Amherst, N.Y.: Prometheus Books, 1993.

<u>1030</u>   *The World's Greatest Religions*

<u>1060</u>   *The Futility of Belief in God*

<u>1061</u>   *The Human Origin of Morals*

<u>1066</u>   *The Forgery of the Old Testament.* Reprinted in *The Forgery of the Old Testament and Other Essays.* Amherst, N.Y.: Prometheus Books, 1993.

<u>1076</u>   *Morals in Ancient Babylon*

<u>1077</u>   *Religion and Morals in Ancient Egypt*

<u>1078</u>   *Life and Morals in Greece and Rome*

<u>1079</u>   *Phallic Elements in Religion*

<u>1084</u>   *Did Jesus Ever Live?* Reprinted in *The Myth of the Resurrection and Other Essays.* Amherst, N.Y.: Prometheus Books, 1993.

<u>1095</u>   *The Sources of Christian Morality*

<u>1102</u>   *Pagan Christs Before Jesus*

1104   *The Myth of the Resurrection.* Reprinted in *The Myth of the Resurrection and Other Essays.* Amherst, N.Y.: Prometheus Books, 1993.

<u>1107</u>   *Legends of Saints and Martyrs*

1110   *How Christianity "Triumphed." Reprinted in The Myth of the Resurrection and Other Essays. Amherst, N.Y.: Prometheus Books, 1993.*

1121   *The Evolution of Christian Doctrine*

1122   *The Degradation of Women*

1128   *The Church and the School*

1130   *The Dark Ages*

1131   *How to Write for the Market*

1132   *New Light on the Cult of Witchcraft*

1134   *The Horrors of the Inquisition*

1135   *Prostitution and the Inquisition*

1136   *Medieval Art and the Church*

1141   *The Reformation and Protestant Reaction*

1142   *The Truth about Galileo and Modern Science*

1927

1140   *The Renaissance: A European Awakening*

1137   *The Moorish Civilization in Spain*

1127   *Christianity and Slavery*

1144   *The Jesuits: Religious Rogues*

1145   *Religion and the French Revolution*

1150   *The Churches and Modern Progress*

1203   *Seven Infidel United States Presidents*

1205   *Thomas Paine's Revolt against the Bible*

1211   *The Conflict between Science and Religion*

1215   *Robert G. Ingersoll: Benevolent Agnostic*

1218   *The Truth about Christianity and Philanthropy*

1224   *Religion in Great Poets*

1229   *The Triumph of Materialism*

1237   *The Beliefs of Scientists*

1243   *The Failure of the Christian Missions*

1248   *The Lies of Religious Literature. Reprinted in The Forgery of the Old Testament and Other Essays. Amherst, N.Y.: Prometheus Books, 1993.*

109   *Facts You Should Know about the Classics*

297   *Do We Need Religion?*

354   The Absurdities of Christian Science

365   Myths of Religious Statistics

366   Religion's Failure of Combat Crime

841   The Failure of Religion

439   My Twelve Years in a Monastery

445   The Fraud of Spiritualism

446   Psychology of Religion

1928

477   The Nonsense Called Theosophy

1262   Is Evolution True? Is Evolution, As a Process, Substantiated by the Facts?
A Debate between George McCready Price, MA, and Joseph McCabe

1929

1455   The End of the World

1450   Do We Live Forever? A Reply to Clarence Wilson

1486   Are Atheists Dogmatic?

1487   A Manual of Debunking

1490   Is Einstein's Theory Atheistic? An Answer to Cardinal O'Connell

1501   Mussolini and the Pope: The Comedy of the Blackshirt and the Blackmailer

1930

1502   Why I Believe in Fair Taxation of Church Property

1504   How to Overcome Self-Consciousness

1509   Gay Chronicle of Monks and Nuns

1510   The Epicurean Doctrine of Happiness

1515   The Love Affair of a Priest and a Nun

1536   Facing Death Fearlessly

1539   Debate with a Jesuit Priest

1543   Is War Inevitable?

1550   How People Lived in the Middle Ages

1559   Can We Change Human Nature?

1931

1561   *That Horrible French Revolution*

1942

1762   *What Is Wrong with the World*

1763   *How an Ape Became a Man*

1764   *The Evolution of Animal Life*

1765   *The World We Live In: The Important Truths of Geology and Astronomy*

1943

1766   *The Body Machine and How It Works*

1767   *The Mysteries of Embryology and Heredity*

1768   *The Plant World Simplified, the Main Principles of Modern Botany*

1769   *Has Man a Mind? The Truth Forced Upon Modern Psychology*

1770   *Man the Creator: Physics As the Basis of Engineering*

1771   *The Wonders of Modern Chemistry, the Principles Upon Which They Are Based*

1772   *How Religion Began: Primitive Man Stumbles into a Blind Alley*

1773   *Philosophers and Their Dreams, the History and Nature of Philosophical Speculations*

1774   *Real and Unreal Moral Law, the New Ethic and Its Timely Revolution*

1775   *How Christianity Grew Out of Paganism, the Real Origin of the Christian Religion*

1776   *The Ancient World, from the Dawn of Civilization to the Greeks*

1777   *The World of the Greeks and Romans: How a New Age Opened 2500 Years Ago*

1778   *The Middle Ages: The Longest Reaction in History*

1779   *Truth about the Rebirth of Civilization: The Material Factors*

1780   *Asia's Great Atheist Religions: An Account of Confucianism and Buddhism*

1781   *Skeptics the Great Leaders of Progress: Historical Absurdity of the Alleged Menace of Skepticism*

1782   *The Making of the Modern World, Civilization Advances As Obscurantism Decays*

1783   *Lies and Bunk about Racial Superiority: The Aryan and Other Races*

1784   *Asia and Its Problems: The Asiatics Just As Capable of Progress As the Whites*

1785   *Japan and America: Why America Was Caught Napping*

1786   *Russia in the Light of War: A Revolution in World-Opinion*

1787   *Socialism and Capitalism: A Short Statement on the Economic Issue*

1788   *Evolution or Revolution: Fallacy of the Slow and Steady Theory of Progress*

1789   *Can We Change Human Nature? Social Psychology Slays a Popular Myth*

1790   *Sham Fighting about Matter and Spirit: Current Bunk about Materialism and the Spiritual*

1791   *Freethought and Agnosticism: Lies and Confusions in Conventional Literature*

1792   *The Literature of Myths and Legends: Books That Dupe Half the World*

1793   *Great Poets and Their Creeds: The Fallacy That Religion Inspires Great Poetry*

1794   *The Theatres and the Cinema: A Critique of Them As Organs of Public Education*

1795   *Pessimism in Modern Literature: Why so Much Cynicism in Brilliant Writers?*

1796   *Fancy Modern Religions: When Do They Become Rackets?*

1797   *The Futility of All Mysticisms: The Claim That There Is a Superscientific Knowledge*

1798   *Fundamentalists and Superior Believers: The Fallacy of the Belief That Refining Orthodoxy Pays*

1799   *Is Our Age Degenerate? A Talk about Superior Early Ages Bunk*

1944

1800   *The Crying Need for School Reform: How to Make Education Attractive and Effective*

1801   *The Question of Democracy: A Critical Study of First Principles*

1802   *The Man and the Woman: Science and Common Sense on the Sex Question*

1803   *What is the End of Life? Bunk about the Aimlessness of Modern Life*

1804   *Bunk about Marriage: The Synthetic Zeal of the Bigots*

1805   *Should the World Federate? The Question of the Federation of all Nations*

1806   *H. G. Wells and His Creed: An Examination of the Chief Constructive Proposals in Literature*

1807   *Is America Religious? A Candid Examination and Critique of Claims*

1808   *Death Control and Birth Control: The Orthodox Attitude Paradoxical and Insincere*

1809   *Bunk about Free Will and Strong Will: Another Revolution in Psychology*

1810   *The Materialistic Determination of History: A Great Philosophy in Brief Outline*

1811   *Man Today Faces His Greatest Opportunity: This Tide in Man's Affairs*

1947

1828   *Bunk about Marriage*. This is a reprint of no. 1804.

1830   *The Mystery of Existence*

1831   *Sex Life in Russia*

1844   *The Erring Husband*

ARTICLES IN RPA/RATIONALIST ANNUALS

1897   From Rome to Rationalism; or, Why I Left the Church.

1898   The Sources of Modern Doubt

1899   The Revival of Ritualism

1900   Shall Rationalism Disarm?

1901   Science and Theology in the Nineteenth Century

1902   The Victory of Christianity

1903   The Abiding Element in Religion

1904   The Cult of the Unknown God

1905   A World without God: An Anticipation

1906   The Artificial Creation of Life

1907   Fore-Gleams of Humanism in Debate

1908   The Lesson of Evolution

1909   New Light on the Nature of Mind

1910   Free-Will in Modern Psychology

1911   The Secret Philosophy of Mark Twain

1912   The Tercentenary of the English Bible

1913   The Sources of the Gospel Parables

1914   The Philosophy of Sir Oliver Lodge

1915   Rationalism and War

1916   Has Rationalism Corrupted Germany?
1917   The Papacy During the Renaissance
1918   What Christianity Has Done for Russia
1919   The Vitality of France
1920   The Churches and the World Unrest
1921   The Psychology of Modern Mysticism
1922   Is England a Christian Country?
1923   Reflections in Athens
1924   Religion at the Antipodes
1925   The Outlook: Progress or Reaction?
1926   The Triumph of Evolution

IMPORTANT ARTICLES IN OTHER JOURNALS

1905   "Sir Oliver Lodge on Haeckel," *Hibbert Journal* 3 (1905): 741–55.
1911   "Is Civilization in Danger?" *Hibbert Journal* 10 (1912): 599–614.

VOLUMES COMPRISING THE *KEY TO CULTURE*

1927

1. Physics
2. Astronomy
3. Geology
4. Biochemistry
5. Palaeontology
6. Botany
7. Zoology
8. Comparative Anatomy
9. Economic Botany and Zoology
10. Evolution
11. Anthropology and Philology
12. Human Anatomy and Physiology
13. Embryology

1928

14. Psychology
15. Human Prehistory
16. Ancient Near East
17. Greece and Rome
18. India and China
19. Middle Ages
20. Rise of Modern Europe
21. Modern Intellectual History
22. American History
23. Political Evolution
24. Economics
25. Economic Theories
26. Economic Life of Man
27. History of Social Ideals
28. Writers in Antiquity
29. Writers in the Middle Ages
30. Great Modern Writers
31. Writers Today and their Message
32. Ancient Art
33. Medieval Art
34. Modern Art
35. Critical Thinking
36. History of Philosophy
37. History of Morality
38. History of Education

1929

39. Applied Psychology
40. Progress of Science

Volumes 1–11	later sold as *The Foundations of Science*
Volumes 15–22	later sold as *A Complete Outline of History*
Volumes 23–27	later sold as *The Elements of Economics*
Volumes 28–31	later sold as *The Outline of Literature*
Volumes 35–40	later sold as *The Art of Thinking Logically*

APPENDIX 2

Articles by McCabe in the *Literary Guide*

N ote: this is by no means a complete list of the articles wrote, but it illustrates the extraordinary breadth of McCabe's journalistic activity.

March 1898	Rationalism and Sentiment
June 1898	On the Growth of Myths
November 1898	The Dread of Materialism
January 1899	The Ascent of Man: Being a Summary of Charles Darwin's *Descent of Man* (*Literary Guide Reprints*)
April 1899	The Meaning of Faith
August 1899	Impersonal Deities
October 1899	Dreyfus and the Political Moralists
April 1900	Dr. Mivart's Religion
	The Answer of the Dying Century
July 1900	The Bible in China
October 1900	Closing the Century of Science
November 1900	Answers to the World-Riddle
January 1901	The Life of Thomas Henry Huxley (*Literary Guide Supplement*)
February 1901	Rome in the New Century
March 1901	A Prehistoric Peep
April 1901	A Temple of Reason

October 1901	The Presidential Speech
November 1901	The French Convulsions
January 1902	The First Year of the Century
January 1903	The Decay of Reverence
	Notes to "The Riddle of the Universe"
April 1903	Science à la Mode
June 1903	Lord Kelvin as Theologian
August 1903	Sir Oliver Lodge on Faith
September 1903	The Thunderbolt Falls
November 1903	The Church Congress
December 1903	"What is Anti-Christianity?"
February 1904	The Pulverisation of Professor Haeckel
April 1904	Sir Leslie Stephen (*Literary Guide Supplement*)
July 1904	Professor Lloyd Morgan on Haeckel
September 1904	Mr. Balfour's Radiation
October 1904	The Rome Freethought Congress: The Significance of the Gathering
November 1904	Mr. Oliver Lodge on Haeckel
January 1905	The Wonders of Life (*Literary Guide Supplement*)
February 1905	The Latest Defense of the Faith
March 1905	The Believing Bishops
August 1905	The Bible and the Child
September 1905	The British Association Meeting
October 1905	The Paris Congress
January 1906	The Solitary Splendor of Sir Oliver Lodge
February 1906	The Pathetic Ballad of Mr. Frank Ballard
March 1906	The Last Tributes to the Life of George Jacob Holyoake
April 1906	The Origin of Life
May 1906	A Defence of Spencer
June 1906	Secular Education and the Bishops Who Need It
August 1906	The Royal Commission of Ecclesiastical Militancy
September 1906	The March of Science
November 1906	The Evolution of the Churchgress
December 1906	Catholic Truth and Scientific Fiction

February 1907	The Scientific Creed of Sir Oliver Lodge
May 1907	Catholicism and Scholarship
July 1907	Death-Bed Conversions
September 1907	The Papacy and Modern Thought
November 1907	Sea-Breezes in the Church Congress
January 1908	The Decadence of Orthodoxy
March 1908	The Law and the Blasphemer
April 1908	More About the Law and the Blasphemer
May 1908	A Catholic View of Us
July 1908	The New Pan-Anglican Apologetic
August 1908	A Museum of Evolution
October 1908	The Growth of Crime in France
November 1908	The Moral Education Congress
December 1908	The Education Compromise and Rationalists
January 1909	Moses and Mr. Tuckwell
February 1909	The Centenary of Darwin
April 1909	Are Men of Science Agnostic?
May 1909	The "Forgeries" of Professor Haeckel
June 1909	My Visit to Jena
July 1909	A Literary Monument to Darwin
September 1909	The *Encyclopedia Biblica* and Its Critics
October 1909	Rationalism Dominant in the American Universities
November 1909	The Martyrdom of Francisco Ferrer
December 1909	In the Days of Mazzini
February 1910	Echoes of the Ferrer Case
March 1910	The Meaning and Range of Telepathy
April 1910	The Reform of the Divorce Law
May 1910	The Story of a Pioneer
June 1910	The Diary of a Pilgrim
July 1910	The Diary of a Pilgrim II
August 1910	The Diary of a Pilgim: In Marvellous Melbourne
September 1910	The Diary of a Pilgrim: Rationalism in Australia
October 1910	The Diary of a Pilgrim: At the Antipodes
November 1910	The Diary of a Pilgrim: The Return to Australia and Home

December 1910	Dr. Wallace's Last Words on Evolution
February 1911	The Creed of Dr. Russel Wallace
March 1911	Haeckel's Embryo Drawings
April 1911	The Brotherhood of Men
May 1911	Christian Evidence and Christian Etiquette
June 1911	William Archer on Ferrer
July 1911	The Parliament of Man
October 1911	The Anti-Rationalism of Bergson
November 1911	Mr. R. J. Campbell on Christ
January 1912	The Inquisition in Spain
February 1912	The Truth about the Jesuits
March 1912	Ferrer Vindicated in Spain
April 1912	Concerning Various Matters
June 1912	The "Titanic" and God
July 1912	Bergson and Science
August 1912	Dr. Horton as a Religious Oracle
September 1912	Christian Influence on Marriage
October 1912	The Dreadful Heresies of Professor Schäfer
November 1912	The Bishops in Churchgress
December 1912	The Church and Divorce Law
January 1913	The Evolution of Christmas
February 1913	Mysticism and Morals
March 1913	Modernism: Catholic and Protestant
May 1913	The Church Bell at Sea
July 1913	Religion at the Antipodes
September 1913	A Tour of Maoriland
November 1913	The End of the Tour
December 1913	The Tactics of the Clergy
January 1914	The Morals of Rationalists
February 1914	Kikuyu
March 1914	A Debate on Miracles
April 1914	The Churches and the People
May 1914	The Task of Rationalism
June 1914	The Revolt against Reason

July 1914	More Rebels against Reason
August 1914	Doubts about Darwinism
September 1914	Armageddon
October 1914	The Clergy and the War
November 1914	German Culture and German Brutality
January 1915	Under the Stars and Stripes
February 1915	The Neutrality of America
March 1915	German Atrocities and British Humanity
April 1915	Rationalism and the War
May 1915	The War and the Population Question
June 1915	After the War
July 1915	The Soul of Germany
August 1915	The Clergy and the War
September 1915	The Ideal of Arbitration
October 1915	The Religious Revival in France
April 1916	The Faith and the War
May 1916	The Humanism of Shakespeare
June 1916	The Ordeal of War
August 1916	A Bit of Catholic Truth
September 1916	Christ and War
November 1916	The Bishop's Progress
December 1916	Do the Dead Live?
January 1917	Ring in the New
February 1917	The Singular Case of Sir W. Crookes
April 1917	Religion in the United States
May 1917	Under the Stars and Stripes
July 1917	William Archer on the New God
	America at War
August 1917	The Bishops and the Psalms
September 1917	Mr. Wells's Metaphysic
November 1917	The Pope's Neutrality
December 1917	The Blight of Pessimism
January 1918	The Burden of the Year
February 1918	The Day of Prayer

March 1918	The Advance of Science
April 1918	The Catholic Appeal to the Nation: An Open Letter to Cardinal Bourne
June 1918	The Machinery of Life
July 1918	A New View of Man's Origin
August 1918	Episodes of the War: The Revival of the Psalms
September 1918	Four Years After
October 1918	An Apology for the Pope
November 1918	A Rationalist Queen of England
December 1918	The Changing Face of Europe
January 1919	The New Year and the New Era
February 1919	The Things that Matter
March 1919	The Coming World Peace
April 1919	Twopenny-Worth of Christian Evidence
May 1919	New Experiments in Religion
June 1919	A Word About Spirituality
July 1919	The Dying Fire
August 1919	The Nation Thanks God
September 1919	Ernst Heinrich Haeckel
October 1919	The Vilification of Rationalists
November 1919	Miss Royden's Theology
December 1919	The Defence of Materialism
January 1920	The Burden of the Year
Feb1920	The Creed of a Dying Woman
March 1920	The Thirst for Immortality
April 1920	The Great Debate
May 1920	Who Are These Spiritualists?
June 1920	The Hope of the Race
July 1920	Clericalism, Behold the Enemy!
August 1920	The New Catholic Menace
September 1920	The Creed of a Rationalist
October 1920	A Gospel of Sweet Reasonableness
November 1920	Mr. Wells's History of the World
December 1920	The Poor Old Church

January 1921	The Spirituality of Sir A. C. Doyle
February 1921	Do We Need Any "Ism"?
March 1921	The Newest Spiritualism
April 1921	The Paganism of Keats
May 1921	Rationalism and the Emotions
June 1921	The Dreariness of Rationalism
July 1921	Mr. Wells As Reformer
August 1921	Rationalism and the New Hope
September 1921	The Youth of Ernst Haeckel
October 1921	More About the Evolution of Man
November 1921	The Twin Superstitions of Our Time
December 1921	Elie Metchnikoff: A Great Rationalist
January 1922	The Harvest of the Year
February 1922	What is Rationalism?
March 1922	The Great Intellectual Adventure
April 1922	The Present Position of Darwinism
May 1922	Mr. Blatchford Recants
June 1922	The Major Prophets of Rationalism
July 1922	Recent Exposures of Spiritualism
August 1922	The Magnificence of Shelley
September 1922	The Ascent of Man
October 1922	Where Cross and Crescent Meet
November 1922	The Catholic Church and Evolution
December 1922	Mr. Wells Sees it Through
January 1923	Lord Balfour's Gifford Lecture
February 1923	The Irreligion of the Age
March 1923	Gospels and Philosophies of Life
April 1923	Birth Control and Piety
May 1923	Materialism Again Annihilated
June 1923	The Shadow of the Holy Cross
July 1923	Sunday at Sea
August 1923	The Human Comedy
September 1923	Under the Southern Cross
January 1924	The Chances of Reaction

May 1924	A Century of Triumph
June 1924	Rationalism and Life's Problems
July 1924	My Impressions of Spain
August 1924	Galvanizing the Corpse of Spiritualism
September 1924	The Miracles of Lourdes
October 1924	The Conflict of Religion and Science
November 1924	Is There a Religious Revival?
December 1924	What is Religion?
January 1925	What of the Future?
February 1925	Apologetics Up to Date
March 1925	New Light of Man's Evolution
April 1925	Religion and the French Revolution
May 1925	The Religion of a Darwinist
June 1925	The Church of Christ
July 1925	Religion and the New Psychology
August 1925	The Great Fight in America
September 1925	Science and Religion
October 1925	Lessons of the Debate
November 1925	Under the Stars and Stripes
December 1925	Rationalism in America
January 1926	The Churches in America
February 1926	The Outlook in America
March 1926	Among the Canadians

APPENDIX 3

Lectures and Debates Given by Joseph McCabe

Abbreviations: ELES, East London Ethical Society; HEI, Hampstead Ethical Institute; NSS, National Secular Society; RPA, Rationalist Press Association; SLES, South London Ethical Society; SPES, South Place Ethical Society; WLES, West London Ethical Society.

Note: As with appendix 2, this list is by no means complete, even for his lectures in England. It merely gives an indication of the prodigious breadth of McCabe's knowledge, and of his stamina.

1900

January 7	"The Catholic Church in France" to SLES
January 28	"Ethics as a Basis of Social Authority" to NLES
March 18	"The Old Testament in Board Schools" to Chatham Secular Society
April 22	"The Bible in Board Schools" to SLES
October 21	"Death and Afterwards" to Camberwell Secular Hall
November 4	"The Problem of the Jew" to Leicester Secular Society
December 9	"The Origin of Life" at 3:00 P.M. and "Death and Afterwards" at 7:00 P.M. to Sheffield Secular Society

1901

Runs a series of eleven lectures for WLES on "Church Discipline"

1903

January 18	"The Future of Catholicism" to SLES
February 2	"The Future of Catholicism" to ELES
March 8	"Early Christian Women" to SLES
March 15	"The Unknown God" at 3:00 P.M. and "The Future of Catholicism" at 7:00 P.M. at Sheffield Secular Society
April 12	"The Bible in School" at Camberwell Secular Hall
May 3	"The Golden Age" at ELES
May 17	"Women in Early Christian Teaching" to ELES
October 4	"The Failure of the Churches" to ELES
October 25	"Citizenship" to SLES
November 29	"The Legend of a Golden Age" at noon and "The Riddle of the Universe" at 6:30 P.M. to Glasgow Secular Society
December 6	"The Riddle of the Universe" to ELES

1904

January 10	"The Legend of a Golden Age" to WLES
February 14	"Japan—A Godless Nation" at Stanley Hall, London
February 15	Leads discussion on "The Religious Temperament of Women" at SPES
February 28	"Modern Priestcraft" at noon and "A Godless People: The Japanese" at 6:30 P.M. to Glasgow Secular Society
April 3	"Ethics in Japan" to SLES and "The Neo-Biblical Study of the Resurrection" to SPES
April 24	"The Ethical Principles of Robert Owen" to North Kensington Ethical Society
May 1	"Church and State in France" to WLES
June 19	"Church and State in France" to SLES
June 26	"The Moral Influence of Europe in Asia" to SPES
July 31	"The Scholastic Side of Dante" to SPES
October 16	"Parsifal and the Holy Grail" to SPES

November 13   "Christian Europe and Pagan Asia" to Glasgow Secular Society

November 20   "The Vatican" to SPES

December 11   "The Struggle in France" to Camberwell branch NSS

1905

January 1   "The Welsh Revival" to SPES

January 15   "The Legend of the Virgin Birth" at noon and "The Religion of Sir Oliver Lodge" at 7:00 P.M. to Liverpool branch of NSS

February 12   "The Decay of the Church of Rome" at noon and "Sir Oliver Lodge on Haeckel" at 6:30 P.M. to Glasgow Secular Society

February 14   "The Welsh Revival" to Glasgow Rationalist and Ethical Union

February 19   "The Devil in Milton and Goethe" to SPES

March 26   "Sir Oliver Lodge and Professor Haeckel" to SLES

April 2   "The Economic Side of War" to SPES

May 21   "The Decay of Catholicism" at 3:00 P.M. and "The Welsh Revival" at 7:00 P.M. to Liverpool branch NSS

June 11   "Paganism—Old and New" at SLES

July 30   "Dr. Barry's *Renan*" to SPES

August 13   "The Bible in School" at 2:45 P.M. and "The Riddle of the Universe" at 6:30 P.M. to Failsworth Secular Sunday School

September 10 "The Residual Conflict of Science and Theology" to SPES

October 22   "Are We Making Social Progress?" to SPES

October 29   "The Bible in School" at noon and "The Evolution of Man" at 6:30 P.M. at Glasgow branch of NSS

November 6, 13, 20, 27, December 4, 11   Gives a series of lectures with lantern slides on "Prehistoric Man: A Sketch of the Ascent of Humanity from the Ape Stage to Civilization" at Essex Hall, London, which "were successful beyond all expectation . . ." (RPA Report, 1906, pp 6–7)

November 12, 19, 26, December 3   Gives a series of lectures on "The Evolution of Man" to Leicester Secular Society

November 28   "The Philosophy and Personality of Professor Haeckel" to SPES

December 24   "The Evolution of Christianity" to SLES and "The Evolution of Christmas" to SPES

1906

February 25	"The New Ideal of Womanhood" to SPES
March 25	"The Ethic of Liberal Thought" to SPES
April 22	"The Novel with a Purpose" to SPES
May 27	"The Historical Attitude of the Priest toward Education" to SPES
June 24	"The Constraints of Goethe and Shakespeare" to SPES
July 29	"The Church and Medieval Art" to SPES
September 23	"The Religion of Epicurus" to SPES
October 14	"The Religious Condition of Italy" to SPES
November 10, 17, 24, December 1	"The Ascent of Man from Ape to Civilization" to the Ethical Society, Fulham Palace Road. November 10, "The Primal Savage." November 17, "The Birth of Art." November 24, "The First Traces of Civilization." December 1, "The Dawn of History."
November 25	"In the Days of the Comet" to SPES

1907

January 6	"The Early Church and the Workers" to SPES
January 13	Unknown topic in Bristol
January 14, 15	Unknown topic in Plymouth
January 16	Unknown topic in Plumstead
January 20	"In the Days of the Comet" to HEI and "Bible Lessons in London Schools" to the Fulham, Hammersmith and Barnes Ethical Society
January 25	Unknown topic in Garden City
January 27	"The Humanism of Goethe and Shakespeare" Hampstead and Battersea
January 30	Unknown topic in Plumstead
February 2	"The Fourth French Revolution" to SPES and "Is Woman Inferior?" to Camberwell Ethical Union
February 3	"The Fourth French Revolution" to SPES
March 17	"A Hundred Years of Education Controversy" to SPES
March 24	"A Hundred Years of Education Controversy" to Camberwell Ethical Society
April 28	"Woman and Politics" to SPES and "A Religion of Happiness" to Camberwell Ethical Society

May 19	"Woman and Politics" to Camberwell Ethical Society and "The Dusk of the Gods" to SPES
June 16	"The Evolution of Toleration" to SPES
June 30	"The Dusk of the Gods" to SLES
July 21	"Art and Ethics" to SPES
September 22	"The Value of Life in Modern Science" to SPES
October 6	"Christian Science" to SLES
October 17	"The High Death Rate in France" to Malthusian League, London
October 20	Unknown topic to Glasgow Secular Society
October 28	"The Beginning of the World" for the Plymouth Rationalist Society on behalf of the RPA
October 29	"The End of the World" for Plymouth Rationalist Society on behalf of RPA
November 17	"The Jesuit in Fact and Fiction" to SPES
November 22	"The Real Cost of War" to SLES and "The Ethics of Maeterlinck" to SPES

1908

January 19	"The Social Work of George Jacob Holyoake" to SPES
February 2	"The Church and Social Questions" at 3:00 P.M. and "Our Earliest Human Ancestors" at 7:00 P.M. to Coventry branch of NSS
February 23	"The Awakening of Spain" to SPES
March 1	"Secularism and Socialism" at noon and "The Jesuit in Fact and Fiction" at 6:00 P.M. toGlasgow Secular Society
March 22	"The Ethic of Enfranchisement" to SPES
March 26	Leads discussion at RPA's offices on "The Prospects of the Education Bill"
March 29	"The Influence of Science and Religion on Social Life" to SLES
April 19	"The Catholic Church in the United States" to SPES
May 24	"Free Will in Modern Psychology" to SPES
June 21	"Prospero and Caliban" to SPES
July 19	"New Theories of Child Training" to SPES
September 13	"The Position of Roman Catholicism" to SPES
October 4	"The New Faust" to SPES

October 5, 6	Debate on "The First Chapter of Genesis and Modern Science" with Rev. John Tuckwell at Essex Hall, London
October 20, 27, November 4, 13	Series of lectures for SPES on "The Evolution of Mind" with 180 lantern slides
October 29, November 5, 12, 19	Series of lectures at Fulham Town Hall on "The Evolution of Mind," with 180 lantern slides
November 6	"Creation Myths" at RPA's offices
November 8	"Heredity and Moral Education" to SPES
November 29	"Free Will and Free Progress" and "The Evolution of Mind" to Glasgow Secular Society
December 20	"The Milton Tercentenary" to SPES

1909

January 24	"The Poetry of William Watson" to SPES
February 21	"The Centenary of Darwin" to SPES
March 5	"Rationalism and Reaction" to RPA HQ
March 7	"The Humanism of Shakespeare" and "The Centenary of Darwin" to Glasgow Secular Society
March 10	"From Microbe to Man" to Exeter RPA
March 28	"The Novels of D'Annunzio" to SPES
April 11	"The Pessimism of Tolstoy" to SPES
May 9	"Swinburne" to SPES
May 16	"The Outlook for Secular Education" at 2:45 P.M. and "The Dusk of the Gods" at 6:30 P.M. at Failsworth Secular School
June 13	"The Law of Divorce" to SPES
July 11	"The Stage and the Censor" to SPES
September 5	"The Trouble in Spain" to SPES
October 3	"Religion in the United States" to SPES
October 6	"The End of the World" to the Birmingham RPA
October 13	"Our Earliest Human Ancestors" to the Birmingham RPA
October 19, 26, November 2, 9	"The Evolution of Morality" to SPES. October 19, "The Origin of Moral Feeling." October 26, "Barbaric Codes of Morality." November 2, "The Threshold of Civilization." November 9, "Morality and the Ethical Religions."

November 11	"A Rational View of the Woman Problem" to an RPA meeting
November 16	"The Life and Work of Senor Ferrer" to SPES
November 29	Debates with G. W. de Tunzelmann on "Theism and the Problem of the Universe" at Essex Hall, London
December 19	"Sir O. Lodge and the Future Life" to SPES

1910

January 2	"Civilization and the Selection of the Unfit" to SPES
February 6	"Watson's Later Poetry" to SPES
March 6	"Anatole France as Artist and Thinker" to SPES
April 3	"Dr. Garnett's *Life of W. J. Fox*" to SPES
June 4, 6, 7, 9, 10	Lectures in New South Wales
June 14	Lectures in Brisbane
June 22	Leaves Sydney for New Zealand; gives twenty-five lectures in as many days
June 6	Gives address to Unitarian Church in Auckland, which is overwhelmed by the two hundred to three hundred people who turn up to listen
June 7	"The Evolution of Man" at Choral Hall, Auckland
June 8	Federal Hall, Auckland, on unknown subject
June 9	Federal Hall on unknown subject; might also have given afternoon address on "Secular Education"
July 2	"Secular Education: The Question of the Hour" at Wellington Town Hall; Stout in Chair
July 3	"Christianity and Social Progress" at His Majesty's
July 4	"The Evolution of Man" at Wellington Town Hall Concert Chamber
July 5	"The Evolution of the Social Position of Women" at Unitarian Church, Ingestre Street, Wellington
July 5	"The Evolution of Morality and Civilization" at Wellington Town Hall
July 11	"The Evolution of Man" in Timaru; Deputy Mayor met McCabe at the station
July 12	"The Present Conflict between Science and Theology" in Timaru; Rev. J. H. G. Chapple of St. Andrews Church in Chair

July	Lectures in Dunedin and Invercargill before returning north
July 25	"Ferrer the Anarchist, Atheist, Wife-deserter, Free Fancier, and Insurrectionist" in Sydney
October 13	Joint RPA/SPES memorial lecture at Conway Hall on Francisco Ferrer, on the anniversary of his death
October 19	Debate on "Ghosts" at Wallingford Literary and Debating Society against unknown opponent
October 23	"An Impression of Australia" to SPES
November 27	"Mark Twain's Anonymous Philosophy" to SPES
December 4	Unknown topics to Glasgow Secular Society, noon and 6:30 P.M.
December 11	Unknown topic to Leicester Secular Society
December 18	"The Mediocrity of the Time" to SPES

1911

January 8	"The Pessimism of Tolstoy" at 3:00 P.M. and "Theology and Recent Science" at 7:00 P.M. at Liverpool branch NSS
January 11	"Mark Twain as a Rationalist" to SLES
January 22	"St Augustine's City of God" to SPES
February 26	"The New Portugal" to SPES
March 9, 10	Debates "Christianity or Secularism: Which is the Better for Mankind?" at Holborn Town Hall with W. T. Lee of North London Christian Evidence League
March 13	"The Evolution of Morality and Civilization" to the Edinburgh RPA
March 19	"*The New Machiavelli*" to SPES
March 26	"The Evolution of Mind" to Stockport Labour Church
April 3	"The Martyrdom of Ferrer" to Cardiff RPA
April 4	"The Evolution of Man" to Penzance RPA
April 23	"The Revival of Nietzsche" to SPES
May 21	"The Tercentenary of the Bible" to SPES
June 18	"Plato's Plea for Immortality" to SPES
July 16	"The Universal Peace Congress" to SPES
September 10	"The New Mysticism of Bergson" to SPES
October 13	"The Struggle in Spain: Ferrer and After" to SPES
October 30	"The Story of Man's Origin" at Essex Hall

November 1, 8, 15, 22	Series of lectures on "The Story of Man's Origin" to Borough Polytechnic Institute
November 7, 14, 21, 28	Series of lectures on "The History and Meaning of Rationalism" to SPES. November 7, "The Psychology of Rationalism." November 14, "The History of Rationalism." November 21, "The Social Record of Rationalism." November 28, "The Future of Rationalism." Many hundreds attended.
November 26	"The Personality of Goethe" to SPES
December 31	"The Mysticism of Bergson" to SLES and "Eugenic Fallacies" to SPES

1912

January 7	"Ethics and Darwinism" to Fulham Ethical Society
January 28	"The Evolution of Religion" to SLES
February 4	"Christ in Modern Scholarship" at 3:00 P.M. and "The Evolution of Religion" at 7:00 P.M. to Liverpool branch NSS
February 11	"The Devil in Milton and Goethe" at 3:00 P.M. and "The Evolution of Morality" at 6:30 to Sheffield Ethical Society
February 25	"The Parables of Christ" to SPES
March 17	"Rome-Rule in Ireland" to SPES
March 24	"The Ethics of the Gospels" at noon and "Life in Other Worlds" at 6:30 P.M. to Glasgow Secular Society; lantern slides
April 14	"Woman's Rights and Woman's Duties" to SPES
May 12	"Dickens as a Moralist" to SPES
June 9	"Browning's Religion" to SPES
July 14	"Russia" to SPES
September 22	"Mysticism and Morals" to SPES
October 14	"Ferrer's Final Vindication" to SPES
October 20	"*Marriage*" to SPES
November 4	"The Origin and Nature of Life" at Essex Hall; Percy Vaughn in Chair
November 24	"The Failure of Carlyle" to SPES
December 22	"The Christmas Revival" to SPES

1913

January 26	"The New Oxford Theology" to SPES

February 2   "The Gospel of Carlyle" to Fulham Ethical Society

February 18   "Wonderful Chapters in the Story of the Earth" to Hampstead
                 Conservatoire

February 23   "The Tyranny of Shams" to SPES

October 5   "Progress at the Antipodes" to SPES

October 26   Unknown topic to Fulham Ethical Society

November 9   "The Religion of Sir Oliver Lodge" to SPES

December 7   "Alfred Russel Wallace" to SPES

December 14   "Science and the Hope of Immortality" at noon and "Wonderful
                 Chapters in the Story of the Earth" at 6:30 P.M. to Hull RPA

December 18   Unknown topic to Peckham and Rye Discussion Society

1914

January 4   "The Religion of G. Bernard Shaw" to SPES

January 19   Debate on "Immortality" at the Little Theatre with J. A.
                 Hobson against G. K. Chesterton and Hilaire Belloc

February 8   "The Ethic of G. Bernard Shaw" to SPES

March 1   "The Religion of Sir Oliver Lodge" and "The Birth and Death
                 of Worlds" in Sheffield

March 9   "The Religion of Sir Oliver Lodge" in Birmingham

March 22   "Evolution and Religion" in Edinburgh

March 23   "Science and Immortality" in Northampton

April 19   "The Education of the Adult" to SPES

May 17   "The Historicity of Christ" to SPES

June 14   "The Melting Pot" to SPES

July 12   "The Religious Philosophy of Eucken" to SPES

October 11   Debates "Is Nature Cruel?" against Rev. L. Clare and speaks on
                 "The Birth and Death of Worlds" at Hull

October 18   "The Place of War in History" to SPES

November 1   "The Influence of Nietzsche" to SPES

1915

January 10   "An Impression of New York" to SPES

February 14   " The Eclipse of Idealism" to SPES

March 14   "The New Papacy" to SPES

March 28	"American Neutrality: A Personal Impression" to SLES
April 11	"Fallacies of Race and Nationality" to SPES
May 9	"Progress Since Waterloo" to SPES
June 27	"The Soul of Germany" to SPES
September 12	"Patriotism" to SPES
October 10	"Nietzsche" to SPES
November 14	"Mr. Balfour on Humanism" to SPES

1916

January 9	"The Pagan and Christian Ideal of Marriage" to SPES
February 20	"The Trial of Democracy" to SPES
March 12	"The Papacy and the Reformation" to SPES
June 4	"The Pope as Peacemaker" to SPES
July 9	"Mr. Shaw and the Teaching of Christ" to SPES
September 10	"Religious Optimism and the War" to SPES
October 15	"Woman in the New Industry" to SPES
October 22	"The Preparation of the Earth for Life" in Wigan for RPA
October 29	"The Early Development of Life" in Wigan for RPA
November 5	"The Rise of the Higher Animals" in Wigan for the RPA
November 12	"The Evolution of Humanity" in Wigan for the RPA. Average turnout for these lectures was 350—"fairly large audiences."
November 26	"The Mission of Hope and Repentance" to SPES
December 3	"Rationalism in the Great Poets" and on "Robert Owen: The Great Welsh Rationalist" at Abertillery
December 31	"The Present Temper of Germany" to SPES

1917

July 1	"The Spirit of the United States" to SPES
July 8	"America's Problems" to SPES
September 2	"The Pope's Terms" to SPES
September 9	"The Evolution of Beauty in Nature" in Wigan for RPA
September 16	"The Evolution of Mind" in Wigan for RPA
September 23	"The Evolution of Morality" in Wigan for RPA
September 30	"Evolution and Religion" in Wigan for RPA

October 28	"The Religion of H. G. Wells and G. B. Shaw" in Sheffield for RPA
October 29	Unknown topic in Ayr
November 18	"The Conversion of Mr. Wells" to SPES
November 25	"The Churches and Social Progress" and "The Religion of H. G. Wells and G. B. Shaw" in Swansea for the RPA
December 2	"The Riddle of Russia" to SPES

1918

January 13	"The Revival of Spiritualism" to SPES
February 10	"Recent Views on the Origin of Religion" to SPES
March 24	"The Conscription of Wealth" to SPES
April 28	"The Vitality of France" to SPES
June 16	"The Dilemma of the Churches" to SPES
July 21	"Rationalism as a Practical Creed" to SPES
September 1	"The League of Nations" to SPES
September 15	"The Churches and the War" at 3:00 P.M. and "The Miracles of Modern Science" at 7:00 P.M. in Wigan for RPA
September 22	Lectures on "Religion after the War" at 3:00 P.M. and "Wonders of Evolution" at 7:00 P.M. in Wigan for RPA
November 3	"The Foundations of Peace" to SPES
November 29	Unknown topic in Sheffield
December 15	"Is It a New England?" to SPES

1919

January 12	"A League of Nations" to SPES
February 2	"*Joan and Peter*: Mr. Wells on Education" to SLES
February 16	"The Socialist State of Queensland" to SPES
March 2	"The Church and the People" to SLES
March 16	"The Medieval Guild" to SPES
April 13	"The Dying Creeds" to SPES
April 20	"The Kingdom of Man" to SLES
May	Speaks to six hundred wounded former soldiers at Buxton. Only eight remain for the concluding hymn.
June 22	"The Russian Constitution" to SPES

1919	Lectures to British troops stationed in the Rhineland for about two months
September 17	"The Reality of Moral Forces" to SPES
September 21	"Science and the Hope of Immortality" and "The Glories of Ancient Athens" at Wigan for RPA
September 28	"Do We Need Religion?" and "Life in Ancient Rome" at Wigan for RPA
September 29	"Theosophy and Christian Science" to RPA at Essex Hall
October 5	"City Temple Theology as Expounded by Miss Mary Royden" to RPA at Essex Hall
October 13	"Sir Oliver Lodge's Defence of Spiritualism" to RPA at Essex Hall
October 19	First of three "Evolution of Man" series to Leicester Secular Society
October 20	"Sir A. Conan Doyle's Evidence for a Future Life" to RPA at Essex Hall
October 22	Unknown topic at Accrington
October 26	Second of three "Evolution of Man" series to Leicester Secular Society
October 28, November 5, 12, 17	"The Evolution of Man" at the People's Palace, London
November 2	Third of three "Evolution of Man" series to Leicester Secular Society
November 9	"The Religion of the Great Artists" at Sheffield
November 16	"The Religion of the Great Artists" to SPES
November 24, December 1, 8	"The Evolution of Man" at Caxton Hall, London
November 27, December 4, 11	First three of four-part series on "The Evolution of Man" to the Woolwich Radical Club
December 7	"The Evolution of Man" at Newport Pagnell
December 14	"The Place of Frivolity in Life" to SPES
December 16	Unknown topic at the Old Vic, London
December 21	Unknown topic at Woking

1920

January 4	Unknown topics at Swiss Cottage at noon and Golder's Green in the evening
January 8	Fourth and last in series of "The Evolution of Man" to Woolwich Radical Club
January 10	Unknown topic in Plymouth
January 12	Unknown topic in Ayr
January 13	Unknown topic in Falkirk
January 14	Unknown topic at Greenock
January 15	Unknown topic in Edinburgh
January 16	Unknown topic in Glasgow
January 18	Unknown topics in Glasgow, morning and evening
January 25	Unknown topics in Swansea, afternoon and evening
January 26	Unknown topic in London
February 2	Unknown topics in Halifax and Leeds
February 3	Unknown topic in Leeds
February 4, 11, 18, 25	Unknown series at Northern Polytechnic, Holloway
February 12, 13	Unknown topics in Bournemouth, with two on the 13th
February 15	Unknown topic in Coventry
February 22	"The Position of the Churches" to SPES
February 28	Unknown topic at Bedford Park
February 29	"The Immortal Story of Athens" at Stockport Labour Church
March 7	Unknown topic at Abertillery
March 11	Debate with Sir Arthur Conan Doyle on "Is Spiritualism Based on Fraud?" at Queen's Hall, London, before a packed audience
March 14	"The Dangers of Spiritualism" to SPES
March 16	Unknown topic at Cambourne
April 18	"The Science of Death and Science of Life" to SPES
May 30	"The Eclipse of the Papacy" to SPES
June 13	"The Virtues and Vices of Patriotism" to SPES
July 11	"The Decay of Literature" to SPES
September 12	"The Church and the Marriage Law" to SPES
October 3	"Theology and Evolution" to SPES

| October 7,
14, 21, 28 | "The Evolution of Man" to Borough Polytechnic |
| October 8,
15, 22, 29 | "The Evolution of Man" at Public Hall, Croydon |

1921

January 23	"Keats as a Pagan Poet" to SPES
February 20	"The Age of the Cinema" to SPES
March 20	"The Chances of Reaction" to SPES
April 17	"Is There an Ethical Decay?" to SPES
May 29	"The Teaching of History" to SPES
June 12	"The Right of Personality" to SPES
July 3	"Modern Priestcraft" to SPES
September 11	"Mr. G. B. Shaw's Pentateuch" to SPES
October 31	"Modernism in the Church of England" to SPES
December 4	"The Chances of Peace" to SPES

1922

January 1	"The Risks of Democracy" to SPES
February 12	"The Decay of Moral Teaching" to SPES
April 23	"Character and Immortality" to SPES
May 14	"Mr. Chesterton on the Modern Spirit" to SPES
June 18	"Modern Pessimism" to SPES
July 9	"Contemporary Superstition" to SPES
September 17	"Impressions of the Sick Lands of Europe" at SPES
October 6, 23, 30, November 6	"The Evolution of Man and the Present State of Science" at Caxton Hall, London
October 2	"Spiritualism" at Liverpool
November 5	"My Impressions of Eastern Europe" at SPES
November 11	Unknown topic at Caxton Hall
December 31	"Bishop Gore on God" at SPES

1923

January 21	"The Cross and the Crescent" at SPES
February 11	"The Collapse of Pacifism" at SPES
March 4	"Renan as a Moralist" to SPES
June 5	"A New Creed for a New World" at Centennial Hall, Brisbane
June 26	Unknown topic at Unitarian Church.
June 27	"The Imposture of Spiritualism" at Auckland Town Hall, presided over by Sir Robert Stout
June 28	"The Wonders of Egypt and Babylon" at Auckland Town Hall, chaired by H Scott Bennett
June 30	"The Evolution of Man" at Auckland Town Hall Concert Chamber
July 1	"The Present Conflict Between Science and Religion" at Auckland Town Hall
July 2	"The Twilight of the Gods" at Auckland Town Hall Concert Chamber

1924

January 6	"The Legend of a Golden Age" to SLES
January 13	"The Real Tut-ankh-Amen" to HEI
February 3	"The Truth about Tutankhamen" to SLES
February 17	"The Power of the Press" to HEI
March 9	"The Reunion of the Churches" to SLES
March 23	"The Power of the Press" to SLES
April 6	"The Reunion of the Churches" to HEI
April 27, May 11	"Mr. Wells as a Prophet" to HEI
October 11	Debate: "Is Democracy a Failure?" to HEI
October 12	"Mr. Shaw's Idea of History" to HEI
October 12	"George Bernard Shaw on Joan of Arc" to SLES
November 16	"Fascism in Spain" to HEI and SLES in evening
December 14	"The Legend of the Lost Atlantis" to HEI in afternoon and SLES in evening

1925

January 18   "Bertrand Russell's *Icarus*" to HEI in afternoon and SLES in evening

February 15   "Can We Change Human Nature?" to HEI in afternoon and SLES in evening

March 3   Opens discussion on "Is a Militant Rationalist Policy Desirable?" at RPA HQ; Herbert Cutner in Chair

March 15   "The Spaniard and the Moor" to HEI in afternoon and SLES in evening

April 19   "The Paradox of the American" to HEI in afternoon and SLES in evening

May 10   "Religion and the French Revolution" to SLES

May 17   "Religion and the French Revolution" to HEI

September 6   Debates George McCready Price on "Is Evolution True?" at Queen's Hall, London; Earl Russell in Chair

October 18   Debates Rev Carlyle Summerbell, D.D., on "Has the Universe a God?" at Auditorium Recital Hall, Chicago. Spends last three months of 1925 lecturing for the Chicago Rationalist University Society

1925–26   Gives forty lectures and holds six debates during this tour

1927

April 10   "My Impressions of Mexico" to SPES

May 1   "My Impressions of the United States" to SLES

1932

October 16   "What's Wrong with the World?" to Leicester Secular Society

1933

March 5   "The Twilight of the Gods" to RPA, Glasgow District

October 24   "Rationalism and the Modern World" to Conway Discussion Circle, SPES

December 17   "The Triumph of Materialism" to Leicester Secular Society

1934

March 18   "The Scientific Reconstruction of Life" to RPA, Glasgow District

June 3   "The Blood-Price of Democracy" to SPES

November   First mention of McCabe returning to RPA lecturing circuit (for March 1935)

November 4 "Light on the Origin of Civilization" to Leicester Secular Society; lantern slides

November 11 "This Tide in Man's Affairs" to SPES

December 4 Debates with Rev. A. W. Harrison, D.D., on "That Christianity Did Not Promote Civilization" at Conway Hall

1935

February 18 "Mexico and its Wonders" at Carnegie Public Library, Ayr

March 3   Unknown topic at fifty-fourth anniversary of Leicester Secular Society's opening of Secular Hall

March 19   "Wanted, a New Voltaire" to Conway Discussion Circle, SPES

March 24   "The Church Trouble in Germany" to SPES

September 15 "Changing Human Nature" to SPES

October 29 "The Chances of a Religious Reaction" to Conway Discussion Circle, SPES

November 3, Series of four lantern slide addresses on "The Evolution of Euro-
10, 17, 24 pean Civilization" at Leicester Secular Society. November 3, "The Sources of Greek Civilization." November 10, "The Glory that was Greece." November 17, "The Splendor that was Rome." November 24, "The Magnificent Arab Civilization."

1936

January 12   "Professor Dewey's Creed for Everyman" to SPES

January 28   "The Menace of the Catholic Church" to SPES

September 20 "The Next War"

October 18   "Can Science Change Human Nature?" to Glasgow RPA

November 3   "Our Fascist Churches" to Conway Discussion Circle, SPES

1937

February 2	Debates "That the Weight of Evidence Is against the Theory of Organic Evolution" with Douglas Dewar at Conway Hall
February 14	"The Red Pope: Pius XI" to SPES
February–March	Debate in L.G. between McCabe and Dr. Vladimir Novak on Rationalism in Czeckoslovakia (February, p. 47, and March, p. 64)
March 14	"Can Science Change Human Nature?" to Leicester Secular Society
March 20	"The New Anglican Theology" to SPES
September 28	"Rationalism and the Churchless Four-Fifths" to Conway Discussion Circle, SPES
December 12	"The Brave New World" to SPES

1938

January 16	"Religion and Revolution" in Glasgow
March	"The Papacy in the World Crisis" to a packed audience in Blackburn
September 9–13	Attends International Freethought Congress in London. Speaks on "The Present Religious Reaction and the Menace of the Vatican" along with three others
October 9	"The Social Record of Skepticism" at Leicester Secular Society
October 16	"The Social Record of Heresy" in Glasgow
November 8	"Rationalism—Rational and Irrational" to Conway Discussion Circle, SPES

1939

January 22	"The Catholic Church and Morals" to Blackburn branch of NSS
February 26	"The Subtle Tyranny of the Press" to SPES
March 12	"Some Bad Popes" to Leicester Secular Society
March 26	"The Popes and the World Crisis" to Manchester branch of NSS
October 3	Debate between McCabe and Rev. Father Vincent McNabb at Welfare Hall, Pyle, Glamorgan on "That Roman Catholicism Is a False Religion"

October 15   Unknown subject to Leicester Secular Society

December 17   "Religion and the World Upheaval" to Manchester branch of NSS

1940

February 18   "God and the War" to Manchester branch of NSS

February 25   "Mr. Wells's New World Order" to SPES

March 3   "Secularism and its New Psychology" at Leicester Secular Society

October 20   "Is the Dark Age Returning?" to SPES

December 22   "The Starry Heavens and the Moral Law" to SPES

1941

March 9   "The Dream of a Golden Age" at Leicester Secular Society

March 16   "Changing Human Nature" to SPES

July 20   "Germany: An Interpretation" to SPES

October 19   "The Pope's Holy War" to Leicester Secular Society

November 30   "Is Science to Blame?" to SPES

December 28   "The Papacy and Russia" to Blackburn NSS

1942

June 28   "American and Japan" to SPES

1943

February 7   "The Centenary of the Death of Richard Carlile'

February 14   SPES 150th anniversary. McCabe speaks along with Lord Snell, Joad, S. K. Ratcliffe, and G. W. Keeton

October 31   "The Shadow of the Coming Peace" to SPES

1944

March 12   Unknown topic to Leicester Secular Society

March 26   "The Papacy and the War" to Blackburn NSS

June 18   "The New Education" to SPES

December 31   "The Old World and the New" to SPES

1945

May 6	"Germany" to SPES
July 29	"The Failure of the Twentieth Century" to SPES
October 9	"Haeckel and Modern Thought" at Conway Discussion Circle, held jointly by RPA and SPES
December 30	"The Vatican Peril" to Blackburn branch of NSS

1946

January 6	"Criticism of Science" to SPES
February 26	Replaces ill Chapman Cohen to lead Conway Discussion Circle on "The Dangers and Fallacies of Race," a combined SPES/RPA activity
April 30	Chairs first session of World Union of Freethinkers Conference in London, on "Rationalism"
May 19	"The Larger Education" to SPES
July 28	"Fifty Years Retrospect" to SPES
October 6	"Applying Science to Life" to SPES
December 29	"Ring in the New" to SPES

1947

January 7	"Rationalism in Post-War Europe" at Conway Discussion Circle
February 23	"Early Christian and Modern Communism" to SPES
March 2	"Responsibilities of Democracy" to SPES
April 13	"Our Timid Historians" to SPES
June 15	"Contemporary Pessimism" to SPES
July 27	"The Growth of Anti-Semitism" to SPES
October 5	"Do Soldiers Rule Us?" to SPES
November 16	"Heresy; Yesterday and Today" to SPES

1948

February 1	"The Revolutions of 1848" to SPES
February 29	"Do Races Wear Out?" to SPES

1949

February 13	"Seventy Years of Education" to SPES
October 23	"The Black Year of 1849" to SPES

1950

June 25	"The Inspiration of Sacred Music" at SPES
December 11	"The Philosophy of Epicurus" at Conway Hall to SPES

1951

July 1	"More's *Utopia*" to SPES
September 23	"Communism" to SPES
Nov	"Religion, Crime, and Secularism" to West London branch of NSS

1952

January 27	"Science and Theology Today" to SPES
April 27	"History and Its Pessimists" to SPES
August 8–12	Addresses Seventh Annual Conference of the RPA at Leicester University College, Oadby, Leicester on "Roman Catholicism and Crime"
September 21	"Juvenile Delinquency" to SPES
November 30	"The Constructiveness of Rationalism" to SPES

1953

April 26	"Forecasts of the Future" to SPES

1954

February 28	"The Character of Popular Revolutions" to SPES

Bibliography

REFERENCE

Catechism of the Catholic Church. Suva, Fiji: Liberaria Editrice Vaticana, 1995.
New Catholic Encyclopedia. New York: McGraw-Hill, 1967.
Atwater, Donald. *The Penguin Dictionary of Saints*. London: Penguin, 1985.
Dahlitz, Ray. *Secular Who's Who*. Melbourne: Ray Dahlitz, 1994.
Eliade, Mircea, ed. *The Encyclopedia of Religion*. New York: Macmillan, 1987.
Kelly, J. N. D. *The Oxford Dictionary of Popes*. Oxford: Oxford University Press, 1986.
Milner, Richard. *The Encyclopedia of Evolution*. London/New York: Facts on File, 1990.
Stein, Gordon, ed. *The Encyclopedia of Unbelief*. Amherst, N.Y.: Prometheus Books, 1985.
Wiener, Philip P., ed. *Dictionary of the History of Ideas*. New York: Charles Scribner's Sons, 1978.

GENERAL BIBLIOGRAPHY

Annan, Noel. *Leslie Stephen*. London: Macgibbon & Kee, 1951.
Appleyard, Bryan. *Understanding the Present: Science and the Soul of Modern Man*. London: QPD, 1992.
Armstrong, Karen. *Through the Narrow Gate*. London: Macmillan, 1981.
Ayer, A. J. *Philosophy in the Twentieth Century*. London: Unwin Paperbacks, 1984.
Ballard, Frank. *"Clarion" Fallacies*. London: Hodder & Stoughton, 1904.
———. *The Miracles of Unbelief*. Edinburgh: T. & T. Clark, 1905.
———. *Haeckel's Monism False*. London: Charles H. Kelly, 1905.
———. "Romanism versus Christianity." *London Quarterly Review* 307 (July 1930): 66–77.

Barry, Very Rev. Canon William. *The Prospects of Catholicism*. London: Catholic Truth Society, 1901.

Bauman, Zygmunt. *Intimations of Postmodernity*. London/New York: Routledge, 1993.

Beaglehole, J. C. *Victoria University College*. Wellington: New Zealand University Press, 1949.

Belloc, Hilaire. *A Companion to Mr. Wells's "Outline of History."* London: Sheed & Ward, 1929.

Berman, David. *A History of Atheism in Britain: From Hobbes to Russell*. London/New York: Routledge, 1990.

Bethell, Nicholas. *The Last Secret: Forcible Repatriation to Russia 1944–47*. London: Andre Deutsch, 1974.

Birx, H. James. *Interpreting Evolution*. Amherst, N.Y.: Prometheus Books, 1991.

———. "Ernst Haeckel." *New Zealand Rationalist and Humanist* (September 1994): 2–4.

Blackham, H. J. *Stanton Coit: 1857–1944*. London: Favil Press, n.d.

Blatchford, Robert. *God and My Neighbour*. Chicago: Charles H. Kerr, 1934.

Blinkhorn, Martin, ed. *Fascists and Conservatives*. London: Unwin Hyman, 1990.

Boardman, John, Jasper Griffin, and Oswyn Murray, eds. *The Oxford History of the Classical World*. London: Guild Publishing, 1986.

Bonner, Hypatia Bradlaugh, ed. *Humanity's Gain from Unbelief*. London: Watts, 1932.

Bowler, Peter. *Evolution: The History of an Idea*. Berkeley: University of California Press, 1989.

———. *The Non-Darwinian Revolution: Reinterpreting a Historical Myth*. Baltimore, Md./London: Johns Hopkins, 1992 [1988].

Brace, C. Loring. *Gesta Christi: A History of Humane Progress Under Christianity* London: Hodder & Stoughton, 1884.

Brandon, Ruth. *The New Women and the Old Men: Love, Sex and the Woman Question*. London: Flamingo, 1991.

Brooke, John Hedley. *Science and Religion*. Cambridge: Cambridge University Press, 1993.

Brome, Vincent. *Six Studies in Quarrelling*. London: Cresset, 1958.

Budd, Susan. *Varieties of Unbelief*. London: Heinemann, 1977.

Burr, John R. "McCabe, Joseph Martin." In *The Encyclopedia of Unbelief*, edited by Gordon Stein. Amherst, N.Y.: Prometheus Books, 1985.

Burrow, J. W. *Evolution and Society*. Cambridge: Cambridge University Press, 1970.

Bury, J. B. *A History of Freedom of Thought*. London: Williams & Norgate, 1913.

———. *The Idea of Progress*. New York: Dover, 1955.

Butterfield, Herbert. *The Whig Interpretation of History*. London: Penguin, 1973.

Calne, Donald B. *Within Reason: Rationality and Human Behaviour*. New York: Pantheon, 1999.

Calvin, William H. *How Brains Think*. London: Wiedenfeld & Nicolson, 1997.

Campbell, Colin. *Toward a Sociology of Irreligion*. London: Macmillan, 1971.

Carr, John Dickson. *The Life of Sir Arthur Conan Doyle*. London: Pan, 1953.

Cassirer, Ernst. *The Philosophy of the Enlightenment*. Boston: Beacon Press, 1960.

Chan, Wing-tsit. *A Source Book in Chinese Philosophy*. Princeton, N.J.: Princeton University Press, 1973.

Chesterton, G. K. *Heretics*. London: John Lane The Bodley Head, 1911.

Clark, Kenneth. *Civilisation*. London: BBC/John Murray, 1971.

Clements, Keith. *Lovers of Discord: Twentieth Century Theological Controversies in England*. London: SCM, 1988.

Clements, Richard. "A Tribute to Joseph McCabe." *Humanist* 83, no. 2 (February 1968): 41–43.

Cliteur, Paul. "The Challenge of Postmodernism to Humanism." *New Humanist* 110 (August 1995): 4–9.

Cobban, Alfred. *In Search of Humanity*. London: Jonathan Cape, 1960.

Cohen, Chapman. *The Other Side of Death*. London: Pioneer Press, 1922.

Conan Doyle, Arthur. *The New Revelation*. London: Hodder & Stoughton, 1918.

Cooke, Bill. "A Rebel to His Last Breath: Joseph McCabe." *New Zealand Rationalist and Humanist* (spring 1997): 2–10.

———. *Heathen in Godzone: Seventy Years of Rationalism in New Zealand*. Auckland: NZARH, 1998.

Coren, Michael. *Gilbert: The Man Who Was G. K. Chesterton*. London: Jonathan Cape, 1989.

———. *The Invisible Man: The Life and Liberties of H. G. Wells*. London: Bloomsbury, 1994.

———. *Conan Doyle*. London: Bloomsbury, 1996.

Cornwell, John. *Hitler's Pope: The Secret History of Pius XII*. London: Viking, 1999.

Coulton, G. G. *Romanism and Truth*. London: Faith Press, 1931.

Crawshay-Williams, Rupert. *Russell Remembered*. London: Oxford University Press, 1970.

Darlington, C. D. *The Conflict of Science and Society*. London: Watts, 1948.

Davies, A. J. *To Build a New Jerusalem: The British Labour Party from Keir Hardie to Tony Blair*. London: Abacus, 1996.

Davies, Norman. *Europe: A History*. Oxford: Oxford University Press, 1996.

Dawkins, Richard. *The Selfish Gene*. Oxford: Oxford University Press, 1976.

———. *The Blind Watchmaker*. London: Longman, 1986.

———. *River Out of Eden*. London: Wiedenfeld & Nicolson, 1995.

———. *Climbing Mount Improbable*. London: Viking, 1996.

De Blaye, Edouard. *Franco and the Politics of Spain*. London: Penguin, 1976.

Dennett, Daniel C. *Consciousness Explained*. London: Penguin, 1993.

———. *Darwin's Dangerous Idea*. London: Allen Lane/Penguin Press, 1995.

De Rosa, Peter. *Vicars of Christ: The Dark Side of the Papacy*. London: Corgi, 1989.

Derrida, Jacques. *The Gift of Death*. Chicago: University of Chicago Press, 1995.

Dewar, Douglas. *A Challenge to Evolutionists*. Croydon: Uplift Books, 1948.

Diamond, Jared. *Guns, Germs and Steel*. London: Vintage, 1998.

Dickson, John. *Shall Ritualism and Romanism Capture NZ?* Dunedin: Otago Daily Times and Witness Newspapers Ltd, 1912.

———. *Our Liberties and Eternal Vigilance*. Napier: G. W. Venables, 1928.

Draper, John William. *A History of the Conflict Between Religion and Science*. London: Watts, 1927.

Drawbridge, C. L. *Common Objections to Christianity*. London: Robert Scott, 1914.

Duffy, Eamon. *Saints and Sinners: A History of the Popes*. New Haven, Conn./London: Yale University Press, 1997.

Ellis, Havelock. *The Task of Social Hygiene*. London: Constable, 1927.

Farrington, Benjamin. *Head and Hand in Ancient Greece*. London: Watts, 1947.

Flew, Antony. *An Introduction to Western Philosophy*. London: Thames & Hudson, 1971.

———. *Darwinian Evolution*. London: Paladin, 1984.

————. *Atheistic Humanism*. Amherst, N.Y.: Prometheus Books, 1993.

Furbank, P. N. *Diderot*. New York: Alfred A. Knopf, 1992.

Gardner, Juliet, ed. *What is History Today?* Basingstoke: Macmillan, 1989.

Gasman, Daniel. *The Scientific Origins of National Socialism*. London/New York: Macdonald & American Elsevier, 1971.

Gay, Peter. *The Enlightenment: An Interpretation*. London: Wildwood House, 1973 [1966].

Gee, Maurice. *Plumb*. London: Faber & Faber, 1978.

Gellner, Ernest. *Reason and Culture*. Oxford: Blackwell, 1992.

————. *Conditions of Liberty: Civil Society and Its Rivals*. London: Hamish Hamilton, 1994.

Gerard, Rev. John, S.J. *Professor Haeckel and His Philosophy*. London: Catholic Truth Society, 1910.

Goldberg, Isaac. *Joseph McCabe: Fighter for Freethought*. Girard, Kan.: Haldeman-Julius, 1936.

Gould, F. J. *The Life-Story of a Humanist*. London: Watts, 1923.

————. *The Pioneers of Johnson's Court*. London: Watts, 1929.

Grunberger, Richard. *A Social History of the Third Reich*. London: Penguin, 1974.

Gunn, John W. "McCabe the Rebel." *New Zealand Rationalist* (June 1952): 7–9. Reprinted from *The American Freeman*.

Haeckel, Ernst. *The Riddle of the Universe*. London: Watts, 1900.

————. *The Wonders of Life*. London: Watts, 1906.

————. *The Evolution of Man*. London: Watts, 1910 [1874].

————. *Last Words on Evolution*. London: Watts, 1910.

————. *Eternity*. New York: Truth Seeker, 1916.

Haldeman-Julius, Emanuel. "My Second 25 Years." *Critic and Guide* (1949).

Hanlon, J. O. "Joseph McCabe . . . A Tribute." *New Zealand Rationalist* (November 1950): 3.

Harris, Frank, Percy Ward, George McCready Price, Joseph McCabe, and Arthur Conan Doyle. *Debates in the Meaning of Life, Evolution, and Spiritualism*. Amherst, N.Y.: Prometheus Books, 1993.

Harvey, David. *The Condition of Postmodernity*. Oxford: Blackwell, 1991.

Haynes, E. S. P. *Pages from a Lawyer's Notebook*. London: Watts, 1939.

Herrick, Jim. *Vision and Realism: A Hundred Years of the Freethinker*. London: G. W. Foote & Co., 1982.

Hill, J. Arthur. *Spiritualism: Its History, Phenomena and Doctrine*. London: Cassell, 1918.

Hiorth, Finngeir. *Introduction to Atheism*. Pune: Indian Secular Society, 1995.

"Historicus." *Did Jesus Ever Live—or Is Christianity Founded Upon a Myth?* New York: United Secularists of America, 1972.

Höhne, Heinz. *The Order of the Death's Head: The Story of Hitler's SS*. London: Pan, 1981.

Holyoake, George Jacob. *Sixty Years of an Agitator's Life*. London: T. Fisher Unwin, 1906.

Howlett, Duncan. *The Fatal Flaw at the Heart of Religious Liberalism*. Amherst, N.Y.: Prometheus Books, 1995.

Humphrey, Nicholas. *A History of the Mind*. London: Chatto & Windus, 1992.

Jackson, John G. *Christianity Before Christ*. Austin, Tex.: American Atheist Press, 1985.

Jameson, Fredric. *Postmodernism or, the Cultural Logic of Late Capitalism*. London: Verso, 1993.

Joad, C. E. M. *The Testament of Joad*. London: Faber & Faber, 1943.
———. *Shaw*. London: Victor Gollancz, 1949.
Keith, Sir Arthur. *A New Theory of Human Evolution*. London: Watts, 1950.
Kelly, Alfred. *The Descent of Darwin: The Popularisation of Darwin in Germany 1860–1914*. Chapel Hill: University of North Carolina Press, 1981.
Kenny, Anthony. *A Path from Rome*. Oxford: Oxford University Press, 1986.
Kerényi, Carl. *Prometheus: Archetypal Image of Human Existence*. Princeton, N.J.: Princeton University Press, 1991.
Kurtz, Paul. *In Defense of Secular Humanism*. Amherst, N.Y.: Prometheus Books, 1983.
———. *Eupraxophy: Living Without Religion*. Amherst, N.Y.: Prometheus Books, 1989.
———. *The Transcendental Temptation: A Critique of Religion and the Paranormal*. Amherst, N.Y.: Prometheus Books, 1991.
———. *The New Skepticism: Inquiry and Reliable Knowledge*. Amherst, N.Y.: Prometheus Books, 1992.
Lecky, W. E. H. *History of the Rise and Influence of the Spirit of Rationalism in Europe*. 2 volumes. London: Longmans, Green, 1904.
Lehman, L. H. *Behind the Dictators*. Auckland: N. V. Douglas, 1946.
Levine, Peter. *Nietzsche and the Modern Crisis of the Humanities*. Albany: State University of New York Press, 1995.
Lewin, Roger. *Complexity: Life on the Edge of Chaos*. London: Phoenix, 1995.
Lloyd-Jones, Mike. "Joseph McCabe: Apostle of Rationalism." *Freethinker* (June 1974): 88–89.
Lodge, Sir Oliver. "The Reconciliation between Science and Faith," *Hibbert Journal* 1 (1902).
———. *Life and Matter: A Criticism of Professor Haeckel's "Riddle of the Universe."* London: Williams & Norgate, 1907.
———. *Raymond, or Life and Death*. London: Methuen, 1916.
Lukes, Steven. *The Curious Enlightenment of Professor Caritat*. London: Verso, 1996.
Luntley, Michael. *Reason, Truth and Self*. London/New York: Routledge, 1995.
MacDonagh, Giles. *Prussia: The Perversion of an Idea*. London: Mandarin, 1995.
MacDonald, George. *Fifty Years of Freethought: The Story of the Truthseeker*. New York: Truthseeker, 1931.
Macey, David. *The Lives of Michel Foucault*. London: Vintage, 1994.
Magee, Bryan. *Confessions of a Philosopher*. London: Wiedenfeld & Nicolson, 1997.
McLoughlin, Emmett. *Famous Ex-Priests*. New York: Lyle Stuart, 1968.
McNabb, Vincent. *The Catholic Church and Philosophy*. New York: Macmillan, 1927.
Maitland, Frederic William. *Life and Letters of Leslie Stephen*. London: Duckworth, 1906.
Mann, Walter. *The Follies and Frauds of Spiritualism*. London: Watts, 1919.
Martin, Kingsley. *Editor*. London: Hutchinson, 1968.
Martin, Michael. *Atheism: A Philosophical Justification*. Philadelphia: Temple University Press, 1990.
Mayr, Ernst. *One Long Argument: Charles Darwin and the Genesis of Modern Evolutionary Thought*. London: Penguin, 1993.
Midgley, Mary. *Science as Salvation*. London: Routledge, 1994.
Millar, Ronald. *The Piltdown Men*. London: Scientific Book Club, 1974.
Miller-Argue, Robert. *Evolution Exploded by Many Infallible Proofs*. Sydney: Commonwealth Christian Evidence Press Association, 1910.

Monk, Ray. *Wittgenstein: The Duty of Genius*. London: Vintage, 1991.

Moulton, J. Hope, ed. *Is Christianity True? A Series of Lectures*. London: Charles H. Kelly, 1904.

Munz, Peter. *Philosophical Darwinism*. London: Routledge, 1993.

Murray, Gilbert. *Humanist Essays*. London: Unwin Books, 1964.

Nietzsche, Friedrich. *Thus Spake Zarathustra*. Buffalo: Prometheus, 1993.

———. *Beyond Good and Evil*. London: Penguin, 1988.

O'Farrell, P. J. "McCabe and Sectarianism," *Manna* 6 (1963).

———. *The Catholic Church and Community in Australia: A History*. Melbourne: Nelson, 1977.

O'Neill, John. *The Poverty of Postmodernism*. London/New York: Routledge, 1995.

Passmore, John. *The Perfectibility of Man*. New York: Charles Scribner's Sons, 1970.

———. *Serious Art*. London: Duckworth, 1991.

Peake, Arthur S. *Christianity: Its Nature and Truth*. London: Duckworth, 1909.

Peake, Arthur S., and R. G. Parsons, eds., *An Outline of Christianity: The Story of Our Civilisation*. 5 volumes. London: Waverley, 1928.

Plimer, Ian. *Telling Lies For God*. Milsons Point: Random House, 1995.

Popper, Karl R. *The Poverty of Historicism*. London: Routledge & Kegan Paul, 1957.

———. *The Open Society and its Enemies*. London: Routledge & Kegan Paul, 1963.

Ratcliffe, S. K. *The Story of South Place*. London: Watts, 1955.

———. "Joseph McCabe: An Appreciation." *Rationalist Review* 1, no. 12 (March 1955): iii–iv.

Reid, W. Nicol. *The Supremacy of Reason*. London: Watts, 1924.

Rhodes, Anthony. *The Vatican in the Age of the Dictators 1922–45*. London: Hodder & Stoughton, 1973.

Robertson, J. M. *Christianity and Mythology*. London: Watts, 1900.

———. *A History of Freethought in the Nineteenth Century*. London: Watts, 1929.

———. *A History of Freethought: Ancient and Modern*. London: Watts, 1936.

Royle, Edward. *Religion, Radicalism and Freethought in Victorian and Edwardian Britain: The Records of the Leicester Secular Society 1852–1943*. Wakefield: EP Microform, 1982.

Ruse, Michael. *Taking Darwin Seriously*. Oxford: Basil Blackwell, 1989.

Russell, Bertrand. *History of Western Philosophy*. London: George Allen & Unwin, 1946.

———. *The Analysis of Mind*. London: George Allen & Unwin, 1951.

———. *Human Society in Ethics and Politics*. London: George Allen & Unwin, 1954.

———. *Religion and Science*. Oxford: Oxford University Press, 1960.

Rylands, L. Gordon. *The Christian Tradition*. London: Watts, 1937.

Sagan, Carl. *The Demon-Haunted World*. London: Headline, 1996.

———. *Billions and Billions*. London: Headline, 1997.

Sanders, E. P. *The Historical Figure of Jesus*. London: Allen Lane/Penguin Press, 1993.

Saul, John Ralston. *The Doubter's Companion*. London: Penguin, 1995.

———. *The Unconscious Civilisation*. London: Penguin, 1997.

Seckel, Al, ed. *Bertrand Russell on God and Religion*. Amherst, N.Y.: Prometheus Books, 1986.

Seward, A. C., ed. *Darwin and Modern Science*. Cambridge: Cambridge University Press, 1910.

Shelley, Percy Bysshe. *The Poetical Works of Percy Bysshe Shelley*. London: Ward, Lock Ltd., n.d. Introduction by Richard Garnett

Shotwell, J. T. *The Religious Revolution of Today*. London: Watts, 1915.

Smith, David C. *H. G. Wells: Desperately Mortal*. New Haven, Conn.: Yale University Press, 1986.

Smith, Gregory Bruce. *Nietzsche, Heidegger and the Transition to Postmodernity*. Chicago/London: University of Chicago Press, 1996.

Smith, Warren Sylvester. *London Heretics 1870–1914*. London: Constable, 1967.

Sokal, Alan, and Jean Bricmont. *Fashionable Nonsense: Postmodern Intellectuals' Abuse of Science*. New York: Picador, 1998.

Spong, John Shelby. *Liberating the Gospel: Reading the Gospels with Jewish Eyes*. New York: HarperSanFrancisco, 1996.

Stein, Gordon. *Freethought in the United Kingdom and the Commonwealth: A Descriptive Bibliography*. Westport, Conn.: Greenwood Publishing Group, 1981.

Stein, Gordon, ed. *An Anthology of Atheism and Rationalism*. Amherst, N.Y.: Prometheus Books, 1980.

Stephen, Leslie. *An Agnostic's Apology*. London: Watts, 1931.

Tallis, Raymond. *Enemies of Hope: A Critique of Contemporary Pessimism*. New York: St. Martin's Press, 1997.

Thomas, Hugh. *The Spanish Civil War*. London: Penguin, 1979.

Thomas, R. Hinton. *Nietzsche in German Politics and Society, 1890–1918*. Manchester: Manchester University Press, 1983.

Thompson, E. P. *The Poverty of Theory*. London: Merlin Press, 1978.

Thompson, David. *The Aims of History*. London: Thames & Hudson, 1969.

Thomson, J. Arthur. *The Gospel of Evolution*. London: George Newnes, 1926.

Thrower, James. *The Alternative Tradition: Unbelief in the Ancient World*. The Hague: Mouton, 1980.

Tribe, David. *100 Years of Freethought*. London: Elek, 1967.

———. *President Charles Bradlaugh MP*. London: Elek, 1971.

Thurston, Herbert. *No Popery: Chapters on Anti-Papal Prejudice*. London: Sheed & Ward, 1930.

Vitzhum, Richard C. *Materialism: An Affirmative History and Definition*. Amherst, N.Y.: Prometheus Books, 1995.

Walker, Martin. *The Cold War*. London: Vintage, 1994.

Wallace, Stuart. *War and the Image of Germany: British Academics 1914–1918*. Edinburgh: John Donald, 1988.

Walter, Nicolas. *Humanism: What's in the Word*. London: RPA, 1997.

Walvin, James. *Victorian Values*. London: Cardinal, 1987.

Watson, George. *The English Ideology: Studies in the Language of Victorian Politics*. London: Allen Lane, 1973.

Wells, H. G. *Anticipations*. London: Methuen, 1902.

———. *The Discovery of the Future*. London: PNL Press, 1989.

———. *Boon, The Mind of the Race, The Wild Asses of the Devil, and The Last Trump*. London: T. Fisher Unwin, 1915.

———. *God the Invisible King*. London: Cassell, 1917.

———. *Christina Alberta's Father*. London: Jonathan Cape, 1925.

———. *Mr Belloc Objects to "The Outline of History"*. London: Watts, 1926.

———. *Experiment in Autobiography*. London: Victor Gollancz/Cresset, 1934.

————. *The Brothers*. London: Chatto & Windus, 1938.

————. *Crux Ansata: An Indictment of the Roman Catholic Church*. London: Penguin, 1943.

Wells, H. G., Julian Huxley, and G. P. Wells. *The Science of Life*. London: Cassell, 1931.

Wertheim, Margaret. *The Pearly Gates of Cyberspace*. Auckland: Doubleday, 1999.

Whitehead, Fred, and Verle Muhrer, eds. *Freethought on the American Frontier*. Amherst, N.Y.: Prometheus Books, 1992.

Whyte, Adam Gowans. *1899–1949: The Story of the RPA*. London: Watts, 1949.

Wilson, A. N. *God's Funeral*. London: John Murray, 1999.

Wilson, Edward O. *Consilience, The Unity of Knowledge*. London: Little, Brown, 1998.

Index

ABC of Evolution, The, 70, 125
Abélard, Peter, 47, 68, 70, 90, 163, 240
Aeterni Patris, 27, 30
agnosticism, 76, 134, 203–204, 241, 244–49
Appleyard, Bryan, 16, 117
Aquinas, Thomas, 27, 30, 252
Archer, William, 217
Armstrong, Karen, 159, 215
Asimov, Isaac, 117, 145, 255
atheism, 19, 20, 76, 80, 97–98, 122, 123, 133, 180–82, 240, 244–49, 250, 261
Augustine, Saint, 63, 90, 102,
Australia, 42, 43–44, 80, 92–93, 200, 217, 222

Ballard, Frank, 81, 118, 125, 131, 137, 193, 212
Bankruptcy of Religion, The, 195–98, 251
Bauman, Zygmunt, 16
Belloc, Hilaire, 42, 104–105, 125, 204
Berman, David, 248–49
Bible in Europe, The, 99–100, 102, 108, 159
Big Blue Books, 61–62, 69, 86, 89, 138, 223–24, 228, 230, 231, 242, 257, 258
Birx, H. James, 123
*Biographical Dictionary of Modern Rational-
ists,* A, 57, 60, 242–43, 257
Blackham, H. J., 68
Blatchford, Robert, 192–93, 241
Bonner, Hypatia Bradlaugh, 48, 49, 55, 58, 77
Bowler, Peter J., 124–25, 129
Brace, Charles Loring, 102, 152–53, 159
Bradlaugh, Charles, 37, 48, 51, 55, 76–77, 245–46, 248
Branden, Ruth, 158
Brooke, John Hedley, 121
Brown, Bishop William Montgomery, 57
Büchner, Ludwig, 134
Budd, Susan, 179–80
Bullett, Gerald, 59, 248
Bury, J. B., 94
Butterfield, Herbert, 95

Campbell, Colin, 76, 179–80
Can We Save Civilization?, 57, 73, 112, 127, 166
Carlyle, Thomas, 53, 111, 180
Chapple, James Henry George, 83
Chesterton, G. K., 42, 83, 152, 164, 193, 204
Christian apologists, 81, 102, 159, 187–88, 192–98, 215

327

attacks on McCabe's integrity, 41, 42, 80, 193–95, 212, 220–23
criticism of McCabe's opinions, 101, 104–105, 182–83, 205
other views of, 92–93, 96–97, 100–101, 102, 104–105, 118, 125, 130–31, 137, 141–42, 152, 187–88, 204–205, 215
Churches and the People, The, 108
Clodd, Edward, 39, 50, 57, 58, 73, 78
Cohen, Chapman, 40, 49, 62, 84, 128, 201–202, 248–49
Coit, Stanton, 37–38, 51, 140
Confucius/Confucianism, 140–41, 186–87, 251–52
Coren, Michael, 200–201
Cornwell, John, 225–231, 233
creationism, 143–44
Crime and Religion, 62, 219, 233
Crises in the History of the Papacy, 219–20, 221

Darlington, C. D., 170–71
Darwinism, 123, 125–30, 143–44
Dawkins, Richard, 20, 73, 120, 123, 130, 131, 143–44, 248
Decay of the Church of Rome, The, 218
Dennett, Daniel C., 20, 123, 137
Derrida, Jacques, 17
dialectical materialism, 91–92, 260
Diderot, Denis, 253, 256–57, 260
Doyle, Sir Arthur Conan, 53–54, 200–203
Duffy, Eamon, 221, 224–31, 233
Durkheim, Emile, 184

education, 75, 76, 107, 172–75, 216
    secular, 42, 44, 216
1825–1925: A Century of Stupendous Progress, 90–91, 92, 93, 117
Eighty Years a Rebel, 36, 58, 67, 211–12, 222
Einstein, Albert, 136
Ellis, Havelock, 69, 106, 158, 162
Encyclopedia of Unbelief, The, 11, 69, 188
Enlightenment, the, 16, 21, 73, 124, 156, 173, 252–53, 256–60, 260–64
enlightenment, true, 12–13

Epicureanism, 77–79, 151, 154
eupraxophy, 77
Evolution of Civilization, The, 95, 259
Evolution of Mind, The, 40, 53, 125, 138
Existence of God, The, 39, 57, 70, 181–82, 184, 246

Ferrer, Francisco, 43, 216–17
Flew, Antony, 20, 122, 123, 248
Foote, G. W., 38, 48–49, 83, 248
Foucault, Michel, 161, 173, 255
Frazer, J. G., 184, 185
Freethinker, 38, 48–49, 62
freethought, 19, 76, 250
From Rome to Rationalism, 35–36, 186, 191

Gellner, Ernest, 244, 256
Gilmour, J. P., 55
Goethe, Johann Wolfgang von, 78, 90, 126, 155, 163–64, 180
Gorham, Charles T., 39, 58
Gould, F. J., 35, 50, 55
great chain of being, the, 100, 130, 131
Growth of Religion, The, 183–85

Haddon, Dr. A. C., 184, 251
Haeckel, Ernst, 36, 43, 79–82, 125, 134–38, 139, 192–93, 198–99
Haeckel's Critics Answered, 80, 193, 199, 212
Haldeman-Julius, Emanuel, 45–46, 51, 56, 57, 58, 61–62, 70, 71–72, 82, 154, 213, 223, 247, 257
Harvey, David, 260
Haynes, E. S. P., 36, 39, 216–17
Heidegger, Martin, 15–16, 92, 254, 262
historicism, 16, 90–92, 112–13
History of Human Morals, The, 56, 58, 107–108, 160–63, 186–87, 252, 261
History of the Popes, A, 58, 204–205, 220, 223–224
Holyoake, George Jacob, 37, 48–49, 51, 55, 74, 75–76, 79, 82, 106, 245
homosexuality, 164
Horton, Rev. R. F., 80, 212
Howlett, Duncan, 182, 197–98

humanism, 16, 68, 77, 108, 118, 130, 202, 249–53, 261–64

Huxley, Julian, 51, 132, 143

Huxley, Thomas Henry, 56, 76, 79, 246, 250, 259

Influence of the Church on Marriage and Divorce, The, 42, 153, 159

Is Spiritualism Based on Fraud?, 200–201, 202

Jameson, Fredric, 92, 161

Joad, C. E. M., 51, 58, 59, 139, 157–58, 254

Kaiser: His Personality and Career, The, 110

Kant, Immanuel, 69, 94, 109

Keith, Sir Arthur, 51, 127, 139, 143

Kenny, Anthony, 30, 215

Key to Culture, 56, 70, 73, 118–19, 129, 140, 257–58

Key to Love and Sex, 56, 154–60, 162, 251

Kurtz, Paul, 77, 123, 202

Lankester, Sir E. Ray, 143, 203

Lecky, W. E. H., 101, 239–40

Lee, Beatrice, 37, 46, 57

Lee, W. T., 101, 105

Leicester Secular Society, 37

Levine, Peter, 162, 256

Life and Letters of George Jacob Holyoake, 48–49, 70, 74, 82, 107

Literary Guide, 36, 38, 39, 47, 49, 51, 52, 53, 54, 58, 59, 84, 170, 202–203, 205, 241

Little Blue Books, 45, 51, 56, 61–62, 70, 82, 89, 182, 189–190, 246

Lodge, Sir Oliver, 80, 122, 134–38, 198–200

Loisy, Alfred, 190, 215–16

Lovejoy, Arthur, 100

Lukes, Steven, 262–63

Luntley, Michael, 16, 258

Lyotard, Jean-François, 112–13

McCabe, Joseph

on atheism and agnosticism, 60, 97–98, 122, 197, 244–49, 256–57, 261

birth, 23–24

on blasphemy, 48–49

on Catholicism, 19, 28, 60, 62, 103, 104, 122, 159–60, 204–205, 211–33

on character, 109–10, 160–61

character of, 12, 24, 25, 32, 36–37, 47, 51–52, 55–56, 67–68, 83, 151, 263–64

on the Dark Ages, 97, 102–103

as Darwinian, 123, 124–30, 143–44

death, 18, 63

as debater, 40–42, 52, 53–54, 200–201

difficulties in studying, 17–21

divorce, 46

on education, 28, 42, 94–95, 172–75

education of, 24–25, 27–28, 30

and Ellen Newton, 11, 46, 63

on emergent evolution, 128

on the Enlightenment, 12, 256–57, 261–64

on ether, 135–38

on eugenics, 128–30

on evolution, 122, 123, 124–30, 143–45, 251

family life, 38–39

as feminist, 20, 42, 151–64

at Forest Gate, 27–29

at Freethought Congresses 42–43

on gender issues, 42, 97, 101,107, 151–64, 174

on God, 180–83, 244–49, 253

on golden ages, 105–106, 160–61, 251, 261

as historian, 89–92, 94–96, 96–100, 160–61, 188–89, 189–92, 219–20, 224–31

on historicity of Jesus, 189–92, 263

on history, 89, 90–92, 96–100, 100–105, 160–61, 261–64

on the humane spirit, 106, 107, 108–109, 250–53, 254

influence, 17, 40, 70, 72–73, 79, 82–86, 125, 144, 200, 257–58

as intellectual pioneer, 17, 18, 20, 100,

156, 160, 162, 189, 233, 244–45, 248
as internationalist, 91, 169, 171–72,
186–87, 249, 251–52
as lecturer, 28, 29, 37, 39–40, 43–44, 62,
85, 144
on laws of progress, 90–92, 93–96, 97,
112–13, 130–33
leisure, 67, 68–69
loss of faith, 26, 28–29, 30–32, 180–81
at Louvain, 29–30
marriage, 37, 38–39, 46
on the Middle Ages, 97, 102–105
on monism and materialism, 60, 77,
125, 133–38, 198–99, 256–57
on the moral law, 78, 109–10, 157, 251,
258
on the nineteenth century, 12, 93,
105–10, 161, 252, 261
novitiate, 25–26
parents, 23–24, 25, 31–32, 67
on politics, 110–11, 165–75
as polymath, 18, 20–21, 72, 244, 257
as popularizer, 18, 19, 51, 73–74, 82–84,
95, 119, 124, 132, 137, 142–45,
174–75, 183, 188, 213, 253–56
pseudonyms used by, 59–60
on race, 111, 127–28, 138–42, 184
on rationalism, 50, 239–44
as rebel, 20, 28, 76, 264
relationship with academics, 73, 98, 99,
127, 138, 253–56
relationship with fellow rationalists, 32,
36–37, 47, 48–49, 53–55, 60–61,
70–71, 73, 152–53, 232
on religion, 179–92
on science, 12, 117–20, 122, 125–26,
143–45, 250
on sex, 53, 69, 101, 151, 154–60,
163–64, 174, 251
sexual abuse of, 24, 164
similarities to Gospel writers, 98–99
as smiter of humbug, 18, 25, 56, 74, 82,
140, 151
on social Darwinism, 125–26, 127–28
on the Soviet Union, 60–61, 168–69,
170–71

translations by, 38–39, 70, 71
truculence of, 46, 50, 51, 52, 55–56, 73
upbringing, 23–26, 67, 93, 257
as writer, 11, 35–36, 38, 39, 43, 69–74
MacDonald, Ramsay, 38
McNabb, Father Vincent, 30, 42, 105,
130–31, 215, 221
Magee, Bryan, 253
Martin, Michael, 20, 245–46, 248
Martyrdom of Ferrer, The, 216–17
Marvels of Modern Physics, The, 136, 145
materialism, 20, 78, 120, 133–38
Mayr, Ernst, 123, 126
Mercier, Mgr. Désiré Joseph, 29–30,
Midgley, Mary, 99, 124, 133, 156
Mill, John Stuart, 30, 83, 239, 259
Miller-Argue, Robert, 92–93
Modern Rationalism, 36, 248, 253
Moran, Cardinal, 43, 222
Munz, Peter, 112, 123

National Secular Society, 37, 62
New Science and the Story of Evolution, The,
57, 71, 125
New Zealand, 42, 43–44, 63, 80, 82,
83–85, 140, 183, 218, 222, 224
New Zealand Association of Rationalists
and Humanists, 17, 61, 82, 84, 224
Nietzsche, Friedrich, 16, 30, 80, 84, 111,
127, 161, 248
Last Man, the, 84, 253–56

O'Farrell, P. J., 222
O'Neill, John, 264
Origin and Meaning of Ideas, The, 61
Owen, Robert, 74–75, 82, 94, 106,
172–73, 217, 262

Paine, Thomas, 23, 76
Papacy in Politics Today, The, 58, 70, 205,
218, 223–24, 225, 230, 232
papal states, 27
Passing of Heaven and Hell, The, 196–97
Peake, Arthur, 100–101
Pearson, Karl, 129, 158
pederasty, 24, 164

Peter Abélard, 36, 70
Piltdown Man, 127, 139, 142–43
popes, 212–13, 219–20, 221, 224–25
  Gregory I (590–604), 103, 219–20
  John Paul II (1978–), 215, 231
  Leo XIII (1878–1903), 27, 30, 215, 216, 226
  Pius IX (1846–1878), 27
  Pius X (1903–1914), 27, 28, 42, 216
  Pius XI (1922–1939), 223–28
  Pius XII (1939–1958), 225, 227–33
Popes and Their Church, The, 215, 221
Popper, Karl, 90, 112, 119, 162, 165, 172, 244
postmodernism, 12, 13, 249
  defined, 16
  differences between McCabe and, 12, 32, 112–13, 120, 133, 144–45, 161, 173, 175, 243, 252–53, 254–56, 258–60, 260–64
  and the Enlightenment, 13, 15–16, 156, 173, 252–53, 260–64
  rationalism and, 17, 90, 105, 112–13, 120, 140, 144–45, 161, 243, 244, 254–56, 258–60, 260–64
Price, George McReady, 52, 144
progress, 16, 38, 92–96, 133, 141–42
progressionism, 130–33
Prometheus/Prometheanism, 78–79, 252, 254

Ratcliffe, S. K., 68, 89, 157
rationalism, 18, 28, 36, 161, 185–86, 188, 189, 232, 239–44
  principles of, 16–17, 41, 50, 75–76, 156, 213, 233, 243, 244, 263–64
  puritan origins of, 67–68, 83, 154
  values of, 16, 18, 161, 169, 263–64
Rationalist Encyclopedia, A, 60, 129, 135, 143, 182, 247
rationalist humanism, 16–17, 140
Rationalist Press Association, 35, 38, 39, 40, 48, 59–61, 69–70, 76, 79–80, 127, 170, 200, 213, 222, 223, 232–33, 240–41, 248
  estrangement from, 47–56, 248

reconciliation with, 57–58
  views on, 36–37, 56, 248
Rationalist Press Committee, 35–36, 38, 240
Reade, Winwood, 95
reason, 15, 243–44, 263
religion, conflict with science, 71, 121–24
Religion in the Twentieth Century, 38, 249
Religion of Woman, The, 97, 151, 156, 249
religious studies, 19
Rhodes, Anthony, 225–31
Riddle of the Universe, The, 36, 39, 79–82, 137, 192–93
Riddle of the Universe Today, The, 58, 71, 125, 128, 143
Rise and Fall of the Gods, The, 56, 58, 97–98, 247, 249, 251, 261
Robertson, Archibald, 205
Robertson, J. M., 38, 39, 48, 50–51, 55, 57, 58, 77, 189–92, 248
Roman Catholic Church, 25–32 81–81, 181, 194, 204, 211–33
  and Nazi Germany, 227–33
  and Fascist Italy, 223–27
  attitude to dissent, 32, 204, 215, 220–23
  Protestant attitudes towards, 193–94, 212, 215–16, 218, 222, 231
Roosevelt, Theodore, 45
Ruse, Michael, 124
Russell, Bertrand, 15–16, 17, 18, 61, 69, 98, 110, 154, 242, 247, 260

Sagan, Carl, 117, 119, 123, 145, 253, 255
Saul, John Ralston, 23, 226
Schiller, F. C. S., 249
science, 13, 16 124, 130, 144–45
  conflict with religion, 71, 121–24
scientism, 16, 117–20, 142–43
secularism, 37, 75, 76
Shaw, George Bernard, 20, 59, 73, 134, 152
Shebbeare, C. J., 118, 182–83, 192
Shelley, Percy Bysshe, 73, 78
Shotwell, James Thomson, 185
Smith, Gregory Bruce, 16, 161, 262
Social Record of Christianity, The, 58, 108

Sokal, Alan, 17, 120, 144, 244
Soul of Europe, The, 111–12, 140
Sources of the Morality of the Gospels, The, 93, 188
South Place Ethical Society, 38, 40, 47, 51, 59, 62, 68, 157
Spencer, Herbert, 30, 131, 246, 259
Spengler, Oswald, 91
spiritualism, 71, 134, 198-203, 203-204
Splendor of Moorish Spain, The, 58, 141
Stead, W. T., 32
Stein, Gordon, 18, 69, 188
Stephen, Sir Leslie, 35–36, 37, 38, 77, 79, 100, 106, 239, 245, 251
stoicism, 77–78, 101–102, 108, 250
Story of Evolution, The, 57, 71, 125, 130, 132, 257
Story of Religious Controversy, The, 182, 189–90, 261
Streeter, B. H., 108, 192, 196

Taint in Politics, The, 166–67
Tallis, Raymond, 105, 118, 120, 183, 260
teleological maps, 99, 133, 253, 259–60
Testament of Christian Civilization, The, 99
Thompson, E. P., 94
Thomson, J. Arthur, 71, 122, 131–33
Thurston, Herbert, 221
Treitschke, Heinrich von, 111–12
True Story of the Roman Catholic Church, The, 213, 223

Twelve Years in a Monastery, 27, 35–36, 57, 152–53, 160, 213–15, 240
Tyranny of Shams, The, 53, 151, 156, 163, 166, 173, 203

United States, 42, 44–45, 52, 82, 151, 166, 249–50

Vitalism, 120, 134–38
Vitzhum, Richard C., 20, 133–38
Voltaire, 23, 223

Wallace, Stuart, 110
Walvin, James, 106
Ward, Percy, 54
Watts, Charles Albert, 50, 51, 52, 54, 58, 73
Weininger, Otto, 152
Wells, H. G., 50, 51, 57, 59, 61, 71, 106, 125, 132, 142, 158, 187, 195, 203–205, 218, 223, 246, 255, 257–58, 261–62
Wertheim, Margaret, 135
Wilde, Oscar, 83, 164
Wilson, A. N., 133, 175
Wilson, E. O., 80, 175, 259, 260
Wittgenstein, Ludwig, 15, 152
Wolpert, Lewis, 120, 123
Woman in Political Evolution, 151, 153